The Spectre of Afghanistan

The Spectre of Afghanistan

Security in Central Asia

Kirill Nourzhanov and Amin Saikal

I.B. TAURIS
LONDON • NEW YORK • OXFORD • NEW DELHI • SYDNEY

I.B. TAURIS
Bloomsbury Publishing Plc
50 Bedford Square, London, WC1B 3DP, UK
1385 Broadway, New York, NY 10018, USA
29 Earlsfort Terrace, Dublin 2, Ireland

BLOOMSBURY, I.B. TAURIS and the I.B. Tauris logo are trademarks of
Bloomsbury Publishing Plc

First published in Great Britain 2021

Copyright © Kirill Nourzhanov and Amin Saikal, 2021

Kirill Nourzhanov and Amin Saikal have asserted their right under the Copyright, Designs and Patents Act, 1988, to be identified as Author of this work.

For legal purposes the Preface on p. vi constitute an extension of this copyright page.

Cover design by Holly Bell
Cover image © Alev Takil/Unsplash

All rights reserved. No part of this publication may be reproduced or transmitted in any form or by any means, electronic or mechanical, including photocopying, recording, or any information storage or retrieval system, without prior permission in writing from the publishers.

Bloomsbury Publishing Plc does not have any control over, or responsibility for, any third-party websites referred to or in this book. All internet addresses given in this book were correct at the time of going to press. The author and publisher regret any inconvenience caused if addresses have changed or sites have ceased to exist, but can accept no responsibility for any such changes.

A catalogue record for this book is available from the British Library.

A catalog record for this book is available from the Library of Congress.

ISBN: HB: 978-1-7883-1765-8
       PB: 978-0-7556-3706-5
       ePDF: 978-1-7883-1766-5
       eBook: 978-1-7883-1767-2

Typeset by RefineCatch Limited, Bungay, Suffolk
Printed and bound in Great Britain

To find out more about our authors and books visit www.bloomsbury.com
and sign up for our newsletters

Contents

Preface		vi
Glossary of Terms		viii
	Introduction	1
1	The Afghanistan Threat	13
2	Afghanistan and Regional Security: The Views from Central Asia	51
3	The Central Asian Policy Response to Security Threats from Afghanistan: Development, Defence and Diplomacy	83
4	Great Powers and the Central Asia–Afghanistan Equation	121
5	Central Asia's Contribution to Peace in Afghanistan: Mission Impossible or the Dawn of Hope?	151
	Conclusion	177
Bibliography		193
Index		231

Preface

The Afghanistan conflict has grown to be the longest in the history of US military interventionism. US involvement in the country began in response to Al Qaeda's terrorist attacks of 11 September 2001. Since then, the United States, backed by NATO and non-NATO allies, has been struggling to transform Afghanistan into a stable and secure state. Yet, it has achieved little so far in this respect. The ongoing conflict has not only inflicted heavy human and material losses on the Afghan people, and on the United States and its allies – far more than was initially anticipated – but has also caused serious security concerns for Afghanistan's neighbours.

The conflict and its consequences have generated a plethora of published work from diverse perspectives. However, few such works have provided an in-depth analytical discussion about the implications of the Afghan turbulence for the Central Asian republics. Indeed, the impact of the conflict on Kazakhstan, Kyrgyzstan, Tajikistan, Turkmenistan and Uzbekistan and their individual and/or collective responses in dealing with security concerns arising from Afghanistan – and from the involvement of outside powers in the country – have been largely overlooked.

This book examines the evolution of the Afghanistan conflict since 2001 and delves into an analysis of the policy behaviour and remedial measures adopted by the five Central Asian republics in coping with the 'Afghan threat'. Whilst its approach focuses on how discourses of dangers are constructed in the region it does not aim to advance new vistas in Securitisation Theory or, for that matter, analyse the Afghan situation and Central Asian responses within any particular normative paradigm. The volume's primary focus is on unpacking and explaining the complexity of the Afghan conflict and the manner in which the Central Asian republics have sought to securitise their positions in relation to the evolving situation in Afghanistan.

This book follows our previous co-edited volume, *Afghanistan and Its Neighbours after the NATO Withdrawal*, which was published in 2016. It has been in the making for several years and we have sought to ensure that it is as up-to-date as possible. The task has nonetheless been complicated by the evolving Afghan situation and shifting regional circumstances, as well as by US policy behaviour under President Donald Trump. The latter was opposed to US intervention even prior to taking office. He is now very keen to bring it to an end, preferably through a political settlement of the Afghan conflict. However, his administration's efforts have not, to date, paid off. The twin goals of an honourable exit for the US and its allies and the establishment of a relatively functioning and sovereign Afghanistan remain elusive.

The research and writing of this book was made possible through a Discovery Project grant awarded to the authors by the Australian Research Council Discovery Projects funding scheme (project DP130104461). We have had the valuable support of three research assistants: Christian Bleuer, Andrew Feng, Philippa Hetherington and Elisabeth Yarbakhsh. While we are very thankful to all three of them, our gratitude also goes to Dr Yarbakhsh for her excellent job in reviewing and editing the entire manuscript and for taking care of the detailed logistics of the project. Further, we would like to thank the Australian National University, which has been our academic home during the course of this project, and are indebted to the anonymous reviewers of the manuscript and the publishing team at I.B. Tauris/Bloomsbury.

Kirill Nourzhanov and Amin Saikal
Canberra, May 2020

Glossary of Terms

6+2 the informal coalition of China, Iran, Pakistan, Tajikistan, Turkmenistan and Uzbekistan, plus Russia and the United States, working between 1997 and 2001 towards finding a solution for the 'Afghan problem'.

ADB (Asian Development Bank) a regional development bank with headquarters located in Mandaluyong, Metro Manila, Philippines.

AKN (Aga Khan Network) also known as the Agha Khan Development Network (AKDN), network of development agencies founded by the Agha Khan.

AKT (Afghanistan–Kyrgyzstan–Tajikistan) a three-country counter-narcotics initiative.

Al Qaeda (the base) a militant Islamist organisation founded by Osama bin Laden in 1988, initially in the context of the Soviet invasion of Afghanistan.

ANATF (Afghan National Army Trust Fund) a NATO run funding stream to channel international financial support to Afghanistan's security forces.

ANSF (Afghan National Security Forces) also known as the Afghan National Defense and Security Forces (ANDSF); comprised of the armed forces, national and local police and the national directorate of security.

Arbaki Afghan term referring to tribal community militia forces.

Bay'a (allegiance) an Arabic religious term referring to an oath of allegiance to a leader.

Bonn Agreement UN-brokered talks in Bonn; gave rise to a compact officially entitled the 'Agreement on Provisional Arrangements in Afghanistan Pending the Re-Establishment of Permanent Government Institutions' (2001).

BRI (Belt and Road Initiative) also known as the One Belt One Road (OBOR) or the Silk Road Economic Belt (SREB); Chinese Government infrastructure and investment initiative across Africa, Asia and Europe.

BSA (Bilateral Security Agreement) a 2014 agreement between Afghanistan and the United States, whereby US troops were to remain in Afghanistan after the end of the international combat mission.

C5+1 Central Asia plus Afghanistan format; platform for discussing regional concerns, as well as developing joint measures for peace (the Central Asia plus United States grouping is also designated C5+1).

CAES (Central Asian Energy System) network comprised of the Soviet-era Central Asian Power System (CAPS) (predominantly hydroelectric) and natural gas pipelines.

CAREC (Central Asia Regional Economic Cooperation) program established in 1997 by the Asian Development Bank to encourage economic cooperation; comprised of eleven countries of the wider Central Asia region.

CASA-1000 (Central Asia–South Asia 1,000 MW) program to allow for the export of excess hydroelectricity from Tajikistan and Kyrgyzstan to Pakistan and Afghanistan.
CENTCOM (Central Command) also known as United States Central Command (USCENTCOM).
CIS (Commonwealth of Independent States) regional grouping comprised of the ten former-Soviet states of Eurasia.
CLJ (Constitutional Loya Jirga) convention of Afghan delegates meeting in Kabul in December 2003 to debate and decide on a draft constitution.
COIN (counter-insurgency) a population-centred military strategy for Afghanistan developed under President Obama.
Corridor 5 transit route between Afghanistan on the one hand and China, Pakistan, Kyrgyzstan, Kazakhstan and Tajikistan on the other.
CPEC (China–Pakistan Economic Corridor) a series of infrastructure projects linking Pakistan and China.
CRRFCA (Collective Rapid Reaction Force for Central Asia) armed forces comprising 5,000 servicemen from mobile and light mountain infantry units stationed in Kazakhstan.
CSTO (Collective Security Treaty Organization) a military alliance of Russia, Armenia, Belarus, Kazakhstan, Kyrgyzstan, and Tajikistan.
DABS (*Da Afghanistan Breshna Sherkat*) Afghan national electricity company
Daesh (*al-Dawlah al-Islamīyah fī al-ʻIrāq wa-al-Shām*) Arabic acronym for ISIS, usually used as a derogatory term.
Dushanbe Four defunct program bringing together Afghanistan, Pakistan, Russia and Tajikistan in support of the Afghanistan government's efforts at national reconciliation.
EEU (Eurasian Economic Union) a political and economic grouping of Eurasian states, including Armenia, Belarus, Kazakhstan, Kyrgyzstan and Russia.
ELJ (Emergency Loya Jirga) a convention of Afghan delegates held in Kabul in June 2002 to elect a transitional administration.
FSB (Federal Security Service) security agency of the Russian Federation.
GBAO (Gorno-Badakhshan Autonomous Oblast) an autonomous region of eastern Tajikistan.
GKNB (State Committee for National Security) national security and intelligence agency in Tajikistan.
Haqqani Network Afghanistan-based militia that is associated with the Taliban.
Heart of Asia/Istanbul platform to discuss issues impacting Afghanistan and thirteen of its regional counterparts.
Hezb-e Islami (the Islamic Party of Afghanistan) Afghan political party and former militia under *mujahideen* leader, Gulbuddin Hekmatyar.
IBB (Imam Bukhari Brigade) Sunni Islamist militia comprised primarily of Uzbeks fighting in Syria and Afghanistan.
IDB (Islamic Development Bank) bank comprised of fifty-seven member countries, with headquarters located in Jeddah.

IMF (International Monetary Fund) international organisation, comprising 189 member countries, with headquarters located in Washington, D.C.; promotes monetary cooperation.

IMU (Islamic Movement of Uzbekistan) Salafi Islamist militia with early aspirations of forming an Islamic state in Uzbekistan; associated variously with al-Qaeda, the Taliban and ISIS.

IRA (Islamic Republic of Afghanistan) official name of Afghanistan since 2004.

IRPT (Islamic Renaissance Party of Tajikistan) Islamist political party in Tajikistan; currently outlawed.

ISAF (International Security Assistance Force) NATO-led security mission in Afghanistan.

ISI (Inter-Services Intelligence) intelligence agency of Pakistan

ISIS (Islamic State in Iraq and Syria) Sunni Islamist militant group that declared an Islamic caliphate and declared a proto-state in Iraq in 2014, extending to Syria in 2015.

ISIS-K (Islamic State in Iraq and Syria, Khorasan) branch of the Islamic State of Iraq and Syria operating primarily in Afghanistan.

Ittehad-e Islami Barayi Azadi-ye Afghanistan (The Islamic Unity for Independence of Afghanistan) Islamist political party formed in Afghanistan in the early 1980s.

JEMB (Joint Electoral Management Body) independent body mandated to oversee the election process in Afghanistan during the transitional period.

JIA (*Jamiat-e Islami-ye Afghanistan*; Islamic Society of Afghanistan) Muslim political party in Afghanistan.

JICA (Japan International Cooperation Agency) organisation that coordinates Japan's official development programs

Jihadi person undertaking *jihad*; an Islamic militant.

Jirga a traditional Pashtun assembly or council.

JMIA (*Junbish-e Milli-ye Islami-ye Afghanistan*; National Islamic Movement of Afghanistan) ethnic Uzbek political party in Afghanistan.

JTJ (*Jama'at al-Tawhid wa-l-Jihad*; Congregation of Monotheism and Jihad) Sunni Islamist militia that masterminded the St. Petersburg attack.

Jund al-Khilafa also known as ISIS-AP; Islamic State in Iraq and Syria, Algeria Province.

KAZBAT Kazakhstan's peacekeeping battalion.

KTJ (*Katibat Tawhid wal Jihad*; battalion of monotheism and Jihad) al-Qaeda-associated battalion comprised mostly of Uzbek fighters.

Lapis Lazuli Corridor trade and transport route which starts in Afghanistan and follows a land and sea route to Turkey and on to Europe.

LeT (*Lashkar-e-Toiba*; Army of the Righteous) an Islamist militant group operating out of headquarters in the Punjab province of Pakistan.

Loya Jirga grand council; an extraordinary traditional Pashtun tribal meeting.

MCTFA (Major Crimes Task Force Afghanistan) a department of the Afghan national police initiated and trained by the US Federal Bureau of Investigation (FBI) and functioning under the auspices of the Afghan Ministry of Interior (MoI).

Meshrano Jirga (House of Elders) upper house of the Afghan National Assembly.

Mujahideen plural of *mujahid*, an Arabic term referring to one engaged in jihad; often associated with the Islamist militant groups fighting the Soviet invasion of Afghanistan.

NDN (Northern Distribution Network) various supply routes to Afghanistan from the north.

NSR (New Silk Road) an Obama-era initiative to develop an integrated Central Asia as a transit route between Europe and East Asia.

NUG (National Unity Government) power-sharing government of President Ashraf Ghani and his Chief Executive Officer (CEO), Abdullah Abdullah, formed after tightly contested elections in 2014.

ODA (Official Development Assistance) a term coined to measure flows of international aid.

OSCE (Organization for Security and Co-operation in Europe) international security organisation comprised of fifty-seven member countries.

PRC (People's Republic of China) China's official name since 1949.

RECCA (Regional Economic Cooperation Conference on Afghanistan) conference held at intermittent intervals since 2005.

SCO (Shanghai Cooperation Organisation) a regional grouping hosted by China; comprised of China, five former Soviet states, Pakistan and India.

SGB (State Security Service) Uzbekistan's national security and intelligence agency; previously National Security Service (SNB).

Shari'a Islamic law.

Shura traditional leadership councils.

SIGAR (Special Inspector General for Afghanistan Reconstruction) US institution providing oversight of US investment in Afghanistan.

SNB (National Security Service) Uzbekistan's national security and intelligence agency; renamed the State Security Service (SGB) in 2017.

SNTV (single non-transferable voting) voting system in which an individual casts one vote for one candidate in a multi-candidate race.

SREB (Silk Road Economic Belt) also known as the One Belt One Road (OBOR) or the Belt and Road Initiative (BRI); Chinese Government infrastructure and investment program across Africa, Asia and Europe.

Taliban (students) Islamic fundamentalist political movement working primarily in Afghanistan and, to a lesser extent, Pakistan.

TAP-500 (Turkmenistan–Afghanistan–Pakistan 500 kV) power transmission line.

TAPI (Turkmenistan–Afghanistan–Pakistan–India) gas pipeline infrastructure project.

TAT (Turkmenistan–Afghanistan–Tajikistan) railway project intended to link the three countries.

TIR (*Transports Internationaux Routiers*, International Roads Transport) convention establishing a customs transit system; comprised of seventy-five countries and the European Union.

TTP (*Tehrik-i Taliban Pakistan*; Students Movement of Pakistan) Islamic militantly movement based in Pakistan; not formally affiliated with the Afghan Taliban.

TUTAP (Turkmenistan–Uzbekistan–Tajikistan–Afghanistan–Pakistan) officially the *Afghanistan: Energy Supply Improvement Investment Program*; a proposed electric power transmission network.

UIFSA (United Islamic Front for the Salvation of Afghanistan) also known as the 'Northern Alliance'; anti-Taliban alliance formed in Afghanistan in 1996.

UNDP (United Nations Development Program) United Nations poverty eradication program.

UNHCR (United Nations High Commissioner for Refugees) United Nations refugee agency.

WB (World Bank) international financial institution; provides loans to countries for capital projects.

Wilayat (province) in Arabic, an administrative division; a state.

Wolesi Jirga (House of the People) lower house of the Afghan National Assembly.

XUAR (Xinjiang Uyghur Autonomous Region) ethnically diverse Muslim-majority autonomous region of northwest China.

Introduction

The Afghan Threat: Conflict and Security in Central Asia

This book, which follows on from the volume *Afghanistan and Its Neighbours after the NATO Withdrawal*,[1] aims to continue some of the themes established in that work, but also to develop different discussions and new pathways. It has a particular focus on Kazakhstan, Kyrgyzstan, Tajikistan, Turkmenistan and Uzbekistan and explores how these Central Asian countries have formulated and implemented their security-driven foreign policies on Afghanistan since 2014.

Central Asia's place as Afghanistan's neighbour is, at present, paradoxical. On the one hand, it is characterized by physical proximity and long-standing ethno-linguistic and cultural connections – what Marlene Laruelle referred to as the 'civilizational fundamentals' underpinning mutual awareness.[2] This awareness has been periodically bolstered by dramatic events such as the Soviet occupation of Afghanistan during the period 1979–1989 and the Tajik civil war of 1992–1997.[3] On the other hand, geographic and historical closeness has not led to the development of sustained and substantial political and economic ties since the Central Asian republics gained independence nearly thirty years ago. Compared to Afghanistan's other neighbours – Iran and Pakistan – the Central Asian Republics have largely stayed aloof from Afghan domestic politics and kept the cross-border flow of people, finances and ideologies at a minimum. The suggestion that 'the former Soviet states came to embrace Afghanistan as an integral part of Central Asia and its most populous country',[4] is an exaggeration informed not so much by evidence from the ground as by wishful thinking on the part of Western experts concerned about geopolitical containment of China and Russia in the region. Afghanistan remains a distinct 'other' to most Central Asian states who, in Rein Müllerson's colourful expression, 'thank Allah that they do not live like their neighbours to the south'.[5]

Christian Bleuer and Said Reza Kazemi's otherwise excellent study pushes the boundary too far in the opposite direction when it states that 'Afghanistan and the countries of Central Asia remain strangers' and claims that neither side has a notable role to play in the other's policymaking.⁶ The Central Asian elites may well wish to have little to do with the conflict-riven southern neighbour yet one dimension of the relationship is inescapable – security. Paula Newberg argued that protecting themselves from the malign effects of Afghanistan's internal problems had formed a core element of the 'strategic calculations' of the Central Asian states since independence.⁷ Unlike Pakistan and Iran, they are neither responsible for the gestation of these problems nor involved in their resolution (or perpetuation) through local proxies. Nonetheless, while not jeopardising Afghanistan's security themselves, the Central Asians are forced to share in its insecurity whether they like it or not.

The impact of the Afghan conflict on Central Asian security receives constant attention from local politicians, experts and the media. There is also a growing corpus of scholarly literature produced in the region.⁸ The same cannot be said about the state of the field in Western academe where Central Asia watchers have tended to refer to Afghanistan cursorily in broad thematic explorations of the region's security or downplayed the security aspects of the neighbourhood dynamics in favour of the 'Great Game' geopolitical approach.⁹ Even the withdrawal of NATO troops from Afghanistan, announced in 2012 by the Obama administration, does not seem to have piqued Western experts' interest in how the Central Asians would assess and react to the changed security landscape.¹⁰

This book analyses the evolution of the Afghanistan conflict and seeks to address the question of how the Central Asian states deal with the threats arising from this perennial conflict. Security is the determining factor in the Afghan policies of regional states, but it is not the only factor; economics, geopolitics, culture, environmental concerns and other considerations also play a part. Following the ousting of the Taliban in 2001 the Central Asians had optimistic expectations concerning what might be achieved under the West's stewardship in terms of Afghan peace and stability. At the time, they contemplated a raft of economic and transport initiatives involving the southern neighbour that could allow them to overcome their landlocked position and reach the Indian Ocean. A decade later, widespread disappointment on both counts was palpable. A senior Kazakhstani diplomat who served as an ambassador to Kabul in 2005–2011 made three points summing up the situation:

- the US-led counterterrorist campaign had failed;
- all transit infrastructure projects had, similarly, failed; and
- Afghanistan had become a major liability and an impediment in Central Asia's quest for access to global markets in the southern direction.¹¹

The announcement of the departure of the International Security Assistance Force (ISAF) from Afghanistan in 2012 and the subsequent withdrawal of most of the US and allied troops by the end of 2014 caused tremendous anxiety in Central Asia's capitals. Scenarios predicting a speedy collapse of the central government in Kabul, the country's descent into anarchy, and the resultant uncontrolled flow of extremists, weapons and narcotics across the border, gained currency across the region.[12] Central Asian leaders seemed to be drifting ever so closer to the alarmist stance of Moscow, which contemplated the disintegration of Afghanistan as a nation-state.[13]

The survival of the Ashraf Ghani and Abdullah Abdullah National Unity Government (NUG) after 2014, and the sustained effort by the United States to make the Afghan security forces more resilient and capable, assuaged these fears somewhat, but by no means restored the Central Asians' faith in Afghanistan as a trustworthy regional partner. Almost no one in the region believed in the salutary conclusion of Afghanistan's transition to self-reliance when international donors' commitments were set to expire. However, a possibility of negotiated peace with the Taliban has brought hope to the Central Asian states that their security might be assured in ways other than erecting an impenetrable defence perimeter on the border with Afghanistan. This book will take stock of the current fluid and indeterminate situation, privileging indigenous perspectives, triangulating and adjusting them critically where appropriate.

Securitisation and Desecuritisation of the Afghan Threat in Central Asia

This book follows a general constructivist premise that security is a politically and socially constructed phenomenon. It does not go into the ontological and epistemological debate within constructivist security studies;[14] for our analytical purposes the adoption of a basic securitisation model as developed by Barry Buzan, Ole Wæver and Jaap de Wilde is sufficient. Securitisation is a process of presenting an issue as an existential threat requiring emergency measures and justifying actions outside the normal bounds of public debate and political procedure.[15] The process involves securitising actors who declare something – a referent object – existentially threatened; this declaration, or the securitising move, must be accepted by the target audience for the issue to be successfully securitised.[16] Desecuritisation is the reverse process of moving an issue out of the threat–danger modality of security and into the logic of regular politics, where compromise, solutions and debate are made possible.[17]

In the case of Central Asia's relations with Afghanistan, national governments or to be more precise the 'foreign policy executives' (FPEs) defined by Steven Lobell as personnel in charge of 'devising grand strategy and maximising national security' are the hegemonic securitising actors.[18] An FPE in the region typically includes the president, his administration, high-ranking officials in the Ministry of Foreign Affairs, the cabinet and the defence and security establishment.

State and society constitute the main referent objects of securitisation moves in Central Asia – that which needs protecting first and foremost from threats emanating from Afghanistan. In the region, 'the object of protection, the state, coincides with the agent in charge of its protection, the government';[19] hence challenges to the foundations of statehood, such as territorial integrity or monopoly on the legitimate use of violence, are merged with regime stability. Rustam Burnashev and Irina Chernykh produced a detailed account of Afghanistan-centred articulations of threat in different Central Asian countries between 1992 and 2005, noting a gradual shift from the military sector of security (the *mujahideen*/Taliban/guerrillas attacking across the border) after 1997, to what they called 'new dimensions of insecurity' undermining the fabric of local societies via the narcotics epidemic, the erosion of secular identity, migration and so on.[20] Ultimately, the constant representation of specific trends and events generated by a chronically unstable Afghanistan as demanding emergency response from the Central Asian governments, resulted in a comprehensive picture of danger – the Afghan issue became macro-securitised. The target audience of securitisation, the populace of Central Asia, was successfully persuaded that the southern neighbour is indeed a threatening 'other'.

Emergency response and going beyond 'normal politics' in the context of securitised instability in Afghanistan refers not just to militarisation and augmentation of the security services' remit and capabilities (although there is a lot of that happening), but also exceptions to declared foreign policy paradigms. The Afghan issue warrants deviation from the balanced conduct of multivector international relations or strict neutrality; the governments in Central Asia periodically rationalise swings and turnarounds in their dealings with great powers such as the United States and Russia, in the name of parrying existential threats from the southern neighbour.

Jef Huysmans (following Carl Schmitt) made an important point that the political practice of securitisation does not necessarily preclude interaction in the economic sphere with the threatening 'other'. The 'friend' and 'enemy' opposition of the former, is different to the 'profitable' and 'unprofitable' opposition of the latter.[21] The political transcends the sector-specific logic though; protection of state and society from existential threats trumps commercial relations. In 2002, Bobo Lo published a pertinent (and in many ways prophetic) study of the 'securitisation' and 'economisation' impulses in Russian foreign policy under Putin, noting that in the interplay between overtly security objectives and economic interests the former are bound to win.[22] In the case of the Central Asian states' policy-making on Afghanistan, Burnashev summed up the Central Asian dilemma well: full isolation of the southern neighbour is impractical and may cost money in lost trading opportunities, yet any increased interaction with Afghanistan, in the form of friendly partnership, carries risks of conflict transfer into the region.[23] In other words, doing business with Afghanistan is acceptable so long as its dangerous problems remain safely contained on its territory behind militarised borders, restrictive visa regimes and information firewalls. In early 2018, Kazakhstan's deputy foreign minister gave a statement which broadly reflected the disposition of FPEs across the region:

> Afghanistan ought not to be regarded *exclusively* as a threat to peace and stability as applied to Central Asia. Afghanistan also presents *one* of the important *opportunities* for our economies to diversify ... *Sooner or later* the situation in Afghanistan *will sort itself out* [*ureguliruetsia*] ... We believe that the Afghan people will make a choice in favour of peace and stability and *this will open* significant prospects for the countries of Central Asia.[24]

References to economic opportunities in Afghanistan in this typical speech act do not amount to desecuritisation either substantively (it is still a threat to peace and stability in Central Asia) or temporally (normalisation lies in an undetermined future). Afghanistan is not an indispensable factor in the region's push for diversification – merely one of the options that can wait until the situation somehow improves. Central Asia's agency in attaining such improvement is minimal.

Achieving desecuritisation of Afghanistan under the present circumstances is a challenging task. An explicit security discourse centred on the country's conflict will not be easy to dismantle. However, in line with Lene Hansen's taxonomy, incremental desecuritising moves are possible in the form of issue *replacement* and *rearticulation* which might eventually lead to 'change through stabilization',[25] whereby the issue of Afghanistan will be defined as inherently solved. Substituting the Islamic State and its affiliates for the Taliban, as the main agents of extremism, and then advocating negotiations to bring the latter into the realm of regular politics is an example of replacement and rearticulation of the Afghan threat pursued by the Central Asian republics since 2015.

The material for analysing patterns of securitisation and desecuritisation in the policy discourse of the Central Asian states concerning Afghanistan comes from official public sources. The selection of texts follows three basic criteria: recent provenance; clear articulation of threat; and wide circulation.[26] Speech acts by heads of state and government functionaries, particularly those that frame a policy as the only possible and legitimate course of action, are obviously important. We agree with Marcel de Haas that programmatic security documents (e.g. military doctrines, foreign policy concepts and national security strategies) are vital and often overlooked sources,[27] and refer to them frequently. Government views on Afghanistan are rarely challenged in public by institutionalised opposition and interest groups, or subjected to parliamentary discussion, scrutiny and oversight. The main source of counter-narratives of security in Central Asia is what Gearóid Ó Tuathail and Simon Dalby called a 'specialised community of security intellectuals'.[28] All countries bar Turkmenistan have think tanks and prominent commentators with access to the media. Some dismiss them as incapable of independent analysis and merely conferring a veneer of expert respectability to the authorities' proclamations.[29] This judgment is too harsh. Even in the most authoritarian settings security intellectuals 'are able to interpret, influence and modify the ideas presented to them [by the government] and communicate these changes back to the sender in a circular ideational exchange'.[30] In Kazakhstan and Kyrgyzstan in particular, independent experts engage with the hegemonic discourse critically and creatively; their opinion should be taken into account.

Outline of the Book

The first chapter provides a comprehensive background to the ongoing conflict in Afghanistan. It examines the process of stabilisation and security building launched in 2001 following the defeat of the Taliban by the US-led coalition. A lack of national reconciliation after regime change, the imposition of exogenous norms and institutions of statehood under the Bonn Agreement, external meddling and proxy wars, corruption and the wasteful use of donor funds have all combined to torpedo Afghan hopes around the implementation of good governance and economic development. Some progress has been achieved in the social sphere but the fundamental problem of security has not been resolved, despite the experimentation of successive US administrations, which saw the surge of US troops on the ground, the handover of responsibility to the Afghan security forces, and Trump's 2017 strategy of prompting the Taliban to the negotiations table from the position of strength. Insurgency has continued to grow resulting in less government control, more terrorist attacks, and mounting military and civilian casualties. The Asia Foundation survey of the Afghan people in 2018, revealed that 61.3 per cent believed the country was moving in the wrong direction, citing insecurity, the parlous state of the economy and problems with governance as the top three reasons for pessimism.[31]

2018 was the fourth consecutive year that the national mood stayed deep in the negative territory, providing yet another indicator that the NUG was not doing well at all. The perennial crisis of the Afghan state, coupled with the uncertainty about the intentions of its chief backer, the United States – which may be eyeing an exit strategy leaving its ally in the lurch – is of great concern to Afghanistan's neighbours to the north. The March 2020 peace agreement between the US and the Taliban as a prelude to a political settlement of the Afghan conflict has not as yet produced tangible results in the desirable direction, especially against the backdrop of deep political turmoil in Afghanistan as a result of the disputed outcome of the September 2019 presidential election.

The second chapter forms the conceptual core of the book. It maps out the process of securitisation and desecuritisation of the Afghan threat in Central Asia. Focusing on six distinct narratives of danger, it contrasts and compares their framing, intensity and hierarchy in all five Central Asian states. The major finding is that since 2014 the issue of the presence of radical Islamist groups on the territory of Afghanistan has been universally elevated to the position of an existential threat to state and society. A particular embodiment of this threat is the Islamic State and its affiliates in Afghanistan, who destabilise internal peace in Central Asia through terrorism and extremist propaganda that radicalizes the local Muslim population. The issue of narcotics trafficking from Afghanistan continues to be securitised robustly in the region, with the exception of Turkmenistan. Spillover of the armed conflict from the territory of Afghanistan is securitised strongly in Tajikistan and Kyrgyzstan owing to the relative weakness of their armed forces and traumatic experiences with violent incursions in 1999 and 2000. Turkmenistan has seen a fair number of violent accidents on the border with Afghanistan since 2014, yet its officials have chosen to silence the matter. Conversely, the Turkmen opposition in exile and independent experts prioritise this threat in their discourse. The expectation of an emergency situation involving refugees fleeing the conflict in Afghanistan has receded greatly compared to the early 2000s. This adverse scenario is now in the category of security risks rather than existential threats (with the partial exception of Tajikistan). The same applies to the ethnofidelity factor: the governments in Central Asia are not too worried about the fate of non-Pashtun minorities in Afghanistan and what a deterioration in their situation could mean for their own stability. An interesting point of divergence is observed in the field of geopolitical concerns, i.e. to what extent the conflict in Afghanistan can be used by the great powers to project into Central Asia. The issue is heavily securitised in Kyrgyzstan and Tajikistan whereas Kazakhstan, Turkmenistan and Uzbekistan feel reasonably comfortable about their sovereignty.

Securitisation implies a positive, if complex, correlation between public discourse and policy practice.[32] Chapter 3 traces the Central Asian states' responses to the Afghan crisis, grouped into three broad categories of measures: economic, military and diplomatic. Their contribution to the stabilisation of Afghanistan via economic development has been limited and amounted largely to catering to the needs of US troops in the country and servicing donor projects. Central Asians have adopted an opportunist and consumerist stance, cashing in on the international aid bonanza without exposing themselves to the risks of investment and open trade. Maintaining and enhancing the security barrier has been the primary response strategy since 2014. All Central Asian republics have invested significantly in bolstering their military and special service capacity to face the Afghan threat at the national, regional, and international levels. Desecuritisation of the Taliban has paved the way for the Central Asian capitals to push actively for negotiations between the NUG and the Taliban for the sake of a peace deal.

Chapter 4 canvasses the role of the United States, Russia and China in the securitisation/desecuritisation practices in Central Asia. They are treated as the *functional actors* i.e. those whose activities have significant effects on security making by the national securitising actors.[33] Washington, Moscow and Beijing have distinct views on the crisis in Afghanistan which they translate to the Central Asian republics in order to mobilise them for a particular course of action. In line with Alexnder Cooley's seminal work,[34] we find that powerful external players cannot force the local interlocutors to adopt policies which they find unpalatable or detrimental to their perceived national interest. Since 2014, Russia and China have been more successful than the United States in finding a common ground on the Afghan threat with the Central Asian states.

The final chapter takes stock of the evolving situation in Afghanistan, including the US efforts to make a military exit within the framework of a political settlement. It also assesses the important developments in Central Asia which took place in 2018, namely a thaw in Uzbekistan's relations with its neighbours and a series of diplomatic initiatives championed by Kazakhstan and Uzbekistan to advance the search for peace in Afghanistan. Should the five states be able to achieve a modicum of regional goodwill and cooperation, which has been missing since 1992, this may eventually lead to a greater and more positive Central Asian involvement in Afghanistan. However, in the short- to mid-term a comprehensive desecuritisation is unlikely and the image of Afghanistan as a source of existential threats will continue to dominate the Central Asian republics' policy vis-à-vis their southern neighbour.

Notes

1 Amin Saikal and Kirill Nourzhanov, eds, *Afghanistan and Its Neighbors after the NATO Withdrawal* (Lanham: Lexington Books, 2016).
2 Marlene Laruelle, 'Introduction', in *The Central Asia–Afghanistan Relationship: From Soviet Intervention to the Silk Road Initiatives*, ed. Marlene Laruelle (Lanham: Lexington Books, 2017), p. xii.
3 A substantial portion of 500,000 Soviet conscripts and officers who served in Afghanistan were drawn from Central Asia. In the 1990s, military contingents from Kazakhstan, Kyrgyzstan and Uzbekistan helped government forces in Tajikistan fight their opponents whose main support bases were in Afghanistan. Veterans of both campaigns are well organised and socially and politically active across Central Asia. Kazakhstan alone has some 19,000 retuned 'internationalist servicemen' who vigorously lobby the state for perks and privileges and contribute to the public debate on the patriotic upbringing of the youth and defending the country against external threats. Gulnar Iksanova, 'Zasedanie komiteta po sottsialno-kulturnomu razvitiiu sovmestno s sotsialnym sovetom pr fraktsii "Nur Otan"', *Mazhilis of the Parliament of the Republic of Kazakhstan*, 27 February 2018, http://www.parlam.kz/ru/blogs/iksanova/Details/6/58025.
4 S. Frederick Starr and Svante E. Cornell, *Modernization and Regional Cooperation in Central Asia: A New Spring?* (Washington DC: Central Asia–Caucasus Institute & Silk Road Studies Program, 2018), p. 31.
5 Rein Müllerson, *Central Asia: A Chessboard and Player in the New Great Game* (London: Routledge, 2007), p. 139.
6 Christian Bleuer and Said Reza Kazemi, *Between Co-operation and Insulation: Afghanistan's Relations with the Central Asian Republics* (Kabul: Afghanistan Analysts Network, 2014), pp. 3, 62.

7 Paula R. Newberg, 'Neither War nor Peace', in *Afghanistan: Challenges and Prospects*, ed. Srinjoy Bose, Nishank Motwani and William Maley (London: Routledge, 2018), p. 36.
8 See, for example, Alexander Knyazev, *Istoriia Afganskoi voiny 1990-kh gg. i prevrashchenie Afganistana v istochnik ugroz dlia Tsentralnoi Azii* (Bishkek: KRSU, 2002); S.M. Akimbekov, *Afganskii uzel i problemy bezopasnosti Tsentralnoi Azii* (Almaty: KISI, 2003); Alexander Knyazev, ed., *Afganistan i bezopasnost' Tsentralnoi Azii* (Bishkek: Friedrich Ebert Foundation, 2010); Saimuddin Mirzoev, *Afganistan: vyzovy i ugrozy* (Dushanbe: Irfon, 2017).
9 Notable works include Ahmed Rashid, *Islam, Oil and the New Great Game in Central Asia* (London: I.B. Tauris, 2002); Reuel R. Hanks, *Global Security Watch: Central Asia* (Santa Barbara: Praeger, 2010); Kristian Berg Harpviken and Shahrbanou Tadjbakhsh, *A Rock between Hard Places: Afghanistan as an Arena of Regional Insecurity* (London: Hurst and Company, 2016).
10 One of the few journal articles which attempted a systematic analysis was Timothy A. Krambs, 'Central Asia and the Afghanistan Security Dilemma: Amelioration, Retrograde, or Status Quo? Central Asia's Role in Regional Security Regarding Afghanistan after 2014', *Connections* 12, 2 (2013), pp. 1–26. Its source base was somewhat limited, using texts in English only.
11 Agybai Smagulov, *Ekspertnaia otsenka vliianiia afganskogo protivostoianiia na politicheskuiu i ekonomicheskuiu situatsiiu v Tsentralnoi Azii* (Bishkek: University of Central Asia, 2013), pp. 37–38.
12 Murat Laumulin, 'Bezopasnost' Tsentralnoi Azii v kontekste situatsii v Afganistane posle 2014 goda', *Tsentralnaia Aziia i Kavkaz* 16, 3 (2013): pp. 7–23.
13 See, for instance, Kirill Nourzhanov, 'Russia's Afghanistan Policy after 2014: Staying at an Arm's Length and Preparing for the Worst', in Amin Saikal and Kirill Nourzhanov (eds), *Afghanistan and Its Neighbors after the NATO Withdrawal* (Lanham: Lexington Books, 2016), pp. 163–178.
14 Thierry Balzacq, 'The "Essence" of Securitisation: Theory, Ideal Type, and a Sociological Science of Security', *International Relations* 29, 1 (2015): pp. 103–112.
15 Barry Buzan, Ole Wæver, and Jaap de Wilde, *Security: A New Framework for Analysis* (Boulder: Lynne Rienner Publishers, 1998), pp. 23–24.
16 Ibid., p. 36.
17 Barry Buzan and Lene Hansen, *The Evolution of International Security Studies* (Cambridge: Cambridge University Press, 2009), pp. 216–217.
18 Steven E. Lobell, 'Threat Assessment, the State, and Foreign Policy: A Neoclassical Realist Model', in *Neoclassical Realism, the State, and Foreign Policy*, ed. Steven E. Lobell, Norrin M. Ripsman, and Jeffrey W. Taliaferro (Cambridge: Cambridge University Press, 2009), p. 57.

19 Mehdi Parvizi Amineh and Henk Houweling, 'IR-Theory and Transformation in the Greater Middle East: The Role of the United States', *Perspectives on Global Development and Technology* 6, 1 (2007): p. 74.
20 Rustam Burnashev and Irina Chernykh, *Bezopasnost' v Tsentralnoi Azii: metodologicheskie ramki analiza* (Almaty: Kazakhstansko-nemetskii universitet, 2006).
21 Jef Huysmans, *The Politics of Insecurity. Fear, Migration and Asylum in the EU* (London: Routledge, 2006), pp. 128–129.
22 Bobo Lo, *Russian Foreign Policy in the Post-Soviet Era Reality, Illusion and Mythmaking* (Basingstoke: Palgrave Macmillan, 2002).
23 Rustam Burnashev, 'Afganistan: chto Kazakhstanu daleko, to Germanii – blizko', *Ostkraft*, 2 June 2014, http://ostkraft.ru/ru/documents/1482.
24 Erzhan Ashikbaev, 'Afganistan ne dolzhen rassmatrivat'sia iskliuchitelno kak ugroza miru', *Tengri news*, 4 January 2018, https://tengrinews.kz/kazakhstan_news/afganistan-doljen-rassmatrivatsya-isklyuchitelno-ugroza-miru-334683/ (emphasis added).
25 Lene Hansen, 'Reconstructing Desecuritisation: The Normative-Political in the Copenhagen School and Directions for how to Apply it', *Review of International Studies* 38, 3 (2012): pp. 541–544.
26 See Lene Hansen, *Security as Practice: Discourse Analysis and the Bosnian War* (Abingdon: Routledge, 2006), pp. 73–77; Aglaya Snetkov, *Russia's Security Policy under Putin: A Critical Perspective* (London: Routledge, 2015), p. 28, n. 2.
27 Marcel de Haas, 'Security Policy and Developments in Central Asia: Security Documents Compared with Security Challenges', *The Journal of Slavic Military Studies* 29, 2 (2016): pp. 203–226.
28 Gearóid Ó Tuathail and Simon Dalby, 'Geopolitics and Discourse: Practical Geopolitical Reasoning in American Foreign Policy', in *The Geopolitics Reader*, edited by Gearóid Ó Tuathail, Simon Dalby and Paul Routledge, (London: Routledge, 1998), pp. 80–81.
29 Ivan Safranchuk, 'Islamistskaia ugroza dlia Tsentralnoi Azii: Afganistan i globalnyi kontekst', *Indeks bezopasnosti* 4, 111 (2014): p. 103.
30 Erin Zimmerman, *Think Tanks and Non-Traditional Security Governance Entrepreneurs in Asia* (Basingstoke: Palgrave Macmillan, 2016), p. 27.
31 Tabasum Akseer and John Rieger (eds), *Afghanistan in 2018: A Survey of the Afghan People* (Washington DC: The Asia Foundation, 2018), pp. 17–25.
32 Hansen, 'Reconstructing Desecuritisation', p. 532; Snetkov, *Russia's Security Policy*, p. 19.
33 Thierry Balzacq, 'Enquiries into Methods: A New Framework for Securitisation Analysis', in *Securitisation Theory: How Security Problems Emerge and Dissolve*, ed. Thierry Balzacq (London and New York: Routledge, 201), p. 35.
34 Alexander Cooley, *Great Games, Local Rules: The New Great Power Contest in Central Asia* (Oxford: Oxford University Press, 2012).

1

The Afghanistan Threat

The 2001 US-led invasion of Afghanistan, as part of what Washington declared to be a wider 'war on terror', initially generated much optimism about the future of the country and the wider region. Yet as the campaign progressed, this initial optimism gave way to disillusionment and despair among many Afghans and democratic forces across the Muslim world. Afghanistan is today confronted with serious domestic challenges and foreign policy complications; its future hangs in the balance. Whether one observes the prevailing situation from the perspective of the Afghans, or assesses it from the vantage point of seasoned analysts of the Afghan conflict and the vagaries of the war on terror, the story so far is one of disappointment.

The Afghan people have many reasons to feel duped. They have been failed by their leaders, and by the foreign actors that have supported those leaders. Upon launching the war on terror, then-US President George W. Bush (2001–2009) vowed to bring peace, stability, security, prosperity and democracy to Afghanistan (and later to Iraq), and to free the world from what he called the terror wreaked upon it by those elements who used and abused Islam. Today, this promise rings more hollow than ever before. After so much investment in blood and resources on the part of the United States and its NATO and non-NATO allies, not to mention the incalculable loss of lives and property suffered by the Afghan people, the situation in Afghanistan bears no resemblance to the future that Bush promised to deliver.

This chapter has three main objectives: The first is to place the 2001 US invasion of Afghanistan in its historic context, recognizing that it occurred at a moment when the country had been shattered by over twenty years of devastating war. The second is to analyse the evolution of the Afghan situation under the US presidencies of Bush, Barack Obama (2009–2017) and Donald Trump (2017–present). The third is to evaluate the overall security profile of Afghanistan after seventeen years of US-led NATO and non-NATO civilian and military efforts to stabilise and secure Afghanistan, and to democratise the country.

The Context

In October 2001, the United States invaded the largely Taliban-controlled Afghanistan in a military intervention called 'Operation Enduring Freedom' under the aegis of the 'war on terrorism' which Bush declared on 16 September. Ostensibly, the invasion and subsequent occupation of the country aimed to remove a regime that Washington believed to be harbouring the terrorist network Al Qaeda, led by Osama bin Laden, which had attacked the United States at the cost of some 3,000 lives on 11 September 2001. However, as the operation's moniker suggests, the Bush administration presented the invasion as more than a purely military and strategic exercise. Quickly following on the tail of security concerns regarding the removal of the Taliban was the notion that the invasion would allow the United States and its international backers (including the United Nations) to turn this seriously 'disrupted state'[1] into 'a stable, free and peaceful' state,[2] so that it would never again become a hub for international terrorism. By implication, then, the aim of the operation was also to contribute to regional stability and security. As a result, despite having initially disavowed any interest in nation-building, Washington committed itself incrementally to the reconstruction of Afghanistan through substantial military, economic and humanitarian involvement.

The Taliban seized power in September 1996 after four years of internecine conflict between various Afghan Islamic resistance forces known as the *mujahideen*, who themselves had waged a protracted war against the Soviet occupation of Afghanistan from late December 1979 until the Soviet army was forced to retreat almost a decade later.[3] The main mujahideen groups, who represented the majority Sunni Muslim population of Afghanistan, were backed by the United States and its Western and regional allies, most importantly Pakistan, which served as a frontline state against the expansion of Soviet communism through Afghanistan.[4]

The Taliban, a group made up of former religious students from the *madrasas* of southern Afghanistan and northern Pakistan, were (and are) largely an ethnic Ghilzai Pashtun group of militant fighters who espoused a rigid and medievalist doctrine of Sunni Islam and claimed moral and religious superiority over the mujahideen groups in Afghanistan.[5] They initially attracted popular support through a promise to bring justice, rule of law and peace to Afghanistan through a strict imposition of their brand of Islamic law and governance. Nasreen Ghufran writes that they were perceived as a 'peaceful, neutral, and nongreedy [sic] force', whose promises of '[disarming] local militia and [enforcing] Islamic law' were 'clear and convincing for the war-weary public'.[6] The group was set up and funded by Pakistan's powerful Interservices Directorate (ISI) in the early 1990s, when the ISI had realised that maverick mujahideen leader, Gulbuddin Hekmatyar's *Hezb-e Islami* (the Islamic Party of Afghanistan), which they had previously supported, was an ineffective medium through which to influence Afghan politics.[7]

After the Soviet withdrawal and three years of fighting an insurgency war against the unstable first mujahideen government of Burhanuddin Rabbani, in September 1996, the Taliban took over Kabul and with it nominal control of most of the country.[8] Within two years, the Taliban were able to gain control of an estimated 85 per cent of Afghanistan, renaming the country 'the Islamic Emirate of Afghanistan'. However, only Pakistan, Saudi Arabia and the United Arab Emirates officially recognised the Taliban as the legitimate rulers of Afghanistan. Despite the Taliban's ongoing demands for international recognition and Islamabad's strenuous lobbying on their behalf, widespread international criticism of the group's hard-line policies, as well as its harbouring of bin Laden and other Al Qaeda operatives, led to several rounds of UN sanctions.[9] Afghanistan became, in the eyes of the rest of the world, an international pariah, officially condemned and largely ignored in the post-Cold War world order.[10]

The US government, while mistrustful of the Taliban, did not, at first, pay it much attention. It continued the policy of disengagement that it had pursued in Afghanistan following the Soviet withdrawal from the country.[11] Strategically, the only interest that the United States had in Afghanistan in this period was as a potential host of a Trans-Caspian oil pipeline.[12] However, this ambivalence evaporated once it became evident that the Taliban had permitted bin Laden, a Saudi Arabian Islamic militant who had organised terrorist attacks against the United States, to establish the bases of his Al Qaeda network in Afghanistan.[13] In August 1998, then-President Bill Clinton ordered cruise missile attacks on suspected Al Qaeda bases in Afghanistan in response to the group's orchestration of two bombings at US embassies in Nairobi and Dar es Salaam.[14] With bin Laden becoming a crucial target for the United States, Washington began placing increasingly tight sanctions and restrictions on the Taliban government in Kabul in an effort to coerce it into handing over bin Laden.[15] These attempts had little effect as the United States could not enlist the support of Pakistan. Whilst the new Bush government was still trying to develop a more effective strategy for dealing with the Taliban and with bin Laden and his organisation, Al Qaeda executed its most spectacular and devastating attacks on New York and Washington on 11 September 2001.

In response, the United States undertook the invasion of Afghanistan. At first, the United States went ahead largely on its own, with some help from Canada and the United Kingdom, and with the endorsement of the United Nations Security Council. However, as it met rapid success in bringing down the Taliban regime (assisted by certain anti-Taliban Afghan groups), its NATO allies quickly formed a multinational force, named the International Security Assistance Force (ISAF) in and around Kabul to help protect the new, internationally backed administration and stabilise Kabul according to UN Security Council Resolution 1386.[16] However, while the United States toppled the Taliban and dispersed bin Laden and his operatives, it did not defeat them altogether. Many managed to melt away in the treacherous Afghan landscape and cross the border into Pakistan. Despite all the military and civilian efforts made by the United States and its allies at very high human and financial costs since late 2001, not to mention the incalculable losses in life and property on the part of the Afghan population, the country remains mired in poor governance, corruption, instability, insecurity, poverty and bloodshed. Meanwhile, the Taliban-led insurgency has become increasingly robust.

The task that the United States had envisaged of transforming Afghanistan into an enduring stable state with a democratic, or even just viable, system of governance, has proven very difficult to achieve. As long as this remains the case, Afghanistan's neighbours, particularly the Central Asian republics, have good reason to be concerned about the spill-over of Afghanistan's problems into their territories. Such concern is further exacerbated by extensive cross-border ethnic, cultural and linguistic ties to Afghanistan and the danger emanating from the activities of the extremist political Islamist groups in the country. The question is: what has prevented Afghanistan's successful transition and dashed the hopes that a majority of the suffering Afghan people had held for their post-Taliban future? To answer this question, it is important to turn to an analysis of the US approach and the Afghan developments from the presidency of Bush to that of Trump.

The George W. Bush Era

The process of stabilisation and security building that unfolded for Afghanistan was problematic from the outset. Immediately following the initial defeat of the Taliban in November 2001, a conference involving four Afghan groups, Afghanistan's neighbours and the United States and its core European allies, was convened in Bonn, under the auspices of the United Nations, and with the purpose of placing an Interim Authority in place in Afghanistan which could smooth the way for building a stable and democratic state. The result was the 'Bonn Agreement' – essentially an inter-elite settlement, involving four Afghan groups, but not the Taliban – and the creation of an internationally backed interim administration under the leadership of Hamid Karzai, a Durrani Pashtun figure who opposed the Taliban and enjoyed the support of the United States. As Barnett Rubin has pointed out, the timeframe for the achievement of each of the key benchmarks of the Bonn Accords – two and a half years – was hardly enough to turn a failed state into a democracy.[17] This was nonetheless the ambitious aim of the drafters of the Accords. Since Bonn, Afghanistan has held several *Loya Jirgas* (traditional Pashtun tribal meetings), where delegates from across the country have approved the Interim Authority, debating, and then finally endorsing, a new constitution. The presidential election in 2004 and parliamentary elections in 2005 led to self-congratulatory speeches by members of the Bush administration regarding Afghanistan's successful transition to stability, security and democracy. However, as many commentators have pointed out, elections, the 'free' status of which is questioned by some, do not in themselves necessarily produce stability and democracy.

The Bonn Agreement

The UN-brokered talks in Bonn gave rise to a compact officially entitled the 'Agreement on Provisional Arrangements in Afghanistan Pending the Re-Establishment of Permanent Government Institutions'. This document outlined plans for an Interim Administration, an Emergency Loya Jirga (ELJ) to select a Transitional Administration to succeed the Interim Administration in June 2002, and a Constitutional Loya Jirga (CLJ) to discuss and endorse a new constitution.[18] It also set a timeframe for the holding of elections, both for the head of state and for the legislative body. In doing so, it projected the development of a secure and viable system of government, and outlined a clear (if ambitious) timeframe for the transition of Afghanistan from failed state to functioning democracy. Commentators have argued that, while the Bonn conference could not produce instant legitimacy for the new Interim Administration, the UN delegation in particular was aware of the nuanced approach needed to develop democratic frameworks that encouraged the expression of popular sovereignty.[19] Indeed, recognition of Afghanistan's unique characteristics and past historical precedents was a major factor in UN efforts to emphasise Afghan ownership of the process (although they may have been curtailed by the US's core security and strategic objectives, which framed the post-Taliban reconstruction effort within the lens of America's war on terror).

The Bonn Agreement also made provision for the establishment of a Supreme Court and gave the Interim Administration authority to establish more courts as required.[20] The re-establishment of the rule of law was considered one of the vital steps towards the construction of a stable government in Kabul. The drafters at Bonn also dictated that the 1964 constitution of King Zahir Shah (1930–1973) should be re-instated, until such a time as an appointed Judicial Commission could work to draft a new constitution.[21] Importantly, however, the Agreement stipulated that no provision of the 1964 constitution which was 'inconsistent with [the Bonn Agreement] or with international legal obligations to which Afghanistan is a party' would be valid, and also invalidated the provisions relating to the monarchy, and to the executive and legislative bodies.[22]

The Emergency Loya Jirga

While many international commentators were left with the impression that the Bonn Agreement had given existing elites a disproportionate share of power in the Interim Administration, it was hoped that the ELJ, convened to select the Transitional Administration, would ensure a sufficient level of representation in the government of Afghanistan's ethnically and culturally heterogeneous population until elections could be held.[23] A 'Jirga' is a traditional Pashtun assembly or council. A 'Loya Jirga' is a grand council, which historically has been used as a mechanism for the discussion and legitimation of issues vital to the nation. It typically adjudicates a number of legal issues from property rights to tribal foreign policy and relations with other governments (both national and international).[24] The Loya Jirga had approved the five previous constitutions of Afghanistan (1923, 1931, 1964, 1977 and 1987) although, with the possible exception of the Loya Jirga of 1964, they had mostly been docile, unassertive bodies whose job was to give a stamp of approval to the dictates of the leader.[25] For the 2002 ELJ, the procedure for the selection of delegates was complex; traditional leadership councils known as *shuras* met to choose electors, who then cast ballots for Loya Jirga delegates from their district.[26] Representatives of the US government, such as US ambassador Zalmay Khalilzad, touted the Loya Jirga as an 'ancient democratic tradition' of Afghanistan, a claim used to legitimise the process back home.[27] Critics, however, from Human Rights Watch to anthropologist Jamil Hanifi, questioned the democratic credentials of the Loya Jirga, pointing out that the shuras which made decisions pertaining to potential delegates at the grassroots level were made up exclusively of male elders 'considered to represent the respected or powerful families in a given region'.[28]

While the 'democratic' status of the ELJ may have been questionable, it did succeed in fulfilling its mandated task of choosing a Transitional Leader and Transitional Administration in June 2002.[29] Karzai, the interim leader appointed by the Bonn Agreement, was confirmed as Transitional Leader, a position he was to occupy until elections planned for 2004. On 19 June, the last day of the ELJ, Karzai announced his Transitional Administration, with the three key security portfolios of Defence, Foreign and Interior ministries going to prominent members of the most influential group in the Bonn conference: the former United Islamic Front for the Salvation of Afghanistan (UIFSA), also known as the 'Northern Alliance'. The latter had been formed by the legendary Commander Ahmad Shah Massoud, who had fought against the Soviet occupation of Afghanistan in the 1980s and subsequently resisted the Taliban and their Pakistani backers. He was assassinated by Al Qaeda agents two days before the 11 September terrorist attacks on the United States.

While some observers hoped that the Transitional Administration would be more representative of the mosaic Afghan society than its Interim predecessor, once again the government which emerged from the ELJ mirrored the security and strategic concerns of Karzai and his American backers.[30] Many delegates complained that they had felt intimidated by members of the security services who were reportedly present inside the Loya Jirga tent, undermining the notion that the electoral process was free and fair.[31] Indeed, the then-UN Under-Secretary-General for Political Affairs, Kieran Prendergast, noted several cases of intimidation in a briefing to the UN Security Council. This was an admission which was corroborated by a report the following year by the International Crisis Group which found that the gathering was '[s]ubject to back-room deals and intimidation on the floor', meaning that 'delegates were unable to fulfil the duties mandated to them under the Bonn Agreement'.[32] In addition, Khalilzad was accused, both in Afghanistan and the international media, of twisting the arm of former King Zahir Shah to convince him not to stand for election as Transitional Leader, leaving the way open for the US government's clear favourite, Karzai, to win.[33] The impression that the US delegation was exerting influence behind the scenes, whether real or imagined, tarnished the legitimacy of the ELJ in the eyes of many in Afghanistan.[34]

The Constitution

Many of the problems faced in the convening of the ELJ resurfaced just a few months later, in December 2003, when the CLJ convened in the same tent to discuss and approve a constitution put forward by a drafting commission that Karzai had appointed. The Bonn Agreement had, as a transitional measure, reinstated the constitution of 1964 with the exception of provisions relating to the monarchy and the sharing of powers between executive and legislature. The draft produced by the Constitutional Commission was based heavily on the 1964 text.[35]

During this process, there was considerable international scrutiny of the proposed constitution, particularly in the United States, where the key questions for many were the role of Islam in the future Afghan state and the protection of international norms of human rights.[36] The central concern was the extent to which the constitution drew on Islam – and in particular *sharia* (Islamic Law) – as a source of law. This focus on the role of Islam in the proposed constitution was reiterated in the US media coverage of the lead-up to the CLJ, a focus which obscured other pressing issues such as the balance between the centre and the periphery in the Afghan state and, particularly the tension between those who advocated a centralised government and those who called for a form of federalism to ease tensions in the ethnically divided country.[37]

The draft constitution presented to the CLJ was viewed by many Afghans as Karzai's attempt to consolidate power in his own hands, backed by the United States, which believed a strong, centralised state would make Afghanistan more amenable to American interests.[38] The concentration of power in the presidency prompted 'nearly universal criticism in Afghanistan from across the political spectrum', particularly from groups such as *Jamiat-i Islami*, *Junbish-i Milli*, the United National Party, and the royalist National Unity Movement, which were all aligned in opposition to the draft constitution.[39] Particularly concerned by the attempt to centralise power in the hands of the Kabul government were non-Pashtun leaders from northern Afghanistan such as: the leader of the *Jamiat-i Islam-i Afghanistan* (JIA, or the Islamic Society of Afghanistan), Rabbani, whose presidency (1992–1996) and mujahideen government continued to be recognized by the UN until Karzai's ascendency in December 2001; the Uzbek warlord and leader of the *Junbish-i-Milli Islami Afghanistan* (JMIA, or the National Islamic Movement of Afghanistan), Abdul Rashid Dostum, who subsequently also served as the first Vice President under President Ashraf Ghani during the National Unity Government (2014–2020); and the Defence Minister and Vice President in Karzai's Interim and Transitional Governments, Mohammed Qasim Fahim. All of these leaders favoured a parliamentary system of governance, with certain levels of power to be transferred to the regional elected leaders and institutions.[40]

In the months leading up to the Jirga, Dostum and his fellow regional leaders such as the strongmen Ismail Khan (Herat Province) and Mohammed Atta (Balkh Province) were vocal about their support of a federalist model of governance that would devolve more power to the regional governments.[41] Nonetheless, pro-Karzai factions loyal to the president were better organized in the CLJ than they had been during the ELJ.[42] The constitution still stipulated a strong executive arm, albeit a less powerful one than the original draft had suggested.[43] Many commentators on Afghanistan have continued to maintain that the political system that was delivered is too centralised, and a federalised system, which would invest greater sovereignty in ethnic minorities, who would otherwise feel alienated from the system, would have been more appropriate for the socially divided country.[44]

Meanwhile, the draft constitution presented to the Loya Jirga in late 2003, while citing Islam as an important influence on the formation of Afghan law, placed considerable emphasis on secular sources of law such as international human rights treaties, and democratic norms such as the rule of law and gender and ethnic equality.[45] Again, this secular focus was perceived by many in Afghanistan to be a result of American influence over the Karzai government, and as an imposed constitutional framework that was inappropriate in a country in which Islam is of great importance in citizens' lives. In the lead-up to the CLJ, a number of groups were calling for a greater role for Islam than what they suspected would be advocated by the Constitutional Commission. Members of JIA and *Ittehad Islami Barayi Azadi Afghanistan* (The Islamic Unity for Independence of Afghanistan), led by another former mujahideen leader with close links to Saudi Arabia, Abdul Rasul Sayyaf, called for the words 'Islamic state' to be used in the constitution, as well as some reference to the *hijab*, while a group of Islamic scholars led by the Deputy Supreme Court Justice Fazel Ahmad Manawi advocated shari'a as the sole source of law in Afghanistan.[46] Ultimately, a compromise was reached between the more secular outlook of the draft constitution and the Islamists within the CLJ. Thus, a number of provisions referencing Islam in the draft were retained, such as one which declared that 'in Afghanistan no law can be contrary to the beliefs and provisions of the sacred religion of Islam'.[47] Significantly, the Supreme Court was given powers of judicial review. As Larry Goodson states, this compromise was key, as it meant that '[t]he great struggle between conservative clerics and more moderate elements within Afghan society [would] not be settled in this Constitution but in its subsequent interpretation.'[48]

Even more than the ELJ, the utility of the CLJ as a symbol of American success in bringing stability and democracy to Afghanistan rested on its status as a fair, representative and unbiased organ of government. However, a number of non-governmental bodies attending the CLJ, as well as journalists and other commentators, reported considerable intimidation, aggressiveness and even violence among delegates; women in particular seem to have been singled out as targets of this behaviour. Others reported similar circumstances inside the tent, whereby delegates who wished to oppose prominent power-brokers were evicted from meetings or threatened with violence.[49] Claims of bias and intimidation, particularly by the American delegation at the CLJ seem to undermine the confident claim that, in Khalilzad's words, democracy was 'bubbling up' and therefore stability and security was around the corner in Afghanistan.[50]

Despite simmering disagreement over the role of the executive in relation to the legislature, the recognition of ethnic specificity and the role accorded to Islam, the fundamental work of the CLJ was done. A largely presidential governmental structure had been set up, with a bicameral National Assembly with an upper house (the *Meshrano Jirga*), one-third of which is appointed by district councils, one-third by provincial councils and one-third by the president; and a lower house (*Wolesi Jirga*) to be elected through a national vote open to all men and women over the age of eighteen. The next step was to hold elections for the president and then for the Wolesi Jirga which were scheduled for June 2004. Yet, given the nature of the strong presidential system of governance that was enshrined, the executive branch was empowered to deflect parliamentary scrutiny and constraints in a country embarking, for the first time in its history, on what soon proved to be a very primitive democratisation path.

The Presidential Elections

The administrative and security effort involved in organizing the presidential elections was enormous, and a number of internal and external bodies helped the Transitional Government in convening the election. These included the Afghan-run Joint Electoral Management Body (JEMB), established by the Electoral Law, which was set up for 'establishing policy guidelines, approving procedures, and exercising oversight over the electoral process'. JEMB was assisted by two US organisations funded by the Reagan-founded National Endowment for Democracy, the National Democratic Institute and the International Republican Institute, as well as the United Nations Assistance Mission to Afghanistan.[51] American and international organisations thus played a significant role in organising and monitoring the Afghan elections, a fact which both supported the Bush administration's claims that the United States was deeply involved in the

Afghan democracy process, and implicated them in any potential failures of the electoral process.

Karzai won the vote by 55.5 per cent, negating the need for a run-off. With an overall majority, Karzai was officially elected President of Afghanistan for a five-year term. Just over eight million Afghans had voted in the election, which constituted 70 per cent of those registered to vote, a high turnout considering the persistent instability in the country.[52] Karzai's victory, which proved his ability to cross ethnic lines and receive votes from non-Pashtun segments of the population, was considered by many a triumph for ethnic pluralism. However, other commentators have noted that his high polling may also have been influenced by the fact that he was implicitly backed by the occupying American forces, against whom there was, as yet, only limited resistance.[53]

The Parliamentary Elections

While the presidential election had occurred without any major upsets, the much larger election for the National Assembly was a bigger challenge. The elections for the 259 members of the Wolesi Jirga (House of the People) were an enormous undertaking which involved 160,000 polling staff who manned 26,500 polling stations in 8,300 locations throughout Afghanistan.[54] Once again, JEMB, the United Nations and international and domestic security forces were involved in the coordination of the elections.[55]

In the lead-up to the election, much debate surrounded the voting system to be used for the selection of candidates. International democracy promoters associated with the UN, independent think tanks and other non-governmental organisations pushed for a party-based system, whereby political parties would pre-select candidates and the voters would vote by party, rather than candidate, at the polling booth.[56] Political parties are often considered a bulwark of democracy development, and those who supported a party-based system argued that it would generate an inclusive political body which was strong enough to check any extreme assertion of power by the executive. On the other hand, the Afghan government and many Afghan citizens were fearful that such an approach would lead to existing ethnic and tribal factions dominating electoral proceedings.[57] In the end, the latter viewpoint won out, and a single non-transferable voting (SNTV) system was put in place. According to this system, voters cast ballots for individuals not parties. Each electorate was assigned a certain number of seats, and on the day the top candidates, up to the number of candidates the electorate was assigned, were elected to the Wolesi Jirga. This voting system, which has proved to be notorious in resulting in the election of candidates with very low number of votes, is practiced in only a handful of other countries, among them Jordan and Vanuatu.

The Afghan elections in October 2005 were viewed by many as a test of this controversial system. In the end, the Wolesi Jirga as elected did not confirm many of the most dire fears of SNTV's opponents, as it consisted of a number of political 'blocs' rather than being completely fragmented. Although social and religious conservatives were the largest group elected to the assembly, they did not constitute a majority, and there were also large groups of traditionalists and liberals elected.[58] In addition, sixty-eight women were elected, nineteen more than the 25 per cent required by the quota system.[59] The turnout was lower than hoped, particularly in light of the high turnout for the presidential elections; 57 per cent of registered voters placed a ballot, a significant decrease from the 70 per cent at the presidential election.[60] Some commentators suggested the lower voter numbers may have been an indication of growing disillusionment with the electoral process, after the success of the presidential election failed to bring about an increase in security and stability in Afghanistan.[61]

Nonetheless, the election of the Wolesi Jirga, and with it the completion of the roadmap outlined at Bonn, was presented by many in the Bush administration and segments of the US and international media as an unmitigated success. Bush himself congratulated Afghanistan on the 'successful parliamentary elections' which he declared 'a major step forward in Afghanistan's development as a democratic state governed by the rule of law'.[62]

Yet even as members of the Bush administration and its supporters were confidently declaring Afghanistan's transition to a working procedural democracy, some NGOs, scholars, journalists, commentators and other politicians were pointing to inherent flaws in the process by which Bonn had unfolded.[63] Many have been cited above; they include accusations of intimidation and vote buying involved in the Loya Jirgas; the impact of weak security on the ability of many to vote, particularly in unstable regions in the Pashtun-dominated south; the lack of protection given to women and other minorities, which silenced many who may have otherwise wanted to play a more active role in the consultative and decision-making processes; and the dangerous potential for conflict as a result of a heavily centralised and powerful executive arm based in Kabul, rather than a system of federalism which would help to enfranchise provincial and minority sections of Afghan society. While highlighting these problems, many of these observers conceded that managing to stage elections and put together a 'rough and ready' legislative body *at all* was an achievement in a country which has suffered such long-term conflict and poverty as Afghanistan.[64] However, this was tempered by the recognition that, far from solving the democracy-deficit in Afghanistan, the Bonn process has left the country in a state 'between stability and volatility',[65] with an inherently flawed governance structure.

In a 2008 report from the New York University Centre for International Co-operations, Barnett Rubin and Jake Sherman asserted that 'after six years of international assistance to the Afghan government the expansion of both the illicit narcotics industry and the insurgency constitutes a powerful indictment of international policy and capacity'.[66] Indeed, the presence of the increasingly powerful insurgency and resultant proliferation of the opium trade was evidence of the lack of embedded democracy in Afghan society and the failure of attempts at developing good governance since 2001, while at the same time severely hampering attempts to strengthen democratic institutions. It was also arguably the most visible evidence of the failure of the Afghan democracy experiment and security-building, as frequent news stories in the international media highlight both rising civilian and military death tolls from the insurgency and the sensational augmentation of narcotics cultivation since 2001.[67]

Symbiotically linked, the insurgency and the narcotics trade were two of the central foci of the 'Afghanistan Compact', a document outlining goals for the development of Afghanistan forged by the Afghan and foreign-donor governments at a conference in London in 2006. Whereas the Bonn Agreement, as noted above, focused almost exclusively on a roadmap for the development of institutional structures for procedural democracy, and national stability and unity, the Afghanistan Compact evinced the international community's realisation that without increased security, and a diminution of the drugs trade that accompanies instability in the region, no attempts at state building would succeed. The Compact pledged to reverse three main deficiencies in contemporary Afghanistan: security; governance, rule of law and human rights; and economic and social development.[68] As such, it represented a welcome turn to addressing previously neglected challenges to the development of substantive democracy in Afghanistan. However, the insurgency and narcotics trade continued to rage, and posed fatal tests for the efficacy of the Compact, and of the Afghanistan democracy experiment as a whole.[69]

The failure of the US nation-building project in Afghanistan bore serious implications for the security and physical safety of Afghan citizens. Weak governance is one of the most common preconditions for the emergence of an insurgency in post-conflict states, and Afghanistan has sadly been no exception to this rule.⁷⁰ According to Antonio Giustozzi, the Taliban were regrouping and planning an insurgent war against occupying American and NATO forces in Afghanistan as early as 2002.⁷¹ Since that time, they grew in strength as a result of three important factors: first, the weak government of a transitional state in which not enough attention was paid to strengthening local government and grassroots democracy – this created a space in which the insurgency could flourish; second, the growing nexus between the insurgents, terrorist networks and the narcotics trade provided the insurgents with funds to finance their campaign; and third, the disaffection of large sections of the Afghan population who saw huge amounts of international aid wasted in their country while basic reconstruction projects lay unfinished. These three factors created a support base for the Taliban insurgents, which would have been unthinkable in 2001.⁷²

It is important to note the direct influence that the substantial growth of poppy cultivation, and the development of Afghanistan as the world's largest producer of illicit opium, has had on the security situation in the country. With the steady increase of the opium crop there has developed concurrently a series of networks of drug traffickers, Taliban insurgents, regional crime bosses and extremist elements, operating in various parts of the country, particularly close to the southern border with Pakistan,⁷³ and through the Afghan borders with neighbouring Central Asian republics, from which narcotics traders find their way to Russia and Europe. This interaction between various anti-state actors has strengthened the insurgency, undermining the control of the government in opium-cultivating provinces and turning Afghanistan into a 'narcotic state', with poppy production, sales and trafficking constituting half of the country's economy.

Finally, the severe deficit in reconstruction at the grassroots level in Afghanistan resulted in a severe disconnect between the expectations of the population and the reality of life under the government in Kabul. Throughout the Bush administration, a majority of Afghan citizens did not see results from either the democracy push or the billions of dollars spent on reconstruction and military operations. The American promise of large-scale development and prosperity continued to elude them, and most continue to live in abject poverty.⁷⁴ International aid budgets, insufficient to begin with, were spent inefficiently and in some cases squandered on salaries for NGO workers and international staff in Kabul, and did not reach those most sorely in need in Afghanistan's rural provinces.⁷⁵ A pervasive culture of corruption and dependency permeated both state and society at all levels. As a result, any attempt by US and NATO forces trying to fight a counter-insurgency to win the 'hearts and minds' of the Afghan people faced failure. This reality pushed some into the hands of the insurgents, who they saw as at least being a stabilising and more religiously palatable force in the country, albeit a potentially repressive one.

The Obama Era

Bush's Democratic successor, President Obama (2009–2017), inherited an intractable Afghan conflict, requiring urgent change in the US policy approach. In his 2008 election campaign, Obama had promised to focus renewed attention on Afghanistan, while labelling the war in Iraq, resulting from the 2003 US invasion of the country, a distraction that needed to be ended. He was not specific on how exactly he would turn Afghanistan around in the face of increasing violence, high opium production, poor governance, corruption and international mismanagement. Nor was he quick to develop a new Afghanistan plan once he took office; it would take almost a full year before Obama announced a new strategy for Afghanistan, in December 2009. Meanwhile, the country continued to deteriorate and the problematic 2009 Afghan presidential election further eroded the legitimacy of the government, now led by an elite that was increasingly at odds with their American funders. President Karzai had failed to depart from the traditional Afghan politics of family, tribal, ethnic and factional connections, nepotism and bribery and lack of rule of law in building the necessary institutions as the foundations for generating national unity, stability and security. The more he failed to deliver on his mandate and the more the US-led foreign forces proved unable to deal a decisive blow to the Taliban-led insurgency and pressure Pakistan to halt its support of the insurgents, the more Karzai glossed over his own shortcomings and increasingly blamed the United States for Afghanistan's woes. The situation was made more unpalatable by the circumstances surrounding Karzai's victory at the 2009 presidential elections, as his main rival and former foreign minister as well as a prominent member of UIFSA, Abdullah Abdullah, decided to withdraw from contesting the second round on the grounds that the Electoral Commission had sided with Karzai and the latter had refused to replace the chair and members of the Commission with neutral ones. The result was that Karzai faced a serious problem of legitimacy, which continued to haunt his second presidential term.

Obama's Reassessment and the Surge

In late 2008, the US government conducted a number of internal reassessments of American policies and strategies in Afghanistan, chaired by Richard Holbrooke and Undersecretary of Defense for Policy, Michèle Flournoy. However, the final evaluation was made by a White House Review Committee in February 2009, chaired by Bruce Riedel, a veteran CIA officer, who was appointed by the newly elected President Obama. This resulted in a new Afghanistan policy in March, when Obama announced an additional 21,000 troops for the war effort. In the northern summer of 2009, General Stanley McChrystal took over as the top US and NATO commander in Afghanistan and initiated another reassessment process that ended with his request for an additional 44,000 US troops.[76] McChrystal's request generated heated internal debates, as the highly experienced US ambassador to Afghanistan, Karl Eikenberry (2009–2011), argued against extra troops. The ambassador, who had also previously served as the commander of all NATO forces in Afghanistan, could not see that extra troop deployments would make much difference under Karzai's dysfunctional and corrupt government.

In December 2009, President Obama finally made his decision. In his 'Address to the Nation' he clearly stated the new strategy:

> I have determined that it is in our vital national interest to send an additional 30,000 U.S. troops to Afghanistan. After 18 months, our troops will begin to come home. These are the resources that we need to seize the initiative, while building the Afghan capacity that can allow for a responsible transition of our forces out of Afghanistan.[77]

In his speech, Obama lamented the distraction of Iraq and stressed the obvious problems in Afghanistan, focusing on those that were of most concern to American interests, namely that the Taliban and Al Qaeda had 'maintained common cause' in their fight against US-led forces and that the Afghan government was 'hampered by corruption, the drug trade, an under-developed economy, and insufficient security forces'.[78] Obama clearly outlined his desired goal of reversing the momentum in the fight against the Taliban and strengthening the Afghan government's capability against the insurgents – but in a mere eighteen-month period. To achieve this, Obama stressed the 'three core elements' of what he called his population-centred counter-insurgency (COIN), as against Bush's 'counterterrorism', strategy. These core elements were: the protection of the main population centres; the expansion of Afghan national security forces, with the aim of achieving self-sufficiency; and 'an effective partnership with Pakistan [that is, to pressure Islamabad to curtail its support for the Taliban and their supporters]'.[79] Regarding the fight against Al Qaeda, Obama contrasted Afghanistan as a war of necessity with the war in Iraq, which he framed clearly as a mistake and a failure. He underscored the necessity of victory in Afghanistan, by warning that failure to achieve the stated mission there would give Al Qaeda a victory and allow it to once again use that country as a base for attacks against the United States.[80] Meanwhile, he made his strategy time-based rather than conditions-based by announcing that the United States would withdraw most of its troops by the end of 2014, which also opened the way for America's allies to do the same.

Planned end-goals, with clearly defined time-frames, then became a hallmark of Obama's Afghanistan campaign. However, the goals, strategies and deadlines in Afghanistan were continually adjusted throughout his time in office.

Corruption and Governance Problems Persist

A subsequent internal US government report, intended to inform policymakers, made clear that the reasons for the continued insurgency in Afghanistan included not just the presence of a safe haven in Pakistan, civilian casualties and resentment over the presence of a foreign army on Afghan soil, but the deficit of good governance in Afghanistan, especially public anger over the predatory corruption of the Afghan leadership.[81] This was an issue that, after his retirement as US ambassador to Afghanistan, Eikenberry reinforced publicly. In an article outlining the numerous failures of US and Afghan leadership in Afghanistan, he described how the United States and its allies created a system whereby President Karzai was not accountable to anyone when it came to poor governance practices. Most systems of governance have incentives and disincentives, but the Afghan leadership was isolated from those checks and balances. The Afghan people do not pay for the functioning of their state; international donors do, funding around 90 per cent of Afghanistan's government expenditures. This isolates the Afghan government from the Afghan people, as it is internationally sourced funds being spent rather than taxes collected from the Afghan people (a basic rentier state arrangement). As for international donors, they have made it clear that they will not introduce any penalties or incentives to induce good governance and reduce corruption, as this would imperil anti-terrorism efforts in the region. This reluctance underpins Eikenberry's argument that 'Karzai has had little reason to improve his state's effectiveness or accountability' and that the Afghan leadership 'consistently oppose foreign efforts to create transparent, rule-bound Afghan institutions because such projects threaten to undermine their political domination and economic banditry'.[82]

With Obama in the White House, it appeared as though this toleration of Afghan corruption and poor governance might come to an end. In his December

2009 address, President Obama announced new standards to which the Afghan government would be held accountable:

> The days of providing a blank check are over. President Karzai's inauguration speech sent the right message about moving in a new direction. And going forward, we will be clear about what we expect from those who receive our assistance. We'll support Afghan ministries, governors, and local leaders that combat corruption and deliver for the people. We expect those who are ineffective or corrupt to be held accountable.[83]

Despite Obama's emphasis on accountability and the promises made by President Karzai in his inauguration address, corruption in Afghanistan during his term did not just persist unabated, but rose to new heights. The Karzai administration continued to resist and interfere with anti-corruption initiatives driven by donor and international agencies such as the Major Crimes Task Force Afghanistan (MCTFA), which was set up by General McChrystal as part of a broader anti-corruption drive. While the MCTFA was formed by several international agencies, it was led by the Afghan government. As a result, it was subject to conflicting directives and objectives, as demonstrated most visibly in 2010, when Mohammad Zia Saleh – a top official in the government – was arrested on bribery charges in an investigation led by the MCTFA. In response, Karzai launched an enquiry to reign in the task force and later intervened to secure Saleh's release. Indeed, Karzai's repeated interventions into anti-corruption investigations led one official from the attorney-general's office to admit that '[u]nfortunately when it comes to high-ranking government officials, we can't do anything'.[84]

Another highly visible example was the culmination of the 2010 Kabul Bank scandal. Various Kabul Bank executives, many tied to President Karzai and his family, defrauded depositors of approximately US$1 billion. The Afghan government elites surrounding Karzai had called Obama's bluff, and the response showed how weak the American position actually was in Afghanistan: a confrontation over the blatant theft of US$1 billion in American taxpayers' money could result in US counterterrorism and counter-insurgency plans being completely derailed. The Kabul Bank scandal, as a symbol of overall corruption and theft in Afghanistan, clearly demonstrated the futility of outside efforts to force good governance upon the ruling elite in Afghanistan. Karzai's response to American demands for new banking and finance oversight measures in Afghanistan was simply to reject them.[85]

In 2006, 42 per cent of Afghans surveyed reported that government corruption was a major problem in daily life. By 2014 the response rate had increased to 62 per cent. The problem here was not just the delegitimisation of the Afghan government, but the legitimisation of the alternative: the Taliban. In the same survey, over 40 per cent of respondents who had sought resolution to a dispute reported that the dispute was over land.[86] Land disputes in Afghanistan are one of the main drivers of conflict, as aggrieved parties seek alternatives to the corrupt government system, including violent conflict.[87] This has given the Taliban a chance to step in as a supporter of one side or the other. It has also provided the insurgency a chance to demonstrate that it could offer a preferable government to the current one. For example, *The New York Times* reported the case of two men in Kandahar, one of whom was accusing the other of stealing his house:

> Despite paying more than $1,000 apiece in lawyers' fees, they found no resolution in the government's judicial system. The tribal courts, informal networks of elders that most rural Afghans rely on, had also come up short. So the two men did what a growing number of Afghans do these days when there is no other recourse: They turned to the Taliban. Within a few days, their problem was resolved – no bribes or fees necessary.[88]

The Surge Fails and Security Worsens

America's most basic strategic goals were outlined by the Congressional Research Service in 2015: 'to prevent Afghanistan from again becoming a safe haven for terrorist organizations' by 'enabling the Afghan government and security forces to defend the country against the continuing Taliban-led insurgency and to govern effectively and transparently'.[89] However, these goals remained unrealised under the Obama presidency. The security situation in Afghanistan continued to deteriorate, maintaining the trend seen during the later years of the Bush administration. The failure of the Obama administration to rectify the problems created during the Bush administration could be seen clearly. Following the troop drawdown by the close of 2014, formerly peaceful provinces soon fell, one after another, into the same level of conflict as the most conflict-ridden areas, such as Helmand. By mid-2015, the Taliban were threatening major population centres in the south and east, and making inroads into northern Afghanistan. They also succeeded in taking, albeit briefly, the northern city of Kunduz. Areas previously safe for Afghan government officials and international development projects soon became off limits. Most problematically for US interests, Afghan security forces showed themselves incapable of operating without foreign support and assistance. Not only is the entire cost of Afghan army and police forces paid for by international donors, but Afghan forces showed, during the offensive to retake Kunduz, that they were not able to organise the counter-attack without American planning, command, air support and special forces.[90]

As the US and allied forces were reduced to a training and supporting role, without necessarily letting their guard down in fighting terrorism, the Afghan forces, which increasingly took the lead in combat, suffered from high levels of casualties and desertion. 2015 set a record for deaths of Afghan police and soldiers.[91] Poor pay and low morale also continued to undermine their effectiveness. Further, it became clear that they could not operate independently without the support of the international forces and especially American air power. In comparison, foreign coalition forces, sustained the lowest number of casualties since the war began. This however did not diminish the recurring 'green on blue' attacks, where Taliban sympathisers infiltrated the armed forces and carried out attacks on local and international forces.[92]

Obama's surge, combined with a new style of population-centric strategy, did not reap the benefits that he had hoped for. This strategy focused on major population areas as key centres of gravity for producing stability. In this view, the chief objective was to develop an area in which the population could enjoy the benefits of stability, and then to transfer security and governance to local forces once this transition was completed. It involved an approach of 'locking in' and securing key areas through development and therefore a clear shift away from a more standard approach which targets insurgents first. Indeed, this approach is epitomised in the strategy's moniker, 'clear, hold, build, transfer'.[93] The promise of the surge (30,000 troops) and the new counter-insurgency (COIN) style of operation, advocated by the US military camp and led by the Commander of United States Central Command, General David Petraeus, did not fit the reality of the operating environment in Afghanistan. Eikenberry, who viewed Obama's chosen tactics and strategy as a failure, subsequently wrote:

> The COIN-surge plan for Afghanistan rested on three crucial assumptions: that the COIN goal of protecting the population was clear and attainable and would prove decisive, that higher levels of foreign assistance and support would substantially increase the Afghan government's capacity and legitimacy, and that a COIN approach by the United States would be consistent with the political-military approach preferred by Afghan President Hamid Karzai. Unfortunately, all three assumptions were spectacularly incorrect, which, in turn, made the counterinsurgency campaign increasingly incoherent and difficult to prosecute. In short, COIN failed in Afghanistan.[94]

The American efforts to push out the Taliban from select areas was often initially successful in forcing the Taliban to retreat. But the follow-up strategy of inserting central government officials and security forces into these areas alongside foreign military forces, was an action that often aggravated locals. The US goal was to protect the population, as outlined in its COIN doctrine. But, as Eikenberry asked:

> Protect it from whom and against what? It certainly meant protecting the Afghan people from marauding Taliban insurgents. But what about criminal narcotraffickers, venal local police chiefs, or predatory government officials? What should be done about tribes that turn to the Taliban for help in fighting more powerful tribes with patrons in the Kabul government? And what about complex cases of ethnic violence with roots dating back a century or more?[95]

The American plan was both too simple and too inappropriate for the social and political realities of Afghanistan. However, the worsening security was also matched by another deteriorating situation: the American relationship with President Karzai.

US-Karzai Relations Worsen

Karzai at first hoped to gain increased control from the surge of troops and money, but once he saw its failure and the resulting backlash of Afghan public opinion, he quickly changed his tactics to harshly criticise the American government and military. Karzai's anger over the American refusal to go after the Taliban inside their Pakistani safe-havens was a sentiment shared broadly by Afghans. But Karzai had other reasons to be unhappy with the US government. The expanded US military operations and accompanying surge of American money often worked to the benefit of power-brokers and commanders outside the government or outside Karzai's own patronage networks, thereby undermining his personal power. US actions were weakening the central government and Karzai's authority to the benefit of newly empowered provincial governors, tribal leaders, police commanders and other authority figures. Karzai often expressed his anger at this new 'parallel government' and American disregard for his power in the form of public criticisms of US strategy that actually had resonance with the Afghan people: civilian casualties, night-time raids, detention of Afghans, tolerance for Pakistan's intransigence, etc.[96]

Publicly, Eikenberry spoke more diplomatically than Karzai, but in private his assessment was harsh. Leaked cables from 2009 show a severely strained relationship with the US ambassador describing Karzai as a weak and paranoid leader surrounded by criminal allies, unskilled in state-building who 'sees himself as a nationalist hero who can save the country from being divided by the decentralization-focused agenda of Abdullah'.[97] Yet Karzai's paranoia may well have been warranted. The second-ranked UN official in Afghanistan, Peter W. Galbraith, proposed to the White House to replace Karzai after the sheer scale of fraud in the 2009 presidential election was revealed.[98] Karzai's paranoia reached its peak as journalists revealed that US and European officials were strongly considering inserting a 'chief executive' in the Afghan government and devolving power and funding to the provincial and district governments in order to circumvent Karzai and his dysfunctional central government. The name of the interior minister, Mohammad Hanif Atmar, a Pashtun nationalist and former communist figure (and an American favourite), was widely circulated. Karzai's response was to declare that such plans were an attempt to create a 'puppet state'.[99] Although Karzai, together with Obama, signed the Enduring Strategic Partnership Agreement between Afghanistan and the United States on 2 May 2012, providing the long-term framework for the Afghan–US relationship after the US troop drawdown by the close of 2014, Karzai's attitude towards Washington nose-dived. Karzai's final act, before the expiry of his two constitutional terms, was his refusal to sign the new Bilateral Security Agreement (BSA) to set the conditions for American forces in Afghanistan after the drawdown. Whilst projecting himself as an Afghan nationalist and being conscious of his legacy in history, he first deferred the agreement to a Loya Jirga, but even when the Jirga approved it almost unanimously on 21 November 2013 he declined to ratify it.[100]

Drawdown and the Bilateral Security Agreement

Going into the 2012 US presidential elections, an article in *Foreign Affairs* by three analysts from the Obama-friendly Brookings Institution stated that, 'Obama can rightly claim that he has ended the Iraq war, persevered in Afghanistan and Pakistan, and essentially decapitated Al Qaeda [by killing bin Laden on 2 May 2011]'.[101] Yet, the same article also noted that a clear success in Afghanistan had proved to be elusive, despite the surge and its accompanying increase in new resources that were injected into Afghanistan. The authors spoke euphemistically of a 'failure to achieve objectives as effectively as possible'.[102] Relatively favourable assessments of American policies in Afghanistan like these became fewer and fewer, and soon gave way to a broad agreement that the Obama administration, building on the failures of the Bush administration, had not succeeded in any significant way in Afghanistan. Still, by late 2013 Obama maintained that the surge, starting in 2009, had made possible the full transition of security responsibilities to Afghan forces that was scheduled for the end of 2014.[103] Eventually, President Obama backtracked on this handover of security responsibilities once it became clear that Afghan forces were in dire need of direct assistance in order to maintain the security of the Afghan government. Obama's second term was dominated by deadlines and plans to transition responsibility to the Afghan government, with the hope that the situation would improve. Yet the opposite occurred and optimistic plans had to be repeatedly contested, scrapped and rewritten as a result of the deteriorating conditions on the ground in Afghanistan. Writing in late 2013, Stephen Biddle argued that handing over the war to the Afghan government and withdrawing, basically replicated the US strategy in Vietnam of scheduling 'a "decent interval" between the United States' withdrawal and the eventual defeat of its local ally'.[104]

Reconsideration of the Drawdown

In November 2014, Obama directed American forces in Afghanistan to directly engage in combat and provide air-support to Afghan security forces, putting aside the sole 'advisory and training' role, to which the United States had hoped they would be able to downgrade. The Afghan government and security forces had shown themselves unprepared to fight the insurgency on their own without the direct participation and support of the Americans. The decision, which was the result of pressure from the US Department of Defense and was facilitated by a more willing partner in Afghanistan, the newly-elected President Ashraf Ghani, provided the basis for the newly-named Operation Resolute Support.[105] The American side had had to moderate its goals of creating a strong, independent and functional state to prevent the weak Afghan government from being overrun by the Taliban and preventing the resurgence of Al Qaeda in the region, which had been reduced to a low level of capability that the US government no longer found threatening.[106]

Factors outside Afghanistan were taken into consideration when making the decision to extend the role and presence of US combat forces. Those critical of the Obama administration pointed to the rise of the so-called Islamic State in Iraq and Syria (ISIS) and its intrusion into Afghanistan in 2016, arguing that it would not have been possible if the United States had kept a military presence on the ground in Iraq.[107] The rhetoric of these critics on the withdrawal from Iraq soon started to match what the Obama administration and its military officials were saying on the situation in Afghanistan. In late 2015, with the Taliban steadily gaining ground and ISIS expanding its operations in Afghanistan, US military officials began to publicly advocate for slowing or even halting the drawdown of American forces from Afghanistan (numbering about 9,800 by September 2015). US Army General John Campbell, the overall US commander in Afghanistan, had presented options to the Obama administration – as early as March 2015 – that included maintaining a minimum of 8,000 US troops in Afghanistan through 2016 and several thousand into 2017. With support from Ghani, top Obama administration officials and Republicans in Congress, the likelihood of the drawdown being slowed seemed increasingly likely. The Taliban's brief capture of Kunduz, the first city to fall to the militia since 2001, highlighted, for NATO countries, the fragility of Afghan security forces and their continued need for outside support. The 2016 withdrawal date became just another discarded deadline.[108]

The Trump Era

The unexpected election victory of President Trump in November 2016, brought great uncertainty to American foreign policy in Afghanistan. Trump had promised to withdraw the United States from foreign entanglements during his electoral campaigning, and in 2012 had tweeted: 'Afghanistan is a complete waste. Time to come home!'[109] However, once in office, he found it imperative to change his position. In August 2017, when he announced his long-anticipated approach to Afghanistan, Trump instead deepened America's military involvement. 'My original instinct was to pull out, and historically I like following my instincts', Trump told troops at Fort Myer. 'But all my life, I've heard that decisions are much different when you sit behind the desk in the Oval Office'.[110] While Trump's plan was light on detail, in reversal of Obama's policy he committed to deal with the Afghan conflict on a conditions-based, rather than time-based, approach. He announced an increase in troop numbers, with no time limit on troop withdrawal from Afghanistan, a greater emphasis on the Afghan government's military capacity-building and a more forceful policy of engagement with Pakistan, in order to pressure Islamabad to stop its support of the Taliban and their affiliates. Meanwhile, he called on India to play a greater role in Afghanistan. For all practical purposes, he relegated the Bush and Obama-era focus on good governance to a back-seat and declared that '[w]e are not nation-building again', but we are there to kill 'terrorists'.[111] In other words, he made it clear that the United States was no longer concerned about who governed Afghanistan and how the country was governed. Concurrently, he retained what Obama had advocated: a political settlement with the Taliban as the most viable means to bring the long-running Afghan conflict to an end. The two figures influencing Trump's approach were his National Security Advisor at the time, Retired General Herbert Raymond McMaster, whom Trump dumped in late May 2018, and the Secretary of Defense, Retired General James Mattis, who resigned in the following December over differences with Trump. Both had served in Afghanistan and had an intimate knowledge of the Afghan conditions, insurgency and America's involvement in the country.

Reactions to Trump's policy in Afghanistan were mixed. For example, Vanda Felbab-Brown of the Brookings Institute described his renewed commitment to Afghanistan and military increase as 'to a large extent correct', but criticised his 'de-emphasis on Afghan governance and political issues' as 'deeply misguided' and, potentially, 'a fatal flaw in the strategy'.[112] *The Diplomat* offered a similarly balanced assessment: 'Trump's speech lays out an encouraging vision, but whether this vision can be translated into reality remains in question, given the many preoccupations of this administration on the domestic front'.[113] However, the policy failed to pay off, despite Trump boosting the number of US troops from some 9,000 to 13,000 and maximising pressure on Pakistan, which saw American economic and military assistance to Islamabad decrease from the heights of billions of dollars under the Bush administration, to a mere US$150 million in security assistance by mid-2018.[114]

Meanwhile, the political and security situation continued to deteriorate in Afghanistan, leading Trump, known for wild policy swings and impulsive decision-making, to revert to his pre-election view of the unviability of the Afghan war. By early 2018, he decided that the sooner he could disentangle the US militarily from Afghanistan the better. But given the complexity of the situation, he preferred this objective to be achieved through a political resolution of the conflict. His administration initiated the process for such a resolution in earnest in September, which after so many turns and twists resulted in the US–Taliban peace deal of 29 February 2019 as a pathway to an all-Afghan comprehensive political settlement. This process and its results are detailed in the Conclusion for reasons of subject and structural fluidity, after having discussed the Central Asian views of, and responses to, the Afghan situation, as well as the great power roles and the Central Asian efforts to see a peaceful Afghanistan.

Evaluation

The problems of Afghanistan are two dimensional: internal and external. Domestically, the country suffers from poor leadership and governance, and is drowned in corruption and malpractice. The internal political games and divisions have continued unabated in the post-Karzai era. The disputed results of the 2014 presidential election are still not fully settled. Of the two leading contenders, Ghani and Abdullah, the latter won the first round of the election by a large margin of 53 to 34 per cent of some seven million votes cast, but in the second round, the results were almost reversed, amid allegations of vote-rigging in favour of Ghani. The intensification of the dispute, which threatened the collapse of the political system, prompted the then-US Secretary of State John Kerry to intervene, in order to avoid a looming crisis. Kerry was able to broker a deal between the two contenders to form a National Unity Government (NUG), with Ghani taking over the presidency and Abdullah assuming the position of Chief Executive (CE), which required a constitutional amendment to transform it legally into the prime ministership. The NUG, unprecedented in Afghan history, did not work well.

Ghani and Abdullah come from totally different backgrounds. The US-educated Ghani hails from a Ghilzai Pashtun tribe, to which the Taliban also belong, in contrast to the historically dominant Durrani Pahstun tribe, of which Karzai is a member. He led a secularist life in the United States as an academic and World Bank official during the entire period from the start of the Soviet occupation through the mujahideen government up to the end of the Taliban rule of Afghanistan. Abdullah, educated in Afghanistan, comes from a mixed Pashtun and Tajik background and had served under the leadership of anti-Soviet and anti-Taliban Commander Massoud, within a moderate Islamic ideological framework and subsequently as foreign minister during Karzai's Transitional and Interim administrations. Unlike the expatriate Ghani, he had an indigenous base of support. The two could not work harmoniously and share power on a fifty-fifty basis as they had initially agreed upon entering a government of national unity. Indeed, their government lay in tatters due to internal rivalries, infighting and ethnic divisions.

In short, under the NUG, the factors of instability, insecurity, poverty, patronage, corruption, national divisions, deception, the narcotics crisis and appalling human rights violations, especially in relation to women, continued to haunt a majority of the Afghan people. In Transparency International's global corruption perceptions index of 2017, Afghanistan ranked 177 out of 180 countries, and is amongst the ten poorest states in the world. There was no improvement in the country's reputation as having steadily become a major source of opium over the last two decades. In 2017 more opium came out of Afghanistan than in any previous year. The United Nations Office on Drugs and Crime reported that in that year:

The total area under opium poppy cultivation in Afghanistan was estimated at 328,000 hectares in 2017, a 63% increase or 127,000 hectares more compared to the previous year. This level of opium poppy cultivation is a new record high and exceeds the formerly highest value recorded in 2014 (224,000 hectares) by 104,000 hectares or 46%.[115]

The influence of 'strongmen', who have traditionally featured in the Afghan landscape in different ways and forms, also remained pervasive – some of them in alliance with the Kabul government, and others in opposition to it. Hence, the country faced an uphill battle to solidify itself as a functioning state with sufficient internal structures and sources of income to be able to survive without ongoing assistance from the United States and its allies.[116] In January 2018, Ghani himself admitted in an interview to American CBS 60 Minutes, that without US support and money, his government would collapse within six months.[117]

Externally, the Afghan conflict remains deeply entangled with regional dynamics, including Indo-Pakistan animosities, the Pakistan-Saudi Arabian strategic partnership, Saudi–Iranian rivalry, US–Iranian enmity, as well as US–Russian competition and a Tehran–Moscow axis, whereby Iran and Russia have come together to ensure that the United States does not succeed in Afghanistan. Trump's encouragement of wider Indian involvement in Afghanistan ignores the fact that Pakistan will not stand idly by and allow its regional foe to gain the upper hand in a country where it has been heavily at work for nearly four decades to ensure it follows a direction that is amiable to Pakistan's domestic and regional policy interests.

As a result, the Pakistan-backed Taliban-led insurgency, which seeks to retake power and re-establish a traditional Islamic Emirate, has not only remained robust, but has also lately been accompanied by the emergence of anther militant Islamic group, the Khorasan branch of the Islamic State of Iraq and Syria (or ISIS-K) on the Afghan landscape. ISIS has increasingly executed deadly operations against the government and the US and allied forces since the origination of ISIS-K in Afghanistan in mid-2016. Whilst the latter still remained relatively small with an estimated 1,000–2,000 fighters, the Taliban and their affiliates, including the Haqqani network, which has been linked to Pakistan's ISI, have steadily made gains since the withdrawal of most of the American and allied troops from Afghanistan by the end of 2014. They have taken over many villages and small towns and threatened some of the main provinces, including Kunduz in the north, and Helmand and Uruzgan in the south. Their expanding operations into northern Afghanistan, on the border with the Central Asian republics of Tajikistan, Uzbekistan and Turkmenistan, have posed a security challenge not only for those republics, but also for their neighbouring states of Kyrgyzstan and Kazakhstan. Given the historically close ties between the Central Asian states and Russia and the proximity to China, Afghan developments have increasingly become a matter of concern for Moscow and Beijing. Afghan government troops, backed by limited foreign forces and American air power, have managed to take back Kunduz three times in the last four years, but have not been able to deliver any full defeat of the insurgent forces in the north or, for that matter, anywhere else in the country.

Meanwhile, bewtween 2016 and 2018, Kabul experienced more insurgent attacks than ever before, resulting in the loss of thousands of civilian lives. According to a UN report, in the first six months of 2018 alone, the number of civilian deaths reached a record level of 1,692[118] – a number that doubled by mid-2019. The insurgents have continued to believe that time is on their side and have acted in ways that have overstretched the Afghan National Security Forces (ANSF), which number around 350,000 and is entirely funded, trained and equipped mainly by the United States and partly by its allies. These strategies are partly responsible for the heavy losses and a high desertion rate that the ANSF has sustained over the last four years.[119]

Conclusion

US intervention in Afghanistan has been fraught with serious problems from 2001 to the present. Whilst it scored some success in the area of structural development, political and social freedoms and empowerment of some ethnic minorities, it has been undermined by multiple missteps. The broader US objective of transforming Afghanistan into a stable, secure and relatively prosperous, if not democratic, country, stated initially by Bush, pursued subsequently by Obama, and then taken up by Trump (although without any emphasis on the democratic aspect), has not produced the desired results. This is largely because it has not been accompanied by a viable strategy, with a clear understanding of the complexities of the Afghan and regional landscapes, as confirmed by the former-US Secretary of Defense Robert Gates (2006–2011).[120] The United States has now been involved in the longest war that it has fought, and yet Afghanistan remains in the doldrums in every respect,[121] with its future hanging in the balance. Given this state of affairs, Afghanistan's neighbours, including the Central Asian republics and, for that matter, major powers – not just the United States, but also Russia and China – have good reason to be wary and watchful of future developments as far as their national and regional security interests are concerned. The discussion in this chapter now leads us to assess the broader topic under consideration – the impact of instability in Afghanistan on the Central Asian republics and their responses in the context of major power rivalry to which their region is subjected.

Notes

1   For a detailed discussion, see Amin Saikal, 'Dimensions of State Disruption and International Responses', *Third World Quarterly* 21, no. 1 (2000): pp. 39–49.
2   George W. Bush and Hamid Karzai, 'Remarks by President Bush and President Karzai of the Islamic Government of Afghanistan', *The White House*, 12 September 2002, https://georgewbush whitehouse.archives.gov/news/releases/2002/09/20020912-6.html.
3   On the 1992–1996 civil war in Afghanistan see Amin Saikal, *Modern Afghanistan: A History of Struggle and Survival* (London: IB Tauris, 2004), pp. 209–225.
4   There is a wealth of literature on the Soviet war in Afghanistan; see Saikal, *Modern Afghanistan*, pp. 187–208; Olivier Roy, *Islam and Resistance in Afghanistan* (Cambridge: Cambridge University Press, 1986); Barnett Rubin, *A Nation is Dying: Afghanistan under the Soviets 1979–1987* (Evanston: Northwestern University Press, 1988).
5   Saikal, *Modern Afghanistan*, pp. 220–221; for a journalistic account of the origins of the Taliban see Ahmed Rashid, *Taliban: Militant Islam, Oil and Fundamentalism in Central Asia* (New Haven: Yale University Press, 2000), pp. 17–67.
6   Nasreen Ghufran, 'The Taliban and the Civil War Entanglement in Afghanistan', *Asian Survey* 41, no. 3 (2001): p. 467.
7   Simon Bromley, 'Connecting Central Eurasia to the Middle East in American Foreign Policy towards Afghanistan and Pakistan: 1979–Present', in *The Greater Middle East in Global Politics*, ed. M. Parvizi Amineh (Leiden: Brill, 2007), pp. 86–87.
8   On the ascendency of the Taliban and their eventual victory in Kabul in 1996 see Saikal, *Modern Afghanistan*, pp. 220–225; Larry Goodson, *Afghanistan's Endless War: State Failure, Regional Politics and the Rise of the Taliban* (Seattle: University of Washington Press, 2001), pp. 77–80; Angelo Rasanayagam, *Afghanistan: A Modern History* (London: I.B. Tauris, 2003), pp. 145–153; Neamatollah Nojumi, *Rise of the Taliban in Afghanistan: Mass Mobilization, Civil War, and the Future of the Region* (New York: Palgrave Macmillan, 2002), pp. 134–152.
9   Although sections of the US government and congress perceived such recognition as potentially amenable to US strategic interests, on the grounds that the Taliban could serve as an effective Sunni bulwark to contain Iran and provide security to

trade routes and potential energy pipelines running through Central Asia, they therefore considered formal recognition of the Taliban. See Ghufran, 'The Taliban and the Civil War Entanglement in Afghanistan', pp. 480–481.
10 On the international reaction to the Taliban takeover see Rasanayagam, *Afghanistan*, pp. 162–177.
11 Amin Saikal, 'The Role of Outside Actors in Afghanistan', *Middle East Policy* 7, no. 4 (2000): p. 51. The US government at first seemed amenable to recognising the legitimacy of Taliban rule, but decided against it when the extreme fundamentalism of the regime became clear. However, this initial reaction is emblematic of the ambivalence with which the United States viewed the Taliban for much of the late 1990s. See Christopher L. Gadoury, 'Should the United States Officially Recognize the Taliban?' *Houston Journal of International Law* 23, no.1 (2000): p. 395.
12 Ralph H. Magnus, 'Afghanistan in 1996: The Year of the Taliban', *Asian Survey* 37, no. 2 (1997): p. 117; Rashid, *Taliban*, p. 179; Rasanayagam, *Afghanistan*, pp. 170–171; Nojumi, *The Rise of the Taliban*, pp. 198–199. Significantly, one of the consultants to UNOCAL at the time was Zalmay Khalilzad, prominent neo-conservative and later US ambassador to Afghanistan.
13 On bin Laden and the Taliban see Rashid, *Taliban*, pp. 132–140.
14 Nojumi, *The Rise of the Taliban*, pp. 199–200.
15 Gadoury, 'Should the United States', p. 398.
16 See NATO, 'ISAF – Chronology' International Security Assistance Force website, accessed 29 July 2008, http://www.nato.int/ISAF/topics/chronology/index.html.
17 Barnett Rubin, 'Crafting a Constitution for Afghanistan', *Journal of Democracy* 15, no. 3 (2004): p. 6.
18 United Nations, 'Agreement on Provisional Arrangements in Afghanistan Pending the Re-Establishment of Permanent Government Institution (Bonn Agreement)', United Nations, 2001, http://www.un.org/News/dh/latest/afghan/afghan-agree.htm, Section I.
19 William Maley, *Rescuing Afghanistan* (Sydney: University of NSW Press, 2006), p. 33.
20 UN, 'Agreement on Provisional Arrangements', United Nations, Section II.
21 Ibid.
22 Ibid.
23 See for example, Marin Strmecki, 'Creating a Government', (Interview), *Newshour with Jim Lehrer*, PBS, 21 December 2001; Ali A. Jalali, 'The Legacy of War and the Challenge of Peace Building', in *Building a New Afghanistan*, ed. Robert I Rotberg (Washington: Brookings Institution Press, 2007), p. 30.
24 Charles H. Norchi, 'Toward the Rule of Law in Afghanistan: The Constitutive Process', in *Beyond Reconstruction in Afghanistan: Lessons from Development Experience*, ed. John D. Montgomery and Dennis A. Rondinelli (New York: Palgrave Macmillan, 2004), p. 117.

25 Rubin, 'Crafting a Constitution', p. 7.
26 'Q & A on Afghanistan's Loya Jirga Process', *Human Rights Watch,* 15 April 2002, http://www.hrw.org/press/2002/04/qna-loyagirga.htm.
27 Zalmay Khalilzad and Daniel Byman, 'Afghanistan: The Consolidation of a Rogue State', *The Washington Quarterly* 23, no. 1 (1999): p. 77.
28 'Q & A on Afghanistan's Loya Jirga Process', *HRW*; M. Jamil Hanifi, 'Editing the Past: Colonial Production of Hegemony through the "Loya Jerga" in Afghanistan', *Iranian Studies,* 37, no. 2 (2004): pp. 295–322.
29 Norchi, 'Towards the Rule of Law', p. 118; Lauryn Oates and Isabelle Solon Helal, 'At the Cross-Roads of Conflict and Democracy: Women and Afghanistan's Constitutional Loya Jirga', (report, International Centre for Human Rights and Democratic Development, Montreal, 2004), p. 16, http://www.wraf.ca/documents/consLoyaJirgaE.pdf. Oates and Helal claim that *shuras* are ad-hoc forms of decision making which are generally comprised of village elders, landlords, khans and military commanders, and rarely include women.
30 For non-governmental commentary on the make-up of the Transitional Government see, for example, 'Afghanistan: Analysis of New Cabinet, Warlords Emerge from Loya Jirga More Powerful Than Ever', *Human Rights Watch*, 20 June 2002, http://hrw.org/english/docs/2002/06/20/afghan4051.htm.
31 Rubin, 'Crafting a Constitution', p. 10; 'Afghanistan: Loya Jirga off to a Shaky Start', *Human Rights Watch*, 13 June 2002, http://hrw.org/english/docs/2002/06/13/afghan4039.htm; Oates and Helal, 'At the Cross-Roads of Conflict and Democracy', p. 15.
32 'The Afghanistan Transitional Administration: Prospects and Perils', (briefing paper 19, International Crisis Group, Kabul/Brussels, 30 July 2002), p. 2.
33 Amin Saikal, 'The United Nations and Democratization in Afghanistan', in The UN Role in Promoting Democracy: Between Ideals and Reality, ed. Edward Neman and Roland Rich (Tokyo: Institute of Samoan Studies, 2004). p. 331. See also Carlotta Gall, 'Former Afghan King Rules out all but Symbolic Role', *The New York Times*, 11 June 2002, http://query.nytimes.com/gst/fullpage.html?res=9F04E1D8113DF932 A25755C0A9649C8B63&sec=&spon=&pagewanted=2; Camelia Entekhabi-Fard, 'As Afghan Council Proceeds, America Predicts a Strong President: A EurasiaNet Q & A with US Ambassador Zalmay Khalilzad', *EurasiaNet*, 22 December 2003, http://www.eurasianet.org/departments/qanda/articles/eav122203.shtml; S. Frederick Starr and Marin J. Strmecki, 'Afghan Democracy and its First Missteps', *The New York Times*, 14 June 2002, http://query.nytimes.com/gst/fullpage.html?res=9F06E1DF123CF937 A25755C0A9649C8B63.
34 Camelia Entekhabi-Fard, 'Accusations of American Meddling Mar Afghan Council', *EurasiaNet*, 6 December 2002, http://www.eurasianet.org/departments/insight/articles/eav061202a.shtml.

35 Rubin, 'Crafting a Constitution', p. 10.
36 See for example, Cheryl Bernard and Nina Hachigan (eds), *Democracy and Islam in the New Constitution of Afghanistan* (Santa Monica: RAND, 2003).
37 See for example Carlotta Gall, 'New Afghan Constitution Juggles Koran and Democracy', *The New York Times*, 19 October 2003, http://query.nytimes.com/gst/fullpage.html?res=9C06E2DC133EF93AA25753C1A9659C8B63&sec=&spon=&pagewanted=2; Victoria Burnett, 'Afghan Constitution Ready for Public Debate: Draft would Establish an Islamic Republic', *The Boston Globe*, 2 October 2003, http://www.boston.com/news/world/middleeast/articles/2003/10/02/afghan_constitution_ready_for_public_debate/.
38 'Afghanistan: The Constitutional Loya Jirga', (briefing paper 29, International Crisis Group, Kabul/Brussels, 12 December 2003), p. 10.
39 Ibid., p. 4.
40 G. Raif Roashan, 'Afghan Constitution an Exercise in Nation Building: A Test in Social Organisation', (report, Institute for Afghan Studies, 27 July 2004), http://www.institute-for-afghan-studies.org/Contributions/Commentaries/DRRoashan/.
41 Grant Kippen, 'The 2004 Presidential Election: On the Road to Democracy in Afghanistan', (briefing paper, Centre for Study of Democracy Queen's University, Kingston, 2006), p. 23.
42 Rubin, 'Crafting a Constitution', p. 9.
43 Ibid., p. 5.
44 See, for example, Saikal, 'The United Nations and Democratization', p. 335; Maley, *Rescuing Afghanistan*, p. 46.
45 Ali Wardak, 'Building a Post-War Justice System in Afghanistan', *Crime, Law and Social Change* 41 (2004), pp. 319–341.
46 'Afghanistan's Flawed Constitutional Process', (briefing paper 56, International Crisis Group, Kabul/Brussels, 12 June 2003), p. 10.
47 Islamic Republic of Afghanistan, 'The Constitution of Afghanistan', 2004, http://www.afghan-web.com/politics/current_constitution.html#chapterone, Chapter 1, Article 3.
48 Larry Goodson, 'Afghanistan in 2003: The Taliban Re-surface and a New Constitution is Born', *Asian Survey* 41, no. 1 (2004): p. 20.
49 'Threats of Expulsion of Loya Jirga Delegate Unacceptable', *Amnesty International*, 29 November 2003, http://asiapacific.amnesty.org/library/Index/ENGASA110292003?open&of=ENG-AFG; 'Afghanistan: Constitutional Process Marred by Abuses', *Human Rights Watch*, 8 January 2004, http://hrw.org/english/docs/2004/01/07/afghan6914.htm.
50 Zalmay Khalilzad, 'Democracy Bubbles Up', *The Wall Street Journal*, 25 March 2004, http://www.state.gov/p/sca/rls/rm/30811.htm.
51 Carol J. Riphenburg, 'Electoral Systems in a Divided Society: The Case of Afghanistan', *British Journal of Middle Eastern Studies* 34, no. 1 (2007): p. 12.

52 Thomas Ruttig, 'The 2004 Afghan Presidential Elections and Challenges for the Forthcoming Parliamentary Elections', in *The Challenge of Rebuilding Afghanistan*, ed. Moonis Ahmar (Karachi: Bureau of Composition, Compilation and Translation, University of Karachi Press, 2005), p. 61.
53 Ibid., p. 63.
54 Michael J. Metrinko, 'Elections in Afghanistan: Looking to the Future', (Issue Paper 20, US Army Peacekeeping and Stability Operations Institute, January 2008), p. 3.
55 Ibid.
56 Hamish Nixon and Richard Ponzio, 'Building Democracy in Afghanistan: The Statebuilding Agenda and International Engagement', *International Peacekeeping* 14, no. 1 (2004): p. 30.
57 Astri Suhrke, 'Democratizing a Dependent State: The Case of Afghanistan', *Democratization* 15, no. 3 (2008): p. 641.
58 Nixon and Ponzio, 'Building Democracy in Afghanistan', pp. 30–31.
59 'Election Watch', *Journal of Democracy* 17, no. 1 (2006): p. 177.
60 Larry Goodson, 'Bullets, Ballots and Poppies in Afghanistan', *Journal of Democracy* 16, no. 1 (2005): p. 31.
61 See Sam Zarifi and Charmain Mohamed, 'Afghan Election Diary', *Human Rights Watch*, 19 September 2005, http://www.hrw.org/campaigns/afghanistan/blog.htm.
62 George W. Bush, 'Statement on the Parliamentary Elections in Afghanistan', *Weekly Compilation of Presidential Documents* 41, no. 38 (26 September 2005): p. 1428.
63 See for example, Suhrke, 'Democratizing a Dependent State'; Kathy Gannon, 'Afghanistan Unbound', *Foreign Affairs,* May/June 2004, https://www.foreignaffairs.com/articles/asia/2004-05-01/afghanistan-unbound; 'Afghanistan's Flawed Constitutional Process', ICG; 'Afghanistan: The Constitutional Loya Jirga', ICG; 'Q & A on Afghanistan's Loya Jirga Process', *HRW*; 'Afghanistan: Analysis of New Cabinet, Warlords Emerge from Loya Jirga More Powerful Than Ever', *HRW*; 'Afghanistan: Constitutional Process Marred by Abuses', *HRW*; Riphenburg, 'Electoral Systems in a Divided Society'; Starr and Strmecki, 'Afghan Democracy and its First Missteps'; Entekhabi-Fard, 'Accusations of American Meddling Mar Afghan Council'; Oates and Helal, *At the Cross-Roads of Conflict and Democracy*; 'Threats of Expulsion of Loya Jirga Delegate Unacceptable', AI; Nixon and Ponzio, 'Building Democracy in Afghanistan'; Andrew Reynolds and Andrew Wilder, 'Free, Fair or Flawed? Challenges for Legitimate Elections on Afghanistan', (report, Afghanistan Research and Evaluation Unit, Kabul, 2004).
64 M. Ashraf Haidari, 'Afghanistan's Parliamentary Election Results Confirm Stunning Gains for Women', *Eurasianet.org,* 28 October 2005, http://www.eurasianet.org/departments/civilsociety/articles/eav102805b.shtml.
65 Saikal, 'The United Nations and Democratization', p. 337.
66 Barnett Rubin and Jake Sherman, 'Counter Narcotics to Stabilize Afghanistan: The False Promise of Crop Eradication', (report, Center for International Co-operation,

New York University, New York, February 2008), http://www.cic.nyu.edu/afghanistan/docs/counternarcoticsfinal.pdf.

67 For example, a sample of news stories from July and August 2008 includes 'Wedding Carnage in Afghan Blast', *BBC News*, 2 August 2008, http://news.bbc.co.uk/2/hi/south_asia/7538905.stm; 'Aid Warning over Afghan Violence', *BBC News*, 1 August 2008, http://news.bbc.co.uk/2/hi/south_asia/7536422.stm; 'Afghan Blast Kills NATO Soldiers', *BBC News*, 1 August 2008, http://news.bbc.co.uk/2/hi/south_asia/7537674.stm; 'Minister Voices Afghan Opium Fear', *BBC News*, 2 May 2008, http://news.bbc.co.uk/2/hi/health/7377817.stm; Carlotta Gall, 'Ragtag Taliban Show Tenacity in Afghanistan', *The New York Times*, 4 August 2008, http://www.nytimes.com/2008/08/04/world/asia/04taliban.html?_r=1&scp=2&sq=afghanistan%20&st=cse&oref=slogin; Carlotta Gall, 'As the Fighting Swells in Afghanistan, so Does a Refugee Camp in its Capital', *The New York Times*, 2 August 2008, http://www.nytimes.com/2008/08/03/world/asia/03afghan.html?scp=5&sq=afghanistan%20&st=cse; Thomas Schweich, 'Is Afghanistan a Narco-State?' *The New York Times*, 27 July 2008, http://www.nytimes.com/2008/07/27/magazine/27AFGHAN-t.html?scp=10&sq=afghanistan%20&st=cse; Editorial, 'Guns and Poppies', *The New York Times*, 5 August 2008, http://www.nytimes.com/2008/08/05/opinion/05tue1.html?scp=1&sq=poppy%20afghanistan&st=cse.

68 NATO, 'The Afghanistan Compact', 31 January–1 February 2006, http://www.nato.int/isaf/docu/epub/pdf/afghanistan_compact.pdf, p. 2.

69 Shayeq Qassem, 'Afghanistan: Imperatives of Stability Misperceived', *Iranian Studies* 42, no. 2 (2009): pp. 247–74.

70 Seth G. Jones, 'The Rise of Afghanistan's Insurgency: State Failure and Jihad', *International Security* 32, no. 4 (2008): p. 8. Jones defines an insurgency as 'a political-military campaign by non-state actors who seek to overthrow a government or secede from a country through the use of unconventional – and sometimes conventional – military strategies and tactics', p. 9.

71 Antonio Giustozzi, *Koran, Kalashnikov and Laptop: The Neo-Taliban Insurgency in Afghanistan* (New York: Columbia University Press, 2000), p. 8.

72 For a detailed discussion of the shortcomings of the US Afghan strategy, see Tim Bird and Alex Marshall, *Afghanistan: How the West Lost its Way* (New Haven and London: Yale University Press, 2011), chs. 3–7.

73 Chester G. Oehme III, 'Terrorists, Insurgents and Criminals – Growing Nexus?' *Studies in Conflict and Terrorism* 31, no. 1 (2008): p. 83.

74 Astri Suhrke, 'Reconstruction as Modernisation: The "Post-Conflict" Project in Afghanistan', *Third-World Quarterly* 28, no. 7 (2007): pp. 1304–1306; 'Editorial: Poorly Directed Aid Increases Afghanistan's Woes', *The Observer*, 20 July 2008, http://www.guardian.co.uk/commentisfree/2008 Obama /jul/20/afghanistan.internationalaidanddevelopment.

75 Richard Ponzio and Christopher Freeman, 'Rethinking Statebuilding in Afghanistan', *International Peacekeeping* 14, no. 1 (2007): p. 175.
76 Kenneth Katzman, 'Afghanistan: Post-Taliban Governance, Security, and U.S. Policy', *Congressional Research Service*, 17 August 2015, p. 23.
77 Barack Obama, 'Remarks by the President in Address to the Nation on the Way Forward in Afghanistan and Pakistan', The White House Office of the Press Secretary, 1 December 2009, https://www.whitehouse.gov/the-press-office/remarks-president-address-nation-way-forward-afghanistan-and-pakistan.
78 Ibid. See also, Trevor McCrisken, 'Justifying Sacrifice: Barack Obama and the Selling and Ending of the War in Afghanistan', *International Affairs* 88, no. 5 (2012): p. 995.
79 Obama, 'Remarks by the President'.
80 Trevor McCrisken, 'Justifying Sacrifice', p. 995.
81 Katzman, 'Afghanistan', p. 16.
82 Karl W. Eikenberry, 'The Limits of Counterinsurgency Doctrine in Afghanistan: The Other Side of the COIN', *Foreign Affairs*, September/October 2013, https://www.foreignaffairs.com/articles/afghanistan/2013-08-12/limits-counterinsurgency-doctrine-afghanistan.
83 Obama 'Remarks by the President'.
84 Lianne Gutcher, 'Afghanistan's Anti-Corruption Efforts Thwarted at Every Turn', *The Guardian*, 20 July 2011, https://www.theguardian.com/world/2011/jul/19/afghanistan-anti-corruption-efforts-thwarted.
85 'Afghanistan's Banking Sector: Central Banks Ability to Regulate Commercial Banks Remains Weak', (audit report, US Special Inspector General for Afghanistan Reconstruction (SIGAR), January 2014), http://www.sigar.mil/pdf/audits/SIGAR%2014-16-AR.pdf.
86 Zach Warren, *Afghanistan in 2014: A Survey of the Afghan People* (San Francisco: The Asia Foundation, 2014), http://asiafoundation.org/resources/pdfs/Afghanistanin2014final.pdf, pp. 91–97.
87 Erica Gaston and Lillian Dang, 'Addressing Land Conflict in Afghanistan', (special report 372, United States Institute of Peace, Washington, June 2015), http://www.usip.org/sites/default/files/SR372-Addressing-Land-Conflict-in-Afghanistan.pdf.
88 Azam Ahmed, 'Taliban Justice Gains Favor as Official Afghan Courts Fail', *The New York Times*, 31 January 2015, http://www.nytimes.com/2015/02/01/world/asia/taliban-justice-gains-favor-as-official-afghan-courts-fail.html.
89 Katzman, 'Afghanistan', p. 16.
90 Travis J. Tritten, 'US Surprised by Kunduz, Weighing More Troops in 2016', *Stars and Stripes*, 6 October 2015, http://www.stripes.com/news/us/us-surprised-by-kunduz-weighing-more-troops-in-2016-1.371913.
91 Luis Martinez, '13,000 Afghan Security Forces Killed in Last Three Years', *USA Today*, 14 August 2015, http://abcnews.go.com/Politics/13000-afghan-security-

forces-killed-years/story?id=33094534; Joseph Goldstein, 'Afghan Security Forces Struggle Just to Maintain Stalemate', *The New York Times*, 22 July 2015, http://www.nytimes.com/2015/07/23/world/asia/afghan-security-forces-struggle-just-to-maintain-stalemate.html.

92 Laviniu Bojor and Mircea Cosma, 'Afghanistan after NATO Withdrawal', *Scientific Bulletin* 20, no. 1 (2015): p. 32.

93 Christine Fair, '"Clear, Build, Hold, Transfer": Can Obama's Afghan Strategy Work', *Asian Affairs: An American Review* 37 (2010): p. 113.

94 Eikenberry, 'The Limits of Counterinsurgency'.

95 Ibid.

96 Ibid.

97 Jon Boone, 'WikiLeaks Cables Portray Hamid Karzai as Corrupt and Erratic', *The Guardian*, 3 December 2010, http://www.theguardian.com/world/2010/dec/02/wikileaks-cables-hamid-karzai-erratic.

98 James Glanz and Richard A. Oppel Jr., 'U.N. Officials say American Offered Plan to Replace Karzai', *The New York Times*, 16 December 2009, http://www.nytimes.com/2009/12/17/world/asia/17galbraith.html.

99 Julian Borger and Ewen MacAskill, 'US will Appoint Afghan "Prime Minister" to Bypass Hamid Karzai', *The Guardian*, 23 March 2009, http://www.theguardian.com/world/2009/mar/22/us-afghan-plan-to-bypass-karzai.

100 Corri Zoli and Emily Schneider, 'Privacy in Muslim Constitutions and Karzai's Refusal to Sign the Bilateral Security Agreement', *The Washington Post*, 2 January 2014, https://www.washingtonpost.com/news/monkey-cage/wp/2014/01/02/privacy-in-muslim-constitutions-and-karzais-refusal-to-sign-the-bilateral-security-agreement/.

101 Martin S. Indyk, Kenneth G. Lieberthal and Michael E. O'Hanlon, 'Scoring Obama's Foreign Policy: A Progressive Pragmatist Tries to Bend History', *Foreign Affairs* 29, no. 91 (2012): p. 34.

102 Ibid., p. 35.

103 Stephen Biddle, 'Ending the War in Afghanistan: How to Avoid Failure on the Plan', *Foreign Affairs* 92, no. 5 (2013): pp. 49–58.

104 Ibid.

105 Mark Mazzetti and Eric Schmitt, 'In Secret, Obama Extends U.S. Role in Afghan Combat', *The New York Times*, 22 November 2014, http://www.nytimes.com/2014/11/22/us/politics/in-secret-obama-extends-us-role-in-afghan-combat.html.

106 Larry Goodson and Thomas H. Johnson, *U.S. Policy and Strategy toward Afghanistan after 2014* (Carlisle: U.S. Army War College Press, 2014), p. 19.

107 Katzman, 'Afghanistan', p. 26.

108 Robert Burns and Lolita C. Baldor, 'Amid Taliban Gains, US Military Favors Longer Presence', *Associated Press*, 30 September 2015, http://bigstory.ap.org/article/259db9

91199d4b6a8652aeb6878eb976/us-military-favors-keeping-troops-afghanistan-past-2016; Paul McLeary, 'Top U.S. Commander: American Troops Need to Stay in Afghanistan', *Foreign Policy*, 6 October 2015, http://foreignpolicy.com/2015/10/06/top-u-s-commander-american-troops-stay-afghanistan/; Gordon Lubold, Margherita Stancati and Habib Khan Totakhil, 'Taliban Offensive in Afghanistan Tests U.S', *The Wall Street Journal*, 29 September 2015, http://www.wsj.com/articles/u-s-warplanes-carry-out-airstrike-in-northern-afghanistan-1443526964.

109 Donald J. Trump, @realDonaldTrump, Twitter Post, 22 August 2012, 12:05am, https://mobile.twitter.com/realdonaldtrump/status/237913235045638144?lang=en.

110 Julie Davis and Mark Landler, 'Trump Outlines New Afghanistan War Strategy with Few Details', *The New York Times*, 21 August 2017, https://www.nytimes.com/2017/08/21/world/asia/afghanistan-troops-trump.html.

111 Philip Ewing and Brian Naylor, '"We Are not Nation-Building Again," Trump says while Unveiling Afghanistan Strategy', *NPR*, 21 August 2017, https://www.npr.org/2017/08/21/545044232/trump-expected-to-order-4-000-more-troops-to-afghanistan.

112 Vanda Felbab-Brown, 'President Trump's Afghanistan Policy: Hopes and Pitfalls', (report, The Brookings Institution, Washington, D.C., September 2017).

113 Rohan Joshi, 'Trump's Afghanistan Policy: The Good, the Bad, and the Ugly', *The Diplomat*, 25 August 2017, https://thediplomat.com/2017/08/trumps-afghanistan-policy-the-good-the-bad-and-the-ugly/.

114 'US Congress Passes Bill to Slash Pakistan's Security Aid to USD 150 million', *The Economic Times*, 3 August 2018, https://economictimes.indiatimes.com/news/international/world-news/us-congress-passes-bill-to-slash-pakistans-security-aid-to-usd-150-million/videoshow/65258721.cms.

115 For a full discussion, see 'Afghanistan Opium Survey 2017: Cultivation and Production', (report, The United Nations Office of Drugs and Crime, New York, November 2017), p. 5. and the rest of the report, https://www.unodc.org/documents/crop-monitoring/Afghanistan/Afghan_opium_survey_2017_cult_prod_web.pdf.

116 For details, see Amin Saikal, 'Afghanistan: A Turbulent State in Transition', in *Modern Afghanistan: The Impact of 40 Years of War*, ed. M. Nazif Shahrani (Bloomington: Indiana University Press, 2018), p. 25.

117 'Afghanistan will Collapse within Six Months without US Support and Money: President Ashraf Ghani', *News18*, 18 January 2018, https://www.news18.com/news/world/afghanistan-will-collapse-within-six-months-without-us-support-and-money-president-ashraf-ghani-1635539.html.

118 'Civilian Deaths in Afghanistan hit Record High – UN', *UN News*, 15 July 2018, https://news.un.org/en/story/2018/07/1014762.

119 For a detailed discussion of the strength and weakness of the Afghan military, see Anthony Cordesman, 'Afghanistan Desertion in the U.S: Assessing the Desertion and "Ghost Soldier" Problems in Afghan National Security Forces', (report, Center for Strategic and International Studies, Washington, 30 October 2017).
120 Robert M. Gates, *Duty: Memoirs of a Secretary at War* (New York: Vintage, 2015), p. 336.
121 Jeremy White, 'Taliban Urges Americans to Pressure Trump and Congress to Pull Troops from Afghanistan', *The Independent*, 14 February 2018, http://www.independent.co.uk/news/world/asia/taliban-us-donald-trump-congress-troops-afghanistan-soldiers-war-a8211081.html.

2

Afghanistan and Regional Security

The Views from Central Asia

The security dimension has dominated policy thinking on Afghanistan in all Central Asian republics since independence. This was especially noticeable during the Taliban rule of 1996–2001, and is again the case following NATO's withdrawal from Afghanistan in 2014. One indicator of a high level of mistrust and apprehension towards their southern neighbour, is public opinion. While there is a great deal of diversity in foreign policy preferences across the region, Afghanistan is universally relegated to the bottom three countries with whom it is felt close positive relations ought to be cultivated (Table 2.1). Even Tajikistan, which has the strongest ethno-cultural bonds with Afghanistan, seems lukewarm to the idea of all-round cooperation.

When asked a direct question about the biggest threat to their country, Afghanistan (together with the United States) topped the charts in Central Asia

Table 2.1 Public opinion in Central Asian states on preferences for closer relations with foreign countries

Kazakhstan	Kyrgyzstan	Uzbekistan	Tajikistan
	Top three choices		
Russia	Russia	Russia	Russia
The European Union	Kazakhstan	South Korea	Kazakhstan
Kyrgyzstan	China	Kazakhstan	China
	Bottom three choices		
United States	India	Tajikistan	Afghanistan
Iran	Iran	Iran	South Korea
Afghanistan	Afghanistan	Afghanistan	United States

Source: Adapted from B. Rakisheva, 'Integratsionnye orientiry molodezhi Tsentralnoi Azii (rezultaty sotsiologicheskogo issledovaniia)', in *Tsentralnaia Aziia v usloviiakh globalnoi transformatsii*, ed. Z. K. Shaukenova (Astana: KISI, 2017), 108–109.

Table 2.2 Biggest perceived threats to Central Asian countries in 2015

Country	Biggest threat	Percentage mentioning
Turkmenistan	Afghanistan	51
Kazakhstan	United States	36
Kyrgyzstan	United States	33
Tajikistan	Syria	31
Uzbekistan	Afghanistan	16

Source: Adapted from N. Esipova and J. Ray, 'Eastern Europeans, CIS Residents See Russia, U.S. as Threats', *Gallup*, 4 April 2016, https://news.gallup.com/poll/190415/eastern-europeans-cis-residents-russia-threats.aspx?version=print.

in 2015 (Table 2.2). Again, Tajikistan was a bit of an outlier, naming Syria – as a code for the ISIS menace. Given the formation of ISIS-K in Afghanistan later in the year, the presence of the Afghan factor in the imagination of danger among Tajik citizens would almost certainly have grown in significance.

In 2017, a political scientist from Tajikistan, summarised the image of Afghanistan in Central Asia as follows:

> Afghanistan has turned into a source of the whole complex of challenges and threats such as religious extremism, international terrorism, illegal circulation of drugs and weapons, illegal migration etc. which constitutes a genuine threat to national security of both individual newly independent states and regional security as a whole.[1]

Official policy documents concur with this assessment. In October 2017, the Collective Security Treaty Organization (CSTO) – which counts among its members Kazakhstan, Kyrgyzstan, Tajikistan and Russia – issued a joint statement on the 'Situation in Afghanistan and the Threat of the Strengthening of International Terrorist and Extremist Organization'. The CSTO expressed concern about the 'deterioration of the security situation in Afghanistan, the high level of terrorist activity and the seizure of new regions around the country by armed opposition fighters', and the consequent 'threats to security and stability in Central Asia'. The organisation highlighted particular alarm about the growing narcotic problem, and called on the international community to 'fight the Afghan drug threat more energetically'.[2] None of these observations was in itself ground-breaking; the declaration was notable in its official and succinct articulation of the Afghan threat to Central Asia. Its logic and vocabulary mirrored the official security discourse not just of the member states but also of Turkmenistan and Uzbekistan, that has remained fairly consistent in the post-ISAF period.

This chapter undertakes a country-by-country analysis of the perceptions of security risks associated with Afghanistan, in Kazakhstan, Kyrgyzstan, Tajikistan, Turkmenistan and Uzbekistan. These perceptions revolve around six distinct narratives of insecurity. These are: 1) terrorism and radicalisation; 2) narcotics trafficking; 3) spillover of fighting from Afghanistan; 4) humanitarian crises and refugee flows; 5) cross-border ethnofidelity; and 6) the risk of becoming involved in great power rivalry centred on Afghanistan. Evidence of all six can be found in official and expert discourse in each Central Asian republic, although their hierarchy and the intensity of securitisation varies by country and over time. Given the particular salience of international terrorism in the perceptions of danger in Central Asia today, it is necessary first to provide a detailed account of ISIS-K in the region, building on the discussion in Chapter 1.

The ISIS Challenge

By mid-2018 the so-called Caliphate of the Islamic State of Iraq and Syria (ISIS) had suffered dramatic and seemingly irreversible territorial losses. Indeed, as early as November 2017, the Iraqi Prime Minister, Hadir al-Abadi, declared military victory over ISIS forces in Iraq, while Iranian President Hassan Rouhani simultaneously announced that Iran had successfully driven ISIS out of Syria.[3] Almost exactly a year later, a drastically reduced core of ISIS fighters were under siege in Hajin, in the Deir ez-Zor province; the last remaining stronghold of ISIS in Syria.[4] This fight for survival was a far cry from the grand ambitions that accompanied the triumphant declaration of an Islamic Caliphate, by Abu Bakr al-Baghdadi, on 29 June 2014.[5] However, while attention has been firmly focussed on Iraq and Syria, ISIS has been building a global network of *wilayats* or provinces. As ISIS suffers immense territorial losses and casualties in the Middle East, these far-flung provinces on the periphery of the Caliphate, continue to breathe life into the crucial territorial ambitions of ISIS.

The *wilayat* Khorasan (ISIS-K), an Afghan-based affiliate of ISIS was declared on 26 January 2015, by Abu Muhammad al-Adnani, ISIS's spokesperson and second in command. The notional geography of Khorasan – a mythohistorical designation – comprises a broad swathe of territory: stretching from Iran in the west, across Central Asia, as far as China in the east. The founding members of ISIS-K were seasoned militants of the Tehrik-i Taliban Pakistan (TTP), along with recruits from existing regional salafist militant groups, who renounced previous ties and swore allegiance to al-Baghdadi. Under the initial leadership of Hafiz Saeed Khan – emir of ISIS's Khorasan province – ISIS-K established a foothold in Nangarhar, near the border with Pakistan, 'recruiting disaffected insurgent Taliban commanders, leveraging local resources, and winning or coercing support from Salafi religious networks'.[6] The group quickly moved to the forefront of a crowded field of armed militant groups in Afghanistan, almost certainly due to the prestige of its association with a globally successful jihadist movement and its capacity to access broader external sources of funding.

In 2018, ISIS-K continued to attract recruits, notwithstanding the 'negative reverberations' caused by the collapse of ISIS in Iraq and Syria.[7] Indeed, contrary to expectations that the destruction of the Caliphate would irreparably cripple ISIS operations elsewhere, there are indications that ISIS-K may, in fact, be an inadvertent beneficiary of territorial losses in Iraq and Syria. Antonio Giustozzi suggests that ISIS's administration is being relocated in 'piecemeal' fashion from Syria to Afghanistan and that 'top-level leaders will follow'.[8] This comes close on the heels of a resumption of funding from Syria to ISIS-K, as ISIS seeks to withdraw its significant financial resources from former territories.

A consequence of the collapse of the Caliphate is the dispersal of ISIS recruits – now battle-hardened – across the globe. The vulnerability of Western countries to violent acts committed by returning jihadists, has been widely flagged.[9] Less attention has been given to the movement of ISIS fighters into the Afghan arena. However, there is a historical precedent of foreign fighters in Afghanistan and the substantial Central Asian ISIS contingent – numbering anywhere between four hundred and five thousand[10] – are well-placed to re-emerge as the experienced foot soldiers of an ascendant ISIS-K.

Militants from Central Asia already have an established presence in ISIS-K. In September 2014, the emir of the Islamic Movement of Uzbekistan (IMU), Usman Ghazi, declared that IMU was forsaking its traditional alliance with the Afghan Taliban, in support of ISIS.[11] In mid-2015, a faction of IMU declared *bay'a* (allegiance) to ISIS and a number of high profile IMU militants have actively promoted ISIS and sought recruits in northern Afghanistan.[12] Defections from other Afghan-based militant groups including Al Qaeda and, even more prominently, the Taliban, have, for the most part, been to the benefit of ISIS-K. Indeed, Paul Lushenko, an intelligence officer in the US army, suggests that any negotiation brokered between the coalition and the Taliban will see a wave of Taliban defections to ISIS-K.[13]

In mid-2017, a succession struggle erupted between Aslam Farooqi, a former commander of the Pakistani Lashkar-e-Toiba (LeT), and former IMU commander, Moawiya. The Central Asian faction, following Moawiya, has operated in northern Afghanistan, while Farooqi's faction dominated eastern Afghanistan.[14] The two factions reconciled in early 2018, under pressure from the top leadership of ISIS and in the context of ongoing coalition and Taliban attacks against the group.

ISIS-K has inherited an expansionist strategy, capitalising on 'weak governance, under-addressed grievances, and poor security' in order to establish itself across the region.[15] It has intentionally sought to exacerbate ethnic, territorial and sectarian disputes to 'indigenize its agenda among marginalized Muslims and secular populations'.[16] According to reports from Kyrgyzstan and Tajikistan, ISIS-K earmarked US$70 million in 2015, to finance sedition and subversion in Central Asia.[17] Giustozzi, among others, has commented on the growing presence of *mujahideen* within Central Asia, the number of which may have reached the 750 mark in 2017, noting that those operating in Kazakhstan, Kyrgyzstan and Uzbekistan depend on ISIS-K while those in Tajikistan tend to follow ISIS-Central.[18] Recent attacks by ISIS-K operatives in South Asia and Tajikistan, and thwarted attacks in the United States are evidence of its reach beyond Afghanistan's borders.

After decades of war and internal chaos, much of rural Afghanistan is seemingly inured to living alongside armed militants and without the presence of a functioning state. However, burgeoning attacks against civilians – including attacks on schools and Shi'a communities – suggest that ISIS-K is prepared to continue the recognised terror-based *modus operandi* of ISIS. For the foreseeable future Afghanistan seems set to remain the backdrop against which the global ambitions of today's militant Islamists are played out. As such, the 'ISIS challenge' features prominently in the security concerns of Afghanistan's northern neighbours.

Kazakhstan

Kazakhstan is the Central Asian state with the weakest ties to Afghanistan, as it shares no common border and has almost no ethnic kin living in Afghanistan. Kazakhstan is located at the opposite end of the greater Central Asian region, with a significant geographical buffer zone in between. From this position of geographical distance, Afghanistan is considered to be more closely tied to South Asia and the Middle East in terms of security, political, social, and economic dynamics. At the same time, Kazakhstan identifies itself as a Eurasian entity whose primary interests connect it with Europe and North-East Asia.

Despite this, Kazakhstan has, since 2001, been pursuing fairly active Afghanistan diplomacy, with an emphasis on multilateral frameworks such as the Organization for Security and Co-operation in Europe (OSCE), the United Nations and the 'Heart of Asia'/Istanbul process.[19] The reasons the Kazakh government have given for its engagement with Afghanistan include both security concerns and possible economic opportunities in Afghanistan. The Kazakh leadership is far quieter in public about the benefits of having served as a transit zone for NATO/ ISAF troops and supplies going to Afghanistan and back. Furthermore, Kazakh leaders have, as Nargis Kassenova argued, been 'seeking status and prestige through positioning [Kazakhstan] as a constructive and responsible stakeholder in the provision of regional and global security'.[20] It is significant to note that, as part of this broader objective, Kazakhstan has provided over US$50 million in aid assistance to Afghanistan in support of reconstruction projects, which include emergency food assistance, social services provision and a long-term project to train Afghan students at Kazakh universities.[21]

In April 2017, President Nursultan Nazarbaev outlined three primary threats facing Kazakhstan in the contemporary world: terrorism, migration and narcotics trafficking. Four million migrants transit through Kazakhstan annually, according to Nazarbaev, with 600,000 guest workers (although the share of Afghans in either category is minuscule). He explicitly highlighted Afghanistan as the primary source of the narcotics problem, and praised the CSTO for its work combatting drug trafficking in the region.[22] According to the Kazakh Interior Ministry, thirty-five tonnes of heroin were intercepted by authorities in 2016, and eleven criminal trafficking groups were stopped. The interdiction rate is generally believed to be as low as 1 per cent.[23]

The radicalisation threat looms large in Kazakhstan, although it has not been subject to the same degree of hyperbole as in other Central Asian republics. In 2016, the head of the Kazakh security service estimated that 800 nationals were receiving training at jihadi camps on the Afghan–Pakistan border.[24] President Nazarbaev suggested in November 2017 that, 'some 400 young Kazakhstanis had been recruited by Islamic State. But now that ISIS is being defeated they are returning'.[25]

The evolution of the views of Erlan Karin, Kazakhstan's eminent public intellectual in the area of Islamic radicalism who has held senior positions in government, think tanks and the media, is illustrative of the dynamics of official discourse securitising Afghanistan. In 2014, he dismissed the Afghan factor as of secondary importance to the security of Kazakhstan.[26] According to Karin, a tiny group of Kazakhstanis belonging to the Jund al-Khilafa gang, operating primarily in Waziristan had been utterly destroyed by Pakistani and US attacks.[27] Three years later, Karin acknowledged Afghanistan's recrudescent relevance to the radicalisation in Kazakhstan. The main threat, according to him, would be ideological: "This will be reflected in the growth of propaganda towards Central Asia. In other words, new propaganda materials targeting Central Asia will appear, the content of radicalizing sources will increase, and we'll have to take this into active account."[28] In 2018, Karin adjusted his position again, saying that those who, one or two years previously, underestimated the threat from ISIS in Afghanistan were wrong: it was no longer just about propaganda but also the direct risk of terrorism about which Central Asians ought to be wary.[29]

Kazakhstan's geographical remoteness ensures that the plight of the few ethnic Kazakhs in Afghanistan and the direct military threat from its territory, are not a major concern in the official security discourse. The 2011 'Military Doctrine of the Republic of Kazakhstan' noted that 'the security situation in Central Asia has the potential to deteriorate due to the ongoing instability in Afghanistan'.[30] In the event that the frontline republics, bordering Afghanistan, were destabilised, this would impact Kazakhstan via a domino effect. The 2017 edition of the 'Military Doctrine of the Republic of Kazakhstan', does not mention Afghanistan at all; it merely refers to the threat of radicalisation in general terms, noting, for example, 'the utilization of Kazakhstani citizens who are members of terrorist and extremist groups for the purpose of destabilizing the internal situation'.[31]

Public discourse centred on the influx of refugees does exist in Kazakhstan and is commonly referred to in local parlance as 'an emergency situation of a social nature'. It had particular salience in 2016, in the context of the migration crisis in Europe. Despite low numbers of refugees – only 700 in January 2016, of whom about 90 per cent were Afghan[32] – the Kazakh government has resolved to erect refugee camps on its southern borders, as a precautionary measure. One official commented that 'this is not to say that refugees will come to us today. This facility is to be held in reserve. If such a situation occurs, our region will be prepared for it.'[33] Funding for the camps came out of a budget line allocated for 'repulsing and resisting terrorism'.[34]

Kazakhstan's status as a comparatively rich nation, and an important regional player in its own right, lessens its concern about adverse impacts flowing from great power rivalry in Central Asia. The multi-vector foreign policy of Nazarbaev is based on maintaining a careful equilibrium of geopolitical balance between Russia, China and the West. Afghanistan is viewed as an opportunity in this context – Astana happily supports diplomatic initiatives coming from all three, believing that ultimately all sides 'may have a common interest and incentive' in achieving lasting peace there.³⁵ At the same time, since 2014, the leadership of Kazakhstan has anticipated the growing presence of Russia and China in the military and security realm, accompanied by the West's decreased engagement. The pecking order of preferred partners to deal with Afghanistan-related risks is clear: Russia and the CSTO, followed by China and the Shanghai Cooperation Organization (SCO), with the United States and NATO relegated to third place.³⁶ Kazakhstan's politicians and experts are fully aware that Moscow and Beijing are likely to exaggerate the actual threats but accept this as 'a way for them to maintain their own domestic stability', rather than a geopolitical ploy.³⁷

Kyrgyzstan

From late 2001 onwards, Kyrgyzstan gave Afghanistan an important place in its foreign policy, but only because of Afghanistan's new relevance to Western countries. The war in Afghanistan offered Kyrgyzstan a chance to boost its international importance and its utility to the United States. The Manas air base in Bishkek was the most important element of this relationship, with the diverted revenue being an important rent for the Kyrgyz leadership and its family network. After Kyrgyz leadership changes – in addition to Russian pressure and deteriorating relations with the United States – in 2014 the Kyrgyz government ended the agreement that had allowed American and European militaries to use Manas.³⁸ After the air base closed Afghanistan was downgraded as a foreign policy concern of Kyrgyzstan.³⁹ However, while Tajikistan and Uzbekistan provide a land barrier between Kyrgyzstan and Afghanistan, Bishkek retains a multifaceted appreciation of the Afghan threat.

The 'Military Doctrine of the Kyrgyz Republic', adopted in 2013 and still in force, names Afghanistan among the 'main threats to military security' in Kyrgyzstan. As a matter of fact, it is the only foreign state mentioned by name in the document. The Doctrine observes:

> Threats of international terrorism, extremism and separatism in the Central Asian region remain pertinent; their formations are capable of rapid adaptation to countermeasures and utilization of new tactics and techniques of subversive acts. Problems of narco-trafficking and illegal migration are transnational in nature and have acquired even greater dimensions. There is a possibility of border incidents and military action on the state frontier and border areas on the basis of the extant unresolved issues.⁴⁰

The 2012 National Security Concept likewise identifies Afghanistan as 'one of the key threats to stability in Central Asia'.[41] The then Vice Premier, Tokon Mamytov, articulated three principles which he said Kyrgyzstan should follow in its approach to Afghanistan. 'First – relations of trust must be established', he wrote in 2013. 'Second – businesslike atmosphere which should follow trust. Third – friendship of the Afghan people.'[42] While these ambitions may seem noble, Mamytov's true feelings to Afghanistan were revealed later in the same document. 'The Kyrgyzstan government's position on Afghanistan consists of extinguishing the fire of tensions and threats to Central Asia at the distant approaches, in Afghanistan itself. When these threats arrive on the Tajik border they'll be unstoppable.'[43]

Memories of Islamist incursions from Afghanistan into southern Kyrgyzstan in 1999 and 2000, known locally as the 'Batken campaigns', continue to trouble the Kyrgyz leadership and public. Clashes between government troops and insurgents from the IMU, who enjoyed support from the Taliban and Al Qaeda, caused Bishkek to revise its military and security planning in order to overhaul its sub-par armed forces.[44] In the post-2014 era, there is still little domestic confidence in their ability to withstand another onslaught from Afghanistan. In August 2017, a serving military officer told a media outlet, on condition of anonymity, 'Hypothetically, if enemies strike from Afghan Badakhshan ... they will reach our city of Osh within 24 hours. The situation is extremely dangerous ... So dangerous that we may wake up one morning and see militants walking in our streets.'[45] These comments align with the typical expert opinion:

> Afghanistan is turning into a hotbed fraught with threat to the entire Central Asia. ISIS plans include the conquest of the region. In Central Asia, Kyrgyzstan has a weak military and economic potential so this country won't be able to stand up to the fighters. Besides, there are 'sleeper fighters' in our country who are waiting for a 'zero hour'.[46]

The official narrative of danger posed presented by sleeper cells and returnee *mujahideen* gained momentum and found reflection in the 2017 launch of a state program designed to combat extremism and terrorism over the five years to 2022.[47] In 2010, seventy-nine people were convicted of terrorism-related offences in Kyrgyzstan; in 2017 that number reached 422. Members of the Uzbek minority are often treated as particularly suspicious. Researchers at the Diplomatic Academy of the Foreign Ministry of Kyrgyzstan wrote.

> Hundreds of young ethnic Uzbeks – citizens of Kyrgyzstan – have joined radical Islamists and are at training bases in Pakistan and Afghanistan. They are ready

to return to the Ferghana Valley in order to take part in armed struggle against secular regimes.[48]

Indeed, ethnic Uzbeks accounted for two-thirds of the 850 or so residents of Kyrgyzstan who joined ISIS abroad; they have recently been implicated in high-profile international terrorist incidents, including an attack on the Reina nightclub in Istanbul in 2016 and the St. Petersburg metro bomb blast in 2017.[49] Sirozhiddin Mukhtarov, the leader of the Jama'at al-Tawhid wa-l-Jihad (JTJ) terror group who masterminded the St. Petersburg attack, as well as the bombing of the Chinese embassy in Bishkek in 2016, has been alleged to have ties with the notorious Haqqani Network in Pakistan and Afghanistan.[50]

Afghanistan is squarely blamed for the deteriorating narcotics situation in the country. In 2014 the main government think tank warned of the imminent danger of Kyrgyzstan 'becoming a hostage to one of the most dynamically progressing drug producers in the world'.[51] According to Kyrgyzstan's top investigative police officer, 30 per cent of Afghan opiates earmarked for export went through Kyrgyz territory, with up to 10–15 per cent of the transit volume staying for local consumption, causing a spike in public safety and health issues.[52] In March 2017, President Almazbek Atambaev engaged in a lengthy televised diatribe. 'Why has the narcotics circulation grown so much, why have shipments of narcotics from Afghanistan to other countries increased?' he asked, going on to answer, 'Because for better or worse the Taliban used to combat poppy cultivation and narcotics growing and when they were replaced by the coalition led by the Americans, the new guys didn't care.' He directed a targeted barb at the US-led coalition for the 'several fold' increase in opium plantation: 'We have to thank those who made a decision to implement a new order in Afghanistan for this.'[53]

Criticising the United States for its Afghan counter-narcotics policy is just one element of the wholesale anti-Americanism evident in the official security discourse of Kyrgyzstan. Bishkek uncritically associates Washington's strategy with the geopolitical ideas of Zbigniew Brzezinski, whereby control of Central Asia is indispensable to the perpetuation of US global hegemony.[54] The United States is held largely responsible for regime changes in Kyrgyzstan in 2005 and 2010. Its plans to cajole Central Asian republics into logistical and infrastructure integration with Afghanistan serves 'the principal objective of subjugating the extractive and transport industries in the region to the American capital'.[55] According to a 2017 poll, some 45 per cent of Kyrgyz citizens view the United States as the greatest economic threat to their country (Figure 2.1), outpacing the second-placed China by some distance.

Which of these countries do you consider to be the most important economic partners and greatest economic threats to Kyrgyzstan?
(Multiple answers allowed)

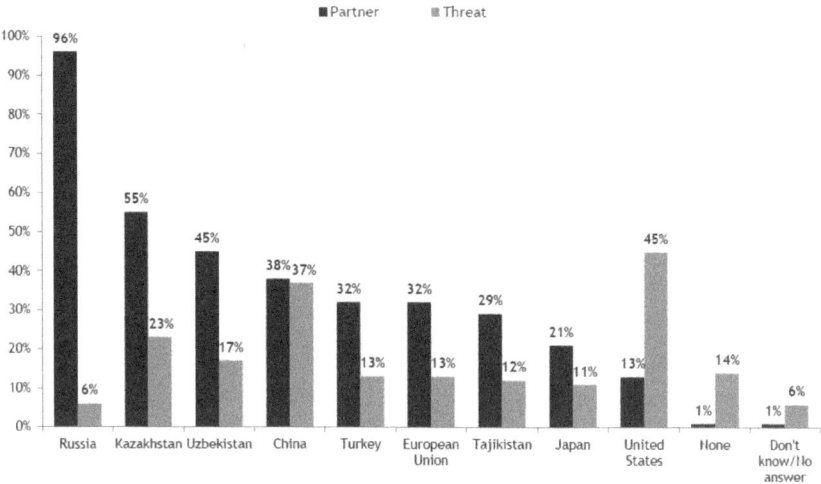

Figure 2.1 Popular views on economic partners and threats in Kyrgyzstan.

Source: *Public Opinion Survey: Residents of Kyrgyzstan*. Washington, DC: Center for Insights in Survey Research, 2017, p. 47.

Finally, there has been some migration from Afghanistan to Kyrgyzstan, although nothing of a volume that could be perceived as a security threat. In May 2016, the government expressed concern about the plight of their ethnic kin, the Pamir Kyrgyzs, who face privation and lack of social services in Afghanistan. An official humanitarian mission was launched with the purpose of 'delivering emergency humanitarian aid to ethnic Kyrgyzs who have found themselves in a difficult life situation'.[56] Thirty-three persons were evacuated to be resettled in Kyrgyzstan. In the same year, 106 Afghans were granted refugee status in Kyrgyzstan.[57]

Tajikistan

Officials and experts in Tajikistan have securitised Afghan threats more systematically and with greater vigour than in any other Central Asian republic. A long and porous 1,344 kilometre shared border and Afghanistan's involvement in the Tajik civil war between 1992 and 1997,[58] naturally contribute to this process. Since 2014, the discourse of menace from Afghanistan has gained in intensity. President Emomali Rahmon's state of the nation address, in December 2017, articulated this perception of Afghanistan, noting that 'the threats in contemporary world, especially the situation in the Middle East and particularly in neighbouring Afghanistan are compelling us to attach fundamental significance to the question of national security.'[59]

He went on to highlight the specific risk of terrorism, in the context of the lengthy Tajik–Afghan border, singling out ISIS as an emerging threat. This construction of Islamist threat has occurred in the context of Rahmon's crackdown on the Islamic Renaissance Party of Tajikistan (IRPT). The IRPT operated as a legitimate political entity in Tajikistan from 1997 up until 2015, at which point the authorities accused it of plotting a coup, proscribed it and had many members arrested. The official narrative portrayed the party as a lynchpin of a grand international jihadi conspiracy affecting the whole of Central Asia and beyond:

> The IRPT is regarded by its foreign sponsors as the centre of Islamist revolutionary activity in the region as a whole given the geopolitical position of Tajikistan which has access to Afghanistan, the Ferghana Valley, and the Xinjiang-Uighur Autonomous Region (XUAR).[60]

Security officials claimed that of 1,000 Tajik citizens in the ranks of ISIS in Syria and Iraq, 521 were IRPT members.[61] Local pro-government experts added to the sense of moral panic by opining that, due in large part to the IRPT propaganda, more than 2,000 Tajik citizens had gone to Afghanistan and Pakistan, joining ISIS-K and other jihadi formations.[62] Having received training and money, they allegedly crawl back across the Afghan–Tajik border 'in small groups of two to three persons ... in order to scout locations for their armed units and terrorist groups'.[63]

Without denying the problem of radicalisation in Tajikistan, independent scholars have questioned its scale and the impact of Afghanistan upon it. The Rahmon government may be bolstering its internal and external legitimacy by presenting itself as a victim of global terrorism and an uncompromising fighter against it.[64] A recent sociological study found that potential support for religious extremist movements in Tajikistan was low and its social base narrow, not exceeding 6–7 per cent of the Muslim population; ISIS recruiters had less success in Tajikistan than in Russia; the Taliban had no influence on the domestic situation at all; and interaction between Islamists in Tajikistan and Afghanistan was weak, occurring mostly through the agency of the Gulf countries' support networks.[65] The study concluded, 'The Afghan factor can only amplify radicalization in the Republic of Tajikistan but it won't play the trigger role – merely an expediting device.'[66]

Also on President Rahmon's radar was the problem of drug production and cross-border trafficking through Tajikistan. Official discourse portrays Tajikistan as a heroic sentinel protecting the rest of Central Asia, Russia and much of the world from a murky torrent of Afghan opiates:

> Since 1994 up until now, the law enforcing bodies and military structures of Tajikistan confiscated 121 tons of narcotics including over thirty-four tons of heroin. Such quantities of drugs could have destroyed lives of fifty-three million people and devastated many families.[67]

The Chief of Staff of Tajikistan's frontier guards spoke in 2016 about 'a serious threat of saboteur operations by international secret services from the territory of Afghanistan aimed at undermining the political situation in the Republic of Tajikistan', working in cahoots with 'Afghan smugglers who create hideouts and caches of narcotics and base camps in their border region from which they transport their deadly wares and recruit accomplices from the population in the [Tajik] border zone'.[68] The Tajik public is frequently reminded that Rahmon has appealed, multiple times, to the international community to create an impenetrable 'security belt' on the border with chaotic and dangerous Afghanistan, but that these pleas have fallen on deaf ears. The picture is one of manifest failure, on the part of the government of Afghanistan and its Western backers, to curb the drug barons inside the country, most of whom have now formed links with terrorists, extremists and subversive agents of all stripes.[69] Against this bleak scenario, President Rahmon, projects an image of Tajikistan, 'resolving the whole world's problems single-handedly'.[70]

Leaving aside the intriguing question of Tajik government officials' role in the narcotics racket,[71] the image of Dushanbe as a world saviour is misleading. Tajikistan accounted for 34 per cent of all opiate seizures (expressed in heroin equivalent) in Central Asia over the period 2011–2015, the largest proportion of opiate seizures in any country in the region,[72] but the northern route via Central Asia conveyed only 25 per cent of Afghanistan's total heroin exports.

There is no doubt that narcotics trafficking from Afghanistan does affect state security in Tajikistan. One of the critical issues at present is that it empowers alternative centres of authority, especially in the Gorno-Badakhshan Autonomous Oblast (GBAO) which has had a chequered history of accepting control from Dushanbe. Heroin seizures in GBAO rose by 89 per cent between 2016 and 2017, indicating a spike in smuggling activity; the remote region was estimated to be a conduit for 16 per cent of Afghan opiates traversing the country.[73] Proceeds from a criminal enterprise in narcotics have enabled the local strongmen to deliver social services and maintain significant, if ambivalent, public legitimacy at loggerheads with the central government.[74]

Narcotics-related skirmishes on the Afghan–Tajik border are common – in the first nine months of 2017, twenty-six armed incidents occurred, with thirteen traffickers killed and nineteen apprehended.[75] Afghan officials accused the Tajik border guards of killing innocent Afghans in order to simulate a fight against contrabandists and receive awards from their leadership: 'Tajik intelligence has promised that they will be awarded medals if they capture or kill a smuggler on the border with Afghanistan'.[76] Dushanbe strenuously denied such allegations and defended its sovereign right to open fire on armed smugglers, adding that such episodes would occur, 'until such time that peace and stability prevail in the Islamic Republic of Afghanistan'.[77] One of the most serious incidents took place in December 2017, when a Tajik Colonel commanding a border guard detachment in the Shuroabad district was shot and killed by Afghan drug mules.[78] The entire border was subsequently closed for several days by Tajik authorities, including the strategic Sher Khan Bandar crossing.

Beyond incursions by Islamists and criminals, the narrative of a spillover risk in Tajikistan has increasingly focused on the Taliban's operations in the north of Afghanistan. In 2016–2018, the Taliban conducted several offensives in the provinces of Balkh, Kunduz, Takhar and Badakhshan, overrunning ANA garrisons and coming right to the border with Tajikistan. Dushanbe interpreted this as a disturbing strategic development, whereby what used to be a secondary front for the Taliban, was now receiving a lot more attention. The main Tajik security agency, GKNB, revised its assessment of the strength of the Taliban in the adjacent areas from 1,200 armed fighters in 2015 to 7,000 in 2018, identifying twenty-nine new training camps, at which some Central Asians were spotted.[79] The fall of Zebak in May 2017, created consternation in Tajik Ishkashim across the river. 'If the Taliban, God forbid, decide to cross the border and attack our districts, we don't have a professionally trained army', said a local Tajik politician, adding, 'but the Taliban are a very disciplined movement and not a single fighter will get onto our territory without receiving an appropriate order'.[80] Such an order has not yet come and is not likely to be issued any time soon, but nervous anticipation on the Tajik side of the border is real enough, and the likelihood of an accidental exchange of fire is high.

Uncontrolled population flows from Afghanistan also cause concern in Dushanbe. Tajikistan faced a refugee crisis due to instability in Afghanistan in

1999 and 2000, with over 10,000 Afghans officially seeking asylum across the border.[81] The total figure was almost certainly much higher, with some suggesting up to 90,000 Afghans may have attempted to seek asylum in Tajikistan – many were denied entry and loitered on islands in the Panj and Amu Darya rivers.[82] According to the United Nations High Commissioner for Refugees (UNHCR), Tajikistan hosts, at present, approximately 3,000 refugees from Afghanistan.[83] The country's ability to accept displaced persons remains precarious. One expert wrote in 2017, that 'the arrival of thousands of refugees could seriously destabilize the situation in Tajikistan and generate large-scale negative consequences … Tajikistan continues to lack the necessary material resources to accept a large number of refugees'.[84]

Among all Central Asian republics, Tajikistan has the strongest connection with Afghanistan in terms of mutual awareness. Nonetheless, despite shared ethnicity, language, religion and history, cross-border connections are not particularly strong. A recent sociological study revealed that communities on two sides of the Amu Darya river consider each other as having different values, political aspirations and economic ambitions, producing a poignant summary: 'A Tajik from Afghanistan and a Tajik from Tajikistan would not have much to share, even if they understood each other's language.'[85] A narrow but vocal stratum of nationalist intellectuals in Dushanbe disagrees and agitates for a united front of Tajiks in both countries against what it sees as a combined onslaught against 'Tajikness' perpetrated by the Taliban, the government in Kabul, ISIS and the West. The first two are culpable of forced Pashtunisation; after all, 'the current war in Afghanistan is the war of two nations – Pashtuns and Tajiks'.[86] The United States and the regime of Ashraf Ghani deliberately and systematically push the Taliban and ISIS to the north of the country in order to destroy ethnic Tajiks there, who had traditionally played the role of a buffer protecting Central Asia and Russia.[87] These intellectuals lionise Ahmad Shah Massoud, Burhanuddin Rabbani, Mohammad Fahim, Atta Mohammad Nur and other Afghan Tajik commanders and posit that peace in Afghanistan, and consequently in Central Asia, is impossible without strong leadership by the Tajiks who are the only group in the country free of external geopolitical patronage.[88]

While pan-Tajik nationalists are active in the media and especially social networks where they engage with anti-Pashtun elements in Afghanistan,[89] their ideas are not openly shared by Dushanbe. It has never questioned the legitimacy of the Karzai and Ghani governments, or otherwise interfered in Afghan domestic politics. As Marlene Laruelle argued, Tajikistan's financial and political reach remains circumscribed and does not stretch beyond moral support to the Tajik Afghans and the provision of a potential rear-operating base for anti-extremist forces, should the situation in Afghanistan spin out of control.[90]

Although Tajikistan officially pursues a multi-vector foreign policy, its policy elite essentially follows the Russian lead in assessing the geopolitical context of the Afghan problem.[91] Its dominant narrative is that of deliberate and purposeful movement of the zone of instability from the south of Afghanistan to the north with the aim of setting up a mini-ISIS wilayat or new Waziristan there. The agency in this process belongs to the United States and its allies, who are preparing to spread instability to Central Asia, 'viewed by the West as a bridgehead for an attack on Russia's and China's interests'.[92]

Turkmenistan

Since its independence in 1991, the government of Turkmenistan has followed the international policy of permanent neutrality; better viewed as self-imposed isolation, occasionally moderated by bilateral transactional diplomacy. It has neglected to cooperate with its Central Asian neighbours in regards to economic or diplomatic relations. Outside the region, Turkmenistan has been careful not to make any serious commitments to multilateral cooperation or international organisations.[93] For Ashgabat, relations with Afghanistan are, however, a necessity conditioned by geography and a shared frontier. Both of Turkmenistan's post-Soviet leaders, presidents Saparmurat Niyazov and Gurbanguly Berdimuhammedov, have – to varying degrees – been worried about war and instability across the border in Afghanistan (including the potential spill-over of conflict onto Turkmen territory).

Examining patterns of securitisation of the Afghan factor in Turkmenistan presents unique methodological challenges, as all security-related issues are taboo for the local media and the expert community, insofar as it exists at all. Officials are equally tight-lipped and do little more than reproduce sound bites from the president which are infrequent and inconsistent. As a result, a lot of information about Ashgabat's dealings with Afghanistan comes to light in a mediated form, through sources in Turkmen opposition and via external observers.

Given the 744 kilometre-long border it shares with Afghanistan, conventional security concerns preoccupy official thinking in Turkmenistan regarding the Afghan threat. Throughout the ISAF era, northwestern Afghanistan, comprising the provinces of Herat, Badghis, Faryab and Jowzjan that abut Turkmenistan, was perhaps the most peaceful and stable part of the country. This all began to change in 2013 with attacks by the Taliban in Faryab. In February 2014, unidentified militants crossed the Murghab River into Turkmenistan for the first time, killing three Turkmen servicemen. Since mid-2014, ISIS-K, or to be more precise pro-ISIS groups in the IMU, have been increasingly active in the region.[94] Russian and Turkmen opposition commentators had suggested that eventually ISIS-K may conduct a raid on Turkmen gas fields in South Yolotan and Dauletabad. These expectations proved alarmist, and the focus of securitisation subsequently moved to the scenario where *mujahideen* crossing the border would ignite an uprising of local Islamist cells under conditions of internal unrest or elite infighting.[95]

After years of denial, the Turkmen authorities have finally recognised the existence of an Islamic underground on its territory. In June 2015, an official statement spoke about the arrest of 150 Turkmen citizens – 'supporters and adherents of bandit entities, the Taliban and Islamic State' – who allegedly planned an attack on a state prison. More than 700 of their sympathisers were also identified. Another group of 100 extremists, was caught with explosive devices and a large sum of cash in hand. The statement concluded with a pithy note that 'modern weapons, high professionalism of the army and security agencies, and, naturally, support by the people' guaranteed the state's efficiency in shielding Turkmenistan from harm.[96]

The pattern of denial continues when it comes to the aggravation on the Afghan–Turkmen border. Multiple reports have described Turkmenistan after 2014, as being 'pre-war and mobilizational', with 70 per cent of the Turkmen army stationed on the border and the upper limit of the national call-up age increased from twenty-seven to thirty, in order to bolster the number of recruits.[97] Nonetheless, Ashgabat reacts nervously to any suggestion that problems exist, regardless of whence it comes. The Turkmen government sent a diplomatic note to Kazakhstan in 2015, registering 'serious concern and lack of understanding' about President Nazarbaev's comments regarding multiple incidents on the Afghan–Turkmen border.[98] When US-funded Radio Azatlyk broke the news about the death of twenty-five Turkmen soldiers in a shoot-out on the border in July 2018, the authorities rebuffed it by parading a local shepherd who saw nothing untoward, and castigating 'electronic media financed by the West'.[99] A Russian news outlet's report on concerns raised by the Commonwealth of Independent States (CIS) border guards commanders about the situation on the Turkmen–Afghan border, was similarly dismissed as not corresponding to reality and an 'unfriendly step towards Turkmenistan'.[100]

Narcotics trafficking and widespread drug use in Turkmen society have been publicly identified as a concern. While former President Niyazov and his head of security, were allegedly directly involved in drug trafficking from Afghanistan during Turkmenbashi's reign,[101] Berdimuhammedov has adopted a strict anti-narcotics government policy. Barely a year into his presidency, Berdimuhammedov created a specialised State Service on Combating Narcotics, which has had a considerable positive impact. In 2015, Turkmenistan was the only country in Central Asia not reported by Moscow as a key transit point for shipments of opiates trafficked from Afghanistan to the Russian Federation (it previously held a regular place of honour on that list).[102] The United States has also praised Turkmenistan's efforts, both in supply and demand reduction: 'President Berdimuhamedov's [sic] regular public statements calling for greater international cooperation and increased efforts against illegal narcotics make clear the importance the Government of Turkmenistan places on its counternarcotics efforts.'[103]

One point of departure from Ashgabat's neutral/isolationist stance, consists of the Turkmenistan–Afghanistan–Pakistan–India (TAPI) gas pipeline. In gestation since 1994, it was supposed to become the main export route for Turkmen hydrocarbons. Despite countless MoUs, negotiations, feasibility studies and opaque commercial deals, the project still has no clear prospects, secure financing or a commercial champion to see it through.[104] Desperate for TAPI to materialise, the Turkmen government quietly helped the US-led effort to vanquish the Taliban in the early 2000s.[105] Since 2016, in even greater desperation, it turned to the Taliban for assurances of security astride the pipeline route; allegedly supplying ammunition to them as a sweetener.[106]

Uzbekistan

Uzbekistan has a strong stake in Afghanistan's stability and security – despite its current modest involvement in that country. In light of its patronage of the IMU, the rise of the Taliban movement was viewed as a serious security challenge by the government of Uzbekistan, in the late-1990s. The IMU was accused of plotting President Islam Karimov's assassination and it carried out attacks on Uzbek soil from Afghan territory. A 2000 incursion into the Surkhandarya region, coming quite close to Tashkent, was a particularly disturbing event: 'Uzbekistan's army managed to repulse the IMU gunmen and drive them back, but suffered considerable losses.'[107]

After 2001, the IMU's fortunes declined, and predictions that Karimov's dictatorial domestic policies and repeated crackdowns on unofficial Islamic groups would turn Uzbekistan into a hotbed of extremism did not materialise – Kazakhstan, Kyrgyzstan and Tajikistan had greater problems with the radical underground by comparison.[108] Nonetheless, Islamists continued to be securitised by the state leadership and media, as the number one threat. Government-sponsored opinion polls showed that citizens agreed with the dominant narrative: 85.8 per cent of respondents in 2016 identified religious extremism as the greatest menace to Uzbekistan.[109] The description of danger shifted from a conventional invasion, to what the Uzbek security service (SNB) termed 'hybrid war' – acts of terrorism, along with anti-government agitation and propaganda, recruitment and disturbances from Afghan territory, by ISIS and what is left of the IMU.[110] Afghanistan was the only foreign country mentioned by name (and not in a good way), in Uzbekistan's Military Doctrine, adopted in January 2018: 'The activity of illegal armed formations in Afghanistan constitutes a particular security threat' which 'may necessitate the deployment of military force [by Uzbekistan]'.[111]

Drug trafficking from Afghanistan has been receding in Uzbekistan's security discourse, especially when compared to other frontline states. In 2012, the growing Afghan opium production was deemed to be 'the decisive factor negatively impacting the narcosituation in the republic,' similar to the extant analysis in Kyrgyzstan and Tajikistan.[112] By 2018, references to the heroin explosion in Afghanistan had all but disappeared, giving way to matter-of-fact praise for law enforcers who 'dedicated their main effort to cutting the contraband of opiates from Afghanistan's northern provinces' – an effort which resulted in the seizure of 56 per cent less narcotics (by weight) between 2016 and 2017.[113] Uzbek authorities claimed that in 2017, there was not a single case of death caused by overdose in the country, whereas between 2001 and 2008 about a hundred people perished annually. The diminution of traffic from Afghanistan, and the resultant loss of supply, was touted as one of the main reasons for this outcome.[114]

The 144 kilometre border that Uzbekistan shares with the Afghan province of Balkh is among the most fortified perimeters in the world, featuring electrified barbed wire, minefields and heavily armed troops, including decommissioned Soviet-era tanks that are used as stationary gun emplacements. In general, since the late 1990s the army has been the centre of attention of the Uzbek leadership and has played an important role in legitimising the regime. After Karimov's death in 2016, Shavkat Mirziyoyev campaigned for presidency under the slogan 'Armed Forces of Uzbekistan are the Reliable Guarantor of Security and Stability', reassuring the electorate that they are completely protected even when 'the threats of terrorism, extremism and radicalism are rising'.[115]

Foreign military analysts agree that Uzbekistan's army is the strongest in Central Asia, but cast doubt on its actual ability to counter spillover from Afghanistan. One point of criticism, is the alleged low morale and lack of combat experience: 'If Afghan Taliban mount an attack, it is quite likely that the martial *mujahideen* will disperse the Uzbek army within a week'.[116] Others highlight the sorry state of equipment, inherited from both the Soviet era and the United States, after its withdrawal from Afghanistan. Unless a radical and expensive program of rearmament is pursued, parrying hypothetical attacks by the Taliban, ISIS-K or the IMU would be difficult.[117] Still others comment that Uzbekistan has been preparing for conventional warfare against Kyrgyzstan, Tajikistan and Kazakhstan, instead of operations against highly mobile militants in difficult terrain: 'Perhaps we can even rejoice that the armaments of the [Uzbek] national army have practically not been renewed since its establishment – less quality equipment will fall into the hands of the Taliban or, God forbid, ISIS-K supporters'.[118]

The criticisms above are harsh and exaggerated, but they raise valid questions which were completely ignored in the public security debate in Uzbekistan. Official statements and the media stretch the iron-clad security guarantee to cover the spillover of fighting from Afghanistan, brooking no possibility of a perimeter breach. Only in 2018 did this situation began to change, as will be discussed in Chapter 5.

Uzbekistan's position vis-à-vis its ethnic brethren in Afghanistan, is quite different to that of Tajikistan. Neither the Uzbek government nor patriotic intellectuals regard the Afghan conflict in ethnic terms. The Uzbek minority in Afghanistan is not discussed in Uzbekistan's media, and their living conditions and potential mass exodus are not securitised. The official discourse portrays the picture of rhapsodic harmony:

> Close ties of friendship based on common history, culture, traditions and values connect us with Afghanistan. It must be noted that today more than five million representatives of the Uzbek nationality reside in the IRA. Ethnic Uzbeks take active part in creative processes occurring in that state.[119]

On the other hand, Tashkent dabbles in domestic politics of the neighbouring country to a far greater extent than Dushanbe. This involvement is not publicised; officially, Uzbekistan 'conducts relations with Afghanistan on the basis of bilateralism and principles of mutual respect and non-interference in each other's affairs'.[120] In practice, the Uzbek government uses local proxies in Afghanistan from time to time, to achieve pragmatic objectives. Tashkent's relations with Abdul Rashid Dostum, an ethnic Uzbek who has been the strongman of Mazar-e Sharif and a senior figure in Afghanistan's national politics for decades, is a good example of cool calculation trumping ethnic solidarity. Dostum received some material support from Uzbekistan in 1996–1997, when he was fighting the Taliban, but after he lost and had to flee he was treated very poorly by Uzbek officials, before they allowed him to go into exile in Turkey. Islam Karimov used to joke that 'if Dostum is an Uzbek general, then I am a Chinese general'.[121] In 2016, Dostum was involved in skirmishes with the governor of Balkh, Atta Mohammad Nur, and made demands on Kabul to increase the representation of ethnic Uzbeks in government structures, at the expense of the Tajiks. He received no encouragement from Tashkent. Leaked reports from a meeting between presidents Mirziyoyev and Ghani in December 2017, revealed that Tashkent agreed to help Kabul in resolving 'some political problems with General Dostum and his entourage', in return for Ghani's commitment to deploy more security forces in the border zone and extradite Uzbek criminals wanted for drug trafficking and extremism.[122] A political analyst from Tashkent, in a rare published comment, characterised Dostum as a useful secular figure, 'fighting bearded *mujahideen*', but added that Uzbekistan's leadership did not over-estimate his significance and certainly did not push for his greater role in Afghan national politics.[123]

Similarly to Turkmenistan, Uzbekistan has been cautious about being involved in geopolitical projects focused on Afghanistan. Having bailed out of the strategic alliance with the United States in 2005 and the CSTO in 2012, Tashkent exhibited reluctance to take part in multilateral or regional security initiatives as a matter of policy. Karimov's '6 + 2' talks (involving China, Iran, Pakistan, Tajikistan, Turkmenistan and Uzbekistan, plus Russia and the United States), launched in 1999 and briefly resuscitated in 2008, and Tashkent's half-hearted involvement in the 'Istanbul Process' since 2011, did not alter the picture at all.[124] A significant change that may have began to occur in 2018, will be covered in Chapter 5.

Conclusion

Unstable and war-torn, Afghanistan is viewed as a source of threat by all Central Asian countries. The discourse of danger focuses on six major themes that are common across the region but vary in terms of visibility and intensity from country to country (Table 2.3). Afghanistan's perceived role as a safe haven and operational base for jihadi groups, particularly ISIS-K, is a particularly strong and commonly shared concern. Narcotics production and trafficking is also a universal theme, although it has been recently desecuritised in Turkmenistan and Uzbekistan. Afghanistan features prominently in the official geopolitical calculus only in Kyrgyzstan and Tajikistan – in both cases, it is seen as a bridgehead for the West to penetrate Central Asia, for the purposes of containing Russia and China. The Turkmen and Uzbek ethnic minorities in Afghanistan are not securitised at all by the eponymous states, and Tajikistan's concern about fellow-ethnics across the border is moderate at best.

A detailed examination of how Central Asian republics construct Afghanistan-related threats is an indispensable component in understanding their actual policies vis-à-vis that country – the book's central assumption is that these policies are primarily security-driven. State-sponsored patterns of securitisation (and desecuritisation) follow complex dynamics, where articulation of threats may serve the agenda of regime maintenance domestically and internationally. Nonetheless, the official discourse analysed above, reflects genuine concerns of Central Asian governments about the situation in Afghanistan. Kazakhstan provides a pertinent story in this regard – which should not be used as an 'authenticity deflator' coefficient at all. When authorities in Astana started to sound alarm bells about the rise of ISIS-K as a mortal menace in 2015, the

Table 2.3 Intensity of Afghanistan-related risks in the security discourse in Central Asia

Risk	Kazakhstan	Kyrgyzstan	Tajikistan	Turkmenistan	Uzbekistan
Islamic radicalism and terrorism	High	High	High	High	High
Narcotics trafficking	High	High	High	Medium	Medium
Spillover of fighting	Low	High	High	Medium	Low
Humanitarian crisis and refugee flows	Low	Low	Medium	Low	Low
Cross-border ethnofidelity	N/A	Low	Medium	Low	Low
Geopolitical risks	Medium	High	High	Low	Low

country's top security intellectuals who enjoyed reasonable autonomy from the state were split: 12 per cent believed that the authorised narrative was an instrument of manipulation by the government to tighten domestic control, but 80 per cent agreed with its veracity.[125]

How the Afghanistan policies of the Central Asian republics come to be influenced by the great powers and how they are implemented in practice, will be the subject of discussion in the next two chapters.

Notes

1   Saimuddin Mirzoev, *Afganistan; vyzovy i ugrozy* (Dushanbe: Irfon, 2017), p. 201.
2   'Joint Statement by the Member States of the Collective Security Treaty Organization on the Situation in Afghanistan and the Threat of the Strengthening of International Terrorist and Extremist Organizations in the Northern Provinces of Afghanistan, issued during the 72nd session of the UN General Assembly', Russian Federation, Ministry of Foreign Affairs, 4 October 2017, http://www.mid.ru/foreign_policy/news/-/asset_publisher/cKNonkJE02Bw/content/id/2886857?p_p_id=101_INSTANCE_cKNonkJE02Bw&_101_INSTANCE_cKNonkJE02Bw_languageId=en_GB.
3   Alex Lockie, 'ISIS has been Militarily Defeated in Iraq and Syria', *Business Insider*, 22 November 2017, https://www.businessinsider.com.au/isis-military-defeat-iraq-syria-2017-11?r=US&IR=T.
4   Linda Dorigo, 'ISIL Continues to Wreak Havoc in Syria's Deir Az Zor', *al-Jazeera*, 14 November 2018, https://www.aljazeera.com/indepth/inpictures/isil-continues-wreak-havoc-syria-deir-ez-zor-181028182030798.html.
5   See, 'A New Era has Arrived of Might and Dignity for the Muslims', *Dabiq* 1, Ramadan 1435/July 2014, https://www.trackingterrorism.org/system/files/chatter/Dabiq%201.compressed_0.pdf, pp. 8–9.
6   Casey Garret Johnson, Masood Karokhail and Rahmatullah Amiri, 'The Islamic State in Afghanistan: Assessing the Threat' (briefing paper, United States Institute of Peace, Washington, D.C., 7 April 2016) https://www.usip.org/publications/2016/04/islamic-state-afghanistan-assessing-threat.
7   Antonio Giustozzi, 'Daesh Moves House: Settling in to Life in Afghanistan', (news brief, Royal United Services Institute, London, May 2018) https://rusi.org/publication/newsbrief/daesh-moves-house-settling-life-afghanistan, p. 1.
8   Ibid., p. 3.
9   See, for example, Daniel L. Byman, 'What Happens when ISIS Goes Underground?' *Brookings Institution*, 18 January 2018, https://www.brookings.edu/blog/markaz/2018/01/18/what-happens-when-isis-goes-underground/.

10 Christian Bleuer, 'To Syria, not Afghanistan: Central Asian Jihadis "Neglect" their Neighbour', *Afghanistan Analysts Network*, 8 October 2014, https://www.afghanistan-analysts.org/to-syria-not-afghanistan-central-asian-jihadis-neglect-their-neighbour/.
11 Damon Mehl, 'The Islamic Movement of Uzbekistan Opens a Door to the Islamic State', *CTC Sentinel* 8, 6 (2015), p. 11.
12 See, Noor Zahid, 'Officials: Son of Slain Uzbek Militant Promotes So-called Islamic State in Afghanistan', *VOA*, 7 February 2017, https://www.voanews.com/a/son-slain-uzbek-militant-promotes-islamic-state-afghanistan-officials-say/3710083.html.
13 Paul Lushenko, 'ISKP: Afghanistan's New Salafi Jihadism', *Middle East Institute*, 26 October 2018.
14 Francesca Manenti, 'The Competition between al-Qaeda and Daesh for the Asian Stronghold', in *The Evolution of Jihadist Radicalization in Asia*, ed. Gabriele Iacovino and Francesca Manenti (Rome: Centro Studi Internazionali/European Foundation for Democracy, 2018), p. 34.
15 Lushenko, 'ISKP'.
16 Ibid.
17 A.A. Kazantsev, 'Tsentralnaia Aziia: sleduiushchii akt dramy?' in *Groza s Vostoka. Kak otvetit mir na vyzov IGIL?* ed. F.A. Lukyanov (Moscow: EKSMO, 2016), p. 128.
18 Antonio Giustozzi, *The Islamic State in Khorasan: Afghanistan, Pakistan and the New Central Asian Jihad* (London: Hurst and Company, 2018), p. 143.
19 Nargis Kassenova, 'Kazakhstan's Policy toward Afghanistan: Context, Drivers and Outcomes', in *Afghanistan and Its Neighbors after the NATO Withdrawal*, ed. Amin Saikal and Kirill Nourzhanov (New York: Lexington Books, 2016), pp. 98–110.
20 Ibid.
21 Reid Standish, 'Kazakhstan Eyes Prestige in Afghanistan's Uncertain Future', *Foreign Policy*, 16 December 2014, http://foreignpolicy.com/2014/12/16/kazakstan-eyes-prestige-in-afghanistan-after-2014-drawdown/; Catherine Putz, 'Will Kazakhstan be a Game-Changer in Afghanistan?' *The Diplomat*, 24 November 2015, http://thediplomat.com/2015/11/will-kazakhstan-be-a-game-changer-in-afghanistan/.
22 'Samye glavnye ugrozy v sovremennom mire nazval Nazarbaev', *Kazakhstanskaia Pravda*, 11 April 2017, http://www.kazpravda.kz/news/prezident1/samie-glavnie-ugrozi-v-sovremennom-mire-nazval-nazarbaev/.
23 'Afganskii geroin prodolzhaiut vezti v Kazakhstan', *Caravan.kz*, 14 June 2017, https://www.caravan.kz/news/afganskijj-geroin-prodolzhayut-vezti-v-kazakhstan-396339/.
24 Erbol Akhantaev, 'V Kazakhstane rastet chislo storonnikov IGIL', *Eurasia News*, 20 April 2017, http://eurasianews.info/analitika/v-kazaxstane-rastet-chislo-storonnikov-igil.html.
25 Nursultan Nazarbaev, '400 kazakhstantsev zaverbovany v "Islamskoe gosudarstvo"', *Nur.kz*, 16 November 2017, https://www.nur.kz/1679518-nazarbaev-400-kazakhstancev-zaverbovany.html.

26 Erlan Karin, 'Afganistan dlia kazakhstantsev–chernaia dyra', *Tengri News,* 31 January 2014, https://tengrinews.kz/kazakhstan_news/erlan-karin-afganistan-dlya-kazahstantsev-chernaya-dyira-249762/.

27 Erlan Karin, *The Soldiers of the Caliphate: The Anatomy of a Terrorist Group* (Astana: KISI, 2016), pp. 36–84.

28 Erlan Karin, 'V 2017 aktualiziruetsia ugroza vozvrata terroristov v Tsentralnuiu Aziiu', KazInform, 9 January 2017, http://www.inform.kz/ru/v-2017-godu-aktualiziruetsya-ugroza-vozvrata-terroristov-v-central-nuyu-aziyu-erlan-karin_a2987055.

29 Erlan Karin, 'Vliianie IGIL v Afganistane rastet', *Atameken Business TV*, 8 January 2018, https://abctv.kz/ru/last/vliyanie-igil-v-afganistane-rastet-%E2%80%93-politolog.

30 Nursultan Nazarbaev, 'Voennaia doktrina Respubliki Kazakhstan', Decree No 161 by the President of Kazakhtsan, 11 October 2011, http://bap.prokuror.kz/rus/o-prokurature/normativnye-pravovye-akty/voennaya-doktrina-respubliki-kazahstan.

31 Nursultan Nazarbaev, 'Ob utverzhdenii Voennoi doktriny Respubliki Kazakhstan', Decree No 554 by the President of Kazakhtsan, 29 September 2017, https://tengrinews.kz/zakon/prezident_respubliki_kazahstan/obopona/id-U1700000554/.

32 Sholpan Orazbekova, 'O zhizni bezhnentsev v Kazakhstane rasskazal predstavitel OON', *Bnews.kz*, 9 December 2016, https://bnews.kz/ru/dialog/interview/o_zhizni_bezhentsev_v_kazakhstane_rasskazal_predstavitel_oon_.

33 Zhanbolat Mamyshev, 'Kazakhstanu rekomendovali rasseliat' bezhentsev v gorodakh, a ne v lageriakh', *Zakon.kz,* 26 February 2018, https://www.zakon.kz/4777441-kazakhstanu-rekomendovali-rasseljat.html.

34 Ibid.

35 B.A. Auelbaev, S.K. Kushkumbayev, K.L. Syroezhkin and V.Y. Dodonov, *Central Asia – 2020: Four Strategic Concepts* (Astana: KISI, 2015), p. 11.

36 G.F. Dubovtsev, *Voennaia bezopasnost' Respubliki Kazakhstan: Opyt, aktualnye problemy, osnovnye napravleniia obespecheniia* (Astana: KISI, 2018), pp. 159–65.

37 Auelbaev et al., *Central Asia – 2020*, p. 20.

38 Christian Bleuer, 'Kyrgyzstan and Afghanistan's Diminishing Relationship', in *Afghanistan and Its Neighbors after the NATO Withdrawal*, ed. Amin Saikal and Kirill Nourzhanov (New York: Lexington Books, 2016), pp. 129–46; Emilbek Dzhuraev and Shairbek Dzhuraev, 'The Kazakh and Kyrgyz Sides of Afghanistan: So Near and Yet So Far', in *The Regional Dimensions to Security: Other Sides of Afghanistan*, ed. Aglaya Snetkov and Stephen Aris (Basingstoke: Palgrave Macmillan, 2013), pp. 173–88.

39 Bleuer, 'Kyrgyzstan and Afghanistan's Diminishing Relationship.'

40 'Voennaia doktrina Kyrgyzskoi Respubliki', Decree No. 165 by the President of the Kyrgyz Republic, 15 July 2013, http://cbd.minjust.gov.kg/act/view/ru-ru/900232.

41 'Kontseptsiia natsionalnoi bezopasnosti Kyrgyzskoi Respubliki', Decree No. 120 by the President of the Kyrgyz Republic, 9 June 2012 http://cbd.minjust.gov.kg/act/view/ru-ru/61367?cl=ru-ru.

42 Tokon Mamytov, 'Doklad', in *Afganistan i Tsentralnaia Aziia v 2014 godu: rol' ODKB v obespechenii regionalnoi bezopasnosti* (Bishkek: Region, 2013), p. 4.

43 Ibid., p. 5.

44 Erica Marat, *The Military and the State in Central Asia: From Red Army to Independence* (London: Routledge, 2010), pp. 70–71.

45 Quoted in Vadim Nochevkin, 'Afganistan: ugroza Kyrgyzstanu rastet s kazhdym dnem', *Delo No*, 30 August 2017, https://delo.kg/afganistan-ugroza-kyrgyzstanu-rastjot-s-kazhdym-dnjom/.

46 Valimzhan Tanyrykov quoted in 'Vneshnie i vnutrennie ugrozy aktualny i dlia Kyrgyzstana', *Gezitter*, 22 December 2015, http://m.gezitter.org/politic/46369_vneshnie_i_vnutrennie_ugrozyi_aktualnyi_i_dlya_kyirgyizstana/.

47 'Programma pravitelstva Kyrgyzskoi Respubliki po protivodeistviiu ekstremizmu i terrorizmu na 2017–2022 gody', Republic of Kyrgyzstan, Ministry of Justice, 21 June 2017, http://cbd.minjust.gov.kg/act/view/ru-ru/100104.

48 K.M Osmonaliev and A. Isamatova, 'Nekotorye problemy obespecheniia bezopasnosti v Tsentralnoi Azii: geopoliticheskie faktory i riski', *Mezhdunarodnoe sotrudnichestvo evraziiskikh gosudarstv* 2, 7 (2016), p. 85.

49 Ely Karmon, 'Central Asian Jihadists in the Front Line', *Perspectives on Terrorism* 11, 4 (2017), pp. 78–86.

50 Ermek Irgaliev, 'Boeviki iz Sirii nachali vozvrashchatsia v Kyrgyzstan', *365info.kz*, 2 November 2017, https://365info.kz/2017/11/boeviki-iz-sirii-nachali-vozvrashhatsya-v-kyrgyzstan/.

51 K.M Osmonaliev, *Trafik afganskikh opiatov cherez territoriiu Kyrgyzstana* (Bishkek: NISI KR, 2014), p. 15.

52 A.A. Botobaev, 'Kharakteristika narkosituatsii v Kyrgyzstane na sovremennom etape', *Problemy sovremennoi nauki i obrazovaniia* 9, 91 (2017), p. 82.

53 Almazbek Atambaev, 'Ekskjliuzivnoe interview telekanalu "Mir"', *Mir 24*, 31 March 2017, https://mir24.tv/news/15910069/eksklyuzivnoe-intervyu-almazbeka-atambaeva-telekanalu-mir-video.

54 Z.T. Muratalieva, 'Proekt SShA po demokratizatsii Tsentralnoi Azii: teoriia na praktike', *Vestnik KRSU* 15, 5 (2015), pp. 20–23.

55 A.T. Isamatova, 'Tsentralnaia Aziia v politike Rossii, SShA i Kitaia', *Vestnik KRSU* 17, 2 (2017), p. 153.

56 The Government of Kyrgyz Republic, Directive No 196-r, 10 May 2016, http://cbd.minjust.gov.kg/act/view/ru-ru/215822.

57 Diana Esenalieva, 'Migratsionnaia sluzhba: v Kyrgyzstane naschityvaetsia 169 bezhnetsev', *Knews.kg*, 3 February 2016, http://www.knews.kg/society/75036_migratsionnaya_slujba_v_kyirgyizstane_naschityivaetsya_169_bejentsev.

58 For a comprehensive account of the history of Tajik–Afghan relations and their impact on domestic politics in Tajikistan after 1991, see Jesse Driscoll, *Warlords and Coalition Politics in Post-Soviet States* (Cambridge: Cambridge University Press, 2015).
59 Emomali Rahmon, 'Poslanie Prezidenta Respubliki Tadzhikistan, Lidera natsii Emomali Rahmona Majlisi Oli Respubliki Tadzhikistan', *Official Portal of the President of Tajikistan*, 22 December 2017, http://president.tj/ru/node/16772.
60 Karim Vohidov, 'Na mezhdunarodnoi konferentsii RATS ShOS terroristichesko-ekstremistskaia organizatsiia PIVT priznana ugrozoi regionalnoi bezopasnosti', *Narodnaia gazeta*, 17 November 2017, https://www.narodnaya.tj/index.php?option=com_content&view=article&id=5448:--------lr----&catid=57:bezopasnost&Itemid=53.
61 Ibid.
62 Cited in A.A. Kazantsev and L. Iu. Gusev, *Ugroza religioznogo ekstremizma na postsovetskom prostranstve* (Moscow: TsIPI MGIMO, 2017), p. 62.
63 A.S. Rahmonov, H. Hojaev and B. Rahmonov, 'Tahdidhoi nav ba amniyati Jumhurii Tojikison: ta'mini rushdi ustuvori kishvar', *Tojikiston va jahoni imruz* 2, 57 (2017), p. 64.
64 D.V. Ovsiannikov and D.G. Popov, 'Sunnitskii Islam i gosudarstvennaia vlast' v Tadzhikistane: voprosy vzaimodeistviia i identifikatsii', *Musulmanskii mir* 2 (2017), pp. 15–17.
65 M.A. Olimov, 'Religioznaia situatsiia v Tadzhikistane: novye vyzovy', in *Evraziiskii perekrestok*, Vyp. 7, ed. V.V. Amelin (Orenburg: IPK 'Universitet', 2017), pp. 31–32.
66 Ibid., p. 32.
67 Rahmon, 'Poslanie Prezidenta Respubliki Tadzhikistan'.
68 Col. Sharaf Faizulloev quoted in Konstantin Gritsan, 'Nachalniki shtabov sveriaiut chasy', *Pogranichnik Sodruzhestva* 4, 88 (2016), pp. 11–12.
69 Shohruh Saidzoda, 'Nezakonnyi oborot narkotikov–prestupleniia, predstavliaiushchie ugrozu bezopasnosti Respubliki Tadzhikistan', *Narkofront* 4 (2017), pp. 32–36.
70 A.A. Alamshozoda, K. Kh. Soliev and M.G. Bukhorizoda, 'Obzor narkosituatsii v Afganistane', *Narkofront* 1 (2017), p. 23.
71 See Filippo De Danieli, 'Counter-narcotics Policies in Tajikistan and their Impact on State Building', *Central Asian Survey* 30, 1 (2011), pp. 129–45.
72 United Nations Office on Drugs and Crime, 'Afghan Opiate Trafficking along the Northern Route', (report, UNODC, Vienna, 2018), p. 46.
73 R.I. Numonzoda and H.D. Muhammadzoda, 'Sravnitelnyi analiz situatsii s prestupnostiu v sfere nezakonnogo oborota narkoticheskikh sredstv, psikhotropnykh veshchestv i prekursorov', *Narkofront* 4 (2017), p. 80.
74 International Crisis Group, 'Rivals for Authority in Tajikistan's Gorno-Badakhshan', (briefing paper 87, Crisis Group Europe and Central Asia, Brussels, 2018), pp. 6–7.

75 Ava Iuldasheva, 'S nachala goda na tadzhiksko-afganskoi granitse proizoshli 26 boestolknovenii, 13 kontrabandistov ubity', *Asia-Plus*, 14 November 2017, https://news.tj/ru/news/tajikistan/security/20171114/s-nachala-goda-na-tadzhiksko-afganskoi-granitse-proizoshli-26-boestolknovenii-13-kontrabandistov-ubiti.

76 'Tajikistan Border Guards Accused of Killing Afghan Civilians', *Fergana News Agency*, 10 November 2017, http://enews.fergananews.com/news.php?id=3597&mode=snews.

77 'Tadzhikistan otvetil na obvineniia Afganistana v obstrele mirnykh zhitelei: eto porozhdenie bolnogo razuma', *Asia-Plus*, 13 November 2017 https://news.tj/ru/news/tajikistan/security/20171113/tadzhikistan-otvetil-na-obvineniya-afganistana-v-obstrele-mirnih-zhitelei-eto-porozhdenie-bolnogo-razuma.

78 Biloli Shams, 'Imenem pogibshego na granitse polkovnika Akhtamova khotiat nazvat' shkolu v ego kishlake', *Asia-Plus*, 6 December 2017, https://news.tj/news/tajikistan/society/20171206/imenem-pogibshego-na-granitse-polkovnika-ahtamova-mogut-nazvat-shkolu-v-ego-kishlake.

79 'GKNB Tadzhikistana: na granitse s respublikoi sosredotocheny 7 tys. Talibov', *EurAsia Daily*, 3 May 2018, https://eadaily.com/ru/news/2018/05/03/gknb-tadzhikistana-na-granice-s-respublikoy-sosredotocheny-7-tys-talibov.

80 'Pamirtsy opasaiutsia perekhoda talibov na territoriiu Tadzhikistana', *Tsentr-1*, 3 May 2017, https://centre1.com/tajikistan/pamirtsy-opasayutsya-perehoda-talibov-na-territoriyu-tadzhikistana/.

81 United States Committee for Refugees and Immigrants, 'USCR Country Report Tajikistan: Statistics on Refugees and Other Uprooted People, June 2001', *ReliefWeb*, 19 June 2001, https://reliefweb.int/report/afghanistan/uscr-country-report-tajikistan-statistics-refugees-and-other-uprooted-people-jun.

82 A.E. Temirkhanova, 'Bezhentsy: Tsentralnaia Aziia vmesto Evropy?' *Uspekhi sovremennoi nauki i obrazovaniia* 1, 4 (2016), p. 131.

83 Nodira Akbaralieva, 'UNHCR and Sheraton Hotel in Tajikistan Offer Afghan Refugees Chance to Shine', *UNHCR*, 25 October 2017, https://www.unhcr.org/en-au/news/latest/2017/10/59edc3de4/unhcr-sheraton-hotel-tajikistan-offer-afghan-refugees-chance-shine.html.

84 Temur Amirov, 'Afganskie bezhentsy. V poiskah luchshei doli', *Asia-Plus*, 7 April 2017, https://www.news.tj/ru/news/tajikistan/society/20170407/afganskie-bezhentsi-v-poiskah-luchshei-doli.

85 Shahrbanou Tadjbakhsh, Kosimsho Iskandarov and Abdul Ahad Mohammadi, 'Strangers Across the Amu River: Community Perceptions along the Tajik–Afghan Borders', (working paper, SIPRI, Stockholm, 2015), p. 37.

86 Fakhriddin Kholbek, 'Gotovte ruzhia! Ili pochemu Nur ne dolzhen uiti?' *Asia-Plus*, 21 December 2017, https://news.tj/ru/news/tajikistan/security/20171221/gotovte-ruzhya-ili-pochemu-nur-ne-dolzhen-uiti.

87 Avaz Yuldashev, 'Ekspert: v Afganistane nabiraet oboroty pushtunskii natsionalizm', *Asia-Plus*, 23 November 2017, https://news.tj/news/tajikistan/security/20171123/ekspert-v-afganistane-nabiraet-oboroti-pushtunskii-natsionalizm.

88 Q. Iskandarov, 'Tojikoni Afghoniston dar ravandi raqobathoi qavmiu siyosii kishvar', *Payomi donishgohi millii Tojikiston* 3, 6 (2017), pp. 12–19.

89 Their most important cyberspace outlet is the 'Tajiks of Afghanistan' portal on the Vkontakte platform. See, https://vk.com/public95755821.

90 Marlene Laruelle, 'Assessing Uzbekistan's and Tajikistan's Afghan Policies: The Impact of Domestic Drivers', in *The Central Asia–Afghanistan Relationship: From Soviet Intervention to the Silk Road Initiatives*, ed. Marlene Laruelle (Lanham: Lexington Books, 2017), p. 126.

91 Kirill Nourzhanov, 'Tajikistan's Multi-Vector Foreign Policy: Constructing Relations with Russia, China, and the United States', in *Tajikistan on the Move: Statebuilding and Societal Transformations*, ed. Marlene Laruelle (Lanham: Lexington Books, 2018), pp. 87–110.

92 Hakim Abdullohi Rahnamo, 'Novoe pokolenie ekstremistov i novye vyzovy bezopasnosti Tsentralnoi Azii', in *Tsentralnaia Aziia v usloviiakh globalnoi transformatsii*, ed. Z.K. Shaukenova (Astana: KISI, 2017), p. 64.

93 Sebastien Peyrouse, 'Political and Economic Pragmatism: Turkmenistan and Afghanistan since 1991', in *Afghanistan and Its Neighbors after the NATO Withdrawal*, ed. Amin Saikal and Kirill Nourzhanov (New York: Lexington Books, 2016), pp. 111–28.

94 Bruce Pannier, 'Insurgent Activities at the Afghan–Turkmen and Afghan–Tajik Borders', in *The Central Asia–Afghanistan Relationship: From Soviet Intervention to the Silk Road Initiatives*, ed. Marlene Laruelle (Lanham: Lexington Books, 2017), pp. 145–48.

95 Iurii Fedorov, 'Afganistan v novykh voenno-politicheskikh realiiakh: chto eto znachit dlia ego sosedei v Tsentralnoi Azii?' *Index bezopasnosti* 21, 1: 112 (2015), pp. 39–40.

96 'Turkmenskie siloviki provodiat reidy protiv bandformirovanii IGIL', *Vesti.kg*, 9 June 2015, https://vesti.kg/analitika/item/34248-turkmenskie-siloviki-provodyat-reydyi-protiv-bandformirovaniy-igil.html.

97 A.A. Kazantsev and I.N. Panarin, *Ugroza mezhdunarodnogo terrorizma i religioznogo ekstremizma gosudarstvam–chlenam ODKB na tsentralnoaziatskom i afganskom napravleniiakh* (Moscow: MGIMO, 2017), p. 21.

98 Andrei Zubov, 'Pochemu Turkmeniia nedovolna slovami Nazarbaeva', *365info.kz*, 16 October 2015, https://365info.kz/2015/10/pochemu-turkmeniya-nedovolna-slovami-nazarbaeva/.

99 'Informatsiia o zhertvakh sredi soldat na turkmeno-afganskoi granitse ne sootvetstvuet deistvitelnosti', *Turkmenportal*, 3 July 2018, https://turkmenportal.com/blog/15087/informaciya-o-zhertvah-sredi-soldat-na-turkmenoafganskoi-granice-ne-sootvetstvuet-deistvitelnosti.

100 'Message for the Media', Republic of Turkmenistan, Ministry of Foreign Affairs, 14 November 2018, https://www.mfa.gov.tm/en/news/1094.
101 Vitalii Volkov, 'Ashkhabad uzhestochaet bor'bu s narkooborotom–shou ili vser'ez?' *Deutsche Welle*, 4 February 2015, https://p.dw.com/p/1EUwJ.
102 UNODC, 'Afghan Opiate Trafficking', p. 47.
103 United States Department of State, 'International Narcotics Control Strategy Report', Vol. I (report, Bureau for International Narcotics and Law Enforcement Affairs, Washington, D.C., March 2017) https://www.state.gov/documents/organization/268025.pdf, p. 277.
104 Luca Anceschi, 'Turkmenistan's Export Crisis: Is TAPI the Answer?' (policy brief 27, Central Asia Program, Washington DC, June 2015), http://centralasiaprogram.org/wp-content/uploads/2015/06/Policy-Brief-27-June-2015.pdf.
105 Pannier, "Insurgent activities", p. 151.
106 Ruslan Tuhbatulin, 'Why Does Turkmenistan Provide Ammunition to the Taliban Movement?' *Chronicles of Turkmenistan*, 16 March 2017, https://en.hronikatm.com/2017/03/why-does-turkmenistan-provide-ammunition-to-the-taliban-movement/.
107 Vitaly V. Naumkin, *Militant Islam in Central Asia: The Case of the Islamic Movement of Uzbekistan*, Berkeley: University of California, 2003, p. 47.
108 Svante E. Cornell, 'Central Asia: Where Did Islamic Radicalization Go?' in *Religion, Conflict, and Stability in the Former Soviet Union*, ed. Katya Migacheva and Bryan Frederick (Santa Monica: RAND, 2018), pp. 75–77.
109 'Uroven' trevogi zhitelei Uzbekistana iz-za rasprostraneniia religioznogo ekstremizma snizhaetsia', *Kun-uz.com*, 18 November 2017 http://kun-uz.com/ru/uroven-trevogi-zhitelei-uzbekistana/.
110 SNB analyst Bakhtier Sharafov quoted in Nigora Yuldasheva, 'Chernaia ten' na zelenykh sklonakh', *Delovaia nedelia*, 4 May 2015, http://www.dn.kz/index.php?option=com_content&view=article&id=2751:2015-05-04-05-00-03&catid=2:2011-10-23-11-43-45&Itemid=17.
111 'Oboronnaia doktrina Respubliki Uzbekistan', Law of the Republic of Uzbekistan No. ZRU-458, 9 January 2018, http://www.lex.uz/docs/3495906.
112 Analytical Center on Drug Control, *Natsionalnyi otchet o narkosituatsii v Respublike Uzbekistan 2012* (Prague: ResAd s.r.o, 2012), p. 6.
113 Analytical Center on Drug Control, 'O narkosituatsii v Respublike Uzbekistan v 2017 godu', NCDC.uz, 2018 http://www.ncdc.uz/ru/protivodeystvie-nezakonnomu-oborotu-narkoticheskikh-sredstv/analiticheskie-obzory/.
114 Andrei Mokii, 'Bolee 8000 narkozavisimykh sostoiat na uchete v Uzbekistane', *Gazeta.uz*, 16 February 2018, https://www.gazeta.uz/ru/2018/02/16/drugs/.
115 Tulkinzhon Karimov, 'Vooruzhennye Sily Uzbekistana–nadezhnyi garant bezopasnosti i stabilnosti, blagopoluchnoi zhizni naroda', *UzDaily*, 25 November 2016, https://www.uzdaily.uz/articles-id-30630.htm.

116 Boris Sokolov, 'Ni chisla, ni umeniia', *Voenno-promyshlennyi kurier* 19, 487 (2013), p. 3.
117 Vitalii Volkov, 'Bezopasnost' v regione: sila i slabost' armii Uzbekistana', *Deutsche Welle*, 10 May 2016, https://p.dw.com/p/1Ikuf.
118 Aleksandr Khramchikhin, 'Mnogovektornyi tupik', *Voenno-promyshlennyi kurier* 14, 629 (2016), p. 5.
119 'Uzbekistan i Afganistan vykhodiat na kachestvenno novyi uroven' sotrudnichestva', Republic of Uzbekistan, Ministry of Foreign Affairs, 1 February 2017, https://mfa.uz/ru/press/smi/2017/02/10085/?print=Y.
120 Suraye Adilkhodzhaeva, 'Obostrenie situatsii v Afganistane: novye ugrozy miru i puti ikh predotvrashcheniia', *Sravnitelnaia politika* 8, 4 (2017), p. 75.
121 Karimov qoted in Arkady Dubnov, 'Dustum idet v nastuplenie', *Institute for War and Peace Reporting*, 21 February 2005, https://goo.gl/hfR5lB.
122 'Na peregovorakh Mirzieeva i Gani podnimalas' "tema Dustuma" i uproshchenie rezhima na granitse', *Fergana News Agency*, 7 December 2017, https://www.ferganaews.com/news/27471.
123 Rafik Saifullin quoted in Viktoria Panfilova, 'General Dustum s'ezdil na istoricheskuiu rodinu', *Nezavisimaia gazeta*, 31 January 2014, http://www.ng.ru/cis/2014-01-31/7_dustum.html
124 Joakim Brattvoll, 'Uzbekistan's Ambiguous Policies on Afghanistan', *PRIO Policy Brief* 1 (2016), https://www.files.ethz.ch/isn/196758/Brattvoll%20-%20Uzbekistans%20ambiguous%20policies%20on%20Afghanistan,%20PRIO%20Policy%20Brief%201-2016.pdf.
125 Anastasiia Reshetniak, *Terrorizm i religioznyi ekstremizm v Tsentralnoi Azii: problemy vospriiatiia* (Astana: KISI, 2016), pp. 28–29.

3

The Central Asian Policy Response to Security Threats from Afghanistan

Development, Defence and Diplomacy

The Central Asian republics' policies to deal with heightened security anxieties about Afghanistan can be grouped into three broad strategies: contributing to its stability via socio-economic development; maintaining a military buffer zone; and expediting a negotiated peace process. The three are not mutually exclusive and are context-specific. The situation in Afghanistan, the domestic political exigencies and the dynamics of regional and international affairs influence the pursuit of these three strategies by each of the Central Asian countries.

Statements to the effect that 'an improvement of the socio-economic situation in Afghanistan is the key factor of stability and security in Central Asia',[1] have been common in the speeches made by regional leaders since the mid-2000s. They are closely tied to the US strategy of bolstering peace by connecting Afghanistan to Central Asia, via a myriad of commercial and trade links resulting in an economic zone of shared prosperity.[2] It is doubtful whether Central Asian presidents sincerely embrace the tenets of liberalism in international relations, but the prospect of the West investing massively in transborder infrastructure projects and of profits from market opportunities in an opened-up Afghanistan are surely attractive in their eyes. The question of their own generosity and openness, as well as the actual efficacy of the connectivity schemes in expediting sustainable development in Afghanistan, is a matter of debate.

Military containment of Afghan threats has entailed two approaches since 2014: building up border defences and cooperation with the government in Kabul, in bolstering the capacity of the Afghan National Security Forces (ANSF). As noted in Chapter 2, activating buffer zones in adjacent territories populated by ethnic Tajiks, Turkmens and Uzbeks has not been a preferred policy choice so far.

Even before the attacks of 11 September 2001, all Central Asian states concurred that the Afghan conflict had no military solution and could be settled only through peaceful political negotiations 'in order to establish a broad-based, multi-ethnic and fully representative Government'.[3] The Tashkent Declaration of 1999 is still invoked today as a basic reference point for many bilateral and multilateral diplomatic initiatives in which the Central Asian states are involved. A major variable among individual countries is their readiness to engage with the Taliban who had been officially designated as a terrorist organisation in the region after 2001.

The Development–Security Nexus

The significance of Central Asia to the stabilisation and reconstruction of Afghanistan was well captured in the five-year National Development Strategy adopted by the government in Kabul in 2008, with active encouragement by its Western backers. The document envisaged the establishment of Afghanistan as a land bridge between Central Asia and South Asia, with specific strategic outcomes including:

- expanded trade in energy covering a significant part of Afghanistan's energy needs and replenishing its coffers through transit fees;
- greater flow of goods, services, investment and technology across the border supporting Afghan economic development; and
- improved border management and customs cooperation reducing trans-border crime.[4]

Taking stock of Central Asia's overall contribution to this vision a decade later, a group of prominent experts representing all Central Asian republics and their colleagues from Germany, Turkey and the United States, observed: 'No particular interest has been shown or noticed from Central Asia to involve in the country's development so far.'[5] The experts' judgment is almost certainly too harsh, but it does reflect the reality that despite verbal commitment to transforming Afghanistan into a regional hub of economic activity, the region's governments have acted rather cautiously and selfishly, focusing on their own national interests, avoiding risk and at times exploiting the weakness of their southern neighbour.

Regional Trade

After the overthrow of the Taliban and the opening of the country, Afghanistan's foreign trade grew strongly. Between 2002 and 2010, its exports increased three-fold and imports five-fold. Trade deficit rose from 9 per cent of GDP to 35 per cent in 2010. The volume of trade was bolstered by the presence of the international coalition, and it was the United States and other international donors who covered the imbalance in commercial exchange.[6] In the first half of 2009, the United States established several new transit corridors for delivery of nonlethal goods to its forces in Afghanistan (and ANSF) via Central Asia. Known as the Northern Distribution Network (NDN), this combination of ports, depots, highways and other elements of transport infrastructure, was to serve as a skeleton for a thriving civilian commercial hub over the five year horizon. Washington, the World Bank (WB) and the Asian Development Bank (ADB) competed with each other to present a magnificent picture of imminent economic benefits accruing from such connectivity: acceleration of GDP growth from 8.8 per cent to 12.7 per cent per annum; raising of exports by $5.8 billion; generation of 771,000 full-time jobs, and so on.[7]

As Tables 3.1 and 3.2 show, trade between Afghanistan and Central Asia did increase by 370 per cent between 2008 and 2016. However, this growth was driven by the Western largesse, and was not necessarily beneficial to the former. In most cases, Afghanistan actually lost ground as an exporter of goods to Central Asia, both in absolute and relative terms. Kazakhstan, Turkmenistan and Uzbekistan ran huge trade surpluses but the nomenclature of commodities they sent to Afghanistan remained limited: the former exported mostly wheat and flour, while the latter two specialised in fuel and electricity. Essentially, the Central Asian countries have followed the lucrative business model developed between 2001 and 2014, profiting from procurement orders by the Afghan government, the remaining US forces, and aid and development organisations. A high point may have been reached in 2012, when the US government spent US$1.3 billion in Central Asia in support of ISAF operations; US$820 million of that sum went to Turkmenistan for fuel purchases to be used in Afghanistan.[8] Kyrgyzstan received US$218.1 million, a substantial portion of which went to a local contractor supplying Russian-made jet fuel to Bagram air base.[9] In other words, the spikes in Afghan import statistics do not reflect the organic and sustainable growth of trade with Central Asia.

State agencies and interests have dominated the exchange on both sides; a dense network of private companies conducting trade according to market rules has simply failed to materialise. According to one interview-based study, there is little mutual interest between merchants in Afghanistan and Central Asia; moreover, 'Afghan traders wishing for closer ties with Central Asian and Russian suppliers ... believe that the current trade regime in Afghanistan is governed by the presence and priorities of the international forces based in Afghanistan'.[10] Tariff and non-tariff barriers have remained. While the quality of roads improved in the decade since the mid-2000s, thanks to the NDN, other measurements of connectivity either stayed static or plummeted. Afghanistan's indicators of cost involved in trading across borders deteriorated by 20 per cent, Tajikistan by 17 per cent and Kazakhstan by 8 per cent.[11] 'Non-standard' border trade, in which small merchants shuttle between Afghanistan and its neighbours, peddling small volumes of products – with a major positive impact on the livelihood of local communities – has remained underdeveloped.[12]

The electric energy sector provides an instructive tale of how Central Asia has contributed positively to stability in Afghanistan, while also showing the motivations for, and limitations to, this contribution.

Table 3.1 Afghanistan's trade with Central Asian countries in 2008

	Export ($ m)	Import ($ m)	Trade balance ($ m)	Share in Afghan import (%)	Share in Afghan export (%)
Kazakhstan	0.34	152.52	−152.18	5.05	0.06
Kyrgyzstan	0.03	5.17	−5.14	0.17	0.01
Tajikistan	6.31	37.18	−30.87	1.23	1.17
Turkmenistan	10.63	12.54	−1.71	0.42	2.01
Uzbekistan	1.52	168.70	−167.18	5.59	0.28

Source: Authors' calculations based on World Bank data.

Table 3.2 Afghanistan's trade with Central Asian countries in 2016

	Export ($ m)	Import ($ m)	Trade balance ($ m)	Share in Afghan import (%)	Share in Afghan export (%)
Kazakhstan	3.99	621.62	−617.64	9.51	0.67
Kyrgyzstan	–	0.08	–	0	–
Tajikistan	0.89	79.68	−78.79	1.22	0.15
Turkmenistan	1.75	355.40	−353.65	5.44	0.29
Uzbekistan	0.41	399.14	−398.73	6.11	0.07

Source: Authors' calculations based on World Bank data.

Regional Energy Cooperation

In 2009, US officials estimated that Afghanistan urgently needed 500 megawatts (MW) of electricity to be injected into its north-east power system, reporting approvingly, that 'Turkmenistan, Uzbekistan, and Tajikistan have stated their willingness to promote stability in Afghanistan by supplying electrical power'.[13] Energy deliveries from Central Asia grew steadily. Between April 2015 and March 2016 (the year 1394, according to Afghanistan's Solar Hijri calendar) imports accounted for 80 per cent of total grid supply; Afghanistan's three northern neighbours covered 78 per cent of these imports.[14] Such expansion was made possible by two factors: a political decision by Kabul and its international backers to bring power to the major cities in the north as quickly as possible and in a no-expense-spared manner; and sudden surplus of electricity created by the disintegration of the Central Asian Energy System (CAES). The CAES was a complex network of gas pipelines and electric power networks, as well as energy producing facilities, developed during Soviet times, which acted as a resource-sharing and coordinating mechanism underpinning regional energy security. In the 2000s, isolationist policies focused on full self-reliance and self-control led to its disruption. Uzbekistan in particular, used its geographic and technological advantages to block electricity and energy supplies to other states, in order to influence foreign policies of the latter.[15] Between 2003 and 2011, Tajikistan, Turkmenistan and Uzbekistan went off the unified grid and their energy exchange collapsed. According to local estimates, the volume of regional energy trade decreased by 73 per cent between 1995 and 2016.[16] Thus, without bolstering production capacity, the Central Asian republics had electricity to sell to Afghanistan.

And sell they did, often at inflated prices and using hastily erected low capacity transmission lines. For much of the 2010s, Uzbekistan provided more than a third of Afghanistan's imported electricity and charged around US$0.1 per kilowatt hour (kWh). Given the high transmission and distribution costs, along with average electricity tariff for consumers of US$0.08–US$0.12 per kWh, Uzbek electricity proved to be rather uneconomical.[17] On the one hand, the flow of energy from Central Asia to important urban centres in the north-east and north-west, who now enjoy better access to electric power than other parts of the country bar Kabul,[18] has undoubtedly bolstered political stability and regime legitimacy. On the other hand, costly imported energy has begun to place a 'huge burden on [the] unstable economy of Afghanistan and its people'.[19]

Tajikistan, Turkmenistan and Uzbekistan operate unsynchronised supply lines, necessitating the construction of expensive convertor stations in Afghanistan.

Moreover, Turkmenistan and Uzbekistan insist on constraining the Afghan side's ability to synchronise domestic generation plants and standardise national transmission facilities, thus complicating the expansion and integration of its power network 'in a rational way'.[20] The sustainability of Central Asian supplies in the immediate future is questionable. Uzbekistan's generation capacity at thermal plants is stretched to the limit, and Tajikistan is energy-deficient in winter months when the demand is at its highest in Afghanistan. Domestic needs in these two countries trump contractual obligations to Afghanistan, which was illustrated by Dushanbe's decision to cut off export in October 2013, due to national shortages. The completion of a nuclear plant in Uzbekistan by 2028, and Roghun hydro power station in Tajikistan by 2033, could resolve these issues but in the meantime disruptions in supply and bickering over prices continue to occur regularly. In late 2017, Turkmenistan announced the doubling of the price of power exports to Afghanistan. When Kabul declined the demand, Ashgabat switched off supplies to four Afghan provinces for two days in a strong-arm negotiations tactic.[21]

One expert characterised the relationship between Uzbekistan and Afghanistan in the energy sphere as 'stable but not reliable, as the Afghan government struggles to do business with its Uzbek counterpart . . . Neither side perceives the other as a trustworthy partner.'[22] As long as the United States and other external stakeholders mediate and pay for expensive Uzbek electricity, cooperation continues. External money may dry up soon however. Between 2002 and 2018, USAID disbursed more than US$1.5 billion in funds to develop the Afghan energy sector, and the Department of Defence threw in another US$527 million. Other donors may have contributed up to US$4 billion. A sizeable portion of this money went to finance transmission and connectivity projects with Central Asia. The US Special Inspector General for Afghanistan Reconstruction (SIGAR) questioned the efficiency and probity with which the money was spent, making a special comment about the adverse effects that the over-reliance on power imports would have on financial sustainability of the Afghan national electricity company, Da Afghanistan Breshna Sherkat (DABS).[23]

Critics of the strategy of importing more electricity from Central Asia have pointed out that the flow-on effect in rural areas has been negligible.[24] 'These huge power lines, however, made no stops – the communities that lost farmland as these high towers had been put up had received financial compensation but did not actually receive any electricity from them,' wrote an American anthropologist observing the towering stanchions that brought energy from Uzbekistan and commenting on the mixed feelings of villagers 'forced to look on a daily basis at the metal giants lurking above their homes while filling up containers with diesel for smoky, ageing home generators or simply going without power at all'.[25] In Afghanistan, the question that is frequently asked is why regional transmission projects are given priority over the development of indigenous generation, creating long-term dependency on imports.[26]

One such project is CASA-1000, a high-visibility project of the Central Asia Regional Economic Cooperation program (CAREC), which joins together five Central Asian republics with Afghanistan, Azerbaijan, China, Georgia, Mongolia, Pakistan and six international development institutions (ADB, European Bank for Reconstruction and Development, International Monetary Fund, Islamic Development Bank, United Nations Development Programme, and WB).

CASA-1000 was first conceived in 2005, envisaging the supply of 1,000 MW to Pakistan and 300 MW to Afghanistan. Its original completion date was 2012. Having faced political and technical difficulties, the deadline moved to 2016 and then 2020. At the end of 2018, the WB, which is the US$1.17 billion project leader and chief financier, reported that construction of the 1,227 kilometre-long high voltage transmission lines and converter stations had not actually started, and rated overall risks associated with the scheme as 'high'.[27] This probably means that another postponement of CASA-1000 is in the offing.

Poor coordination among the stakeholders has been one of the factors dampening CASA-1000's progress. At the outset, its strongest cheerleaders were Kyrgyzstan and Tajikistan, and lending organisations with the capital to invest. The US government came on board promoting the venture as beneficial to Afghanistan's stability and energy security and running community support programs on the ground.[28] Uzbekistan, under Islam Karimov, resolutely opposed the scheme, resenting competition and benefits accruing to regional rivals. Afghanistan was lukewarm and eventually decided not to receive electricity through this project, as it would require additional expenses that could be better used to build its own hydroelectric power plant.[29]

The change of position by Tashkent in November 2018, when it announced the removal of objections to CASA-1000 was good news for the project. Nonetheless, questions remain as to what extent projects like this serve commercial interests of external stakeholders, rather than the stated purpose of stabilising and reconstructing Afghanistan. Would the projected US$40–45 million a year in transit fees be a sufficient return on investment? In what seems to be a lesson drawn from the CASA-1000 experience, CAREC has recently resolved to pay greater attention to aligning national strategies with the international financial institutions' preferences, in the pursuit of regional cooperation.[30]

Economic Assistance, Transport Solutions and Hydrocarbon Projects

The Central Asian republics have consistently signalled their approval of the continuous effort by the international community to render financial support to peace, state-building and development in Afghanistan. Their representatives participated in all global donor conferences, from London in 2006 to Brussels in 2016, as well as countless lesser fora. At the same time, they have not been particularly generous in providing assistance to Afghanistan themselves.

Kazakhstan's Ministry of Foreign Affairs recorded the following activities for the period spanning 2008 to 2014: a grant of US$2.4 million to fund the construction of one school in Samangan and one hospital in Bamian, and road repairs in Kunduz; humanitarian and emergency aid totalling US$17 million; and a US$50 million program to train 1,000 Afghan students in Kazakhstan between 2010 and 2020.[31] In December 2014, Kazakhstan adopted the law 'On official development assistance'. Its first project carried out in line with international standards for providing official development assistance (ODA), targeted Afghanistan where it sought to expand women's economic independence and rights. Other partners in this US$0.4 million program included Japan and the United Nations Development Program (UNDP).[32] In 2017, Nursultan Nazarbaev issued a presidential decree on the main principles of ODA for the next three years, which identified Afghanistan, alongside four Central Asian states, as a priority recipient of Kazakhstan's aid; the 'creation of a belt of good-neighbourliness athwart the perimeter of Kazakhstan's frontiers', being the chief rationale behind such decision.[33] Kazakhstan is likely to remain the only Central Asian state to channel regular development assistance to Afghanistan, however modest, in the near future.

Despite a flurry of positive political statements, high-level official talks, trade fairs and exhibitions and the signing of a framework agreement between Kazakhstan and Afghanistan on the encouragement and mutual protection of investment in 2012, the flow of capital between the two countries has remained virtually non-existent. Risk-averse Kazakhstani entrepreneurs invested a miserly US$0.3 million between 2005 and 2018 in Afghanistan.[34]

Kazakhstan has served as a key chain in the NDN network since 2010. While US cargoes have transited from its Caspian ports to Afghanistan by rail via Uzbek territory without too much difficulty, the same cannot be said about Kazakhstani goods. Tashkent has periodically slapped high tariffs on Kazakh grain and flour destined for Afghanistan and denied access to its railway system, citing congestion. Out of desperation, Kazakh authorities advised its exporters to use a route via Turkmenistan which, while much longer, would reduce the delivery time to ten to twelve days, down from twenty to thirty days.[35] To be fair, Tashkent has supported a radical plan of improving connectivity by building a new Mazar-e Sharif–Kabul–Peshawar railway line proposed by Kazakhstan and Russia, who are reportedly ready to provide at least some financing.[36] Given the tentative price tag of US$3 billion this line does seem to be the latest in a series of pipe-dream projects promising to turn Afghanistan into a transport connector between Europe and South Asia, with less than average chances of success given that the United States and the European Union are not likely to be involved.

Kyrgyzstan's involvement in the stabilisation of Afghanistan via development, exists solely in the discursive realm. As a report by the main government think tank put it, 'our state has been declaring its readiness to implement closer cooperation with Afghanistan for a long time. Dimensions such as energy, transit and transport, training specialists in different areas, and sales of electricity are voiced', before concluding that 'real action is not taking place at present'.[37] Kyrgyzstan did not even open an embassy in Kabul until 2013. Joint statements from official meetings are painful to read as they are short on substance, big on platitudes and highly repetitive. Communiqués from negotiations held in November 2017 and August 2018 were identical:

> During the talks, the sides discussed the current state and prospects for the development of Kyrgyz–Afghan relations in which special attention was paid to the widening and deepening of cooperation in the trade/economic and cultural/humanitarian spheres, including the question of rendering support to ethnic Kyrgyz residing on the territory of Lesser and Greater Pamirs in Afghanistan.[38]

Should CASA-1000 be finished, Kyrgyzstan's economic relations with Afghanistan may acquire some substance, but so far they have been negligible.

A similar verdict can be passed for the case of Tajikistan, with important caveats. As mentioned above, even in the absence of CASA-1000, the republic exports significant quantities of energy to Afghanistan. In 2017, Dushanbe sold US$50 million worth of electricity to Kabul, which accounted for 78 per cent of its total exports to Afghanistan.[39] A strategic bridge built with US funds in 2007, increased the throughput capacity of a border crossing at Lower Panj from five trucks a day to 1,000. The bridge was actively used by the international coalition prior to 2014 to supply ISAF and ANSF and has been designated by CAREC as a mainstay of the 'Corridor 5' project, which is supposed to serve transit trade between Afghanistan on the one hand and China, Pakistan, Kyrgyzstan,

Kazakhstan and Tajikistan on the other hand. An ADB audit conducted in 2015 called Corridor 5 'the most challenging CAREC corridor' listing the reluctance by Tajik authorities to issue visas and road passes to Afghan truck drivers (due to concerns such as narcotics and smuggling), huge waiting times at the Lower Panj crossing point, and a ban by Kyrgyzstan on third party truck transit through Karamyk on the Kyrgyz–Tajik border, as reasons for the route's underperformance.[40]

The Aga Khan Network (AKN) sponsored the construction of five smaller bridges in the 2000s–2010s. In Aga Khan's words, these bridges 'give people an opportunity to unite in order to exchange the best practices in societal development. You may acquire the best possible experience in education, health, economic development, finances and agriculture across borders'.[41] The Afghan governors of Balkh and Badakhshan – Atta Mohammad Nur and Shah Waliullah Adeeb, respectively – registered their appreciation in a more down to earth form, praising the creation of small border markets next to the bridges,[42] although the combined annual turnover of these border markets may not have exceeded US$10 million.

Similarly to Kyrgyzstan, Tajikistan does not fly high as a provider of investment or technical assistance to its southern neighbour. An economist from the Tajik Academy of Sciences argued, in 2013, that Tajikistan could help Afghanistan in areas such as seed technology, livestock quality improvement, silk production, veterinarian control in northern provinces, tourism and the running of free economic zones.[43] Practically nothing from this reasonable bucket list has been realised so far.

One area of cooperation which looked promising in the early 2010s was the Turkmenistan–Afghanistan–Tajikistan railway project (TAT), which was touted by the leaders of the three states as being 'of great importance for the strategic, political and economic interests of all parties' eventually opening 'a new corridor between Central Asia and world markets through the sea ports on the coast of the Indian Ocean'.[44] In reality, Tajikistan would be the main beneficiary from the project, as it could allow it to overcome transport blockade imposed by Uzbekistan. The country's Ministry of Transport reported in 2014 that 423 kilometres of tracks, fifteen stations, 235 kilometres of electric lines, eight locomotives and accompanying infrastructure were lying idle because Tashkent had severed all rail transit.[45] A 160 kilometre-long bypass (with 143 kilometres on Afghan territory) costing US$243 million, would resolve Tajikistan's predicament. The bulk of the financing was to come from international donors working on the reconstruction of Afghanistan. The ADB made a tentative commitment of US$100 million, and Presidents Hamid Karzai, Emomali Rahmon and Gurbanguly Berdimuhammedov attended a ceremony in March 2013 launching the construction and burying a time capsule with a pithy message to future generations. In late 2015 the ADB halted the credit line saying that 'we do not intend to finance construction of a railway in a country [Afghanistan] where security is not guaranteed', adding: 'We will probably return to this project when the security situation in Afghanistan improves.'[46] This may never happen now that Tajikistan and Uzbekistan experienced a rapid and radical thaw in bilateral relations in 2018, which will be discussed in Chapter 5.

Turkmenistan hosted the Seventh Regional Economic Cooperation Conference on Afghanistan (RECCA) ministerial gathering in 2017, where it took an opportunity to stress the need for 'further advancing regional economic cooperation as an effective means to achieve economic prosperity in Afghanistan'.[47] The final declaration listed seven priority investment projects in energy and transport, in four of which Turkmenistan plays a pivotal role: the Turkmenistan–Afghanistan–Pakistan–India gas pipeline (TAPI); Turkmenistan–Afghanistan–Pakistan 500 kilovolt (kV) power transmission line (TAP-500); TAT, and the Lapis Lazuli corridor.

TAPI has been on the drawing board for over twenty years. If completed, the 1,735 kilometre-long pipeline will deliver 33 billion cubic meters (bcm) of Turkmen natural gas to Afghanistan, Pakistan and India annually. By 2015, all technical documentation had been prepared and agreements signed among the four contracting countries. The project has received strong international support from the United States, United Kingdom, European Union, the Gulf countries and even Moscow, which has repeatedly stated that it would like to see Russian companies involved as sub-contractors. Washington's position on the scheme's significance and salubrious impact couldn't be clearer: 'The U.S. supports the TAPI project because we think it has the potential to be a transformative project for the entire region in terms of energy security for countries and commercial ties.'[48] Even the Taliban have come on board, saying that the movement 'views the project as a vital foundational economic element for the country and considers its proper implementation as good news for the Afghan people'.[49] Turkmen opposition sources believe that Ashgabat, which maintained good working relations with the Taliban while they were in power, may have reached an informal understanding with the insurgents about the pipeline protection, in exchange for payment of US$300–400 million a year.[50]

Afghanistan stands to buy 5 bcm of gas from Turkmenistan at a competitive rate and receive up to US$500 million in transit fees each year. The stumbling blocks to TAPI's implementation are finances and the absence of a reputable international operating company. The ADB (acting for Afghanistan), Pakistan and India have committed US$1.5 billion to the US$10 billion project, which means that Ashgabat has to come up with the remainder on its own. In desperation to diversify its gas exports away from China, the Turkmen government appointed its own gas company, Turkmengaz, as the project operator, revised the costs down to US$7 billion in 2018, and announced that by the end of 2019 the Afghan section of the pipeline would be complete and gas deliveries would start. There is much apprehension about this timeline as well as unverifiable reports by the Turkmen government about fresh investors and the actual construction work performed on Turkmen territory.[51]

The story of TAP-500 closely follows that of TAPI. In 2013, President Berdimuhammedov approved a program of building fourteen new thermal power stations operating on gas which would add 3,854 MW to the country's generation capacity and increase its electricity export potential five-fold.[52] The lion's share of this surplus is supposed to go to Afghanistan and Pakistan via a new transmission line running in parallel to TAPI. Just like TAPI, TAP-500 has been stalled by financial and security concerns and no actual work took place in Afghanistan as of late 2018. A long-term power purchase and sales agreement signed between Ashgabat and Kabul in 2015, envisages that the latter will have to buy TAP-500 electricity at the rate of US$0.056 per kWh in 2019 and US$0.071 in 2028, which is rather problematic given that Afghanistan struggled with US$0.04 in 2017, as mentioned above.[53]

The Lapis Lazuli corridor is a trade and transport route which starts in Aqina and Turghundi 'dry ports' in the Afghan provinces of Faryab and Herat, that used to thrive as entrepôts for ISAF supplies prior to 2014. It then proceeds to the seaport of Turkmenbashi in Turkmenistan, crosses the Caspian Sea to Baku, whence it loops to the Black Sea before reaching Turkey and Europe. The inter-government agreement for this cross-modal transportation scheme was signed in Ashgabat on the margins of RECCA-VII in 2017, after three years of preparatory work. It was viewed as a coup for the United States, which positioned this particular corridor 'as the shortest, cheapest, and most reliable route for Afghanistan's trade with Europe', which happened to bypass Iran and Russia.[54] The first test caravan of nine trucks loaded with dried fruit and cotton left Herat for Turkey under the Transports Internationaux Routiers or International Road Transports (TIR) system through Turkmenistan in December 2018, revealing that there was still much to be done by way of reducing imposts and obtaining visas for drivers.[55] Whether this route could compete with the established transit corridors going through Uzbekistan and Iran might depend on the Afghan government's ability to keep offsetting 50 per cent of transport costs of its exporters in the Lapis Lazuli corridor.

Turkmenistan doesn't have a regular aid program aimed at Afghanistan. However, it provided earthquake relief in 2015, built a maternity ward in Torghundi in 2016, and funded the construction of a mosque in Aqina in 2018. Small-scale trade or free people-to-people exchanges across the heavily militarised border don't occur, and Berdimuhammedov's constant references to 'the presence of all possibilities to widen cultural and educational scientific contacts', along with, 'the potential for mutually beneficial contacts between entrepreneurs', and 'the readiness to give Afghanistan effective support in its peaceful renaissance and socio-economic development', ought to be treated as statements of intent at best.[56]

'Tashkent's major interest in the Afghanistan conflict is not economic, but political: to prevent the IMU from benefitting from the fighting in Afghanistan and from de-stabilising Uzbekistan',[57] claimed one analytical report in 2015. This is a fair summary of Uzbekistan's stance under President Karimov, prior to his death in September 2016. Since then, the country has moved towards greater openness in economic relations, although the extent to which the portrayal of Afghanistan as a market opportunity corresponds with Uzbekistan's contribution to its development is a moot point.

Under Karimov, all foreign economic activity was tightly regulated by the state. Obsession with sovereignty, internal stability and total control over the flow of goods and people across borders severely constrained commercial interaction with foreign partners. Figures voiced by an Uzbek foreign trade official are instructive: in 2017, Uzbek capital was represented in about 600 joint ventures across Central Asia and Afghanistan. The figure for the latter was six, which was two less than in Tajikistan after two decades of intense confrontation between Tashkent and Dushanbe.[58] The head of the Balkh provincial Chamber of Commerce and Industries spoke with obvious frustration in 2013 about 'Uzbekistan's far-from-satisfactory business links with Afghanistan,' complaining that 'Afghan entrepreneurs were given bad treatment in Uzbekistan'.[59]

Karimov's successor, Shavkat Mirziyoyev, advised in one of his earlier speeches that 'we [people of Uzbekistan] must guard our priceless treasure – peace and tranquility – like the apple of our eye. It's no secret that forces exist who want to destabilize [the country], sow hatred and conflicts and even spill blood'.[60] With this categorical imperative in mind, the new president has undertaken steps to develop economic ties with Afghanistan in a neo-mercantilist way. His strategy became evident during the official visit of Ashraf Ghani to Tashkent in December

2017. One of the tangible outcomes of the leaders' talks was the signing of forty commercial contracts worth US$500 million – all about the increased export of Uzbek goods to Afghanistan.[61] On its part, the Uzbek side agreed to reduce the price of electricity to US$0.05 per kWh (which is not a huge sacrifice given that it simultaneously signed a deal with Tajikistan to import its energy at US$0.02 per kWh) and cover half the costs of vocational training of one hundred Afghan specialists in Termez. Mirziyoyev presented a gift to the Afghan people in the form of twenty-five buses and three tractors which were gratefully accepted as 'Uzbekistan's contribution, within its ability, to the cause of economic reconstruction of Afghanistan that will expedite the improvement of life of the Afghan people and its return to the normal path of peaceful development'.[62]

Tashkent has indicated its readiness to invest US$500 million in a 657 kilometre Mazar-e Sharif to Herat railway line costing approximately US$1.8 billion. The line is an extension of the Hairatan–Mazar-e Sharif project, which came into existence thanks to the NDN.

By 2011, Hairatan on the Afghan–Uzbek border was a boom town serving as the gateway for perhaps half of Afghanistan's external trade. This high volume was achieved by handling about 40 per cent of ISAF fuel and gear transit. The seventy-five kilometre railway linking Hairatan with Mazar-e Sharif (the first in Afghanistan) was financed by an ADB grant and constructed by the Uzbek state rail monopoly on a noncompetitive single source basis. With sixty-two check posts, round the clock armed patrols, fencing, watchtowers and security cameras, it is probably one of the most heavily protected transport lines in the world.[63] Tashkent retained operational control over the railway, collected customs duties in Hairatan, and banned access by Afghan exporters to its rolling stock. Following the NATO withdrawal, Hairatan has hit hard times becoming a barometer of economic depression in Afghanistan's north.[64] With rail traffic down by 48 per cent between 2012 and 2014, and the port of Hairatan accounting for just 20 per cent of Afghan imports in 2017,[65] plans to extend the railway to Herat looked increasingly unlikely. An independent evaluation commissioned by the ADB in 2015 found that the Hairatan–Mazar project had been executed hastily and without a link to a long-term master plan for Afghanistan's transport development, overestimated the demand for freight, underestimated operational costs, and pronounced it 'less than likely sustainable'.[66] The offer of US$500 million by Tashkent, should be seen as a sweetener and an inducement for Kabul to lobby aid providers to deliver the bulk of the cash – a tactic quite similar to Turkmenistan's efforts in pushing its mega-projects through. As one Uzbek expert put it, 'there is absolutely no doubt that donor states and international institutions must implement their obligations in order to improve the socio-economic situation in Afghanistan.'67

In general, it can be safely said that, lofty rhetoric notwithstanding, the Central Asian states' attempts to mitigate security risks in Afghanistan by contributing to its development have been rather half-hearted. Instead, they have sought to capitalise on the many needs of the neighbouring country and resolve their own issues by taking advantage of the billions of dollars in donor funding made available by the West. In light of the imminent decline of the international community's interest in Afghanistan chances are that the regional zone of prosperity with Kabul at its core will not materialise. Many of the 'connectivity' projects contemplated in the early 2010s may never be implemented, and those that do could change their course and go around Afghanistan rather than traversing it. Potentially sounding the death knell for the NDN legacy schemes, the Uzbek government suggested in September 2018 that an integrated system of managing transport flows across Central Asia be created under the aegis of the SCO.[68] Some of the new transit initiatives associated with China's Belt and Road Initiative will be considered in Chapter 4.

'Fortress Central Asia': Military and Security Response to the Afghan Crisis

Between 2001 and 2014, the Central Asian republics relied on NATO and ANSF to contain threats affecting them from the Afghan soil. In the post-ISAF period, when the security situation patently worsened, they might have felt compelled to give extra support to the National Unity Government to compensate its diminished ability to fight the insurgents. This hasn't happened. The region's governments 'hoped to benefit from a secure Afghanistan and the new economic opportunities that presented', wrote Ivan Safranchuk, 'however, the Central Asians do not want to share in Afghanistan's insecurity. Their basic interest is to store problems on the Afghan side of the border, preferably with a buffer zone between them.'[69]

There exists a universally strong resentment against any kind of direct military involvement in the Afghan conflict across Central Asia. In her fascinating ethnographic study, Madeleine Reeves noted that for historical and geopolitical reasons the Afghan border is an 'exceptional' boundary beyond which lies darkness: 'For my interlocutors in the Ferghana Valley, Afghanistan was often the contrastive other against which civilization and development were charted; and the Afghan–Tajik and Afghan–Uzbek borders often served as referents for the kind of borders that should properly be closed to dangerous seepages of people and ideas.'[70] In 2008, Astana approved the dispatch of four officers from the country's peacekeeping battalion (KAZBAT) to ISAF headquarters. Political and public backlash was so strong that the normally pliable upper house of the national parliament blocked the initiative. By contrast, KAZBAT's five-year deployment on a NATO mission in Iraq stirred no resentment at all.[71]

Kazakhstan is the only country in the region to maintain a semblance of military-security cooperation with Kabul. It undertook to train seventy-five law enforcement officials as part of the 1,000 student intake between 2010 and 2020 as mentioned above. Astana remitted US$2 million to the Afghan National Army Trust Fund (ANATF) in 2016 – a widow's mite that nonetheless earned Nazarbaev praise from the US President Donald Trump for sharing the American burden in bolstering Afghan security.[72] Two bilateral meetings of high-level security officials in 2013 and 2017, issued duplicate statements about the desirability of training of Afghan junior military personnel in Kazakhstan and advantages of potential 'exchange of information or opinion on the security situation'[73] with no discernible action ensuing.

Other Central Asian republics do even less by way of practical cooperation with Afghanistan on security matters. Normally it takes external agency and funding to bring them together. For example, the Japan International Cooperation Agency (JICA) has provided a US$4.6 million grant to Tajikistan for the purposes of effective management of its border with Afghanistan, part of which was spent on 'knowledge co-creation' between the two countries' security bodies.[74] In 2009, the OSCE set up the Border Management Staff College in Dushanbe, which occasionally offers short-term joint courses for Tajik border troops and Afghan border police.[75]

Turkmenistan alone in Central Asia has a dedicated joint commission with Afghanistan on security issues. Set up in 2013, it meets once a year mostly to discuss the safety of infrastructure projects. Since 2015, analysts have noted a change in Ashgabat's behavior which apparently lost confidence in Kabul's ability to improve or even affect the situation in northern Afghanistan.[76] The Berdimuhammedov government, obsessed with TAPI, has been reported to negotiate directly with local actors including district heads, village chiefs and, as mentioned before, even the Taliban. One particular interlocutor are the *arbaki*, tribal community militia forces which for a while were nurtured by the United States as the 'Critical Infrastructure Police' before proving to be too predatory, disruptive and disloyal to the central authorities.[77] One expert summed up the dynamics of Ashgabat's Afghan stance as follows: 'It looks like they've seen the situation degenerate to such an extent that they're willing to make some sacrifices in the neutrality policy.'[78]

Storing up problems on the Afghan side of the border entails the robust defense of this border. The Central Asian countries have historically relied on a combination of national measures and international cooperation in achieving this objective. The declining input of the United States has been pronounced in the post-ISAF period. American security aid to the region plummeted from a high point of US$255 million in 2012 to US$19 million in 2018 – a drop of 93 per cent, the most recent figure falling below the 2001 level.[79] Even lavish assistance during the 'fat years' did not necessarily contribute to the upgrade of the regional defence, counterterrorism and counter-narcotics capacities in the most efficient way because the underlying rationale behind Washington's generosity was gaining physical access to local facilities and balancing Moscow and Beijing.[80] At present Turkmenistan and Uzbekistan prioritise self-sufficiency while the others engage in collective security arrangements more readily when devising measures to contain the Afghan threats.

The deterioration of the situation in Afghanistan after 2014, has caused Ashgabat to embark upon an ambitious reform of its armed forces using its hydrocarbon revenues. Details are scarce but analysts have commented on a move away from a conscript-dominated army and the improved quality of special units, 'which may provide Turkmenistan with an enhanced capability to take on the militant forces threatening the country's border'.[81] Berdimuhammedov appointed the country's head of state security as the Minister of Defence in 2015, ostensibly to tighten control over all uniformed services. He also launched an expansive rearmament program sourcing modern equipment from at least eight foreign states, including Turkey, China and Russia.[82] The resumption of military ties with the latter is particularly noteworthy as it came after a decade of deep freeze. The Russian Defence Minister visited the country in 2016 and apparently reached an understanding on training Turkmen military personnel, operational drills and information exchange, in addition to weapons supply.[83] In 2017 the two countries signed a strategic partnership agreement and several additional protocols; one Russian expert claimed that in 2018 over twenty such documents were in force, amounting to Moscow's guarantee to help in a crisis situation.[84]

Defending oneself according to one's own means and seldom compromising on national interest was the essence of what Bernardo Fazendeiro called 'defensive self-reliance' by Uzbekistan under Karimov.[85] Following his death the new government may have started to reconsider its position in the context of the

Afghan situation. President Mirziyoyev inherited the largest army in the region which had been bolstered by a significant donation of US military vehicles worth US$150 million in late 2014, 'to support their efforts at counter terrorism and counter narcotics'.[86] Nonetheless, aside from one small National Security Service commando unit descended from a Soviet military intelligence brigade, the country's regular armed forces had problems with combat readiness, intelligence and command and control crucial in counterterrorist and counter-insurgency operations.[87] The new government started a program of reforms aiming at the creation of a smaller, but modern and highly mobile, army supplied by the indigenous military-industrial complex. It also confirmed its principled adherence to non-membership in any military blocs, inadmissibility of foreign bases and personnel on its territory, and permanent ban on peacekeeping operations beyond its borders.[88] The army manoeuvres held in the southern Surkhandarya and Qashqadarya regions in November 2018 – the largest in Uzbekistan's history – showed progress of these reforms and demonstrated that 'Tashkent treats the problem of the fighters' relocation from Syria and Iraq to Afghanistan seriously.'[89]

The course of self-reliance has not prevented Tashkent from seeking targeted collaboration with external actors on Afghanistan-related threats. The most important of them is Russia, which in 2016 agreed to sell armaments to Uzbekistan at domestic prices – a privilege that theretofore was accorded only to the CSTO and Eurasian Economic Union (EEU) members. Russian experts have stressed that the 'military-technical cooperation aims, first and foremost, at repelling Afghan fighters', citing deliveries of Mi-35 helicopter gunships 'ideally suited for the harsh operational theatre' and an agreement on the joint use of airspace for military purposes as concrete examples.[90] At the same time, Tashkent has been adamant that there is no chance of Uzbekistan's returning to the CSTO which it quit in 2012: 'The question of renewing our CSTO membership is not on the agenda ... There are no plans to discuss or review this matter in the future,' the country's Foreign Minister stated recently in a televised interview.[91]

By contrast, the CSTO is an essential element of the military and security strategy to contain threats from Afghanistan when it comes to Kazakhstan, Kyrgyzstan and Tajikistan. Since 2014, this bloc has paid increasingly close attention to Central Asia's southern borders. Its collective security strategy adopted in 2016 expanded the list of threats warranting immediate joint action to include terrorism, cross-border incursion of illegal armed formations and narcotics trafficking; Afghanistan was the only menacing country in the document mentioned by name.[92] The CSTO's joint statement issued at the UN General Assembly in 2017 registered the members' particular alarm about:

[T]he Islamic State (ISIS) and the terrorist organizations connected with it in Afghanistan, as well as their proliferation around the country and the attempts to gain a foothold in the northern provinces of Afghanistan, which is creating numerous threats to security and stability in Central Asia.[93]

The CSTO's principal military means of mitigating threats from Afghanistan consists of the Collective Rapid Reaction Force for Central Asia (CRRFCA) comprising 5,000 servicemen from mobile and light mountain infantry units stationed in Kazakhstan, Kyrgyzstan, Russia and Tajikistan. In theory they can deploy anywhere in the region within twelve to twenty-four hours, to support national security forces in a zone of crisis. The CSTO conducts military drills, expedites transfer of Russian weapons to member states, maintains an integrated database of terrorist groups and individuals, and carries out annual police and special service operations to intercept illegal migrants, monitor extremist recruitment in cyberspace and seize narcotics.[94] In 2018, the CSTO 'Canal–Red Dune' operation unfolded over four days in southern Kazakhstan and Kyrgyzstan astride the northern route of drug trafficking from Afghanistan and reportedly netted five tons of opium and forty kilograms of heroin.[95]

Kazakhstan positions itself as an equal partner with Russia in the CSTO. It has been a driving force behind its many initiatives in Central Asia including the formation of CRRFCA.[96] Nonetheless, Nazarbaev has made it clear that while he supports and appreciates the bloc's activities in handling the problems of terrorism, trafficking and ISIS returnees proliferating from Afghanistan, he won't allow it to become overly politicised and acquire anti-NATO overtones.[97] Astana's agenda as the chair of the CSTO for 2018 included greater engagement with the UN, OSCE and SCO and enhanced risk monitoring in Afghanistan.[98]

As smaller and weaker frontline states, Kyrgyzstan and Tajikistan are much more dependent on the CSTO and Russia in maintaining their border security. Moscow operates the 999th airbase in Kyrgyzstan which doubles as an air force component of the CRRFCA. In 2017 the bilateral Status of Forces agreement came into effect whereby the base and four other smaller Russian units 'together with the Armed Forces of Kyrgyzstan ensure the protection of sovereignty and security of the republic including the repulsion of military attacks on the part of international terrorist formations.'[99] In 2012, the Kremlin promised Bishkek US$1billion to modernise its armed forces. Only a portion of that money has been disbursed so far: between 2014 and 2018, Kyrgyzstan received US$125 million worth of weapons.[100] In 2016, President Atambaev lobbied Moscow for the opening of a second base:

I told Putin that if you really want to think about common security then we are interested in building some contingency platforms in the south of the country. This would be real aid. This conversation first took place with the Russian Minister of Defence five to six years ago. Perhaps, the issue is that of finances. But I believe our position is the correct one. We don't need to strengthen the [already existing] Russian base in Kant. If any place is in need of protection then it has to be the border between Kyrgyzstan and Tajikistan. This is my principled position. I have bad premonitions about Afghanistan and whether Tajikistan will hold the blow from there.[101]

Atambaev took special pride in his country's contribution to the CSTO collective security recalling how a Kyrgyz infantry unit marched on foot through difficult terrain to a military exercise on the Tajik–Afghan border in 2016: 'This way we tested whether our soldiers can come to the assistance of our friends in Tajikistan if the situation became tense.'[102]

Kyrgyzstan joined the EEU in 2015. Its southern border became the common customs and control zone for the entire organisation. Moscow allocated US$48 million to upgrade and equip facilities there, which according to the commander of Kyrgyzstan's border guards, 'will enable us to increase the level of border security manyfold, adequately react to potential threats and challenges, and significantly decrease the level of conflict in border areas'.[103]

Similarly to Kyrgyzstan, Tajikistan relies on Russia and the CSTO to a considerable extent to protect itself from Afghanistan's insecurities. In 2014, Moscow announced a long-term program of free arms transfer to the Tajik army worth 70 billion roubles which was equivalent to US$1.2 billion at the time. Deliveries commenced in 2017 at the rate of around US$100 million a year (slightly less than the country's entire military budget), featuring mostly refurbished stock from the Russian Central Military District.[104] The same year Russia's 201st base situated on the territory of Tajikistan, was formally directed to assist the Tajik armed forces in protecting the border with Afghanistan.[105] The base, the largest operated by Russia outside its borders and with 6,500 servicemen, was reinforced, received new weapons including heavy artillery and became otherwise 'optimized to support [Tajik] government forces covering the most dangerous segments of the border'.[106]

Despite some effort by the United States and the European Union to enhance the capacity of the Afghan border police between 2009 and 2014, the Afghan–Tajik frontier remained woefully unprotected with just one patrolman assigned to every kilometre of border – 4.5 times lower than on the border with Pakistan, and 2.1 times lower than on the border with Turkmenistan.[107] On the other side, Tajikistan had roughly ten times more manpower (16,000 – still only about half of the Soviet-era complement, and 16 per cent lower than the number of Russian border guards who were stationed there during 1992–2005), while remaining desperately short of weapons and facilities. When the Taliban captured Kunduz and overpowered border garrisons in Takhar and Badakhshan in 2015, Dushanbe was worried. Rahmon made it the first item on the agenda of his talks with Putin:

> I would like to raise security issues in the CSTO zone of responsibility because the Tajik–Afghan border falls into this zone. The situation in Afghanistan is worsening every day. Fighting is taking place along 60 per cent of the border opposite the Tajik side ... We are very concerned, so today I'd like to discuss the issues of ensuring security in the region in particular.[108]

The CSTO has adopted an interstate program of strengthening the Tajik–Afghan border, and Belarus and Armenia have even provided uniforms and trucks within its framework, but Russia has been slow in committing to action, despite another Taliban offensive in Kunduz in 2017. The main reason for this could be that Moscow would like to see the return of its own forces to guard the border, rather than help the Tajiks. Dushanbe has resisted this move, ostensibly in deference to the negative US position on the matter.[109] Rahmon has repeatedly voiced his frustration with the program's slow progress, which impeded his country's valiant fight against narcotics, terrorism, extremism, organised crime and other negative phenomena linked to the aggravated situation in Afghanistan.[110] He may have found an alternative in China, which has agreed to construct eleven outposts of different sizes on the Tajik–Afghan border.[111] The details of the agreement, including its value and duration are not known but one of the outposts was already active in 2018, and Tajik border guard units displayed a few dozen military vehicles donated by China. This shouldn't be interpreted as a sign of growing Sino–Russian competition in their roles of security providers, because quiet understanding if not formal distribution of responsibilities exists between Moscow and Beijing, in shoring up Tajikistan's border security.[112]

China holds bilateral military drills with Kazakhstan, Kyrgyzstan and Tajikistan at the rate of once every two or three years. Russia conducted fifty-one such events in 2018 alone.[113] Moscow, Beijing and all Central Asian republics except Turkmenistan, have regularly participated in the joint SCO exercises once or twice a year since 2006, practicing both conventional warfare and antiterrorist scenarios.[114] The CSTO and SCO have been trying to harmonise their operations in Central Asia vis-à-vis the Afghanistan problem to avoid duplication and to deal with the intersection of terrorism, insurgency and organised crime in a holistic manner, with limited success so far.[115]

Since 2014, all Central Asian republics have worked hard to erect a military barrier between themselves and troubled Afghanistan. They don't have much trust in the ability of the US-backed government in Kabul to defeat insurgents and stabilise the country, and thus have abstained from committing resources to, and fostering meaningful cooperation with, the ANSF. The West's security footprint in Central Asia has shrunk considerably leaving Russia and in some instances China to underwrite defensive needs of regional states. What has been largely missing from the picture is the collective action by the Central Asian countries themselves, beyond bloc structures run from the outside. Some positive developments in that direction may have started to emerge in 2018; they will be discussed in Chapter 5.

Looking for Diplomatic Solutions to the Afghan Crisis

All Central Asian republics conduct active diplomacy in search of greater stability and security in Afghanistan. The venues for it include major international initiatives, multilateral consultation mechanisms and bilateral negotiations with Kabul. In addition to the UN, the most important Afghanistan-focused (and Afghanistan-led) forum frequented by the region's foreign policy professionals has been the Heart of Asia (HoA), launched in 2011 by fifteen countries who adopted six task forces on counterterrorism; counter-narcotics; disaster management; education; regional infrastructure; and trade, commercial and investment opportunities. Between 2011 and 2015, the HoA held five ministerial conferences, sixteen senior officials and twelve ambassadorial meetings, dozens of symposia, seminars and exhibitions and many other side events predominantly financed by the outer circle of supporting states and organisations such as the United States and the ADB. The actual practical outcome of these activities was negligible or at least intangible: 'All of these events have been instrumental in creating regional political coherence and a sense of amity among the HoA countries.'[116] It is reasonably difficult to measure the extent to which Iran and Saudi Arabia, or India and Pakistan, laid aside their differences in the name of stabilising Afghanistan. One critical report warned about HoA turning into 'a charity organization that countries participate in to brand themselves as altruistic towards Afghanistan, or to please larger geopolitical powers'.[117]

Washington used to be the largest geopolitical actor the Central Asian republics tried to please within the HoA framework: 'The Istanbul Process consciously aims to support the New Silk Road vision of the United States. It seeks to transform the recently constructed Northern Distribution Network ... into enduring enhancements in regional trade links between Central Asia and Afghanistan.'[118] Muratbek Imanaliev, the former Foreign Minister of Kyrgyzstan and SCO Secretary-General, commented that in the early 2010s, the Central Asian elites were still happy to accept the image of improving Afghanistan cultivated by HoA, CAREC and RECCA, and were optimistic about its core role in connectivity projects, on conditions that the United States would provide security and financial sponsorship and Russia and China would support them politically. When neither condition was met, 'the realization that the "Afghan problem" once delegated to the US ... must be taken up by themselves has started to form and take root in the Central Asian countries', argued Imanaliev, adding a further observation on how the region's policymakers felt in 2014:

> By and large, all assess the situation in Afghanistan correctly, anticipate its negative evolution, and offer their own vision of what that country should look like in future. A standard set of characteristics features a peaceful, stable and developing state. Nobody can say how this might be achieved though.[119]

The Central Asians' quest for an optimal multilateral foreign policy mechanism vis-à-vis Afghanistan has exhibited a great deal of diversification since 2014. In 2015, five states and Washington formed a C5 + 1 consultative mechanism supported by a US$15 million appropriation from the US Congress which, among other things, aims to 'explore ways to strengthen cooperation in the promotion of a stable, peaceful, and economically prosperous Afghanistan'.[120] At the same time, Kazakhstan, Kyrgyzstan and Tajikistan became more active in the CSTO Foreign Ministers Council's Working group on Afghanistan pushing for 'a common approach and consolidation of efforts by Afghans and all interested parties', in order to defuse the poor security situation.[121] The Afghanistan contact group in the SCO resumed its annual meetings in 2017, after eight years of inactivity, where four Central Asian republics alongside others, 'exchanged opinions on issues related to the fight against security challenges and threats in the region as well as assistance in the rebuilding of Afghanistan as a peaceful, stable and prosperous state'.[122]

Uzbekistan's president Mirziyoyev provides a good example of the multivocality of Central Asian diplomacy. When visiting Moscow on a state visit in 2017, he said:

> Tranquillity, peace and stability in Afghanistan are very important to us. We are going to help and support in every possible way everything that Russia is promoting vis-à-vis Afghanistan. Everything that is being done by Russia on Afghanistan is of great delight to us.[123]

A year later Mirziyoyev came to Washington and met Trump at the White House. According to the official precis of their conversation,

> President Mirziyoyev reaffirmed his full support for President Trump's South Asia strategy and discussed Uzbekistan's initiatives to strengthen bilateral cooperation, share burdens, and address regional security issues, including stability in Afghanistan ... President Mirziyoyev assured continued support for the Northern Distribution Network and its contribution to achieving peace and stability in Afghanistan ... [President Trump] offered political support and planning consultations regarding Uzbekistan's railroad and infrastructure projects in Afghanistan.[124]

Tashkent feels confident and competent enough to incorporate Russia and the United States in its Afghan calculus: the former as a security guarantor, and the latter as a backer for lucrative infrastructure projects in Afghanistan, that just might arise from the rubble of the Obama-era NSR scheme. The United States may be reducing its own expenditure, but it retains a critical voice in how huge development funds are distributed, and all Central Asian republics are interested in keeping them flowing their way. Uzbekistan's Deputy Foreign Minister reflected the collective wish of his regional colleagues, when he said, 'It is exceptionally important that donor countries and international institutions did not lower their attention and assistance to Afghanistan.'[125]

There are many 'platforms', 'formats' and 'dialogues' combining one or more of the Central Asian republics, on the one hand, and external actors, on the other hand, which touch upon the Afghan problem in one way or another. Practically all of them have limited lifespan, do not go beyond the routine exchange of information and are inconsequential to mitigating the local security concerns. Who would remember the 'Dushanbe Four' for instance which brought together Afghanistan, Pakistan, Russia and Tajikistan ostensibly 'in support of the Afghanistan government's efforts at national reconciliation' and had an entire roadmap worked out to achieve that?[126] What is remarkable is the absence of intra-regional multilateral diplomacy focused on Afghanistan which is the result of deep-seated divisions among the Central Asian countries themselves. One of the few exceptions is the Afghanistan–Kyrgyzstan–Tajikistan counter-narcotics initiative (AKT), which was set up in 2012 and has featured regular ministerial meetings and a handful of joint drug interdiction operations.[127] In December 2017, Tashkent proposed the creation of a new consultative Central Asia plus Afghanistan format (with a confusing designation of 'C5 + 1') 'intended to be an effective platform for discussing the entire range of regional issues, as well as developing joint measures for peace and sustainable development with the support of the United Nations'.[128] This intention had not borne fruit as of late 2018.

The Central Asian states maintain strong bilateral ties with Kabul. Kazakhstan and Uzbekistan have special envoys on Afghanistan in their foreign policy executive. All republics use official visits, embassies and other forms of formal diplomacy to articulate their security concerns and offer advice to the Afghan government. At the same time, they realise the limits to this engagement: their interests on the ground, as one Central Asian expert put it, 'cannot be accomplished in any way other than through approbation from the US which has monopolized control over all processes in Afghanistan'.[129] One area where Central Asian statesmen and diplomats have been increasingly active since 2014, is the inclusion of the Taliban in the political process in Afghanistan.

The softening of the regional capitals' stance on the Taliban, was caused by the growing pessimism about the prospects of counter-insurgency campaign in Afghanistan, and the perception of the Taliban's utility in containing the much more acute threat of the IMU, ISIS-K and other international jihadi groups. They had to tread carefully though, because of the official designation of the Taliban as a terrorist organisation at home and the need to avoid jeopardising good relations with the government in Kabul. Karimov led the way in 2015. Having stressed that Uzbekistan always conducted relations with Afghanistan on the basis of respect to its national interests and non-interference in its domestic affairs, he gave the following counsel to the southern neighbour as a friend and wise senior statesman:

> Today's situation in Afghanistan may be characterized as a low intensity conflict of opposing forces – primarily government troops and the Taliban. Quick withdrawal of the ISAF contingent and concomitant drop in external financial support to Afghanistan has exacerbated the situation. The logical result we can observe is that the vacuum created by the departure of foreign troops is being filled by aggressive terrorist groups squeezed from the Middle East ... It is imperative to resume the negotiations process between the Afghan government and the Taliban. The sides must not link the commencement of the talks to any preconditions. Any circumstances should be the subject of negotiations and not an obstacle to them. Political will and readiness for mutual concessions and

compromise must also be present. Compromise and compromise again is what could lead the Afghan issue out of a deadlock.[130]

All Central Asian republics have offered themselves as mediators for talks with the Taliban. Parallel to that, they have stepped up informal contacts with the rebels first, via special services and recently at the political level, as well – Turkmenistan's deal with the Taliban over TAPI has been mentioned above. Tashkent refused to blame the Taliban alone for a bomb blast that destroyed a pylon of the power transmission line connecting Uzbekistan with the Baghlan province of Afghanistan. As a senior Uzbek diplomat explained, local Taliban commanders had approached DABS to electrify villages under their control via a small offshoot from the main line and only when their request was denied they blew up the pylon – they didn't do that out of spite to Uzbekistan.[131]

Tajikistan has encouraged its southern neighbour to learn from the process of national reconciliation which put an end to the Tajik civil war of 1992–1997. At the same time, it has been more reticent than others on the issue of direct talks between the Kabul government and the Taliban because it views the latter as a Pashtun movement which would skew the ethnic balance of power in Afghanistan, if a power-sharing agreement is reached. This hasn't stopped its security agencies from clandestine contacts with the Taliban for the purpose of intelligence gathering and keeping an eye on criminal gangs.[132] Afghan authorities have repeatedly accused Dushanbe of supplying weapons to the Taliban (both directly and as agents for Russia), repairing their equipment and giving medical treatment to their wounded.[133] Tajik officials have vehemently denied these allegations,

> which demonstrate shortsightedness, incompetence and a lack of elementary knowledge, cause deep regret, hinder the creation of a constructive atmosphere and the fulfillment of earlier agreements and, by doing so, do damage to bilateral relations based on the principles of friendship and neighborliness.[134]

In 2017, the Afghan Ambassador in Moscow, an uncle of President Ghani, insulted Tajikistan by referring to it as a petty Russian mafia-state. Kabul had to issue an official retraction saying the diplomat's words did not represent the policy of the Afghan government.[135]

Conclusion

Building up a protective perimeter has dominated the Central Asian countries' response to the evolving situation in Afghanistan in the wake of the NATO withdrawal. Not having much confidence in the Afghan government's ability to rein in terrorists, rebels, bandits and drug traffickers on its territory, they use internal resources and international cooperation to better prepare their defences should the situation across the southern border deteriorate further. Among the external security providers, the role of Russia and China has grown, while that of the United States has receded.

The Central Asian republics played a significant role in stabilising Afghanistan between 2001 and 2014, by providing supplies and transit routes to the coalition forces and ANSF. They continue to do so, albeit on a reduced scale. Their contribution to sustainable development of Afghanistan is more equivocal. Despite the verbal commitment to achieving stability via economic means, it is more appropriate to see their approach as mulcting the donor community, in current instability, and planning for revenues through connectivity projects, once stabilisation does occur. With the exception of Turkmenistan, they are not prepared to commit serious resources of their own to energy schemes and transport corridors, the future of which hangs, for the most part, in the air.

The Central Asian leaders are fully committed to the idea of territorial integrity of Afghanistan. They have abstained from entertaining ideas about ethnic buffer zones on Afghan territory. Kabul enjoys Central Asia's wholehearted support in international diplomacy when it comes to maintaining the global focus on the Afghan issue and lobbying for development funds. Over the past few years regional capitals have been pushing actively for negotiations between the NUG and the Taliban for the sake of a peace deal. They are aware of their limitations – Central Asia will never have the leverage capacity of Pakistan or Iran in Afghan politics. However, its importance should not be underestimated. Central Asia figures prominently in the Afghanistan strategies of Russia, China and the United States, and this factor may act as a force multiplier for the region, if only temporarily. The next chapter will discuss the role of the Central Asian republics in the Afghan calculus of Moscow, Beijing and Washington.

As a final note, and keeping in mind that public opinion is not the main driver of policy decisions in Central Asia, it could be instructive to learn what ordinary people there make of their governments' stances on Afghanistan. In 2015–16, young people in four republics – unburdened by the troubling memories of the Soviet–Afghan war – were asked to pass judgment. The results showed that there was no public appetite for a radical revision of the status quo (Table 3.3). A plurality of respondents in Tajikistan who favoured closer relations with Afghanistan, once again illustrated the relative importance of ethnofidelity as a policy- consideration in that particular republic.

Table 3.3 Central Asian youth's opinion on relations with Afghanistan, (% of responses to the question 'What kind of relations should our country have with Afghanistan?')

	Closer	More restrained	The same as now	Hard to say	Refused to answer
Kazakhstan	10.6	28.8	51.2	1.5	7.9
Kyrgyzstan	6.1	31.7	50.6	4.2	7.4
Tajikistan	33.3	17.1	41.7	3.1	4.8
Uzbekistan	15.6	24.6	47.8	1.2	10.8

Adapted from: Botagoz Rakisheva, *Molodezh' Tsentralnoi Azii. Sravnitelnyi obzor*. Almaty: Friedrich Ebert Stiftung, 2017, pp. 81–84.

Notes

1 Republic of Kazakhstan, Ministry of Foreign Affairs, 'MID RK raz'iasnil prioritety Kazakhstana v SB OON', *BNews.kz*, 3 January 2017, https://bnews.kz/ru/news/mid_rk_razyasnil_prioriteti_kazahstana_v_sb_oon.

2 S. Frederick Starr, 'A Partnership for Central Asia', *Foreign Affairs* 84, 4 (2005): pp. 164–178.

3 'Tashkent Declaration on Fundamental Principles for a Peaceful Settlement of the Conflict in Afghanistan', *United Nations General Assembly*, Document A/54/174 S/1999/812, 22 July 1999, https://peacemaker.un.org/sites/peacemaker.un.org/files/AF_990719_TashkentDeclaration%28en%29.pdf.

4 Islamic Republic of Afghanistan, *Afghanistan National Development Strategy 1387–1391 (2008–2013): A Strategy for Security, Governance, Economic Growth & Poverty Reduction* (report, Afghanistan National Development Strategy Secretariat, Kabul, 2008), p. 143.

5 Central Asia Institute for Strategic Studies, 'Top Security Concerns in Central Asia – 2017', *CAISS Paper* 1 (2017) http://caiss.expert/top-security-concerns-in-central-asia-2017/top-10-ca/.

6 Roman Mogilevskii, *Trends and Patterns in Foreign Trade of Central Asian Countries* (Bishkek: UCA, 2012), pp. 13–14.

7 S. Frederick Starr, 'Introduction', in *The New Silk Roads: Transport and Trade in Greater Central Asia*, ed. S. Frederick Starr (Washington, D.C.: Johns Hopkins University–SAIS, 2007), pp. 7–10; Andrew C. Kuchins, Thomas M. Sanderson and David A. Gordon, *The Northern Distribution Network and the Modern Silk Road: Planning for Afghanistan's Future* (Washington, DC: Center for Strategic and International Studies, 2009), pp. 19–21.

8 Joshua Kucera, 'Turkmenistan Big Beneficiary of Pentagon Money, While Uzbekistan Lags', *Eurasianet*, 3 December 2012, https://eurasianet.org/turkmenistan-big-beneficiary-of-pentagon-money-while-uzbekistan-lags.

9 Walter Pincus, 'Red Star's Bagram Contract Extended Again', *The Washington Post*, 20 March 2012, https://www.washingtonpost.com/blogs/checkpoint-washington/post/red-stars-bagram-contract-extended-again/2012/03/20/gIQAN91cPS_blog.html?utm_term=.3d8a7a9dca25.

10 Saeed Parto, Jos Winters, Ehsan Saadat, Mohsin Usyan and Anastasiya Hozyainova, *Afghanistan and Regional Trade: More, or Less, Imports from Central Asia?* (Bishkek: University of Central Asia, 2012), p. 32.

11 Montague Lord, 'Regional Economic Integration in Central Asia and South Asia', (paper no. 66436, Munich Personal RePEc Archive, Munich, 15 May 2015), https://mpra.ub.uni-muenchen.de/66436/1/MPRA_paper_66436.pdf, p. 100.

12 United Nations Economic and Social Commission for Asia and the Pacific, 'Afghanistan and Central Asia: Strengthening Trade and Economic Ties', (report, UNESCAP, Bangkok, 27 March 2015), https://www.unescap.org/sites/default/files/Afghanistan%20and%20Central%20Asia-Strengthening%20Trade%20and%20Economic%20Ties.pdf, p. 6.

13 Wikileaks, 'Powering Afghanistan: Considering the Contribution of Central Asia to Stability and Growth', Astana Embassy *Wikileaks Cable 09ASTANA1373_a*, 11 August 2009, https://wikileaks.org/plusd/cables/09ASTANA1373_a.html.

14 Islamic Republic of Afghanistan, Ministry of Economy, 'Electricity Imports', (report, Afghanistan Inter-Ministerial Commission for Energy, Kabul, 2016, https://sites.google.com/site/iceafghanistan/electricity-supply/electricity-imports.

15 Farkhod Aminjonov, 'Limitations of the Central Asian Energy Security Policy: Priorities and Prospects for Improvement', *CIGI Papers* 103 (2016): pp. 1–4.

16 Central Asia Regional Economic Cooperation Program, 'Energy Sector Progress Report and Work Plan (June 2017–May 2018)', (report, CAREC, Senior Officials' Meeting, Bangkok, 27–28 June 2018), https://www.carecprogram.org/uploads/S3b_Energy-Sector-Progress-Report.pdf, p. 17.

17 Asian Development Bank, 'RRP Sector Assessment (Summary): Energy', (report, ADB, Mandaluyong, 2015), https://www.adb.org/sites/default/files/linkeddocuments/47282-001-ssa.pdf.

18 Tabasum Akseer and John Rieger (eds), 'Afghanistan in 2018: A Survey of the Afghan People', (report, The Asia Foundation, Washington, D.C., 2018), pp. 90–92.

19 Saadatullah Ahmadzai and Alastair McKinna, 'Afghanistan Electrical Energy and Transboundary Water Systems Analyses: Challenges and Opportunities', *Energy Reports* 4 (2018): p. 460.

20 World Bank, 'Islamic Republic of Afghanistan Energy Security Trade-Offs under High Uncertainty: Resolving Afghanistan's Power Sector Development Dilemma', (report, ACS19167, Washington, DC, 25 April 2016), http://documents.worldbank.org/curated/en/136801488956292409/pdf/ACS19167-WP-PUBLIC-P146249.pdf, p. 14.

21 Qutbuddin Kohi, 'Turkmenistan Extends Power Export to Afghanistan for a Month', *Pajhwok*, 2 January 2018, https://www.pajhwok.com/en/2018/01/02/turkmenistan-extends-power-export-afghanistan-month.
22 Farkhod Aminjonov, 'Afghanistan's Energy Security: Tracing Central Asian Countries' Contribution', (report, Friedrich-Ebert-Stiftung Afghanistan Office, Kabul, 2017).
23 Special Inspector General for Afghanistan Reconstruction, 'Quarterly Report to the United States Congress', (report, SIGAR, 30 April 2018), https://www.globalsecurity.org/military/library/report/sigar/sigar-report-2018-04-30.pdf, pp. 164–171.
24 'Afghanistan Renewable Energy Development: Issues and Options', *World Bank*, 26 June 2018, http://documents.worldbank.org/curated/en/352991530527393098/pdf/Afghanistan-Renewable-Energy-Development-Issues-and-Options.pdf, p. 97.
25 Noah Coburn, *Losing Afghanistan: An Obituary for the Intervention* (Stanford: Stanford University Press, 2016), p. 91.
26 Mohsin Amin, 'Power to the People: How to Extend Afghans' Access to Electricity', (report, Afghanistan Analysts Network, Kabul, 3 February 2015), https://www.afghanistan-analysts.org/power-to-the-people-how-to-extend-afghans-access-to-electricity/.
27 The World Bank, 'Central Asia South Asia Electricity Transmission and Trade Project (CASA-1000) (P145054)', (report, The World Bank Implementation Status & Results Report, Washington, D.C., 22 December 2018), http://documents.worldbank.org/curated/en/565831545491068302/pdf/Disclosable-Version-of-the-ISR-Central-Asia-South-Asia-Electricity-Transmission-and-Trade-Project-CASA-1000-P145054-Sequence-No-09.pdf.
28 Zafar Bhutta, 'CASA-1000 Project: US to Pour Millions into Afghan Support Programmes', *The Express Tribune*, 30 March 2014, https://tribune.com.pk/story/688934/casa-1000-project-us-to-pour-millions-into-afghan-support-programmes/.
29 Afghan Minister of Energy and Water Ali Ahmad Osmani cited in, 'Afghanistan Reportedly Refuses to Receive Electricity through CASA 1000 Project', *Asia-Plus*, 12 May 2016, http://www.news.tj/en/news/afghanistan-reportedly-refuses-receive-electricity-through-casa-1000-project.
30 'CAREC 2030: Connecting the Region for Shared and Sustainable Development', (report, MandaluyongAsian Development Bank, Mandaluyong, 2017).
31 Republic of Kazakhstan, Ministry of Foreign Affairs, 'Pozitsiia Respubliki Kazakhstan po Afganistanu', *MFA.gov.kz*, 9 May 2014, http://mfa.gov.kz/ru/content-view/uregulirovanie-situatsii-v-afganistane.
32 Malika Orazgaliyeva, 'Kazakhstan Launches First ODA Project in Afghanistan, with Support from UNDP and Japan', *Astana Times*, 23 February 2017, https://astanatimes.com/2017/02/kazakhstan-launches-first-oda-project-in-afghanistan-with-support-from-undp-and-japan/.

33 Nursultan Nazarbaev, 'Ob utverzhdenii osnovnykh napravlenii gosudarstvennoi politiki Respubliki Kazakhstan v sfere ofitsialnoi pomoshchi razvitiiu na 2017–2020 gody', *Presidential Decree No. 415*, 31 January 2017, http://nomad.su/?a=3-201702100039.

34 'Kazakhstan i Afganistan dolzhny ukrepliat' sotrudnichestvo', *Kapital.kz*, 3 August 2018, https://kapital.kz/business/71132/kazahstan-i-afganistan-namereny-ukreplyat-sotrudnichestvo.html.

35 Aliia Khodzhaeva, 'Kazakhstan: KTZh predlagaet eksportirovat' muku v Afganistan cherez Turkmenistan', *Agrarny Sektor*, 4 December 2018, https://agrosektor.kz/agriculture-news/kazahstan-ktzh-predlagaet-eksportirovat-muku-v-afganistan-cherez-turkmenistan.html.

36 Aygul Ospanova, 'Kazakhstan, Russia Back Afghanistan's Transportation System', *Caspian News*, 13 December 2018, https://caspiannews.com/news-detail/kazakhstan-russia-back-afghanistans-transportation-system-2018-12-13-59/.

37 M. Tiulegenov and U. Omuraliev, *Regionalnoe sotrudnichestvo v Tsentralnoi Azii s uchastiem Afganistana posle 2014 goda: perspektivy dlia Kyrgyzskoi Respubliki* (Bishkek: NISI, 2013), p. 34.

38 'Kyrgyzstan i Afganistan dogovorilis' prodolzhit' rabotu po aktivizatsii dvustoronnikh sviazei', *Kabar.kg*, 12 November 2017, http://kabar.kg/news/kyrgyzstan-i-afganistan-dogovorilis-prodolzhit-rabotu-po-aktivizatcii-dvustoronnikh-sviazei/; 'Stats-sekretar' MID KR i posol Afganistana obsudili voprosy rasshireniia sotrudnichestva', *Kabar.kg*, 9 August 2018, http://kabar.kg/news/stats-sekretar-mid-kr-i-posol-afganistana-obsudili-voprosy-dal-neishego-rasshireniia-i-uglubleniia-sotrudnichestva/.

39 Kamila Aliyeva, 'Volumes of Tajik Electricity Exports to Afghanistan Disclosed', *AzerNews*, 1 February 2018, https://www.azernews.az/region/126427.html.

40 CAREC, 'Corridor Performance Measurement and Monitoring', (annual report, CAREC, ADB, Mandaluyong, 2015), https://www.carecprogram.org/uploads/2015-CAREC-CPMM-Annual-Report.pdf, pp. 34–37.

41 Aga Khan IV quoted in G. Gafurova, 'Tadzhiksko-afganskoe sotrudnichestvo v oblasti transportnoi kommunikatsii v gody nezavisimosti', *Uchenye zapiski Khudzhandskogo gosudarstvennogo universiteta* 4, 37 (2013): p. 155.

42 Sharif Said, *Kurs na partnerstvo* (Dushanbe: Orbita, 2013), p. 316.

43 Khojamahmad Umarov, *Torgovo-ekonomicheskie otnosheniia mezhdu Respublikoi Tadzhikistan i Islamskoi Respublikoi Afganistan* (Bishkek: University of Central Asia, 2013), pp. 7–8.

44 'TAT Railway Has Strategic Importance', *Daily Outlook Afghanistan*, 22 April 2014, http://outlookafghanistan.net/national_detail.php?post_id=9953.

45 *Investitsionnyi proekt na stroitelstvo zheleznodorozhnoi linii, soediniaiushchei Respubliku Tadzhikistan s Islamskoi Respublikoi Afganistan i Turkmenistanom (cherez Beshkent)* (Dushanbe: Ministry of Transport of the RT, 2014), p. 3.

46 The ADB Country Director for Tajikistan, Si Si Yu, quoted in Payrav Chorshanbiyev, 'Construction of the TAT Railway Remains Questionable, says Tajik Railway Official', *Asia-Plus*, 26 July 2016, https://asiaplustj.info/en/news/tajikistan/economic/20160726/construction-tat-railway-remains-questionable-says-tajik-railway-official.

47 'The Seventh Regional Economic Cooperation Conference on Afghanistan', (conference report, RECCA, Ashgabat, 14–15 November 2017), http://recca.af/wp-content/uploads/2017/12/RECCA-VII-Report-27-12-2017-1300.pdf.

48 US Deputy Assistant Secretary of State Daniel Rosenblum, 'Remarks at Ashgabat Media Event', *US Department of State*, 5 September 2014, https://2009-2017.state.gov/p/sca/rls/rmks/2014/231328.htm.

49 Faridullah Hussainkhail, 'TAPI Seen as a Project of Empathy and Integrity for Afghans', *Tolo News*, 24 February 2018, https://www.tolonews.com/business/tapi-seen-project-empathy-and-integrity-afghans.

50 Dmitrii Verkhoturov, 'Dan' Talibam za TAPI?' *Gundogar*, 4 May 2016, http://gundogar.org/?02340516865000000000000011000000.

51 Bruce Pannier, 'Analysis: TAPI and Other Turkmen Tales', *RFE/RL*, 1 December 2018, https://www.rferl.org/a/tapi-turkmen-tales-pipeline-qishloq-ovozi-pannier/29632356.html.

52 'Razrabotana Kontseptsiia razvitiia elektroenergeticheskoi otrasli Turkmenistana na 2013–2020 gody', *Turkmen Business*, 14 April 2013, http://www.turkmenbusiness.org/news/razrabotana-kontseptsiya-razvitiya-elektroenergeticheskoi-otrasli-turkmenistana-na-2013-2020-go.

53 'Turkmenistan's Plan B: Electricity Exports', *Eurasianet*, 28 February 2018, https://eurasianet.org/turkmenistans-plan-b-electricity-exports.

54 Shoaib Ahmad Rahim, 'The Geopolitics of the Lapis Lazuli Corridor', *The Diplomat*, 22 December 2017, http://thediplomat.com/2017/12/the-geopolitics-of-the-lapis-lazuli-corridor/.

55 Haidarshah Omid, 'Afghan Goods to Arrive in Turkey via Lapis Lazuli Corridor', *Tolo News*, 25 December 2018, https://www.tolonews.com/business/afghan-goods-arrive-turkey-%C2%A0lapis-lazuli-corridor.

56 'Turkmeno-afganskie peregovory na vysshem urovne', *Turkmenistan segodnia*, 27 August 2015, http://tdh.gov.tm/news/articles.aspx&article2416&cat11.

57 Arvid Bell, *Afghanistan and Central Asia in 2015. An Overview of Actors, Interests, and Relationships* (Frankfurt: Peace Research Institute, 2015), p. 37.

58 B. Achilov, 'O predprinimaemykh Uzbekistanom merakh po dalneishemu ukrepleniiu regionalnogo vzaimodeistviia, razvitiu torgovo-ekonomicheskogo sotrudnichestva', in *Sbornik dokladov mezhdunarodnoi konferentsii 'Tsentralnaia Aziia – glavnyi prioritet vneshnei politiki Uzbekistana'*, (Tashkent: Ministry of Foreign Affairs of Uzbekistan, 2017), pp. 100–108.

59 Mohammad Hashim Barna quoted in Zabihullah Ihsas, 'Trade Barriers Linked to Political Tiffs', *Pajhwok*, 16 July 2013, https://www.pajhwok.com/en/2013/07/16/trade-barriers-linked-political-tiffs.
60 Quoted in Farkhod Aminjonov, 'Stability Over Prosperity and Security over Development in Uzbekistan', in *Current Challenges to Central Asia and Afghanistan: Towards a Better World*, ed. Anna Gusarova (Almaty: Friedrich-Ebert-Stiftung, 2017), p. 49.
61 Navruz Melibaev, 'Chto sviazyvaet Uzbekistan i Afghanistan krome obshchei granitsy i voprosov bezopasnosti?' *CABAR*, 6 April 2018, https://cabar.asia/ru/chto-svyazyvaet-uzbekistan-i-afganistan-krome-obshhej-granitsy-i-voprosov-bezopasnosti/.
62 'Uzbekistan peredal Afganistanu 25 avtobusov, 3 traktora i navesnuiu tekhniku', *UzReport*, 12 January 2018, https://www.uzreport.news/society/uzbekistan-peredal-afganistanu-25-avtobusov-3-traktora-i-navesnuyu-tehniku.
63 Asian Development Bank, 'Unstoppable: The Hairatan to Mazar-e-Sharif Railway Project', (report, ADB, Mandaluyong, February 2014), p. 4.
64 Guillaume Decamme, 'No Work, no Trade on Empty Silk Road in Northern Afghanistan', *Business Insider*, 25 May 2016, https://www.businessinsider.com/afp-no-work-no-trade-on-empty-silk-road-in-northern-afghanistan-2016-5/?r=AU&IR=T.
65 Zarmina Mohammadi, 'MoF Collected 11 Billion AFs From Balkh Customs', *Tolo News*, 2 January 2018, https://www.tolonews.com/business/mof-collected-11-billion-afs-balkh-customs.
66 Asian Development Bank, 'Afghanistan: Hairatan to Mazar-e-Sharif Railway Project', (validation report PVR-439, ADB, Independent Evaluation Department, Mandaluyong, December 2015), https://www.adb.org/sites/default/files/evaluation-document/178419/files/pvr-439.pdf.
67 Farrukh Juraev, 'Ekspet: Uzbekistan vosprinimaet Afganistan kak perspektivnogo partnera, a ne istochnik opasnosti', *Podrobno.uz*, 12 June 2017, https://podrobno.uz/cat/politic/ekspert-uzbekistan-vosprinimaet-afganistan-kak-perspektivnogo-partnera-a-ne-istochnik-opasnosti/.
68 'Uzbekistan predlozhil sozdat' transportnuiu strategiiu Tsentralnoi Azii', *Gazeta.uz*, 20 September 2018, https://www.gazeta.uz/ru/2018/09/20/transport/.
69 Ivan Safranchuk, *Afghanistan and its Central Asian Neighbours: Toward Dividing Insecurity* (Lanham: CSIS and Rowman & Littlefield, 2017), p. 29.
70 Madeleine Reeves, *Border Work: Spatial Lives of the State in Rural Central Asia* (Cornell University Press: Ithaca and London, 2014), p. 179.
71 Matthew Stein, 'The History of Central Asian Peacekeepers: The Development of Kazakhstan, Kyrgyzstan, and Tajikistan's Peacekeeping Units by Fits and Starts', *The Journal of Slavic Military Studies* 31, 2 (2018): pp. 260–263.

72 Donald Trump, 'Remarks by President Trump and President Nursultan Nazarbayev of Kazakhstan in Joint Press Statements', *The White House*, 16 January 2018, https://www.whitehouse.gov/briefings-statements/remarks-president-trump-president-nursultan-nazarbayev-kazakhstan-joint-press-statements/.

73 'Ministry oborony Kazakhstana i Afganistana obsudili sotrudnichestvo v voennoi sfere', *Forbes.kz*, 10 April 2013, https://forbes.kz/news/2013/04/10/newsid_24726; 'Afganistanu predlozhili gotovit' voennykh spetsialistov v Kazakhstane', *InformBuro*, 18 July 2017, https://informburo.kz/novosti/afganistanu-predlozhili-gotovit-voennyh-specialistov-v-kazahstane.html.

74 'JICA Supports the Effective Management of Tajikistan's Common Border with Afghanistan', *Bakhtar News*, 28 November 2018, http://bakhtarnews.com.af/eng/business/item/35783-jica-supports-the-effective-management-of-tajikistan%E2%80%99s-common-border-with-afghanistan.html.

75 'Tajik and Afghan Border Officers Complete OSCE Training-of-Trainers Course', *OSCE Programme Office in Dushanbe*, 7 September 2017, https://www.osce.org/programme-office-in-dushanbe/338251.

76 Safranchuk, *Afghanistan and its Central Asian Neighbours*, p. 23.

77 Toon Dirkx, 'The Unintended Consequences of US Support on Militia Governance in Kunduz Province, Afghanistan', *Civil Wars* 19, 3 (2017): pp. 377–401.

78 Bruce Pannier, 'Majlis Podcast: Turkmenistan's Afghan Dilemma', *RFE/RL*, 2 July 2016, https://www.rferl.org/a/majlis-podcast-turkmenistan-afghan-dilemma/27834187.html.

79 Data obtained from Security Assistance Monitor, http://www.securityassistance.org/data/country/military/country/2001/2018/all/Central%20Asia//.

80 Mariya Omelicheva, 'U.S. Security Assistance to Central Asia: Examining Limits, Exploring Opportunities', *PONARS Policy Memo No. 487*, October 2017, http://www.ponarseurasia.org/memo/us-security-assistance-central-asia.

81 Gabriel Dominguez, Jeremy Binnie and Samuel Cranny-Evans, 'Update: Turkmenistan Parades Ground Vehicles for Special Forces', *Jane's Defence Weekly*, 1 November 2017, https://janes.ihs.com/DefenceWeekly/Display/FG_675609-JDW.

82 'Turkmenistan: Vooruzhennye Sily i razvitie voenno-tekhnicheskogo sotrudnichestva kak osnovy obespecheniia boevogo potentsiala armii', *RGP Kazspetseksport*, 7 September 2017, http://kaspex.kz/ru/news/118-turkmenistan-vooruzhennye-sily-i-razvitie-voenno-tekhnicheskogo-sotrudnichestva-kak-osnovy-obespecheniya-boevogo-potentsiala-armii.html.

83 'Ministry oborony Rossii i Turkmenistana obsudili sotrudnichestvo na Kaspii', *RIA Novosti*, 9 June 2016, https://ria.ru/20160609/1444885718.html.

84 E. Ionova, 'Turkmeniia: poisk novykh gazoeksportnykh marshrutov', *Rossiia i novye gosudarstva Evrazii* 3 (2018): p. 96.

85 Bernardo Teles Fazendeiro, 'Uzbekistan's Defensive Self-Reliance: Karimov's Foreign Policy Legacy', *International Affairs* 93, 2 (2017): pp. 409–427.

86 The Deputy Assistant Secretary of State for Central Asia, Daniel Rosenblum, quoted in Casey Michel, 'The Obama Administration Is Gifting War Machines to a Murderous Dictator', *The New Republic*, 4 February 2015, https://newrepublic.com/article/120911/obama-administration-gives-uzbekistans-karimov-military-machines.

87 Dmitry Gorenburg, 'External Support for Central Asian Military and Security Forces', (report, SIPRI, Stockholm, 2014), pp. 8-11.

88 'Provodimye v Uzbekistane voennye reform v tsentre vnimaniia voenno-politicheskikh krugov SShA i diplomaticheskogo korpusa v g. Vashingtone', *Ministry of Foreign Affairs of Uzbekistan*, 5 December 2018, https://mfa.uz/ru/press/news/2018/12/16950/.

89 Viktoria Panfilova, 'Armiiu Uzbekistana podniali po trevoge', *Nezavisimaia gazeta*, 26 November 2018, http://www.ng.ru/cis/2018-11-26/6_7448_training.html.

90 Aleksandr Khrolenko, 'Bronia krepka: dinamika voenno-tekhnicheskogo sotrudnichestva Moskvy i Tashkenta', *Sputnik.tj*, 16 October 2018, https://tj.sputniknews.ru/columnists/20181016/1027123825/Bronya-krepka-dinamika-voenno-tekhnicheskogo-sotrudnichestva-Moskvy-i-Tashkenta.html.

91 Abdulaziz Kamilov quoted in Mukhammadsharif Mamatkulov, 'Uzbekistan says won't Rejoin Russia-led Security Bloc', *Reuters*, 6 July 2017, https://www.reuters.com/article/us-uzbekistan-russia-bloc/uzbekistan-says-wont-rejoin-russia-led-security-bloc-idUSKBN19Q2DL.

92 'Strategiia kollektivnoi bezopasnosti ODKB na period do 2025 goda', *CSTO Official Portal*, 14 October 2016, http://odkb-csto.org/documents/detail.php?ELEMENT_ID=8382.

93 'Joint Statement by the Member States of the Collective Security Treaty Organization on the Situation in Afghanistan and the Threat of the Strengthening of International Terrorist and Extremist Organizations in the Northern Provinces of Afghanistan, issued during the 72nd session of the UN General Assembly', *Ministry of Foreign Affairs of Russia*, 4 October 2017, http://www.mid.ru/en_GB/foreign_policy/international_safety/conflicts/-/asset_publisher/xIEMTQ3OvzcA/content/id/2886857.

94 I.N. Panarin and A.A. Kazantsev, *Ugroza mezhdunarodnogo terrorizma i religioznogo ekstremizma gosudarstvam – chlenam ODKB na tsentralnoaziatskom i afganskom napravleniiakh*, (Moscow: IMI MGIMO, 2017), pp. 10–15.

95 'Operatsiia ODKB "Kanal – Krasnyi barkhan"', *CSTO Official Portal*, 15 September 2018, http://www.odkb-csto.org/news/detail.php?ELEMENT_ID=13166&SECTION_ID=91.

96 Zh. Kembaev, 'The Implementation of the Commitments Undertaken by the Republic of Kazakhstan within the Framework of the Collective Security Treaty', in *Collective Security Treaty Organisation and Contingency Planning after* 2014, ed. A.F. Douhan and A.V. Rusakovich (Geneva and Minsk: The Geneva Centre for the Democratic Control of Armed Forces, 2016), pp. 145–154.

97   Nursultan Nazarbaev, 'Ekskliuzivnoe interviu prezidenta kazakhstana (telekanal "Mir")', *Zakon.kz*, 12 April 2017, https://www.zakon.kz/4853349-jekskljuzivnoe-intervju-prezidenta.html.

98   Zhanibek Imanaliev, 'ODKB: obespechenie natsionalnoi bezopasnosti Kazakhstana cherez instrumenty kollektivnogo sotrudnichestva', *Ministry of Foreign Affairs of Kazakhstan*, 12 April 2018, http://mfa.gov.kz/ru/content-view/znibek-imanliev-ks-zymdyk-yntymaktastyk-kraldary-arkyly-kazakstanny-lttyk-kauipsizdigin-kamtamasyz-etu.

99   Vladimir Gundarov, 'Kyrgyzstan pereshel pod rossiiskuiu zashchitu', *Nezavisimaia gazeta*, 3 February 2017, http://nvo.ng.ru/nvoevents/2017-02-03/2_935_news.html.

100 Elena Tsoy, 'Za chetyre goda srosiiskoi storony v KR postupila voennaia tekhnika na summu bolee #dl125 mln', *Kabar.kg*, 19 June 2018, http://www.env.kabar.kg/news/za-chetyre-goda-s-rossiiskoi-storony-v-kr-postupila-voennaia-tekhnika-na-summu-bolee-125-mln/.

101 Almazbek Atambaev quoted in Nochevkin, 'Afganistan.'

102 Almazbek Atambaev, 'Ekskliuziv: o EAES, Afganistane i "Mire"', *TV Mir*, 31 March 2017, https://mir24.tv/news/15903439/eksklyuziv-almazbek-atambaev-o-eaes-afganistane-i-mire.

103 Colonel Ularbek Sharsheev quoted in S. Abdykarieva, 'Sotrudnichestvo v deistvii', *Chegarada* 9, 163 (2017): p. 2.

104 Vladimir Mukhin, 'Rossiia speshno narashchivaet voennuiu pomoshch' Tadzhikistanu', *Nezavisimaia gazeta*, 19 December 2017, http://www.ng.ru/world/2017-12-19/2_7140_tajikistan.html.

105 'Putin: Russia's Military Base in Tajikistan to Ensure Security of Border with Afghanistan', *TASS*, 27 February 2017, http://tass.com/politics/932980.

106 Senior Russian diplomat quoted in 'Rossiia usilila voennye bazy v Tsentralnoi Azii v sviazi s "ugrozami iz Afganistana"', *Kommersant*, 7 February 2018, https://www.kommersant.ru/doc/3541501.

107 George Gavrilis, *Afghan Narcotrafficking: The State of Afghanistan's Borders* (New York: East West Institute, 2015), p. 11.

108 Transcript of Putin's meeting with Rahmon. Vladimir Putin, 'Vstrecha s Prezidentom Tadzhikistana Emomali Rahmonom', *Official portal of the President of Russia*, 6 October 2015, http://www.kremlin.ru/events/president/news/50453.

109 Akbarsho Iskandarov, Kosimsho Iskandarov and Ivan Safranchuk, *Novyi etap krizisa v Afganistane i bezopasnost' Tadzhikistana* (Moscow: Valdai Discussion Club, 2016), p. 11.

110 'Emomali Rahmon obratil vnimanie glav gosudarstv ODKB na voprosy ukrepleniia tadzhiksko-afganskoi granitsy', *Avesta*, 9 November 2018, http://avesta.tj/2018/11/09/emomali-rahmon-obratil-vnimanie-glav-gosudarstv-odkb-na-voprosy-ukrepleniya-tadzhiksko-afganskoj-granitsy/.

111 'China to Build Outposts for Tajik Guards on Tajikistan–Afghanistan Border', *South China Morning Post*, 26 September 2016, https://www.scmp.com/news/china/diplomacy-defence/article/2022718/china-build-outposts-tajik-guards-tajikistan.
112 'China's Increasing Security Buffer on Its Western Frontier', *Stratfor*, 11 January 2018, https://worldview.stratfor.com/article/chinas-increasing-security-buffer-its-western-frontier.
113 Press service of the Central Military District of Russia, 'Intensivnost sotrudnichestva TsVO so stranami Tsentralnoi Azii v 2018 godu vozrosla na tret', *Official portal of the Ministry of Defence of Russia*, 25 December 2018, https://function.mil.ru/news_page/country/more.htm?id=12209621@egNews.
114 Marcel de Haas, 'War Games of the Shanghai Cooperation Organization and the Collective Security Treaty Organization: Drills on the Move!' *The Journal of Slavic Military Studies* 29, 3 (2016): pp. 378–406.
115 Orhan Gafarlı, 'Multi-Faceted Linkages between Afghanistan and Central Asian States', in *Evolving Situation in Afghanistan: Role of Major Powers and Regional Countries*, ed. Sarah Siddiq Aneel (Islamabad: IPRI, 2016), pp. 127-142; Mariya Omelicheva, 'Eurasia's CSTO and SCO: A Failure to Address the Trafficking/Terrorism Nexus', PONARS Policy Memo No. 455, January 2017, http://www.ponarseurasia.org/memo/eurasia-csto-and-sco-failure-address-trafficking-terrorism-nexus.
116 'The Heart of Asia–Istanbul Process Progress Assessment 2011–2015', (report, Islamic Republic of Afghanistan, Ministry of Foreign Affairs, Kabul, 2016), p. 24.
117 Richard Ghiasy and Maihan Saeedi, *The Heart of Asia Process at a Juncture: An Analysis of Impediments to Further Progress* (Kabul: Afghan Institute for Strategic Studies, 2014), p. 42.
118 Richard Weitz, 'Almaty Hosts "Heart of Asia" Conference', *Eurasia Daily Monitor* 10, 84 (2013): https://jamestown.org/program/almaty-hosts-heart-of-asia-conference/.
119 M.S. Imanaliev, 'Problemy bezopasnosti v Tsentralnoi Azii i kyrgyzsko-afganskie otnosheniia', *Vestnik Diplomaticheskoi Akademii MID KR* 4, 4 (2014): pp. 52–54.
120 'C5+1 Fact Sheet: Central Asian–U.S. Forum to Enhance Regional Economic, Environmental, and Security Cooperation', *US Mission Uzbekistan*, 24 July 2018, https://uz.usembassy.gov/c51-fact-sheet-central-asian-u-s-forum-to-enhance-regional-economic-environmental-and-security-cooperation/.
121 'Rabochie gruppy po Afganistanu pri SMID ODKB i po bor'be s terrorizmom pri KSSB', *CSTO official portal*, 19 April 2018, http://www.odkb-csto.org/news/detail.php?ELEMENT_ID=12568&SECTION_ID=91.
122 'Press Release on a Meeting of the SCO–Afghanistan Contact Group', *The Ministry of Foreign Affairs of the Russian Federation*, 12 October 2017, http://www.mid.ru/en/foreign_policy/news/-/asset_publisher/cKNonkJE02Bw/content/id/2898520.

123 Mirziyoyev quoted in Viktoria Panfilova, 'Tashkent i Moskva dogovorilis' na 16 milliardov dollarov', *Nezavisimaia gazeta*, 5 April 2017, http://www.ng.ru/cis/2017-04-05/6_6967_uzbekistan.html.

124 'The United States and Uzbekistan: Launching a New Era of Strategic Partnership', *The White House*, 16 May 2018, https://www.whitehouse.gov/briefings-statements/united-states-uzbekistan-launching-new-era-strategic-partnership/.

125 G. Fazilov, 'O podkhodakh Uzbekistana v otnoshenii uregulirovaniia konflikta v Afganistane, predprinimaemykh merakh i usiliiakh po sodeistviiu sotsialno-ekonomicheskomu vosstanovleniiu IRA', in *Sbornik dokladov mezhdunarodnoi konferentsii 'Tsentralnaia Aziia – glavnyi prioritet vneshnei politiki Uzbekistana'*, (Tashkent: Ministry of Foreign Affairs of Uzbekistan, 2017), p. 94.

126 '"Dushanbinskaia chetverka" priniala "dorozhnuiu kartu"', *Vesti.uz*, 5 September 2011, https://vesti.uz/2011-09-05-13-05-09/.

127 'Kyrgyzstan, Afghanistan i Tadzhikistan obsudili "severnyi marshrut" narkotrafika', *Afghanistan Today*, 31 May 2016, http://afghanistantoday.ru/hovosti/kyrgyzstan-afganistan.

128 'Central Asia–Afghanistan Dialogue Format to Be Created', *The Tashkent Times*, 12 December 2017, http://tashkenttimes.uz/world/1793-central-asia-afghanistan-dialogue-format-to-be-created.

129 Aleksandr Kniazev quoted in Viktoria Panfilova, 'Tashkent i Kabul sodaiut zonu svobodnoi torgovli', *Nezavisimaia gazeta*, 18 July 2018, http://www.ng.ru/cis/2018-07-18/6_7269_uzbiekistan.html.

130 Islam Karimov, 'Edinstvennoe reshenie afganskoi problemy – mirnye peregovory s talibami', *FerganaNews*, 13 December 2015, https://www.fergananews.com/news/24249.

131 Vladimir Norov, 'V stabilnosti Afganistana zainteresovan ves' region', *EurAsia Daily*, 30 March 2018, https://eadaily.com/ru/news/2018/03/30/vladimir-norov-v-stabilnosti-afganistana-zainteresovan-ves-region.

132 Vitalii Volkov, 'Pomogut li kontakty s talibami stabilizirovat' Tsentralnuiu Aziiu?' *Deutsche Welle*, 13 June 2018, https://p.dw.com/p/2zOLv.

133 'Tajik Envoy Denies Reports that Russia Allegedly Sells Weapons to the Taliban as Baseless', *Asia-Plus*, 14 February 2017, https://www.asiaplus.tj/tj/node/236627; 'TV interview with Kunduz MP Engineer Kamal', *Ashna – Voice of America Dari Service*, 4 April 2018, https://www.darivoa.com/a/4331976.html.

134 'Dushanbe Objects to Afghan Ambassador in Moscow's Remarks on Tajik People', *Interfax*, 12 January 2017, http://www.interfax.com/newsinf.asp?d=1&id=726895.

135 Mujib Mashal and Jawad Sukhanyar, 'Afghanistan's Approach to Russian Diplomacy: Keep It in the Family', *The New York Times*, 27 February 2017, https://www.nytimes.com/2017/02/27/world/asia/afghanistan-moscow-putin-ghani-kochai.html.

4

Great Powers and the Central Asia–Afghanistan Equation

A scholar from Kyrgyzstan wrote recently that peace and stability in Afghanistan are sui generis positive values for the Central Asian republics, whereas great powers abuse them in order to project their hegemony.[1] The statement may appear overly idealistic and essentialist but its author has a point: the regional countries do not operate in a vacuum, and overlay by stronger external actors has a bearing on how they securitise threats and devise policy responses to them.

In 2015, Kazakhstan's main foreign policy think tank, working in tandem with security intellectuals from Kyrgyzstan, Tajikistan and Uzbekistan, published a report modelling Central Asia's security landscape in the mid-term perspective. Their 'strategic sketches' posited that 'the basic features of the current geopolitical environment of Central Asia are an outcome of the West, Russia and China influences. This configuration of a three power centre is to remain for the foreseeable future'.[2] The Afghanistan factor would play a significant role in the relative standing within this 'triarchy': following the completion of ISAF mission, the United States would lose interest and weaken its presence while Russia and China, facing an unstable Afghanistan, would ratchet up 'their engagement in the regional security because it is a way for them to maintain their own domestic stability'.[3] While this analysis is sound and widely shared by policy makers and security intellectuals in the region, it does leave some important questions unanswered. What exactly do Washington, Moscow and Beijing try to achieve in Afghanistan? Do their policies follow zero-sum game logic? Will the United States disengage completely? To what extent are Russian and Chinese positions harmonised? What kind of agency do the Central Asian countries have vis-a-vis the great powers' pressure? This chapter will attempt to provide some answers.

The United States: Central Asia as the Afghanistan Sideshow

Counter-Insurgency in Afghanistan as the US Priority

'U.S. policy toward Central Asia in the 2000s became a function of supporting its war effort in neighbouring Afghanistan', wrote Alexander Cooley.[4] The region acquired strategic importance as a site for NATO bases performing combat, reconnaissance and logistical tasks; for ISAF supply routes; and as an essential element in the scheme to stabilise Afghanistan via grandiose transport and energy projects. Since 2014, the level of importance assigned to the region has decreased precipitously. The NATO drawdown and the stalling of pipeline, electricity and railway schemes has reduced Central Asia's significance in the eyes of Washington to one of maintaining the Northern Distribution Network (NDN) to transit the diminished volumes of cargo for the Afghan National Security Forces (ANSF) and the remaining US troops in Afghanistan. The change of Central Asia's position in official US thinking is well attested by the US National Security Strategies. Its 2006 version proclaimed:

> Increasingly, Afghanistan will assume its historical role as a land-bridge between South and Central Asia, connecting these two vital regions ... Central Asia is an enduring priority for our foreign policy ... In the region as a whole, the elements of our larger strategy meet, and we must pursue those elements simultaneously: promoting effective democracies and the expansion of free-market reforms, diversifying global sources of energy, and enhancing security and winning the War on Terror.[5]

In 2017, the official rhetoric was much more subdued: 'We will work with the Central Asian states to guarantee access to the region to support our counterterrorism efforts.'[6]

The rise and fall of the New Silk Road (NSR) initiative was the most spectacular story of the US engagement with Central Asia on Afghanistan in the interim. As mentioned in the previous chapter, the idea of establishing Afghanistan as a regional trade and transit hub started to gain ascendancy among US experts and policy makers in 2005. By 2011, it had transformed into an official strategy enunciated by the Secretary of State, Hillary Clinton, using the mantra that 'lasting stability and security go hand in hand with economic opportunity'.[7] Promoted as a long-term vision for Afghanistan beyond the transition from ISAF, it envisaged the creation of a regional energy market in Central Asia, Afghanistan and South Asia. With the NDN as a starting point, the NSR would facilitate trade and transport corridors, ease customs and border procedures, and promote people-to-people ties.⁸ However, the United States did not commit its own funds to any of the NSR flagship projects (the US$15 million allocated to CASA-1000 can be viewed as a token gesture at best), confining its role to lobbying the Asian Development Bank (ADB), the World Bank (WB) and private investors to jump on the bandwagon. The political, legal, logistical and security problems have deterred such investors so far and, coupled with the ambivalence of regional stakeholders such as India, Pakistan, China and Russia, the future of the Turkmenistan–Afghanistan–Pakistan–India (TAPI) pipeline, the Turkmenistan–Uzbekistan–Tajikistan–Afghanistan–Pakistan (TUTAP) regional connectivity project, the Tajikistan–Afghanistan–Turkmenistan (TAT) railway project, Mazar-e Sharif to Herat railway and other ambitious schemes remains bleak.⁹ From the viewpoint of transport economics, the NSR backers did not seem to have pondered on the simple truth that the construction or rehabilitation of roads does not create traffic per se, nor does the increase of traffic to or from South Asia signify any potential for long-term trade.¹⁰

Most significantly, the NSR's underlying assumptions about the alleged benefits of the NDN and its future expansion for Central Asia were completely wrong. Essentially, these benefits did not stretch beyond profiteering from the International Security Assistance Force (ISAF) bonanza and fleecing Afghanistan and its donors. At the same time that Clinton outlined brilliant vistas of connectivity, independent researchers conducting fieldwork established that the NDN failed to incentivise regional cooperation and border reforms, bred corruption, did not make transhipment of non-military cargoes any more efficient and disproportionately enriched elite insiders, yielding no perceptible trickle-down benefits to ordinary Central Asian citizens.¹¹ The NSR appears moribund at present, and is likely to be remembered only as a geopolitical narrative about an American 'mission', obscuring the limited nature of actual US involvement on the ground.¹²

Following the closure of the last US airbase in Central Asia at Manas airport in 2014, Washington has reduced and recalibrated its security cooperation with the region's countries. In his testimony to the US Congress, US Central Command (CENTCOM) General Joseph L Votel said that 'several … governments continue to support the transit of supplies to U.S. troops in Afghanistan and engage the United States on shared interests related to access, border security, counterterrorism, counter-narcotics, and counter-insurgency'.¹³ Votel noted that cooperation had all but ceased with Kyrgyzstan, was largely confined to medical exchanges with Turkmenistan, was complicated by the Russian 201st base 'looming large' in Tajikistan, but was doing reasonably well in Uzbekistan

Table 4.1 US official security assistance to Central Asian countries in 2014 and 2019 (in millions of dollars)

Country	Year 2014	Year 2019
Kazakhstan	78.5	1.7
Kyrgyzstan	10.6	1.4
Tajikistan	34.7	2.7
Turkmenistan	1.5	0.4
Uzbekistan	37.2	0.8

Source: Adapted from Security Assistance Monitor, http://securityassistance.org/.

(bolstering its special operations forces) and Kazakhstan (training NCOs).[14] Official data shows a major drop in the amount of aid earmarked for security cooperation with Central Asia (Table 4.1); budgetary appropriation for bolstering the region's counter-narcotics capacity appears to have stopped completely. CENTCOM has its own discretionary budget which it used, for example, to fund the delivery of US$18 million worth of 'engineering, machinery, equipment, and construction materials that will directly contribute to strengthening the border' between Tajikistan and Afghanistan in 2018.[15] Nonetheless, at present American assistance is dwarfed by what Russia and China have to offer the Central Asian military-security apparatus, in terms of fighting threats from Afghanistan.

Trump's Afghan Strategy and Negotiations with the Taliban

'The situation in Afghanistan today is deeply troubled and fraught', wrote Michael O'Hanlon in 2016, 'but it is not measurably worse than one might have expected say back in 2012, when the Taliban resistance had already proven itself resilient in the face of a NATO troop surge.'[16] The apocalyptic predictions of Afghanistan's total collapse in the wake of the security handover did not come to pass. On the other hand, the country didn't show many signs of improvement, either in the realm of counter-insurgency and counterterrorism or in the area of good government and governance. Propped up by Washington, the authorities in Kabul lurched from one crisis to another, retaining control, however tenuous, over major urban areas. Christine Fair commented that 2017 was not radically different to 2016:

> Security remains elusive, as the battle with the Taliban remains stalemated. The National Unity Government, like the previous Karzai government, has failed to deliver unity or credibility and has been unable to follow through on much-

needed reforms. Afghanistan's neighbors seem more interested in prosecuting their own agendas then in securing the country, while the US continues to struggle to learn the lessons of past mistakes. The international community continues to fixate on its military role, while failing to appreciate the urgent need to begin focusing on a plan for economic sustainability.[17]

'A stalemate where the equilibrium favours the government', was how the US to commander in Afghanistan, General John Nicholson, described the situation in February 2017.[18] In order to tilt the equilibrium decisively, President Donald Trump adopted a new Afghanistan policy which entailed the halting of the withdrawal and the deployment of extra US troops with no end-date for their mission; increasing military pressure on the Taliban; taking a hard line on Pakistan for supporting the Taliban; and obliterating Al Qaeda and other terrorist groups.[19] As the year wore on, the goalposts for victory moved. Success was reconfigured to forcing the Taliban to the negotiations table – at first from the position of strength, and eventually without preconditions. In February 2018, Afghan President Ashraf Ghani, egged on by Washington, offered recognition of the Taliban as a legitimate group and their incorporation into the constitutional political field, in order to start peace talks.

Islam Karimov's wish of the 2015 vintage seems to have been granted. An observation that 'all of Afghanistan's immediate and extended neighbours will be content to support a U.S. effort at pursuing reconciliation with the Taliban so long as their own particular interests are protected',[20] applied in full measure to the Central Asian republics. However, apart from a National Unity Government (NUG)-Taliban compromise, their particular interests included issues such as ethnic composition of the post-reconciliation government, fighting against jihadi and criminal groups, the narcotics situation and economic relations. The United States was reluctant to see these items on the agenda, holding to the view that negotiations ought to be an internal affair between Kabul and the Taliban. Under such circumstances, the Central Asian states decided to participate in the 'Moscow format' of informal regional consultations on Afghanistan, which in April 2017, brought together representatives from Afghanistan (at a junior level), China, India, Iran, Kazakhstan, Kyrgyzstan, Pakistan, Russia, Tajikistan, Turkmenistan and Uzbekistan. The meeting pondered various ideas about the peace process and voiced general support for direct dialogue between Kabul and the Taliban. A press release from the Russian hosts stated that 'the coordination of regional efforts to assist the process of national reconciliation', was the gathering's primary concern and mentioned that 'an invitation to participate in these discussions was also extended to the United States, which did not attend them for unclear reasons'.[21] Essentially, the Kremlin was trying to put on the mantle of chief spokesperson for a bloc of nations with a stake in the Afghanistan settlement. Turkmenistan did not participate in the second meeting in November 2018, but a Taliban delegation did, causing Kazakhstan's foreign ministry to comment about the 'unique' nature of the 'Moscow format'.[22]

Dealing with Geopolitical Adversaries

The US reluctance to have anything to do with the 'Moscow format' is a reflection of the deep mistrust Washington has towards Russia in general. As late as 2013, some of the Kremlin's proposals for cooperation in areas such as the fight against terrorism and drug trafficking, the training and equipping of the ANSF, transit for US troops and exchange of intelligence information, might still have been considered.[23] After the Ukraine crisis, Russian deployment in Syria and the scandal of the 2016 presidential election campaign in the United States the view of the Kremlin as a geopolitical foe and spoiler had become so entrenched that anything Moscow suggests is rejected out of hand. One potential area of engagement at present could be combating ISIS, yet Washington baulks at it because calling Russia a 'partner' in the counterterror fight anywhere in the world would hand Moscow 'a huge PR victory'.[24]

'We know that Russia is attempting to undercut our military gains and years of military progress in Afghanistan, and make partners question Afghanistan's stability', stated General Nicholson, and added: 'It is no secret that Russia seeks any opportunity it can find to drive a wedge between the United States and our Central Asian partners, including Afghanistan.'[25] The narrative of Russia as a US spoiler, centres on two interconnected themes: Russia enables the Taliban, and it disseminates false information about US support to ISIS-K. Speculation about the Russian weapons deliveries to the insurgents started in early 2017 and has continued since 2018.[26] This speculation has relied on Taliban propaganda and the anecdotal testimonies of Afghan officials. 'We've had stories written by the Taliban that have appeared in the media about financial support provided by the enemy', Nicholson said. 'We've had weapons brought to this headquarters and given to us by Afghan leaders and said, "This was given by the Russians to the Taliban".'[27] Ismail Khan, a former Afghan *mujahideen* leader and influential politician in Herat Province, has claimed that armaments were flowing not just from Russia but from Iran and Turkmenistan as well.[28] The intensity and volume of the alleged Russian shipments have never been disclosed; the US Joint Chiefs of Staff Chairman General Joseph Dunford admitted that there was no 'specificity on support to the Taliban' rendered by Moscow.[29]

Russia has dismissed US accusations as 'baseless' and 'idle gossip', and the Taliban leadership while acknowledging 'significant contacts' with Moscow has insisted that Moscow's involvement did not extend beyond 'moral and political support'.[30] Independent experts have commented on the near-impossibility of documenting any linkages to the Russian government as far as Russian-made weapons seized in the battlefield are concerned – many of them date back to the period of Soviet occupation.[31] The US Department of Defence supplied hundreds of thousands of Russian-made weapons to the ANSF before they switched to the NATO standards in 2010. In 2014, US military auditors claimed that more than 100,000 of these 'excess weapons' were poorly inventoried, and warned that 'there is a real potential for these weapons to fall into the hands of insurgents'.[32] The Taliban may have been procuring the bulk of their armaments and ammunition by dealing with the corrupt ANSF officials, with or without financial help from Moscow.[33]

Russia has been accused of exaggerating the number of ISIS-K fighters in Afghanistan, with the aim of justifying support to the Taliban and denigrating the achievements of the ANSF and the United States in destroying the jihadis.[34] In 2016, an independent Afghan analyst, working from extensive interviews with local security sources, estimated ISIS-K's manpower was 4,500–5,000 and noted that 'the Taliban's resistance was one of the main reasons preventing Daesh from capturing swathes in Afghanistan and will continue to keep Daesh's expansion in check'.[35] In December 2017, Moscow counted some 10,000 ISIS-K militants in the country, while the US assessment was 1,100.[36] A UN Security Council report published shortly after cited figures of 'between 1,000 and 4,000 fighters', commenting that 'the number and geographic dispersal of ISIL-affiliated elements in Afghanistan has increased'.[37] Particularly worrying for Russia (and Central Asia) was ISIS-K's expansion to the north of the country. The ANSF and the United States continued to fight the jihadis primarily in their original stronghold in Nangarhar. In 2017–2018, the battle for control in Jawzjan unfolded between Kabul, the Taliban and ISIS-K, the government being 'the weakest party in this triangle'.[38] The Taliban eventually drove Daesh from the province, earning surprising praise from General Nicholson: 'We also note that the Taliban is fighting ISIS, and we encourage that because ISIS needs to be destroyed.'[39] On that rare occasion Russian, Central Asian and American interests reached a point of convergence.

Compared to those with Russia, US disagreements with China on Afghanistan are less venomous but at the same time run deeper. These disagreements revolve around two issues: Beijing's strategic alliance with Islamabad, and its reluctance to commit to the US-led economic ventures in Afghanistan.

Changing Pakistan's behaviour and forcing it to cut ties with the Taliban was a central component of Trump's Afghanistan's strategy. The United States and President Ghani, reached out to China in the hope that it would help achieve this objective. They were disappointed.[40] Moreover, Beijing undertook active steps to ease pressure exerted by Washington on Islamabad, thus postponing 'a much-needed paradigm shift in its suicidal Afghan policy'.[41] This axis of disagreement does not affect the Central Asian countries directly, unlike the second item of contention – China's rejection of the NSR.

China has allocated billions of dollars for infrastructure projects in Central Asia none of which is aligned with the American vision of regional connectivity, with Afghanistan at its core. 'Beijing seems to see little to no gain from coordinating its efforts in Central Asia with the United States', Thomas Zimmerman observed.[42] Once the China–Pakistan economic corridor is completed, Afghanistan runs the risk of becoming an irrelevance in the north–south transit route game, as far as Central Asia is concerned.

Russia: Central Asian Stability as an Overriding Concern

Moscow's Pragmatic Afghanistan Policy

Since 2014, Western assessments of the Kremlin's position on Afghanistan have oscillated between the 'Great Game' and 'realist' poles. The Great Gamers view the situation through the prism of a never-ending proxy war, where Russia challenges the United States for regional or perhaps even global domination.[43] In its extreme variant, this stance acquires civilisational dimensions: 'Afghanistan remains a pawn in the struggle between Eastern and Western ideologies.'[44] The Realists' position is that Russia pursues limited and rational objectives in Afghanistan predicated solely on its national security interest. Anthony Cordesman has summed up this notion well:

> One needs to be careful about assuming that either Russia or China is seeking to sabotage American efforts in Afghanistan, rather than react to the growing possibility that the United States will win every battle, lose the war, and leave out of eventual frustration and exhaustion. ... To put it bluntly, the United States now has no regional friends on the borders of Afghanistan, and few common interests with Russia or China. The only good news for the United States is that the Russian and Chinese roles in Afghanistan are much more driven by self-interest than hostility.[45]

A closer look at the official Russian policy discourse decidedly supports the Realist viewpoint. The 2016 Foreign Policy Concept identified the persisting instability in Afghanistan after NATO withdrawal as a 'major security threat to Russia *and other members of the CIS*' and promulgated Russia's commitment to efforts by the government in Kabul and the international community to restore peace to the country, adding the following caveat: 'Implementing comprehensive measures to mitigate the terrorist threat emanating from Afghanistan against other States, including neighbouring countries, as well as eliminate or substantially reduce illicit production and trafficking of narcotic drugs is an integral part of these efforts.'[46]

Russia's concerns about the growing flow of Afghan narcotics are legitimate and understandable – Russia is a major market consuming as much as 20 per cent of Afghanistan's annual opium production. The securitisation of terrorist groups in Afghanistan, as a challenge to Russia, is more equivocal. ISIS-Central is a clear menace because of the presence of several thousand Russian citizens in its ranks, its connections with the so-called Caucasus Emirate on the territory of Russia and the emergence of clandestine cells of local Muslims and migrants radicalised by Daesh propaganda. However, as Ekaterina Stepanova convincingly argued, 'none of these direct threats by ISIS to Russia's security is linked to Afghanistan as such'.[47] ISIS-K and affiliated groups there matter to Russia only insofar they constitute a threat to Central Asian security, which is intrinsically connected to Russian security.

Russia's former ambassador to Afghanistan, Mikhail Konarovsky, has summed up his country's pragmatic position as follows: 'Russia will accept any government in Kabul, bar the most odious that would implement policies aimed at destabilizing the situation in the southern underbelly of the country, i.e. in Central Asia.'[48] Moscow worked with the United States to topple the Taliban regime. It supported the Karzai government and continues to regard the NUG as the only legitimate locus of power. During a meeting with Ghani, President Vladimir Putin said that 'over these last decades, Russia and Afghanistan have developed what are undoubtedly ties between friendly countries ... You know that we support full normalization of the situation in Afghanistan and establishment of the conditions needed for steady growth', which was followed by Ghani's reassurance that Kabul regarded Moscow as a 'strategic partner'.[49] Limited contacts with the Taliban can be viewed in the same pragmatic light – Moscow is hedging its bets trying to jump-start a long-overdue peace process by talking to them among other stakeholders. The Afghan Head of the National Security Council, Hanif Atmar, came to Moscow in March 2017 to persuade his

Russian colleagues that the Taliban and ISIS-K were equally bad terrorists. He did not succeed but, by his own admission, left completely reassured that Russia was not talking with insurgents behind Kabul's back and working against it.[50] Later that year Atmar enjoined the Russian Security Council Secretary Nikolai Patrushev to help in bringing the Taliban to the negotiating table and admitted that Afghan officials had no evidence of Moscow sending weapons to the enemy.[51] In Stepanova's opinion, the rumours about arms transfer spread by the United States, 'may be dictated by the desire not only to shift the blame for its own policy failures on someone else but also to discredit positive peace-making efforts by Moscow at the regional level'.[52]

Despite Moscow's commitment to supporting Afghanistan's peace through economic development, its material contribution to the cause has been negligible. Having written off the Soviet-era Afghan debt of US$11.1 billion by 2010, it has shown little interest in promoting commercial and investment exchange. Tellingly, Kazakhstan gives more aid to Afghanistan than Russia. Between 2012 and 2016, the already anaemic trade turnover collapsed by 73 per cent with few avenues for improvement due to Russian companies' apprehension about business climate in the country.[53] US economic sanctions imposed on Russian companies since 2014 effectively ban them from conducting maintenance of Soviet and Russian helicopters operated by the ANSF and complicate their potential participation in infrastructure projects in Afghanistan.

Central Asia's Place in Russian Security Thinking

Unlike the United States, Russia has permanent and immediate stakes in Central Asian security. Since the late 1990s, instability in Central Asia has been strongly securitised by Moscow. Any challenge to social order and internal peace there is regarded as a menace by the Kremlin.[54] The Central Asian countries' views on threats emanating from Afghanistan discussed in Chapter 2 are fully shared by the Russian governing elite. In fact, the narratives of danger promoted by Moscow and regional capitals are mutually reinforcing. According to the Russian Foreign Minister, Sergei Lavrov, his country's position on regional security is either identical or 'very close' to those across Central Asia, and bilateral and multilateral cooperation in dealing with terrorism, narcotics trafficking and organised crime 'is acquiring special significance in light of the lingering instability in Afghanistan and the influx of ISIS fighters from Syria and Iraq'.[55]

A certain exaggeration of ISIS-K threat by Russian officials stems from three considerations. First, there is prudent alarmism: as Patrushev put it, in 2014 many believed that ISIS would not present a serious danger in Iraq and Syria; it is better to be safe than sorry in Afghanistan.⁵⁶ Second, inflated figures are mostly voiced by representatives of agencies interested in increased budgets for conventional defence counter-measures such as the Collective Security Treaty Organization (CSTO) and the armed forces. Russian Defence Minister Sergei Shoigu has stated that 'at present, the main threat to the military security of the Russian Federation on the Central Asian strategic theatre consists of the growing activity of international terrorist organizations', and thus rationalised the need for extra funding, weapons and combat training for the Central Military District which has operational control over the 201st and 999th military bases.⁵⁷ Finally, and this is an often overlooked point, Russian talking heads frequently broadcast numbers provided by Central Asian colleagues who exaggerate for reasons of their own. Deputy Director of the Russian Federal Security Service (FSB) quoted the figure of 8,000 terrorists who had relocated to Afghanistan, referring to intelligence provided by Tajikistan.⁵⁸ The comparable (and also inflated) figure bandied around by the CSTO at the time was 2,500. Dushanbe counted members of the proscribed Islamic Renaissance Party (IRPT) as international jihadis, because as far as it was concerned the IRPT and ISIS were 'two sides of the same coin'.⁵⁹ The FSB spokesman did not bother to go into that level of detail.

In March 2018 the head of Uzbekistan's security service, the SGB, addressed the country's Senate with an uncharacteristically gloomy speech: 'The increased activity of Daesh … and other armed groups in northern Afghanistan … is becoming a source of new threats to Uzbekistan.'⁶⁰ The sharpness of his statement may have had something to do with the fact that he had just replaced a heavyweight from the Karimov era whose legacy needed to be thoroughly purged under the banner of fighting complacency.

Since 2017, Russian officials have repeatedly accused the United States of airlifting ISIS fighters to northern Afghanistan and providing them and allied Taliban factions with weapons and ammunition. They have reserved judgment on the reasons for the purported suspicious behaviour merely asking Washington for an explanation. The corroborative evidence consists of flight records for unmarked helicopters (the United States controls Afghan airspace) and testimonies by local residents.⁶¹ One witness is the former Afghan president, Hamid Karzai, who explicated that the 'US wants to expand terrorism into Russia by using Afghanistan as substrate'.⁶² These allegations have the same quality as the American claims about Russian supplies to the Taliban – they are unverified and likely unverifiable. Nonetheless, the heads of Security Councils from Russia and Central Asia have agreed 'to share concrete information about such facts which shed light on the true attitude by the US and its coalition towards ISIS bandits'.⁶³

Russia's efforts to work in concert with the Central Asian republics to deflect Afghanistan-related threats were covered in the previous chapter, but a short recap is needed to highlight three types of security cooperation. It exists at a bare minimum with isolationist Turkmenistan which keeps Russia in mind as a last resort. Uzbekistan pursues the policy of self-reliance but since 2016 the intensity of military–security ties has grown considerably. Finally, there are three CSTO members – Kazakhstan, Kyrgyzstan and Tajikistan – who very closely coordinate policy response and practical action with Moscow. At the same time, Kazakhstan can be placed in a separate sub-category as an equal partner in the security relationship with the Kremlin. Bishkek and Dushanbe are content to play a more passive role of the 'shield' protecting Russia's 'soft underbelly' which is still congruent with their own security interests. In the words of Omurbek Babanov, Kyrgyzstan's former Prime Minister, 'Central Asia ... is becoming a bulwark of Russia's defence which absorbs the initial shock of local conflicts, drug trafficking and contraband that first and foremost target Russia'.[64]

Confronting America?

The view of Afghanistan and its northern neighbours as a battlefield for a geopolitical 'Great Game' is not popular in either Russia or Central Asia. Kazakhstan's prominent public intellectual, Erlan Karin, observed: 'In reality, cut-throat competition doesn't exist among these countries [Russia, China and the US] ... External actors maintain a strategic balance and are not interested in the region's destabilization.'[65] What Washington considers to be Russian strategic sabotage in Afghanistan is conceived as normal diplomacy by Moscow itself. At present the Kremlin prefers to see a power-sharing deal with the Taliban leading to a stable Afghanistan, rather than a never-ending stalemate where ISIS-K carves space in the Hobbesian world of multilateral warfare.

As Ambassador Extraordinary and Plenipotentiary Konarovsky put it, 'Moscow's long-term position regarding Afghanistan derives from concerns about the persistence of a crisis situation in the IRA and absence of progress in resolving the conflict through peaceful means.'[66] Russia believes it exercised strategic patience by supporting the United States and ISAF in their counter-insurgency campaign between 2001 and 2014, which was not crowned with success. The Kremlin expected chaos in Afghanistan after NATO's withdrawal but fortunately this didn't happen. The NUG has managed to survive due to continuous financial and military support from Washington, but there is no chance it will be able to conduct meaningful socio-economic reforms and achieve stability without internal peace. Moscow is doing its best to bring Kabul, the Taliban, and all external stakeholders to the negotiations table in the hope of advancing the peace process 'in an open and transparent manner', implying that they 'will avoid the temptation of gaining unilateral advantage at the expense of other partners including factions inside Afghanistan'.[67]

In December 2017, Putin stated that the situation in Afghanistan was continuing to deteriorate but added that without the US presence there 'perhaps it may have been even worse'.[68] Putin's Special Representative on Afghanistan, Zamir Kabulov, signalled his country's readiness to resume collaboration with Washington on the Afghan issue saying that 'it wasn't us who stopped this cooperation, this was our American colleagues' choice despite the fact that our interaction had proved efficient in the preceding period'.[69] What the Kremlin saw as the main vector of this cooperation became clear in Kabulov's subsequent statements – negotiating with the Taliban and all regional stakeholders including Pakistan without waiting for Trump's new strategy to break the stalemate. 'Moscow is not competing with Washington in settling the conflict in Afghanistan. The US has had enough time, seventeen years, to accomplish its plans,' Kabulov offered. He continued:

> This is not some kind of sporting interest on the part of Russia. The US is far away, and Afghanistan is our literal soft underbelly where national interests of Russia and its allies are at stake ... We let the US know that it is not doing that well and for this reason we are calling for a regional approach to the solution of the Afghan issue.[70]

Kabulov questioned the utility of deploying more American troops on the ground because none of the previous surges had managed to break the stalemate with the Taliban.

The Russian public discourse on Afghanistan does contain elements of anti-Americanism and Geopolitics. Sometimes high-ranking politicians chime in such as Frants Klintsevich – a Soviet veteran of the Afghan war and a member of the upper house of the Russian parliament. In a TV program with a telling name 'Conspiracy Theory' he claimed that Washington's activities in Afghanistan amounted to the 'new US project of destabilizing our [sic] former Soviet Central Asia'.[71] The most active proponents of such narratives are experts and commentators representing the 'national-patriot' or Eurasianist spectrum of the public opinion. Eurasianist media platforms, for example, advance the thesis that the West has deliberately encouraged the cultivation of opium in Afghanistan in order to destroy the demographic potential of its main geopolitical foe, Russia, via a heroin epidemic. The US decision to maintain a military presence in Afghanistan has nothing to do with combating the Taliban – it is to provide cover for poppy plantations.[72] An academic from a prestigious university in Moscow welcomed Trump's strategy and chastised Putin's misguided pragmatism:

> Naturally, the current situation in Afghanistan has been 100 per cent created by the Americans themselves – well, let them deal with it on their own. Let them pay for it with their money and blood. Do we really care about their money and blood? ... If [Islamic] radicals begin expansion from Afghanistan into Central Asia, we'll inevitably have to fight there because it's better to lose one thousand servicemen near Bishkek than ten thousand later on near [the southern Russian cities of] Ufa and Astrakhan. These most obvious considerations are somehow beyond comprehension for a section of our compatriots but little can be done about this. It just so happens that the Kremlin also cannot comprehend that having no losses near Bishkek at all is the best option – let the Americans sustain losses in Afghanistan instead ... Moreover, the deeper the Americans become embroiled in Afghanistan the less active they will be in Syria, Ukraine and the Korean peninsula. This is not difficult to understand yet something complicates such simple comprehension ... Let the US send not four but forty thousand servicemen to Afghanistan. Let them fight there for fifteen more years. Let them have another couple of thousand troops killed ... And let them kill as many terrorists as possible in the process. This is something to which we should give a standing ovation because this is in complete alignment with our national interests.[73]

The views above have little to do with Moscow's official stance. Klintsevich was demoted from his position as the first deputy chairman of the Russian Senate committee on defence and security because the Ministry of Defence and the Senate leadership took umbrage at his public statements that reflected his personal rather than institutional opinion.[74] Nonetheless, tabloids in Central Asia propagate Russian conspiracy theories amplified by local experts' allusions to the American 'Plan B', aimed at destabilizing the region through ISIS ('Plan A' was about forceful democracy promotion in the 2000s).[75]

China: Limited Involvement

Beijing's Security Concerns

In her extensive survey of Chinese scholarship and expert debate in the lead-up to the NATO drawdown, Elizabeth Wishnick came to a conclusion that pessimism infused Beijing's assessment of post-2014 scenarios for Afghanistan, and that caution and non-interference was the key principle of their policy toward that country, 'making it unlikely for China to lead any major initiative on Afghanistan, though it may choose to cooperate with others in support of Chinese immediate interests'.[76] Although it may have climbed a few steps in the PRC's foreign policy hierarchy, Afghanistan still remains merely 'a more important non-priority'.[77] Despite much hype in the 2000s about China's interest in Afghanistan's raw materials and energy sources[78] none of the contemplated projects has come to fruition and is unlikely to be of critical significance to the Chinese economy even if realised in future. Afghanistan plays a salient role in Beijing's strategic relationship with Pakistan, and is tangentially connected to the Belt and Road Initiative (BRI) but its main relevance to China lies in the security sphere. Even here the direct flow of drugs, terrorist personnel and subversive ideology from war-torn Afghanistan through a 92 kilometre-long border in mountainous Wakhan region remains circumscribed.[79]

The Afghan issue matters to China insofar as it affects Central Asia – a crucial link in Xi Jinping's regional foreign policy also known as 'new neighbourhood diplomacy'. Anti-government activism by Muslim ethnic minorities in the Xinjiang Uyghur Autonomous Region (XUAR) is the single most important threat to China's domestic security. One of Beijing's greatest phobias is that Muslim opposition groups would find operational space and support in neighbouring Kazakhstan, Kyrgyzstan and Tajikistan. At present these groups are either suppressed or tightly controlled by the national law enforcement agencies in Central Asia.[80] Moreover, the local governments have abstained from criticising Chinese strategies of combating separatism, extremism and terrorism in Xinjiang some of which recently created moral outrage in the West in light of large-scale extrajudicial internment of Uyghurs, Kazakhs and Kyrgyzs in the so-called re-education camps.[81] Any instability or loss of governmental control in Central Asia would be unwelcome news for Beijing. The PRC authorities believe that 'Afghanistan remains the greatest external destabilizing factor for central Asian countries. If terrorism and extremism in Central Asia are allowed to grow unchecked, Xinjiang will certainly be affected very seriously'.[82] This kind of securitisation based on self-interest and concern about the preservation of the status quo clearly aligns Beijing's stance with that of the region's states and Russia.

The convergence in the interests of Russia, China and the Central Asian states has acquired its most visible manifestation in the activities of the Shanghai Cooperation Organization (SCO). The organisation's key utility to its members rests not so much on practical cooperation on the security front as on the constantly evolving normative consensus about threat identification. SCO's multilateral documents legitimise and wherever possible harmonise pre-existing shared perspectives and domestic rules of dealing with these threats.[83] The SCO 2016 summit in Tashkent registered common heightened concerns about the situation in Afghanistan noting that 'the rise of terrorist groups in the Middle East, the Islamic State in particular, and the rampancy of the Taliban in Afghanistan and Pakistan pose real threats to Central Asia'.[84] The Qingdao SCO summit in 2018 issued a declaration supporting Afghanistan's effort to counteract terrorism, extremism and drug crimes and emphasised that 'there is no alternative to settling the situation in Afghanistan beyond political dialogue and an inclusive peace process by the Afghan people themselves and under their guidance'.[85] Kabul has had an observer status in the SCO since 2012 and aspired to full membership since 2015. As far as China and Russia are concerned, the main obstacle to it consists of the undue influence by the United States on Kabul's foreign policy – they don't want to see Washington's Trojan horse in the ranks. Uzbekistan has misgivings about the Islamic factor in Afghanistan's political system – the same objection it raised against the Islamic Republic of Iran's membership.[86]

The SCO Regional Antiterrorist Structure (RATS) counted 3,000 ISIS-K fighters in northern Afghanistan in early 2018, and mentioned 4,200 'persons of interest' from China, Russia and Central Asia in its unified database, who were planning either to join international terrorist groups or to return home from jihad. The Director of RATS praised solid cooperation with the UN agencies and added that 'at present no contacts with representatives of the American special services are taking place'.[87]

China has contributed more than Russia and Central Asia to Afghanistan's stabilisation, yet it hardly pulls its weight. Before 2014, there was practically no military or security cooperation between the two countries – Beijing left the business of counterterrorism and counter-insurgency to ISAF. After the drawdown, the PRC has taken a greater role in Afghanistan's security, carefully avoiding military intervention. It has sponsored limited training programs for de-mining, counter-narcotics and police specialists.[88] Following a series of high-level meetings in 2016, the PRC announced a US$79 million grant to build 10,000 flats for the families of ANSF personnel killed in action and a further US$72 million donation to provide vehicles, spare parts, and ammunition.[89] These disbursements as well as similar projects in the pipeline while significant in themselves do not match the US contribution or the many needs of the Afghan army and police. As mentioned in the previous chapter, Beijing has agreed to help Tajikistan reinforce its border with Afghanistan and conducted joint anti-terror drills with Dushanbe in 2016. This showed the PRC's mounting concerns about ISIS-K in northern Afghanistan. Motivated by the same perception of threat, Beijing decided to help Afghanistan establish a mountain brigade in Badakhshan, with a training camp and other facilities in the Wakhan Corridor. It was adamant though, that 'there will be no Chinese military personnel of any kind on Afghan soil at any time'.[90]

Since 2014, China has provided approximately US$80 million in aid to Afghanistan annually,[91] which put it roughly on par with disengaging Australia on the list of Kabul's benefactors. As of mid-2017, China's cumulative direct investment stood at US$425 million – a big disappointment after the high expectations of the late 2000s, when Chinese companies won the US$3 billion contract to extract copper from the Mes Aynak mines in Logar province. In today's Kazakhstan and Uzbekistan, the media portray Afghanistan as an opportunity for commerce as well as a source of threats. Its dominant framing in China continues to be as a 'highly unstable and poor country, where terrorism is rampant',[92] which inhibits the appetite of Chinese companies to do business there.

Connecting Central and South Asia

The greatest Chinese business project of them all is the Belt and Road Initiative (BRI), envisaging ambitious infrastructure development in Eurasia and Africa. Its land-based component, the Silk Road Economic Belt (SREB), was first announced by Xi Jinping in Kazakhstan in 2013. Richard Hoagland, US Principal Deputy Assistant Secretary of State for South and Central Asian Affairs during 2013–15, reminisced that initially Washington's view of SREB was 'rather lackadaisical "They do hardware; we do software"', expecting that Beijing would fund expensive railways and pipelines identified in Clinton's NSR initiative, while the United States would look after governance and technical capacity issues.[93] The PRC interlocutors were polite and even friendly but essentially refused to use the NDN as a template for their connectivity project. They preferred to work with Russia and Pakistan in plotting transport corridors traversing Central Asia in the east–west and north–south directions bypassing Afghanistan. 'Look at most maps of Xi Jinping's keynote foreign policy concept cutting a route across Eurasia,' noted Raffaello Pantucci, 'and they tend to go tidily around Afghanistan.'[94]

The China–Pakistan Economic Corridor (CPEC) is of particular importance to Central Asia as it may provide them with access to the Indian Ocean and global trade routes via the Pakistani port of Gwadar. CPEC was launched in 2015, when Beijing and Islamabad signed more than fifty agreements on Chinese investments, totaling US$46 billion over the next ten to fifteen years. At the centre of the project is the road, rail and pipeline corridor from Kashgar in XUAR to Gwadar.⁹⁵ An upgrade of the Karakoram highway between Kashgar and Islamabad has progressed quickly and is likely to be finished in 2020. Kyrgyzstan and Tajikistan already have roads connecting them to the Karakoram highway. Trial runs of trucks carrying Central Asian cargos along the CPEC were reported in 2018.⁹⁶ For Kyrgyzstan and Tajikistan, it is a preferred way to overcome their landlocked position. According to Kazakhstan's foreign ministry, connecting with the CPEC is a priority in the country's effort to advance its 'transit-transport potential' in the southern direction alongside the Uzbekistan–Turkmenistan–Iran–Oman route; Afghanistan is not mentioned as a transit option at all.⁹⁷ Tashkent hedges its bets listing the trans-Afghan route (Mazar-e Sharif–Kabul–Peshawar–Gwadar) together with the Turkmenistan–Iran–Oman and China–Pakistan options in its five-year trade route diversification plan.⁹⁸

A Patient Mediator

Chinese diplomats are in a privileged position compared to their American and Russian colleagues – they are free to work with all actors interested in the process of finding a negotiated solution to the conflict in Afghanistan. They take part in the 'Moscow format' consultations which the United States spurns, and participate in the Quadrilateral Coordination Group (Beijing, Islamabad, Kabul and Washington) where Russia is not invited. They converse with the Taliban and the NUG, Iran and India, and maintain many other bilateral, trilateral and multilateral engagements. Beijing's solid credentials of non-interference have spared it accusations of supporting a faction or running a proxy inside Afghanistan. However, this multifaceted position has some drawbacks. Nobody is completely sure what China's strategic position is beyond tactical maneuvering and transactional politics to ensure Xinjiang's stability. Michael Clarke captured this fundamental uncertainty well, pointing out that it was quite possible for China's foreign policy intellectuals to share an interest with the United States on counterterrorism in Afghanistan and Central Asia and at the same time uphold a fundamental incompatibility between Washington and Beijing over Afghanistan's role in the BRI.⁹⁹ It appears that despite feverish diplomatic activity China is ready to settle for the extremely limited role of honest broker, facilitating communication and biding time until one of the many avenues for a resolution proves optimal for it.¹⁰⁰

Similarly to Russia, China perceives ISIS-K as a more acute threat than the Taliban. The former incorporate Uyghur fighters and try to export their radical ideology to Xinjiang and Central Asia. The latter's goals are limited primarily to the borders of Afghanistan. Beijing maintained ties with the Taliban in the 1990s while they were in government and after 2001 when they were pushed back to Pakistan. Since 2013, China has held trilateral meetings in Beijing, Urumqi and Peshawar with the Taliban and representatives of the government in Kabul to stop the flow of radicalised Muslims from XUAR and disrupt terrorist acts on its territory, with considerable success.[101] Unlike Russia, China believes it is necessary to maintain military pressure on the Taliban and does not share hope that they will help contain the international jihadis in the country.[102]

China states its commitment to the principle of 'Afghan-led and Afghan-owned' peace process promulgated by the United States and the NUG, implying that the Taliban must be forced to negotiate directly with Kabul.[103] At the same time, Beijing is open-minded about exactly who should act as a political sponsor of such talks and also benefit from their outcome. In July 2017, Presidents Xi Jinping and Putin issued a 'Joint Statement by the Russian Federation and the People's Republic of China on the Current Status of Global Affairs and Important International Issues' following their regular summit. A whole section was dedicated to Afghanistan which:

- expressed concern about the growth of ISIS-K in Afghanistan;
- called on international donors to help the socio-economic situation;
- endorsed the 'Afghan-led and Afghan-owned' reconciliation expedited by regional states;
- registered Russian support to China's policy vis-à-vis Pakistan which is conducive to Afghan peace; and
- recorded high praise from China for the 'Moscow format' of regional consultations.[104]

The point about Pakistan, the Taliban's main supporter, as a benign stakeholder in the peace process struck a raw nerve in Washington just as Trump's new Afghan strategy was about to be unfurled. 'Accepting Pakistan as the solution rather than the problem to the Afghan conflict will doom any US military effort in Afghanistan', said one Western analyst. 'The US needs to realize it is facing a hostile tripartite alliance of Pakistan, Russia and China in Afghanistan.'[105] Despite such harsh judgment, China's position is quite flexible and thus appeals to the Central Asian countries. Regional leaders do have a stake in the Afghan peace but they don't want to make a stark choice between Washington's militaristic approach and Moscow's push for the Taliban's legitimisation. Beijing-style unhurried open-ended diplomacy reduces the risks of error and, as one

Chinese foreign policy expert put it, new possibilities will eventually present themselves.[106]

Multipolar and Multilayer Dynamics of Central Asia's Response to the Afghan Issue

Of the three great powers, the United States appears to be the most inflexible and geopolitically-minded in Afghanistan. In its search for a negotiated solution to the conflict, it has become locked into two principles – the 'anyone but Russia' and 'anyone but the Taliban' tests, to paraphrase Cooley.[107] Towards the end of 2018 reassuring signs did emerge that Washington may start talks with the Taliban on counterterrorism and foreign military presence, thus paving the way for negotiations between Kabul and insurgents on the political compromise. There is no evidence, however, that it is prepared to engage with China, Iran and Russia in augmented regional diplomacy – US global posturing prevents such innovation and risk-taking that is essential for the success of peace process.[108]

Washington expects the Central Asian states to support its military operations in Afghanistan logistically, contribute to the country's reconstruction through the participation in the NSR infrastructure projects, and abstain from enabling and legitimising the Taliban either on their own or in collusion with Russia. Moscow's main points of pressure on its Central Asian partners include maintaining an impenetrable defence perimeter against Islamists and narcotics, and the prevention of the return of US military bases to the region. China has similar security agenda (with a special reference to Xinjiang) augmented by the promotion of the CPEC as the strategic north-south transport corridor.

The Central Asian governments have an impressive capacity to deny, adapt or subvert external demands that they deem not quite congruent with their national interests. 'Perhaps great powers assign particular strategic roles to Central Asia today like they used to do it in the past,' wrote a local analyst, 'but they are being corrected by the region's countries themselves.'[109] Uzbekistan bailed out of the CSTO in 2012 when it thought that the bloc no longer served its security needs. Kyrgyzstan terminated the US base in Manas in 2014 for the same reason. President Rahmon repurposed special units trained and equipped by the Pentagon to serve as his 'pretorian guard', because he believed his personal safety had higher priority than counterterrorism.[110] Kazakhstan refused to give custodial sentence to an ethnic Kazakh from China who illegally crossed the border fleeing from a re-education camp in XUAR, causing a comment in human rights circles that 'the Kazakh authorities can stand up to China'.¹¹¹ Local elites have mastered the game of safeguarding state sovereignty and legitimacy to perfection; it is all but impossible for a great power to impose its views without some sort of suasion and quid pro quo.

This autonomous agency can be sapped should geopolitical competition heat up again. Kazakhstan's preeminent Sinologist, Konstantin Syroezhkin, outlined a nightmare scenario circa 2025: the United States, wary of China's inexorable rise to the position of a global challenger, will activate support for Uyghur groups in Central Asia under the slogans of 'freedom' and 'democracy promotion'. Beijing will react by sending troops across the border, and the United States won't be able to help against this 'aggression'.¹¹² It is interesting that Syroezhkin does not include Russia in his apocalyptic vision. This could be either because that country would cease to matter or, more likely, because Beijing and Moscow would act in unison.

There is a near-universal consensus among Central Asian politicians and experts that there are no contradictions between Russia and China on approaches to regional security threats, especially those associated with Afghanistan. In his own 2025 forecast, a prominent Kazakh diplomat and scholar, Murat Laumulin, confidently predicted that the military role of Russia in a well-aligned tandem would still significantly exceed that of China.¹¹³ A Chinese expert concurred, at least for the present, arguing that Russia has more policy assets and resources, such as the CSTO and privileged political relationship with the Central Asian leaders. Therefore, Beijing will build security relations with the region's states through Russia, on the proviso that both sides 'defer to each other's interests and rely on the principle of farsightedness and voluntary nature of decision-making'.¹¹⁴

Russian experts are generally positive about Sino-Russian security cooperation in Central Asia on Afghanistan. One point of criticism they raise is that Beijing does not do enough to expose the faults of the US military campaign and 'provides military cover only for its own short border with Afghanistan'.¹¹⁵ Others have commented on Beijing's reluctance to expand the capacity of the SCO institutions, in particular RATS, and its growing predilection for alternative bilateral and multilateral security arrangements.¹¹⁶

'The U.S. has written off Central Asia', opines Cordesman.¹¹⁷ He is contradicted by other Western commentators: 'The Trump administration intends to recapture the high level of influence that the US enjoyed in the Central Asian region until 10 years ago.'¹¹⁸ Even if this is a case of 'do more with less resources', there is a degree of scepticism in the region about whether Trump's Afghanistan policy could get much traction on the ground: its 'most obvious vulnerability . . . is the predominant sense of superiority and exclusivity that not only breeds a desire for world hegemony but also dulls the perception of reality.'[119]

Conclusion

The United States, Russia and China have distinct views on the crisis in Afghanistan which they translate to the Central Asian republics in order to mobilise them for cooperative action. The diminished pool of resources at the disposal of American decision-makers saps the effectiveness of their political communication. This is most clearly illustrated by the demise of the NSR dream. Moscow and Beijing have been more successful in promoting their frames, in large part due to the fact that their securitisation of Afghanistan-related risks coincides with that of the Central Asian elites.

Great powers cannot force the local partners to adopt policies which they find unpalatable or detrimental to their perceived national interest. It's another matter whether the Central Asian republics themselves can produce workable solutions to their security predicament that would transcend models offered by external actors and prove to be better suited to their specific needs. As Syroezhkin put it, 'there may be political will for it and perhaps the realization of genuine threats... hence the need arises for mechanisms allowing us to pool our efforts'.[120]

Notes

1. M.S. Tuleev, 'Tsentralnaia Aziia: Afganistan i sovremennye aspekty geopolitiki', *Vestnik KRSU* 16, 6 (2016): p. 187.
2. B.A. Auelbaev, S.K. Kushkumbayev, K.L. Syroezhkin and V.Y. Dodonov, *Central Asia – 2020: Four Strategic Concepts* (Astana: KISI, 2015), p. 6.
3. Ibid., p. 20.
4. Alexander Cooley, *Great Games, Local Rules: The New Great Power Contest in Central Asia*, (Oxford: Oxford University Press, 2012), p. 49.
5. *The National Security Strategy of the United States of America*, (Washington, DC: The White House, 2006), p. 40.
6. *National Security Strategy of the United States of America*, (Washington, DC: The White House, 2017), p. 50.
7. Hillary Rodham Clinton, 'Remarks at the New Silk Road Ministerial Meeting', *US Department of State*, 22 September 2011, https://2009-2017.state.gov/secretary/20092013clinton/rm/2011/09/173807.htm.

8 William J. Burns, 'Deputy Secretary of State William J. Burns on Economic Connectivity in Central Asia. Remarks at Asia Society New York', *Asia Society Policy Institute*, 23 September 2014, https://asiasociety.org/policy-institute/deputy-secretary-state-william-j-burns-economic-connectivity-central-asia.
9 Eugene Rumer, Richard Sokolsky and Paul Stronski, *U.S. Policy toward Central Asia 3.0*, (Washington, DC: Carnegie Endowment for International Peace, 2016), pp. 49–50.
10 Sebastien Peyrouse and Gaël Raballand, 'Central Asia: The New Silk Road Initiative's Questionable Economic Rationality', *Eurasian Geography and Economics* 56, 4 (2015): pp. 405–420.
11 Graham Lee, *The New Silk Road and the Northern Distribution Network: A Golden Road to Central Asian Trade Reform?* (New York: Open Society Foundations, 2012).
12 Marlene Laruelle, 'The US Silk Road: Geopolitical Imaginary or the Repackaging of Strategic Interests?' *Eurasian Geography and Economics* 56, 4 (2015): pp. 360–375.
13 'Statement of General Joseph L. Votel, Commander, U.S. Central Command before the House Armed Services Committee on the Posture of U.S. Central Command Terrorism and Iran: Defense Challenges in the Middle East', US House of Representatives, 27 February 2018, https://docs.house.gov/meetings/AS/AS00/20180227/106870/HHRG-115-AS00-Wstate-VotelJ-20180227.pdf, p. 14.
14 Ibid., pp. 14–16.
15 Negmatullo Mirsaidov, 'Rahmon–Votel Meeting Highlights Tajikistan's Key Role in Central Asia', *Caravanserai*, 15 May 2018, http://central.asia-news.com/en_GB/articles/cnmi_ca/features/2018/05/15/feature-01.
16 Michael O'Hanlon, 'Improving Afghanistan Policy', *The Brookings Foreign Policy Brief* 2, 1 (2016): p. 7.
17 Christine Fair, 'Afghanistan in 2017: Another Year of Running in Place', *Asian Survey* 58, 1 (2018): p. 119.
18 'Statement for the Record by General John W. Nicholson, Commander, U.S. Forces–Afghanistan before the Senate Armed Services Committee on the Situation In Afghanistan', US Senate Committee on Armed Services, 9 February 2017, https://www.armed-services.senate.gov/imo/media/doc/Nicholson_02-09-17.pdf, p. 2.
19 Kate Clark, '"Not nation-building," but "killing terrorists": Trump's "New" Strategy for Afghanistan', *Afghanistan Analysts Network*, 23 August 2017, https://www.afghanistan-analysts.org/not-nation-building-but-killing-terrorists-trumps-new-strategy-for-afghanistan/.
20 Ashley J. Tellis and Jeff Eggers, *U.S. Policy in Afghanistan: Changing Strategies, Preserving Gains*, (Washington DC: Carnegie Endowment for International Peace, 2017), p. 19.
21 'Press Release on Regional Consultations on Afghanistan in Moscow', Russian Federation, Ministry of Foreign Affairs, 14 April 2017, http://www.mid.ru/foreign_policy/news/-/asset_publisher/cKNonkJE02Bw/content/id/2726953.

22. 'Kazakhstan prinial uchastie v zasedanii moskovskogo formata konsultatsii po Afganistanu', Republic of Kazakhstan, Ministry of Foreign Affairs, 9 November 2018, http://www.mfa.kz/ru/content-view/kazakhstan-prinal-ucastie-v-zasedanii-moskovskogo-formata-konsultacij-po-afganistanu.

23. Yulia Nikitina, 'Cooperative Transregionalism and the Problem of the "In Betweens"', in *Getting Out from 'In-Between': Perspectives on the Regional Order in Post-Soviet Europe and Eurasia*, ed. Samuel Charap, Alyssa Demus and Jeremy Shapiro (Santa Monica: RAND, 2018), p. 46.

24. Colin P. Clarke, 'Russia Is Not a Viable Counterterrorism Partner for the United States', *RAND*, 28 February 2018, https://www.rand.org/blog/2018/02/russia-is-not-a-viable-counterterrorism-partner-for.html.

25. Nicholson quoted in Jeff Seldin, 'US General: Russia Trying to "Undercut" Progress in Afghanistan', *Voice of America*, 1 September 2018, https://www.voanews.com/a/us-general-russia-trying-to-undercut-progress-in-afghanistan/4554004.html.

26. 'Top U.S. Commander in Afghanistan Accuses Russia of Aiding Taliban', *National Public Radio*, 26 March 2018, https://www.npr.org/sections/thetwo-way/2018/03/26/596933077/top-u-s-commander-in-afghanistan-accuses-russia-of-aiding-taliban.

27. Nicholson quoted in 'The General in Charge of the Afghanistan War said Russia Is Arming the Taliban', *National Post*, 22 March 2018, https://nationalpost.com/news/world/us-will-have-role-in-afghan-reconciliation-with-taliban.

28. Ahmad Majidyar, 'Iran and Russia Team up with Taliban to Undermine U.S.-led Mission in Afghanistan', *Middle East Institute*, 24 March 2017, https://www.mei.edu/publications/iran-and-russia-team-taliban-undermine-us-led-mission-afghanistan.

29. Dunford quoted in Rebecca Kheel, 'Mattis: More Evidence Needed on Russian Support for Taliban', *The Hill*, 10 March 2017, https://thehill.com/policy/defense/353702-mattis-more-evidence-needed-on-how-deep-russian-support-for-taliban-is.

30. 'Russia Dismisses as "Idle Gossip" Claims it is Helping Afghan Taliban', *The Moscow Times*, 25 March 2018, https://themoscowtimes.com/news/russia-calls-claims-it-is-aiding-taliban-in-afghanistan-idle-gossip-60931.

31. Krishnadev Calamur, 'Is Russia Really Arming the Taliban?' *The Atlantic*, 25 August 2017, https://www.theatlantic.com/international/archive/2017/08/russia-taliban-weapons/537807/.

32. Special Inspector General for Afghanistan Reconstruction, 'Afghan National Security Forces: Actions Needed to Improve Weapons Accountability', (audit report, SIGAR 14-84, Arlington, July 2014, https://www.sigar.mil/pdf/Audits/SIGAR-14-84-AR.pdf.

33. 'Russia, Taliban "Laughed" at US Claims of Moscow Arming Fighters', *Al Jazeera*, 31 March 2018, https://www.aljazeera.com/news/2018/03/russia-taliban-laughed-claims-moscow-arming-fighters-180330113642328.html.

34. Ayaz Gul, 'US Military Rejects Russian Claims About Number of IS Fighters in Afghanistan', *Voice of America*, 24 February 2018, https://www.voanews.com/a/us-

military-rejects-russia-numbers-of-islamic-state-fighters-in-afghanistan/4268999.html.

35 Hekmatullah Azamy, 'Challenges and Prospects for Daesh in Afghanistan and its Relations with the Taliban', in *Countering Daesh Extremism*, ed. Beatrice Gorawantschy, Rohan Gunaratna, Megha Sarmah and Patrick Rueppel (Singapore: Konrad-Adenauer-Stiftung, 2016), pp. 50, 55.

36 J.P. Lawrence, 'Russia Using ISIS Fears to Undermine NATO's Afghan Mission, Analysts Say', *Stars and Stripes*, 28 March 2018, https://www.stripes.com/news/russia-using-isis-fears-to-undermine-nato-s-afghan-mission-analysts-say-1.519163.

37 Kairat Umarov, 'Letter dated 17 January 2018 from the Chair of the Security Council Committee pursuant to resolutions 1267 (1999), 1989 (2011), and 2253 (2015) concerning Islamic State in Iraq and the Levant (Da'esh), Al-Qaida and associated individuals, groups, undertakings and entities addressed to the President of the Security Council', *United Nations Security Council*, 26 January 2018, http://daccess-ods.un.org/access.nsf/GetFile?OpenAgent&DS=S/2018/14&Lang=E&Type=DOC.

38 Obaid Ali, 'Qari Hekmat's Island: A Daesh enclave in Jawzjan?' *Afghanistan Analysts Network*, 11 November 2017, https://www.afghanistan-analysts.org/qari-hekmats-island-a-daesh-enclave-in-jawzjan/.

39 Phillip Walter Wellman, 'ISIS Flees Taliban Onslaught, Surrenders to Afghan Government Forces', *Stars and Stripes*, 1 August 2018, https://www.stripes.com/news/isis-flees-taliban-onslaught-surrenders-to-afghan-government-forces-1.540428.

40 Vanda Felbab-Brown, 'President Trump's Afghanistan Policy: Hopes and Pitfalls', (report, The Brookings Institution, Washington, D.C., September 2017), p. 10.

41 Vinay Kaura, 'China, US Differ on Road to Peace in Afghanistan', *Middle East Institute*, 9 January 2018, https://www.mei.edu/publications/china-us-differ-road-peace-afghanistan.

42 Thomas Zimmerman, *The New Silk Roads: China, the U.S., and the Future of Central Asia*, (New York: New York University, 2015), p. 14.

43 Stephen Blank and Younkyoo Kim, *Making Sense of Russia's Policy in Afghanistan*, (Paris: IFRI, 2018).

44 Jeffrey T. Fowler, 'Afghanistan: Has "The Great Game" Returned Between Russia and the US?' *In Homeland Security*, 1 March 2018, https://inhomelandsecurity.com/afghanistan-great-game/.

45 Anthony Cordesman, 'Are Russia and China Sabotaging American Policy in Afghanistan?' *The Hill*, 9 January 2018, https://thehill.com/opinion/international/404716-are-russia-and-china-sabotaging-american-policy-in-afghanistan#bottom-story-socials.

46 'Foreign Policy Concept of the Russian Federation (approved by President of the Russian Federation Vladimir Putin on November 30, 2016)', Russian Federation, Ministry of Foreign Affairs, 1 December 2016, http://www.mid.ru/en/foreign_

policy/official_documents/-/asset_publisher/CptICkB6BZ29/content/id/2542248, emphasis added.
47 Ekaterina Stepanova, *Russia's Afghan Policy in the Regional and East–West Contexts*, (Paris: IFRI, 2018), p. 22.
48 M.A. Konarovsky quoted in Alexey Vasiliev, *Russia's Middle East Policy: From Lenin to Putin*, (Abingdon: Routledge, 2018), p. 371.
49 The Kremlin, 'Meeting with President of Afghanistan Ashraf Ghani', *Official portal of the President of Russia*, 10 July 2015, http://en.kremlin.ru/events/president/news/49910.
50 Vitalii Volkov, 'O chem "seryi kardinal" Afganistana dogovorilsia s Kremlem', *Deutsche Welle*, 20 March 2017, https://p.dw.com/p/2ZYAg.
51 Henry Meyer, 'Now Putin Is Being Asked to Bring Peace to Afghanistan', *Bloomberg*, 23 November 2017, https://www.bloomberg.com/news/articles/2017-11-23/russia-must-pressure-taliban-to-seek-peace-afghanistan-says.
52 Ekaterina Stepanova, 'Faktor IGIL i dvizhenie Taliban v politike Rossii po Afganistanu i v bolee shirokom regione', in *Problemy terrorizma, nasilstvennogo ekstremizma i radikalizatsii*, ed. Ekaterina Stepanova (Moscow: IMEMO RAN, 2017), p. 228.
53 N. Asef, 'Vozvrashchenie Rossii v Afganistan: perspektivy dvustoronnego ekonomicheskogo sotrudnichestva', *Vestnik RUDN* 17, 4 (2017): pp. 781–792.
54 Kirill Nourzhanov, 'Central Asia's Domestic Stability in Official Russian Security Thinking under Yeltsin and Putin: From Hegemony to Multilateral Pragmatism', in *China, Xinjiang and Central Asia: History, Transition and Crossborder Interaction into the 21st Century*, ed. Colin Mackerras and Michael Clarke (London and New York: Routledge, 2009), pp. 151–172.
55 Sergei Lavrov, 'Partnerstvo, ispytannoe vremenem', *Rossiskaia gazeta*, 4 October 2017, https://rg.ru/2017/10/04/lavrov-pomoshch-rf-centralnoj-azii-prevysila-6-milliardov-dollarov.html.
56 Nikolai Patrushev, 'V Afganistane idet terroristicheskaia voina, za god pogibli tysiachi chelovek', *TASS*, 28 September 2018, https://tass.ru/politika/5605150.
57 'Shoigu nazval glavnuiu ugrozu v Tsentralnoi Azii dlia bezopasnosti Rossii', *RIA Novosti*, 25 May 2018, https://ria.ru/20180525/1521394049.html.
58 Gen. Sergei Smirnov quoted in 'FSB: Na sever Afganistana perebrosheny 8000 boevikov iz Sirii', *EurAsia Daily*, 5 April 2018, https://eadaily.com/ru/news/2018/04/05/fsb-na-sever-afganistana-perebrosheny-8000-boevikov-iz-sirii.
59 Sohibi Sharifali, 'Nahzat va "Davlati Islomi" – du jodai yak paimon!' *Jumhuriyat* 168, 24 August 2018, http://jumhuriyat.tj/index.php?art_id=34802.
60 Ikhtier Abdullaev quoted in 'Glava uzbekskikh spetssluzhb nazval vragov gosudarstva', *Vesti.uz*, 2 April 2018, https://vesti.uz/glava-uzbekskikh-spetssluzhb-nazval-vragov-gosudarstva/

61 Maria Zakharova, 'Russia Records Unidentified Helicopters Delivering Weapons to Taliban, IS in Afghanistan', *TASS*, 23 August 2018, http://tass.com/defense/1018368.
62 'Afghanistan Would Be Used as Substrate to Shift Terrorism into Russia: Karzai', *Ariana News*, 18 March 2017, https://ariananews.af/afghanistan-would-be-used-as-substrate-to-shift-terrorism-into-russia-karzai/.
63 Ivan Egorov, 'Ugroza s iuga', *Rossiiskaia gazeta*, 25 November 2018, https://rg.ru/2018/11/25/sekretari-sovbezov-sng-rasskazali-kto-pomogaet-boevikam-v-afganistane.html.
64 Omurbek Babanov, 'Tsentralnoaziatskie vyzovy dlia Rossii', *Russian International Affairs Council*, 13 September 2017, http://russiancouncil.ru/analytics-and-comments/analytics/tsentralnoaziatskie-vyzovy-dlya-rossii/.
65 Erlan Karin, *Dilemmy bezopasnosti Tsentralnoi Azii*, (Paris: IFRI, 2017), p. 9.
66 M.A. Konarovsky, 'Afganistan posle 2014 goda', *Vestnik mezhdunarodnykh organizatsii* 12, 3 (2017): pp. 248–249.
67 Ibid., p. 252.
68 Vladimir Putin, 'Esli by v Afganistane ne bylo SShA, bylo by khuzhe', *Kommersant*, 26 December 2017, https://www.kommersant.ru/doc/3508527.
69 Kabulov quoted in 'MID Rossii zaiavil o gotovnosti k vzaimodeistviiu s SShA po Afganistanu', *Kommersant*, 23 December 2017, https://www.kommersant.ru/doc/3507622.
70 Kabulov quoted in 'Rossiia ne sorevnuetsia s SShA v Afganistane, zaiavili v MID', *RIA Novosti*, 12 November 2018, https://ria.ru/20181112/1532592756.html.
71 Klintsevich quoted in 'SShA gotoviat "novyi proekt" po destabilizatsii Srednei Azii – Klintsevich', *TV Zvezda*, 13 September 2017, https://tvzvezda.ru/news/vstrane_i_mire/content/201709131818-9qjs.htm.
72 Kirill Sokov, 'Afganskii narkotrafik kak sredstvo voiny s Rossiei', *Ritm Evrazii*, 13 July 2016, https://www.ritmeurasia.org/news--2016-07-13--afganskij-narkotrafik-kak-sredstvo-vojny-s-rossiej-24638.
73 Aleksandr Khramchikhin, 'Afganskaia lovushka Ameriki', *Nezavisimaia gazeta*, 27 April 2018, http://nvo.ng.ru/concepts/2018-04-27/1_994_afgan.html.
74 Ivan Safronov, 'Frants Klintsevich postradal "za otkrytost"', *Kommersant*, 12 February 2018, https://www.kommersant.ru/doc/3547099.
75 Aidar Ermekov, 'SShA pereshli k planu 'B' po destabilizatsii Tsentralnoi Azii', *MK Kazakhstan*, 14 November 2018, https://mk-kz.kz/politics/2018/11/14/ssha-pereshli-k-planu-b-po-destabilizacii-centralnoy-azii.html.
76 Elizabeth Wishnick, 'Post-2014 Afghanistan Policy and the Limitations of China's Global Role', *Central Asian Affairs* 1, 1 (2014): p. 152.
77 Thomas Ruttig, 'Climbing on China's Priority List: Views on Afghanistan from Beijing', *Afghanistan Analysts Network*, 10 April 2018, https://www.afghanistan-analysts.org/climbing-on-chinas-priority-list-views-on-afghanistan-from-beijing/.

78 Justyna Szczudlik-Tatar, 'China's Evolving Stance on Afghanistan: Towards More Robust Diplomacy with "Chinese Characteristics"', *Strategic File* 22, 58 (2014): https://www.pism.pl/files/?id_plik=18261, p. 3.
79 Zhu Yongbiao, 'China's Afghanistan Policy since 9/11 Stages and Prospects', *Asian Survey* 58, 2 (2018): p. 292.
80 Konstantin Syroezhkin, *Sintzian: bolshoi vopros dlia Kitaia i Kazakhstana* (Almaty: IMEP, 2015), pp. 132, 298.
81 Adrian Zenz, '"Thoroughly Reforming them towards a Healthy Heart Attitude": China's Political Re-education Campaign in Xinjiang', *Central Asian Survey* (2018) DOI: 10.1080/02634937.2018.1507997.
82 Zhao Huasheng, 'Afghanistan and China's New Neighbourhood Diplomacy', *International Affairs* 92, 4 (2016): p. 900.
83 Roy Allison, 'Protective Integration and Security Policy Coordination: Comparing the SCO and CSTO', *The Chinese Journal of International Politics* 11, 3, (2018): p. 313.
84 Wang Hui, 'SCO Meeting Likely to Deepen Regional Security Cooperation', *China Daily*, 22 June 2016, http://www.chinadaily.com.cn/opinion/2016-06/22/content_25798646.htm.
85 'Qingdao Declaration of the Council of Heads of State of Shanghai Cooperation Organisation', *SCO Secretariat*, 10 June 2018, http://eng.sectsco.org/load/443667/.
86 Igor Subbotin, 'Status Afganistana v ShOS: situatsiia mozhet izmenitsia', *Afghanistan.ru*, 9 June 2018, http://afghanistan.ru/doc/121292.html.
87 Evgenii Sysoev, 'IG stremitsia sozdat' novoe kvazigosudarstvo na territoriiakh Afganistana, Pakistana i stran Tsentralnoi Azii', *RATS SCO*, 28 February 2018, http://ecrats.org/ru/situation/status/7083.
88 Dirk van der Kley, *China's Foreign Policy in Afghanistan*, (Sydney: Lowy Institute, 2014), pp. 7–8.
89 Akram Umarov, 'Assessing China's New Policy in Afghanistan', *Central Asian Affairs* 4, 4, (2017): p. 392.
90 Minnie Chan, 'China Is Helping Afghanistan Set up Mountain Brigade to Fight Terrorism', *South China Morning Post*, 28 August 2018, https://www.scmp.com/news/china/diplomacy-defence/article/2161745/china-building-training-camp-afghanistan-fight.
91 Sudha Ramachandran, 'Is China Bringing Peace to Afghanistan?' *The Diplomat*, 20 June 2018, https://thediplomat.com/2018/06/is-china-bringing-peace-to-afghanistan/.
92 Azeta Hatef and Luwei Rose Luqiu, 'Where Does Afghanistan Fit in China's Grand Project? A Content Analysis of Afghan and Chinese News Coverage of the One Belt, One Road Initiative', *The International Communication Gazette*, 80, 6 (2017): p. 564.
93 Richard E. Hoagland, 'Central Asia: Not in Our Backyard, Not a Hot Spot, Strategically Important', *CIGI Papers* 87, (2016), https://www.cigionline.org/sites/default/files/cigi_paper_no.87web_3.pdf, p. 8.

94 Raffaello Pantucci, 'China in Afghanistan: A Reluctant Leader with Growing Stakes', *ISPI*, 18 October 2018, https://www.ispionline.it/en/pubblicazione/china-afghanistan-reluctant-leader-growing-stakes-21456.

95 Daniel S. Markey and James West, 'Behind China's Gambit in Pakistan', *Council on Foreign Relations*, 12 May 2016, https://www.cfr.org/expert-brief/behind-chinas-gambit-pakistan.

96 'CPEC Is now Connected with Central Asia by Road Network while Bypassing Afghanistan', *The Dispatch News Desk*, 17 February 2018, https://dnd.com.pk/pakistan-is-linked-now-with-central-asia-by-road-network-while-bypassing-afghanistan/139428.

97 'Mnogostoronnee ekonomicheskoe sotrudnichestvo', Republic of Kazakhstan, Ministry of Foreign Affairs, 26 April 2018, http://mfa.gov.kz/ru/content-view/mnogostoronnee-ekonomiceskoe-sotrudnicestvo.

98 'Transportno-kommunikatsionnaia strategiia Uzbekistana predstavlena v Vashingtone', Republic of Uzbekistan, Ministry of Foreign Affairs, 16 December 2018, https://mfa.uz/ru/press/news/2018/12/17089/.

99 Michael Clarke, '"One Belt, One Road" and China's Emerging Afghanistan Dilemma', *Australian Journal of International Affairs* 70, 5, (2016): p. 564.

100 Mordechai Chaziza, 'China's Peace-Maker Role in Afghanistan: Mediation and Conflict Management', *Middle East Policy* XXV, 3, (2018): p. 149.

101 M.V. Kazanin, *Kitai–Pakistan:voenno-tekhnicheskoe i ekonomicheskoe sotrudnichestvo v nachale XXI veka*, (Moscow: Institut Blizhnego Vostoka, 2017), pp. 81–82.

102 Angela Stanzel, *Fear and Loathing on the New Silk Road: Chinese Security in Afghanistan and Beyond*, (London: The European Council on Foreign Relations, 2018), p. 3.

103 Wang Yi, 'Push for New Steps and New Breakthroughs in Afghanistan's Reconciliation Process at an Early Date', *Ministry of Foreign Affairs of the People's Republic of China*, 12 December 2018, https://www.fmprc.gov.cn/mfa_eng/zxxx_662805/t1624843.shtml.

104 The Kremlin. 'Sovmestnoe zaiavlenie Rossiiskoi Federatsii i Kitaiskoi Narodnoi Respubliki o tekushchei situatsii v mire i vazhnykh mezhdunarodnykh problemakh', *Official portal of the President of the Russian Federation*, 4 July 2017, http://kremlin.ru/supplement/5219.

105 Paul Casaca quoted in Shamil Shams, 'China and Russia want US out of Afghanistan', *Deutsche Welle*, 14 June 2017, https://www.dw.com/en/china-and-russia-want-us-out-of-afghanistan/a-39250894.

106 Zhao Huasheng, 'What Is Behind China's Growing Attention to Afghanistan?' *Carnegie Endowment for International Peace*, 8 March 2015, https://carnegieendowment.org/2015/03/08/what-is-behind-china-s-growing-attention-to-afghanistan-pub-59286.

107 Cooley, *Great Games, Local Rules*, p. 176.
108 James Schwelmlein, 'The U.S. and Afghan Government Must Re-engage With the Peace Process', *Carnegie Endowment for International Peace*, 19 November 2018, https://carnegieendowment.org/2018/11/19/u.s.-and-afghan-government-must-re-engage-with-peace-process-pub-77752.
109 Tuleev, 'Tsentralnaia Aziia', p. 187.
110 Dmitrii Popov, 'Dvustoronnie otnosheniia SShA i Tadzhikistana na sovremennom etape', *Novaia Evraziia* 5, 50 (2018): pp. 99–100.
111 Lily Kuo, 'Kazakh Court Frees Woman who Fled Chinese Re-education Camp', *The Guardian*, 2 August 2018, https://www.theguardian.com/world/2018/aug/01/kazakh-court-frees-woman-who-fled-chinese-re-education-camp.
112 Syroezhkin, *Sintzian: bolshoi vopros*, pp. 299–300.
113 Murat Laumulin, 'Central Asia–2025. Part 2', *Central Asia's Affairs* 5 (2017): p. 14.
114 Xiaofen Qiu, 'Kontseptualnye podkhody Rossii i Kitaia v Tsentralnoi Azii: skhodstvo i razlichiia', *Problemy postsovetskogo prostranstva* 4 (2015): p. 82.
115 V.V. Evseev and A.A. Kuznetsov, 'Rekomendatsii po optimizatsii deiatelnosti Shankhaiskoi organizatsii sotrudnichestva', in *Aktualnye problemy razvitiia Shakhaiskoi organizatsii sotrudnichestva*, (Moscow: Institut stran SNG, 2018), p. 69.
116 A.O. Vonogradov, *Resheniia XIX s'ezda KPK i perspektivy rossisko-kitaiskikh otnoshenii*, (Moscow: IDV RAN, 2018), p. 108.
117 Anthony Cordesman, 'America's "Chaos Strategy" in the Middle East and South Asia', *Centre for Strategic and International Studies*, 26 February 2018, https://www.csis.org/analysis/americas-chaos-strategy-middle-east-and-south-asia.
118 M.K. Bhadrakumar, 'The Afghan War: Trump and Putin Battle for Uzbek Support', *Asia Times*, 25 December 2017, http://www.atimes.com/article/afghan-war-trump-putin-battle-uzbek-support/.
119 Laumulin, 'Central Asia–2025. Part 2', p. 15.
120 Konstantin Syroezhkin, *Nuzhno li Kazakhstanu boiatsia Kitaia: mify i fobii dvustoronnikh otnoshenii*, (Astana and Almaty: IMEP, 2014), p. 384.

5

Central Asia's Contribution to Peace in Afghanistan

Mission Impossible or the Dawn of Hope?

In 2018, after four years of indeterminacy and pessimism in the wake of NATO's withdrawal from Afghanistan, glimmers of hope began to emerge that the Central Asian republics may be moving towards more positive and productive engagement with Afghanistan.

One piece of good news was Kazakhstan's non-permanent seat on the United Nations Security Council, which it used to good effect to rekindle global interest in finding a negotiated solution to the Afghanistan imbroglio. Another encouraging development was Uzbekistan's move out of self-imposed isolation following President Islam Karimov's death in September 2016. His successor, Shavkat Mirziyoyev, embarked upon a program of reforms which entailed normalisation of relations with regional neighbours and commitment to a cooperative approach to peace in Afghanistan. The positive momentum generated by the two largest Central Asian republics, had the potential to offset the defensive caution of Kyrgyzstan and Tajikistan, as well as Turkmenistan's growing domestic turbulence, which distracted it from regional issues.

It is too early to say with much certainty that the Russian-promoted vision of Afghanistan as a threat will be decisively discarded across the region. Any shift will remain limited as long as the Afghan government continues to lack direction and stability. Yet in a regional context long plagued by despondency, recent occurrences suggest more constructive relations between Central Asia and Afghanistan are no mission impossible.

One of the most reassuring signs came in January 2018, with a UN Security Council Presidential Statement, stewarded by Kazakhstan, on 'Building Regional Partnerships in Afghanistan and Central Asia'.[1] Delegates at the meeting struck an optimistic note. Hekmat Khalil Karzai, Deputy Foreign Minister of Afghanistan, spoke of a 'new dynamism' in Afghanistan's relations with Central Asian countries;

Erlan Abdyldayev, Minister of Foreign Affairs of Kyrgyzstan, stressed that 'the countries of Central Asia were ready to become actively involved in the process of building peace and stability in Afghanistan'; Kairat Abdrakhmanov, Minister for Foreign Affairs of Kazakhstan, emphasised the need for a 'regional approach', with cooperation 'imperative ... given the threats that did not recognize borders'; and even Sergey Lavrov, Russia's Foreign Minister, conceded that 'the situation in Afghanistan required a complex approach and cooperation with all the neighbouring States, in particular Central Asian countries'.

This final chapter will take stock of recent developments in each of the Central Asian republics, assess prospects for regional cooperation on Afghanistan and make tentative predictions as to what the future might hold.

(Re)Assessing Afghanistan: Are the Central Asian Perspectives Shifting?

At the end of 2017, leading political scientists and security analysts from across Central Asia, participated in a conference intended to explore the possible direction of the region in the coming decade. It was a landmark event – the first of its kind, with participants not only striving to overcome national particularism in search of a common vision, but also criticising external perspectives on Central Asia. Dismissing the Russian viewpoint as excessively gloomy and the Western (and Indian) scenarios for the fragile neighbour as too rosy, delegates toed the middle ground, a vision grounded in present realities but not without hope for the future. The conference demonstrated a growing self-confidence by the expert community in the region, summed up in the somewhat belligerent statement that, 'only representatives from the region itself can understand, study and particularly prognosticate Central Asia'.[2] A central theme that emerged was frustration over the solutions pursued by global powers to the ongoing Afghan crisis and a desire for a greater say in how to deal with threats emerging from the south.

Regional fears about imminent state failure in Afghanistan – palpable in the lead up to the NATO drawdown in 2014 – appear to have given way to the notion that, notwithstanding an absence of substantive progress, Afghanistan is somehow or other muddling through. The ruling coalition in Kabul may be weak, lurching from crisis to crisis; the Taliban may be expanding and the Islamic State has not melted away, but for now, the government of Ashraf Ghani remains intact. Ghani's February 2018 offer of peace talks with the Taliban, followed by a series of negotiated ceasefires later in the year, have been interpreted by the international community – including the Central Asian republics – as a sign of promising political progress.³

The frequency and density of direct contacts between politicians and officials from Central Asia and their Afghan counterparts increased dramatically in 2018. This was particularly evident in the military and security spheres. Army chiefs from Kazakhstan and Uzbekistan visited Kabul in February, for the first time in the post-Soviet period. President Ghani hailed the visit as 'a new chapter of relations and cooperation in the military sector' between the three countries.⁴ Several months later Tajikistan and Afghanistan announced the creation of a joint intelligence working group; this occurred after the head of Tajik security services held talks with his Afghan counterparts which emphasised 'the unified position on security matters by political leaders in both countries'.⁵ However, the clearest indication of the Central Asian elites' desire to be more directly involved in resolving the Afghan conflict, came at a diplomatic forum organised by Uzbekistan in March 2018.

Bringing together diplomatic representatives of twenty-one states, the United Nations and the European Union (but, pointedly, excluding the Taliban), the Tashkent Conference on Afghanistan provided a platform for discussion on a wide range of issues regarding the Afghan peace process, counterterrorism and counter-narcotics efforts and regional economic cooperation. In terms of practical deliverables, the conference did not achieve much: its final Declaration voiced support for the Government of National Unity in Afghanistan, hailed its efforts to begin direct talks with the Taliban and acknowledged the Kabul Process as the main vehicle for achieving peace. No groundbreaking initiatives were announced, and the usual lack of consensus among major international actors, was on display. The Russian Foreign Minister was typically alarmist about the state of affairs in Afghanistan; the US delegation talked tough about continuing the fight against the Taliban and, departing from the conference agenda, the Iranians and Saudis engaged in a shouting match, blaming each other for all sorts of unpleasantness in the Middle East.⁶ Yet, despite its shortcomings, the event was truly unprecedented: for the first time a major international forum on Afghanistan took place *in* Central Asia. In the words of the UN Secretary-General's Special Representative for Afghanistan, Tadamichi Yamamoto, this showed the increasing political influence of Central Asia and, in particular, Uzbekistan's positive transformative effects on the situation in Afghanistan.⁷

The actual extent of influence and positive impact that Afghanistan's northern neighbours will be able to exercise, depends on three connected factors: the first is internal political dynamics in each of the Central Asian republics; the second is their ability to act in unison at the regional level and the third is pressure exerted by external stakeholders, which will undoubtedly continue to influence Central Asian perspectives and policies on Afghanistan.

Afghanistan and the Politics of Security and Reform in Individual Central Asian States

As far as their stance towards Afghanistan is concerned, there continue to be some notable commonalities and points of agreement between the five Central Asian republics: they are still reluctant to become economically exposed to the reconstruction of Afghanistan; their concerns about terrorism, narcotics trafficking, and conflict spillover across the border have not evaporated; and the maintenance of a military-security barrier remains a priority for frontline states. The areas where they can make a positive contribution, individually and collectively, include expediting the intra-Afghan dialogue; enabling infrastructure projects funded by the West and China and pursuing small-scale initiatives that encourage incremental peace in Afghan society. If the Central Asian states' willingness and ability to engage with Afghanistan is to be visualised as a spectrum, Kazakhstan and Uzbekistan – the most willing and able – would be located at one end, Kyrgyzstan and Tajikistan at the other, with Turkmenistan located somewhere in the middle.

Kazakhstan

As the richest and most developed nation, Kazakhstan occupies a special position in Central Asia. Classified as an upper-middle-income country by the World Bank since 2005, it was finally assigned to the 'very high human development' category by the UNDP in 2018 – the only state in the region to have achieved the latter distinction, so far. Kazakhstan has been active in the international arena since independence, pursuing a so-called 'multi-vector' foreign policy. Multi-vectorism – denoting an extreme form of pragmatism in foreign policy, concerned solely with state security and economic development – is the *mot juste* of political leaders across Central Asia. It is commonly accepted, however, that in formulating and implementing it, President Nursultan Nazarbaev has, 'shown the greatest sensitivity, skill and persistence'.[8]

In 2018, Astana's pragmatism was on full display in terms of military and security considerations. First, it opened two of its ports on the Caspian Sea, Aqtau and Kuryk, as transit points for the delivery of non-military goods from the United States to Afghanistan, effectively prolonging the 2010 Northern Distribution Network (NDN) agreement.[9] At the same time, Kazakhstan went out of its way to reassure Russia (and Iran), that under no circumstances would American military presence be allowed on its territory. The Convention on the legal status of the Caspian Sea, signed by all littoral states including Kazakhstan, in Aqtau in August 2018, unequivocally banned the deployment of third party armed forces in the region. While expanding ties with the Ghani administration and professing faith in a bright future for Afghanistan, Kazakhstan also began construction of a defence perimeter on the border with Turkmenistan. By 2020, more than a third of Kazakhstan's 450 kilometre-long southern frontier will be covered by reinforced concrete walls, helipads and advanced security engineering systems.[10] Kazakhstan's chairmanship of the Collective Security Treaty Organization (CSTO), in 2018, was marked by a series of military drills that were unprecedented in scale. These drills involved deployment of the Collective Rapid Reaction Force, including Kazakhstani units, in a variety of scenarios of direct armed conflict on the border and a cross-border 'peacekeeping mission'.[11]

A noteworthy development has been the subtle desecuritisation of threats from Afghanistan. Terrorism, extremism, narcotics and weapons trafficking and transnational crime have not evaporated – indeed, they may well have intensified. However, rather than being framed as direct and immediate threats to Kazakhstan, they are being reconfigured as challenges to Central Asia as a whole, to Eurasia and to the global community. This spatial shift, in official discourse, puts Astana in an enviable position as an indispensable element of any regional or global strategy to stabilise Afghanistan. President Nazarbaev's 2018 book, *Era nezavisimosti* (translated in English as *The Age of Independence*), surveyed twenty-six years of Kazakhstan's foreign policy, since independence, and catalogued dozens of examples of Astana's assistance to Afghanistan, as well as to frontline Central Asian states and to Russia, China, the United States, the Organization for Security and Cooperation in Europe (OSCE), CSTO and NATO.[12] In the words of Kazakhstan's ambassador to the United Nations, Nazarbaev's priority was 'to create a model of a regional zone of peace, security, cooperation and development in Central Asia and Afghanistan, balancing the interests of all stakeholders'.[13]

Nazarbaev's position on Afghanistan had much to do with the imperatives of domestic politics. Since independence, Kazakhstan's governing elite has sought to enhance its claim to legitimacy by redirecting external recognition inward to domestic audiences.¹⁴ The mantle of a respectable international statesman, complements the President's image as a father of the nation and a guarantor of internal peace and economic development. Kazakhstan's chairmanship of the OSCE in 2010 and its non-permanent seat on the UN Security Council in 2017–2018, were important accomplishments for Nazarbaev, demonstrating his country's ability to punch above its weight and influence the global agenda. Since 2016, Nazarbaev has played host to the 'Astana Peace Process' – a series of talks between the Syrian government and opposition, which has yielded some positive results in the form of local ceasefires and de-escalation zones. As Kazakhstan's Ministry of Foreign Affairs, Kairat Abdrakhmanov, explained,

> Astana was chosen as a suitable platform to host these negotiations due to the fact that Kazakhstan is objective and neutral in its approach, as well as a reliable partner for all nations. Kazakhstan has friendly relations with Russia, Turkey, European Union states, as well as the United States ... Kazakhstan has experience acting as a mediator. The country has already hosted two rounds of talks involving representatives of the Syrian opposition in 2015. President Nursultan Nazarbaev also played a central role in mending relations between Russia and Turkey. Without President Nursultan Nazarbaev's contribution, it is unlikely that these talks would have been arranged.¹⁵

Afghanistan presented another public relations opportunity for Nazarbaev. Personalisation of foreign policy and its identification with the perennial Leader of the Nation reached its apex when Kazakhstan's representative at the UN Security Council called on other members to adopt the so-called 'Nazarbaev Codex', as an international norm governing counterterrorist activities in Afghanistan and, in the long-term, globally.¹⁶ Containing a vast number of platitudes about the importance of preventative diplomacy, prophylactic work with youth, disruption of terrorists' finances and intelligence sharing, the Codex put great store in the need to expedite economic development to forestall the spread of extremist ideas.

The nexus between security and development in Afghanistan is, of course, acknowledged by every international actor these days. In Abdrakhmanov's words, 'it is possible to integrate Afghanistan into economic ties with the countries of Central Asia ... We must, using collective effort, adopt a complex development program with broad involvement of international business in the realization of concrete economic projects.'¹⁷ Kazakhstan would rather play the role of a fixer and beneficiary than a donor in this collective effort. Indeed, despite the rhetoric, Kazakhstan has been quite parsimonious in contributing materially to Afghanistan's rehabilitation. In 2018, its officials still had to cite a few million dollars spent in 2008–2012 on humanitarian aid, a single school in Samangan and an unfinished hospital in Bamiyan, as evidence of Astana's unswerving generosity.[18] The much-touted US$50 million education program for Afghan students in Kazakhstan, launched in 2010, proved less than successful, having produced only 50 per cent of the planned graduates. It was repackaged in 2018, as part of the 'Astana Initiative on Empowering Women in Afghanistan', promising more scholarships to female students.[19]

Kazakhstan's direct investment in Afghanistan between 2005 and 2017, totalled a paltry US$300,000. Trade turnover between the two countries in 2017, stood at US$565 million, with Kazakhstan's exports to Afghanistan amounting to US$563 million (75 per cent of which fell on agricultural products, mostly wheat and wheat flour), and imports from Afghanistan not exceeding US$2 million.[20] In the National Export Strategy of Kazakhstan for 2018–2022, Afghanistan is assigned a 'moderate' ranking, the second lowest category of prospective markets.[21]

It is unlikely that Astana will contribute to the stabilisation of Afghanistan in tangible material ways in the immediate future. However, it is probable that it will continue to play an important role in the security architecture maintained by Russia and the CSTO, designed to contain threats from the Afghan conflict through military means. Where Nazarbaev's multi-vectorism holds greatest promise for Afghanistan, is in Kazakhstan's willingness to share intelligence with Kabul, expedite the diplomatic process in all formats, act as a mediator between great powers and participate in large-scale infrastructure projects, provided they are fully funded by external agencies.

Uzbekistan

Uzbekistan represents a curious case. On one hand, the Afghan issue continues to be robustly securitised in domestic discourse. The Military Doctrine adopted in January 2018 states:

> The extant challenges and threats of terrorism, extremism, narcotraffic and transborder crime negatively affect the situation in Central Asia. The activity of illegal armed formations in Afghanistan poses a particular threat to security in the region.[22]

On the other hand, under the presidency of Mirziyoyev, who began his term in office in December 2016, relations between Tashkent and Kabul have experienced a dramatic turnaround. As a prominent Uzbek foreign affairs journal put it, 'thanks to the political will of the President of Uzbekistan and with firm support from Afghanistan's leadership a "systemic breakthrough" occurred in the Uzbek–Afghan ties'.[23]

Between 2003 and 2016, then President Islam Karimov met his Afghan counterpart for talks only twice. High-level political contacts were made difficult by the closure of the American base in Uzbekistan in the wake of the Andijan massacre in 2005. By contrast, Mirziyoyev and Ghani met five times in 2017 alone. This breakthrough however should be viewed in the wider context of Mirziyoyev's reform agenda which incorporated normalisation of relations with all of Uzbekistan's neighbours. In his very first programmatic speech as Acting President before the parliament of Uzbekistan in September 2016, Mirziyoyev emphasised that the national interests of his country demanded, 'the conduct of open, good-natured and pragmatic policy vis-à-vis Turkmenistan, Kazakhstan, Kyrgyzstan and Tajikistan'.[24] Breaking the mould of self-isolation, suspicion and acrimony in dealing with other Central Asian republics, was top priority. Mirziyoyev himself likened the task to thawing a twenty-year-long freeze.

The achievement to date has been impressive. Uzbekistan has made good progress in resolving the seemingly intractable territorial disputes, and issues with border delimitation enclaves and water management. Opening borders and restoring transport links have revitalised trade and made life easier for hundreds of thousands of ordinary people across Central Asia. Significantly, after a long hiatus, Tashkent has shown interest in regional security planning and collaboration. By the end of 2018, it had signed bilateral agreements on military cooperation and held joint drills with all regional neighbours bar Turkmenistan. The 'Jaihun-2018' exercise with Tajikistan was truly historical: armed units from two countries that had been bitter foes for greater part of the post-independence period, trained together for the first time; moreover, they practiced to thwart what was described as a shared external security threat – a breakthrough of militant groups from the territory of Afghanistan.[25]

Uzbekistan has also improved relations with Russia, China and the United States. President Mirziyoyev's first official visit to Washington in May 2018, and his statements about a new era of strategic partnership with America,[26] generated a torrent of enthusiastic comments in the Western media. A comparative analysis of Tashkent's recent diplomatic activities, reveals that, at this stage, there might not be much substance behind this effusiveness, and that Moscow and Beijing have gained more from the political window of opportunity as economic and security partners of Uzbekistan.[27] In 2018, Tashkent resumed its participation in counterterrorism exercises with Russia and the SCO, that had been suspended in 2010 and 2012 respectively.

Apart from regional thaw and re-energised multi-vectorism, the third dimension of the context in which Uzbekistan's Afghan policy is conducted entails Mirziyoyev's restructuring of the country's security apparatus. Its central element, the National Security Service (SNB) was thoroughly purged and renamed the State Security Service (SGB), and its authority diminished. The primary reason was the president's drive to consolidate his grip on power and pave the way for domestic reforms.[28] However, the SNB's ineffectiveness in dealing with Afghanistan-related threats played its role. Its top brass, especially in the Surkhandarya border region, had been mired in corruption and formed close links with drug barons across the southern border.[29] The SNB's heavy-handed treatment of pious Muslims in the past, which resulted in their radicalisation and exodus to Afghanistan and the Middle East, where they swelled the ranks of the IMU and ISIS, contradicted Mirziyoyev's more liberal line. General Shuhrat Ghulomov, former First Deputy Head of the SNB, who used to be regarded as Uzbekistan's top specialist on international jihadi threats, was put on trial and received a life sentence, for his links to organised crime.[30] In the meantime, authorities removed 18,000 Uzbekistani citizens from extremist blacklists.

Uzbekistan is in the process of reforming its armed forces and has increased defence spending to 4 per cent of GDP, in 2018. Mirziyoyev justified the need for greater combat readiness by referring to 'the increased threats of international terrorism, extremism and radicalism around us'.[31] The president had more than seventy generals and senior officers sacked for incompetence and unprofessionalism and enjoined others to work hard on lifting the mobility and efficiency of their units for autonomous action in difficult and mountainous terrain.[32] Counter-insurgency rather than conventional warfare against the Central Asian neighbours, appears to dominate military planning in Tashkent at present.

Taking into account domestic, regional and international aspects of Mirziyoyev's course, the unfreezing of relations with Kabul, while undoubtedly a positive development, should not be overstated. Afghanistan is still viewed as a source of threat; it is not in the same category of regional countries, whose good will and cooperation must be cultivated at all costs to ensure Uzbekistan's well-being. What has changed is the perception of how this threat can be mitigated, and the rhetoric about Afghanistan providing an economic opportunity for Uzbekistan.

On the first account, just as in the case of Kazakhstan, officials and security analysts in Uzbekistan no longer regard the collapse of the central government in Afghanistan as imminent. At the same time, they have apprehensions about the current regime. A government researcher thus summarised the current situation:[33]

> One of the principal factors of enhancing the Uzbek-Afghan bilateral cooperation consists of personal relations of trust between the heads of state. However, when constructing a foreign policy line on the Afghan vector we ought to pay attention to the observable decline of the Ashraf Ghani administration's positions and its growing unpopularity among the people and main political forces of the country.

In his speech to the Tashkent Conference, Mirziyoyev stressed that a direct dialogue, without preliminary conditions, between the government in Kabul and the Taliban was the only way forward to stabilise Afghanistan and added that the start of this process can no longer be postponed.[34] He praised, in equal measure, the Kabul process, the Istanbul process, the Moscow format, the International Contact Group, the SCO–Afghanistan Contact Group and other multilateral platforms, suggesting, however, that his country might be better suited as a site for intra-Afghan dialogue, for reasons of centuries-long cultural affinity between fraternal Uzbek and Afghan peoples.

The Tashkent Conference was praised by Moscow, Washington and other stakeholders in predictable terms, as a follow-up to the efforts by the international community to promote stability in Afghanistan. In the months that followed, it turned out to be more than just another platform for peace talks. In August 2018, a Taliban delegation, led by the head of the movement's political office in Doha, Sher Mohammad Abbas Stanekzai, came to Tashkent for formal talks at the Uzbek Foreign Ministry. The official nature of the visit and the broad range of discussion which included 'the withdrawal of foreign forces and how to achieve peace in Afghanistan' as well as 'current and future national projects such as security for railroad and power lines',[35] significantly increased the stature of the Taliban, as legitimate interlocutors, increasing the likelihood of direct intra-Afghan dialogue. The visit was agreed to, at least implicitly, by Kabul, Washington and Moscow, indicating to many that Uzbekistan, which tries to stay away from geopolitical games and remain equidistant to Russia and the United States, can be an optimal platform for the talks.

Notwithstanding lofty rhetoric about the importance of trade to security, Uzbekistan's economic policy towards Afghanistan has distinct mercantilist overtones. Tashkent views the latter as an important element of the new economic strategy which envisages a move from import substitution to an export-oriented model. Using mostly Chinese investment and technology transfer, Uzbekistan is setting up a manufacturing sector which may not target mature markets, but will have a competitive advantage and consumer appeal in poor countries nearby.[36] In March 2018, Uzbek Minister of Foreign Trade voiced an intention to supply half of Afghanistan's imports in the nearest future,[37] up from a 7 per cent share in 2017. The introduction of a free trade regime between the two countries, which began to be considered in 2018, would undoubtedly help in this agenda and further skew the balance of trade in favour of Uzbekistan. Rather than committing itself to risky large-scale infrastructure projects, such as the Turkmenistan–Afghanistan–Pakistan–India pipeline (TAPI) or CASA-1000, in the name of stabilising Afghanistan through economic development, Tashkent focuses on small initiatives where external funding is guaranteed and profit can be made. The Surkhan–Pul-e Khumri power transmission project, fully funded by the Asian Development Bank (ADB), is one example.[38]

Uzbekistan's pragmatism may also be seen in its stance on new transport corridors connecting it to global markets. The much discussed extension of the Hairatan–Mazar-e Sharif railroad (built by the Uzbek railway monopoly in 2011) to Herat has been put on hold, despite political lobbying from Kabul and Washington. While calling the project 'important,' Mirziyoyev has identified the Russia–India, via Uzbekistan, and the Uzbekistan–Kyrgyzstan–China routes as higher priorities.[39] Media reports and comments from Afghan officials about Tashkent's plans to invest US$500 million to offset the costs of the US$1.8 billion railroad extension, which circulated in early 2018, were met with silence from the Uzbek side. In addition to financial and geopolitical risks, the project's future hangs on security arrangements including Uzbekistan's concerns about the counter-narcotics regime astride the railroad.[40]

In Uzbekistan, the perception of Afghanistan as a threat, competes with its newly promoted image as a land of economic opportunity. If the Tashkent process or similar initiatives do not jump-start a meaningful Afghan dialogue soon, robust securitisation of chaos and instability across the southern border will resume. The news that two Uzbek militant groups – the Imam Bukhari Brigade (IBB) and Katibat Tavwhid wal Jihad (KTJ) – had returned from Syria to Afghanistan in 2018 and were fighting not far from the Uzbek border, must have been particularly worrying for Mirziyoyev. It compelled prominent Western analysts to conclude that, 'it is likely that Uzbekistan will have to deal with Uzbek jihadists threatening its border areas in the long term'.[41]

Tajikistan

If Uzbekistan and Kazakhstan provide reasons for optimism around greater engagement between Central Asian countries and Afghanistan, the same cannot be said for Tajikistan. The current Tajik approach to their southern neighbour has been characterised by high levels of agitation and apprehension. Tajikistan's Foreign Minister Sirojiddin Aslov told the OSCE in late 2017 that while his country is 'interested in lasting peace, political stability and economic reconstruction of Afghanistan', for now the deteriorating situation was 'becoming a serious threat both to Tajikistan and the OSCE's southern borders'.[42]

In 2017 there were thirty-one combat incidents on the Tajik–Afghan border; the figure for the first half of 2018 reached seventeen.[43] While the majority of these were relatively low-key events, involving exchange of fire between small groups of contrabandists and border guards, the potential for escalation was illustrated by an airstrike carried out from Tajik territory in August 2018, against Taliban targets in the Darqad district near the border, ostensibly in retaliation to mortar fire which had killed two Tajik civilians.[44] Tajikistan's counter-narcotics officials reported a significant increase in the flow of opiates from Afghanistan: drug seizures rose by 63 per cent in the border region of Khatlon and by 89 per cent in the Gorno-Badakhshan Autonomous Oblast (GBAO) in 2017 compared to the previous year.[45] They predicted further growth of illicit trade and commented on the evolving technical and tactical sophistication of criminal groups. A 2018 UN report painted a similar picture of rising professionalism, integration and mutual trust between drug-trafficking syndicates in Tajikistan and northern Afghanistan, noting the latter's connection with the ongoing insurgency – led not so much by the Taliban as by 'a variety of local powerbrokers and warlords, many of whom have historical and long-standing connections to the drug trade'.[46]

Transborder crime is a particularly acute threat to the government of Emomali Rahmon in the GBAO. Ever since the end of the civil war in 1997, Dushanbe's control over the region has been tenuous. A steady trickle of drugs and weapons from Afghanistan's Badakhshan, has enabled local strongmen to defy central authorities, leading to armed clashes, most recently in 2014. In what can be seen as a preemptive action, Rahmon descended upon Khorog, the administrative centre of GBAO, in September 2018, removing the region's top police and state security officials and eventually the governor and threatening large-scale deployment of the regular army into the autonomous region, should basic law and order fail to be restored within a month.[47]

Tajik authorities are even more alarmed than Moscow about the threat of ISIS in Afghanistan. In April 2018 its intelligence services estimated the number of ISIS fighters who had moved from Syria to Afghanistan at 8,000 persons, while the Russian assessment at the time was 4,500.[48] ISIS claimed responsibility for a deadly attack on Western tourists in southern Tajikistan as well as a prison riot that claimed dozens of lives.[49] In addition to that, the commanding officer of the Border Guards, General Rajabali Rahmonali, spoke about 6,825 fighters concentrated at twenty-nine training bases in northern Afghanistan in the provinces of Balkh, Kunduz, Tahar and Badakhshan, stressing that 'many of these militants are originally from the countries of Central Asia'.[50] Summing up the official view of the current conditions in Afghanistan, the head of the main analytical centre under the President of Tajikistan wrote:

> The military–political situation in the Islamic Republic of Afghanistan is characterized by the growing potential of international terrorist organizations in the northern provinces of Afghanistan which share border with the Central Asian countries; the increased activity of the military units of the Taliban movement and a loss of the prospect of their political dialogue with government forces. The information we have gives us reason to forecast a further complication of the situation in the IRA and the evolution of the threat of terrorist activities spreading in the direction of Central Asia and the Russian Federation.[51]

Tajikistan received US$122 million worth of weapons from Russia in 2017, and deliveries continued throughout 2018. Russian Major General Aleksandr Kshimovsky, who oversaw the transfers stressed that they occurred gratis and with some urgency: 'The armaments and military materiel supplied will enhance the capacity of Tajikistan's armed forces to repel terrorist threat and create a reliable buffer on the Tajik–Afghan border.'[52] The Russian 201st base was reinforced and otherwise 'optimized to carry out the task of supporting [Tajik] government forces which protect the most dangerous sections of the border'.[53]

A thaw in relations with Tashkent in 2018 further reassured Dushanbe about its ability to deal with security threats from Afghanistan. At the August summit, Uzbek President Mirziyoyev declared that the 'disconsolate' situation in Afghanistan forced both Central Asian republics 'to have very deep thoughts about the security of our borders'.[54] An unprecedented bilateral military exercise that took place shortly afterwards, was attended by Defence Ministers who stated that Tajikistan and Uzbekistan were a 'bulwark' of Central Asia, shared the same operational territory and were ready 'to repel and vanquish terrorism through friendly joint effort and cooperation of military units'.[55]

The lifting of the transport and trade blockade by Uzbekistan against Tajikistan, has had an unintended effect of dampening Dushanbe's enthusiasm about possible economic ventures in Afghanistan. Excess production of Tajik electricity, cement and other products can now be shipped to Uzbekistan. When Tajikistan's ambassador in Tashkent indicated his country's reluctance to proceed with the US$2 billion Tajikistan–Afghanistan–Turkmenistan (TAT) railway project (in gestation since 2010) it was hardly a surprise: 'The TAT route only really made sense when Tajikistan and Uzbekistan were at loggerheads, but now that those two countries are enjoying something of a honeymoon, there are more obvious and direct outlets to Afghanistan and onward to the Persian Gulf available to Tajikistan.'[56] Ashgabat was not pleased with the announcement and even stopped transit of trucks from Iran to Tajikistan on its border for several weeks.

Barring major improvements in Afghanistan's stability, there seems little prospect for Tajikistan changing its defensive posture and turning the 1,400 kilometre-long border into a zone of friendly engagement and mutually beneficial economic activity.

Kyrgyzstan

The election of a new president, Sooronbay Jeenbekov, in November 2017 and a consequent change of government, has not altered Kyrgyzstan's cautious position on Afghanistan. Similarly to Tajikistan, officials in Bishkek show increased nervousness about threats from the south. The country's Security Council Secretary identified the growth of ISIS in Afghanistan as the single most important factor jeopardizing sustainable development in Central Asia, and noted Kyrgyzstan's salience, as a transit point for ISIS attacks on neighbouring republics and on Xinjiang, as supplier of fresh recruits and as a zone of jihadist insurrection in its own right.[57] The last point became a source of moral panic in 2018, when officials and security intellectuals alike started to talk about the ISIS grand strategy consisting of despatching emissaries and resources from Afghanistan to cultivate sleeping cells in Kyrgyzstan instead of striking directly and rashly.[58] A popular Bishkek tabloid commented that, 'ISIS fighters do not even need to invade Kyrgyzstan: "sleepers" – also known as the "fifth column" – will do everything themselves'.[59]

Apart from rendering generic diplomatic support to international initiatives on Afghanistan, Bishkek doesn't have either the desire or capacity to improve relations with Kabul. The upgrade of the Tashkent–Andijan–Osh–Kashgar automobile corridor and the construction of the new Uzbekistan–Kyrgyzstan–

China railway (paid for by China) could be welcome news for Afghanistan, but for the government of Kyrgyzstan both projects have inherent value regardless of whether they would link up with transport corridors in that country.[60] Bishkek doesn't seem to have much interest in bolstering bilateral economic ties or contributing to the security sector in Afghanistan. The Kyrgyz Foreign Minister mentioned only one collaborative venture during a meeting with OSCE colleagues in October 2018 – a 'regional centre on Afghanistan studies in Bishkek which may become an independent academic node for regional and international experts who work on elaborating confidence-building measures among the region's states'.[61] The timeline and sources of financing for this centre are yet to be revealed.

President Jeenbekov gave a wide-ranging interview in May 2018, in which he highlighted the need for 'intergovernment coordination' in the struggle against 'challenges and security threats from Afghanistan to the Central Asian states'.[62] Bishkek has been in talks with Russia about a new Russian military base in the country for some years now, and Jeenbekov admitted a final decision is yet to be made. He said pointedly:

> In our opinion, the situation in Afghanistan, its challenges and threats demand a collective response ... Our position on the need to open a second Russian base in the southern region of the republic aims at the formation of the collective reaction force to respond to the Afghan threats such as terrorism, extremism and drug trafficking. And also to increase the level of interaction with army units of Kyrgyzstan.

In the meantime, the 'collective response' contemplated by Bishkek, was put on display during the 'Issyk-Kul Antiterror 2018' military exercise of Kyrgyz and Russian units, modelling a situation whereby large terrorist formations crossed the Tajik–Afghan border and moved north to set up an ISIS outpost on the territory of Kyrgyzstan. Hypothetical terrorists were successfully destroyed through a joint effort of some 2,000 servicemen, 400 armoured vehicles and, for the first time, the firing of tactical ballistic missiles.[63]

Turkmenistan

In April 2018, President Gurbanguly Berdimuhammedov reiterated his state's neutrality, suggesting that Ashgabat could provide a useful forum for progressing Afghan peace talks. 'Turkmenistan as a neutral state is ready to provide political space for the conduct of national Afghan dialogue under the aegis and leadership of the United Nations,' he said.⁶⁴ Apart from this less than ground-shattering statement, the leadership of the most reclusive Central Asian republic abstained from passing value judgment on the performance and future of central government in Kabul. It sent a low-level representative to the Tashkent conference, did not take part in any military exercises in the region, and refrained from wholehearted endorsement of any new initiatives. As far as Turkmenistan's Afghan policy goes, Berdimuhammedov's attention appears to have been centred, to the point of obsession, on the long-suffering TAPI megaproject.

The official foreign policy journal of Turkmenistan argued that the international community must finance TAPI to the hilt because this 'is, in fact, a direct support to Afghanistan's desire to overcome the long-term stagnation and regress. The future of this country [Afghanistan] depends largely on the extent and scope of international involvement'.⁶⁵ In reality, TAPI is equally important to Turkmenistan. The pipeline does not need to be built at all, to bring tangible political goods to Kabul and Ashgabat. As Luca Anceschi demonstrated, TAPI is 'a pipeline for regime stability, a non-"socially constructed artefact"'⁶⁶ which generates symbolic capital for authoritarian leaders, enthuses the masses and keeps partners in existing energy schemes on their toes, through recurrent discursive practices. Berdimuhammedov's officials went into overdrive in 2018, promising that TAPI gas deliveries would start as early as 2019, despite the absence of substantial progress on many intractable issues related to the project's finances, technical challenges and especially security of the 774 kilometre-long section in Afghanistan, where no actual work had been done. Rosy prospects and pipe dreams spouted by government spokesmen, were designed to paper over a deep economic crisis unfolding in Turkmenistan, accompanied by rampant unemployment, food shortages and a budget deficit.⁶⁷ Once export prices for natural gas rise, leading to greater revenues from China, and relations with two other major customers – Russia and Iran – improve, chances are that the TAPI project will return to the normal state of somnolence, amid sheafs of press releases and meaningless memoranda of understanding.

In the meantime, reports about the rise of clandestine Islamist cells in Turkmenistan, including in the armed forces, have been multiplying. Some of these reports are difficult to verify, and Ashgabat does not comment on them at all yet the overall picture is that of growing instability. A group of seventy 'religious extremists' including twelve officers was exposed in the 22nd Motorised Rifle Division, in 2017.⁶⁸ The number of Turkmenistani citizens who have joined ISIS and the IMU, in the Afghan border provinces of Badghis and Faryab may have reached 350–400.⁶⁹ In April and May 2018, the Taliban's offensives in Faryab and Jowzjan displaced thousands of ethnic Turkmen families and exacerbated fears about cross-border security.[70] The number of armed clashes on the border grew, and Turkmenistan's security forces did not always show sufficient skill, professionalism and motivation in defence of the motherland, which may have forced Ashgabat to resort to the traditional tactic of buying off Afghan field commanders.[71]

Developments inside Turkmenistan have caused sufficient concern among its Central Asian neighbours and Russia, to step up contingency planning. One example of this was the 'Unbreakable Brotherhood' CSTO exercise in November 2018 which rehearsed 'a peacekeeping operation … in the Central Asian region on the territory of the state that is not a CSTO member'.[72] Given that in the region only Turkmenistan and Uzbekistan are non-members, and that the drill featured riot control and food distribution in addition to the routine counterterrorist operation, the focus on the former country was rather transparent.

Prospects for Regional Cooperation and the Afghan Question

Reforms and increased openness in post-Karimov's Uzbekistan have revived the political debate across Central Asia about the prospects for regional cooperation. One example of this trend was an informal summit of five states (Turkmenistan was represented by the speaker of parliament) which took place in Astana in March 2018. Nazarbaev, lamenting the fact that such a gathering was taking place after a decade-long hiatus, noted, 'There is no need to invite a third party around in order to solve issues affecting the Central Asian countries. We can deal with all issues ourselves – that's exactly why we are meeting here.'[73] Some pundits took the Kazakh president's words as an indication of a paradigm shift in dealing with the 'elephant in the room' – Russian influence in Central Asia – and the 'skeleton in the closet' – the situation in Afghanistan.[74]

Such perceptions are misleading, and any talk about 'anchoring Afghanistan in Central Asia's emerging cooperative structures,'[75] seems premature. The summit was convoked on the initiative of Mirziyoyev, as part of his drive to normalise relations with Uzbekistan's neighbours. Normalisation does not necessarily lead to cooperation, especially in its formal and structured variant. Mirziyoyev spoke in general terms about improving business climate in the region, but said nothing about further development of the meeting's format; Tashkent's cautious attitude to any kind of multilateral mechanisms of cooperation continued. Nazarbaev also made it very clear that the resumption of high-level consultative meetings would not lead to any kind of institutionalisation, even at the most basic level: 'We are not going to create any [permanent] organ or secretariat.'[76]

Nazarbaev, speaking on behalf of all participants, emphasised that, 'we all have two big partners and neighbours – Russia and China. We will always work together with them, and all our agreements with them will remain in force.'[77] The regional consultative agenda at the moment does not include external relations; its items are rather parochial and quotidian, for example, maintenance of irrigation systems, seasonal agricultural labour migration and management of border crossings. Many of these problems are a product of decades of confrontation and directly affect the lives of thousands of people on the ground but are of little significance to external players. 'Talk to politicians in Moscow about how peasants on different sides of the border are trying to resolve problems of horticulture and animal husbandry – they'll yawn', quipped a political commentator from Kazakhstan, and added, 'As to Washington and Beijing, these matters may excite only ethno-cultural curiosity there.'[78]

It is unrealistic to expect that the Central Asian republics will be able to elaborate a consensual, comprehensive and implementable strategy vis-à-vis Afghanistan in the near future that would depart from the defensive posturing of 2014. When asked to identify reasons for optimism and pessimism about the prospects of regional cooperation in Central Asia, local security intellectuals put 'objective historical patterns' at the top of the former category, and 'the Afghanistan factor' – at the top of the latter.[79] Naturally, if the current thaw continues and a sustainable level of mutual trust is established, the Afghan issue just may be extracted from the too-hard basket and put on the table for a coordinated and autonomous response by the five countries. Potentially this may result in a reprise of the Greater Central Asia project favoured by the United Stated. It's also possible, however, that the amelioration of internal tensions in Central Asia will enhance what Roy Allison called 'protective integration' of the region under the aegis of the CSTO and the SCO, whose reputation as security providers had suffered because of intra-state crises since 2000.[80] A group of scholars from Kazakhstan came to a similar conclusion independently, predicting a further strengthening of the positions of Russia and China in the region in the external security sector.[81]

Conclusion

During almost two decades of turmoil in Afghanistan after 11 September, there have been several false dawns for improved Central Asia–Afghanistan relations.

The year 2018 witnessed significant developments which, if nurtured and sustained, can turn Afghanistan's northern neighbours into important actors in fostering peace and stability in the country.

All five republics now have greater knowledge of the political processes in Afghanistan and challenges and opportunities it provides. They are more confident about dealing directly with the government in Kabul on operational security matters, than was the case five years ago. Uzbekistan in particular has shown the will and capacity to bolster trade links with Afghanistan.

Kazakhstan and Uzbekistan have emerged as the greatest champions of a negotiated settlement of the Afghan conflict, which is congruent with their national interests. They have managed to position themselves as honest brokers who are not involved in the geopolitical proxy wars and at the same time are acceptable to great powers as mediators.

It is precisely this neutral position that should be cherished and preserved. Cajoling Central Asian countries into pan-regional stabilization schemes, sponsored by the West, would be counterproductive. Clumsy attempts by Washington and its allies to lump them together with Afghanistan into an artificial geographic whole, failed in the past. Tomohiko Uyama has argued persuasively that if the United States stops treating Central Asia as a mere adjunct to Afghanistan and a field for rivalry with Russia and China, and starts attaching 'special importance and respect to them' in their own right,[82] the results could be rewarding. Additionally, if Astana and Tashkent were encouraged to continue with pragmatic diplomacy and small practical steps to improve the lives of Afghans, rather than participate in risky, geopolitically oriented projects, this would be more conducive to incremental peace in Afghanistan.

Notes

1 'Building Regional Partnerships in Afghanistan and Central Asia', *United Nations Regional Centre for Preventive Diplomacy for Central Asia*, 20 January 2018, https://unrcca.unmissions.org/building-regional-partnerships-afghanistan-and-central-asia.
2 T.T. Shaimergenov and M.A. Abisheva, *Tsentralnaia Aziia 2027: meniaiushchiisia strategicheskii landshaft* (Astana: Izdatelstvo biblioteki Pervogo Prezidenta RK–Elbasy, 2017), p. 8.
3 Ed Hadley and Christopher D. Kolenda, 'Political Process in Afghanistan. What Role for International Partners?" in *Incremental Peace in Afghanistan*, ed. Anna Larson and Alexander Ramsbotham (London: Conciliation Resources, 2018), pp. 85–90.

4 Syed Zabiullah Langari, 'Ghani Discusses Terrorism with Uzbek and Kazakh COAS', *Tolo News*, 12 February 2018, https://www.tolonews.com/afghanistan/ghani-discusses-terrorism-uzbek-and-kazakh-coas.
5 'Vizit glavy GKNB Tadzhikistana Ggenerala Yatimova v Kabul', *Akhbor*, 10 May 2018, http://akhbor-rus.com/-p681-118.htm.
6 Farkhod Tolipov, 'The Tashkent Conference on Afghanistan: Too Much Diplomacy, Too Little Solution', *The Central Asia–Caucasus Analyst*, 29 May 2018, https://www.cacianalyst.org/publications/analytical-articles/item/13521-the-tashkent-conference-on-afghanistan-too-much-diplomacy-too-little-solution.html.
7 Tadamichi Yamamoto, 'Statement to the Tashkent Conference on Afghanistan by the Secretary-General's Special Representative for Afghanistan', UNAMA, 27 March 2018, https://unama.unmissions.org/un-envoy-yamamoto-tashkent-conference-afghanistan.
8 Reuel R. Hanks, '"Multi-Vector Politics" and Kazakhstan's Emerging Role as a Geo-Strategic Player in Central Asia', *Journal of Balkan and Near Eastern Studies* 11:3 (2009): p. 260.
9 Arman Kaliyev, 'Opening of Caspian Ports Highlights Strengthening Relations between US, Kazakhstan', *Caravanserai*, 29 March 2018 http://central.asia-news.com/en_GB/articles/cnmi_ca/features/2018/03/29/feature-01.
10 Tamara Stepanova and Salamat Bekbaev, 'K 2020 godu na kazakhstansko-turkmenskoi granitse vozvedut 160 km zabora', *24.kz*, 11 May 2018, http://24.kz/ru/news/social/item/239343-k-2020-godu-na-kazakhstansko-turkmenskoj-granitse-vozvedut-160-km-zabora.
11 'Strany ODKB usiliat bor'bu s mezhdunarodnym terrorizmom i ekstremizmom', *InfoShOS*, 21 September 2018, http://infoshos.ru/ru/?idn=19366.
12 Nursultan Nazarbaev, *Era nezavisimosti* (Astana: LEM, 2017).
13 Kairat Umarov, 'Kazakhstan's Presidency of the United Nations Security Council: A Success of Global Diplomacy by the Leader of the Nation', Republic of Kazakhstan, Ministry of Foreign Affairs, 12 April 2018, http://mfa.gov.kz/en/content-view/stata-kajrata-umarova-predsedatelstvo-kazahstana-v-sovete-bezopasnosti-oon-uspeh-globalnoj-diplomatii-elbasy.
14 Edward Schatz, 'Access by Accident: Legitimacy Claims and Democracy Promotion in Authoritarian Central Asia', *International Political Science Review* 27, 3 (2006): p. 270.
15 'Kazakhstan's Contribution to Resolving the Conflict in Syria', Republic of Kazakhstan, Ministry of Foreign Affairs, 1 March 2017, http://mfa.gov.kz/en/zagreb/content-view/vklad-kazahstana-v-uregulirovanie-sirijskogo-krizisa.
16 'Kazakhstan predlozhil Sovbezu OON priniat' kodeks Nazarbaeva', *Kursiv*, 24 August 2018, https://kursiv.kz/news/politika/2018-08/kazakhstan-predlozhil-sovbezu-oon-prinyat-kodeks-nazarbaeva.

17 Kairat Abdrakhmanov, 'Afganistan dolzhen byt' integrirovan v ekonomicheskie sviazi v TsA', *Kursiv*, 5 September 2018, https://kursiv.kz/news/politika/2018-09/kayrat-abdrakhmanov-afganistan-dolzhen-byt-integrirovan-v-ekonomicheskie.
18 Zhanna Akhmetova, 'Kazakhstan's Assistance to Afghanistan Helps Strengthen Regional and Global Security, Diplomat says', *The Astana Times*, 25 September 2018, https://astanatimes.com/2018/09/kazakhstans-assistance-to-afghanistan-helps-strengthen-regional-and-global-security-diplomat-says/.
19 'Astana Declaration on Empowering Women in Afghanistan', Republic of Kazakhstan, Ministry of Foreign Affairs, 5 September 2009, http://mfa.gov.kz/en/content-view/astaninskaa-deklaracia-o-rassirenii-prav-i-vozmoznostej-zensin-v-afganistane.
20 *Vneshniaia torgovlia Respubliki Kazakhstan, 2013-2017*. Astana: Kazstat, 2018, pp. 8, 11, 98.
21 Andrei Korolev, 'Eksportnyi potentsial Kazakhstana rastet', *Liter*, 25 July 2018, https://liter.kz/ru/articles/show/49012-eksportnyi_potencial_kazahstana_rastet.
22 'Oboronnaia doktrina Respubliki Uzbekistan', Law of the Republic of Uzbekistan No. ZRU-458, 9 January 2018, http://www.lex.uz/docs/3495906.
23 E. Aripov, 'Uzbeksko-afganskie otnosheniia: novyi etap dinamichnogo razvitiia', *Xalqaro munosibatlar* 1, 71 (2018): p. 22.
24 Shavkat Mirziyoyev, 'Vystuplenie premier-ministra na zasedanii palat parlamenta', *Gazeta.uz*, 9 September 2016, https://www.gazeta.uz/ru/2016/09/09/speech/.
25 'Pogranichniki Tadzhikistana i Uzbekistana proveli pervye sovmestnye voennye ucheniia', *Fergana News Agency*, 17 August 2018, http://www.ferganaews.com/news/32081.
26 'The United States and Uzbekistan: Launching a New Era of Strategic Partnership', The White House, 16 May 2018, https://www.whitehouse.gov/briefings-statements/united-states-uzbekistan-launching-new-era-strategic-partnership/.
27 Mariusz Marszewski. 'Thaw in Uzbekistan. Reforms by President Mirziyoyev', (report, OSW Commentary 276, Centre for Eastern Studies, Warsaw, 2018), pp. 7–8.
28 Timur Toktonaliev and Turonbek Kozokov, 'Uzbek President Reins in Security Service', *IWPR*, 4 April 2018, https://iwpr.net/global-voices/uzbek-president-reins-security-service.
29 Rafael Sattarov, 'Vidimost' liustratsii: zachem vlasti Uzbekistana nachali massovye chistki silovikov', *Moscow Carnegie Centre*, 28 September 2018, https://carnegie.ru/commentary/77365.
30 Artur Priimak, 'Muftiiatu Uzbekistana otrezali "ushi" spetssluzhb', *Nezavisimaia Gazeta*, 7 March 2018, http://www.ng.ru/ng_religii/2018-03-07/12_438_uzbekistan.html.
31 Shavkat Mirziyoyev, 'Kazhdyi komandir obiazan umet' operativno prinimat' samostoiatel'nye resheniia', *Uz24*, 11 January 2018, http://uz24.uz/ru/politics/shavkat-

mirziyoev:-kazhdiy-komandir-obyazan-umety-operativno-prinimaty-samostoyatelynie-resheniya.
32 Oleg Stolpovskii, 'Kak uzbekskaia armiia stala silneishei v Tsentralnoi Azii', *Ritm Evrazii*, 20 May 2018, https://www.ritmeurasia.org/news--2018-05-20--kak-uzbekskaja-armija-stala-silnejshej-v-centralnoj-azii-ii-36538.
33 A. Umarov, 'Initsiativy Respubliki Uzbekistan v afganskom napravlenii: potentsialnye vozmozhnosti i riski', *Xalqaro munosibatlar* 1, 71 (2018): p. 38.
34 Shavkat Mirziyoyev, 'Address by the President of the Republic of Uzbekistan at the International Conference on Afghanistan "Peace Process, Security Cooperation and Regional Connectivity"', *Uzbekistan National News Agency*, 27 March 2018, http://uza.uz/en/politics/address-by-the-president-of-the-republic-of-uzbekistan-shavk-27-03-2018.
35 Timur Dadabaev, 'Uzbekistan as Central Asian Game Changer? Uzbekistan's Foreign Policy Construction in the Post-Karimov Era', *Asian Journal of Comparative Politics* 4, 2 (2018): p. 171.
36 Timur Dadabaev, 'Uzbekistan as Central Asian Game Changer? Uzbekistan's Foreign Policy Construction in the Post-Karimov Era', *Asian Journal of Comparative Politics* (2018) DOI: 10.1177/2057891118775289, p. 10.
37 Zhamshid Khodzhaev, 'Tovary is Uzbekistana mogut pokryt' polovinu importa Afganistana', *Narodnoe Slovo*, 24 March 2018, http://xs.uz/ru/post/import_from_uzb.
38 Mir Haidarshah Omid, 'ADB Pledges $70m to Fund Surkhan-Pul-e-Khumri Power Line', *Tolo News*, 17 February 2018, https://www.tolonews.com/business/adb-pledges-70m-fund-surkhan-pul-e-khumri-power-line.
39 Shavkat Mirziyoyev, 'Privetstvie Prezidenta Uzbekistana uchastnikam mezhdunarodnoi konferentsii 'Tsentralnaia Aziia v sisteme mezhdunarodnykh transportnykh korridorov: strategicheskie perspektivy I nerealizovannye vozmozhnosti', Republic of Uzbekistan, Ministry of Foreign Affairs, 20 September 2018, http://m.mfa.uz/ru/press/news/2018/09/16115/.
40 Semen Kukol, 'Opyt Uzbekistana po bor'be s narkougrozoi v Tsentralnoi Azii', *Problemy natsionalnoi strategii* 1, 46 (2018): pp. 103–104.
41 Svante E. Cornell and Jacob Zenn, *Religion and the Secular State in Uzbekistan* (Washington, DC: Central Asia–Caucasus Institute, 2018), p. 40.
42 Quoted in 'MID Tadzhikistana obespokoen aktivnost'iu afganskikh terroristov u svoikh rubezhei', *TAG News*, 8 December 2018, https://tajikta.tj/ru/news/mid-tadzhikistana-obespokoen-aktivnostyu-afganskikh-terroristov-u-svoikh-rubezhey.
43 Avaz Yuldashev, 'Za polgoda na tadzhiksko-afganskoi granitse proizoshli 17 boestolknovenii', *Asia-Plus*, 24 July 2018, https://news.tj/ru/news/tajikistan/security/20180724/za-polgoda-na-tadzhiksko-afganskoi-granitse-proizoshli-17-boestolknovenii.

44 'Air Strike On Tajik–Afghan Border Kills Eight Militants', *RFE/RL*, 27 August 2018, https://www.rferl.org/a/afghan-officials-tajik-or-russian-plane-bombs-afghan-border-area/29455399.html.
45 F.R. Rahimzoda and H.D. Muhammadzoda, 'Kriminologicheskaia kharakteristika narkoprestupnosti v Respublike Tadzhikistan: struktura, dinamika i prognoz', *Narkofront* 1 (2018): p. 21.
46 'Afghan Opiate Trafficking along the Northern Route', (report, United Nations Office on Drugs and Crime, Vienna, 2018), p. 119.
47 Takhmina Okhonvalieva, 'V GBAO smenilsia glava oblasti', *Asia-Plus*, 1 October 2018, https://news.tj/ru/news/tajikistan/20181001/v-gbao-smenilsya-glava-oblasti.
48 'Tadzhikskie spetssluzhby soobshchaiut o massovom peremeshchenii siriiskikh boevikov v Afganistan', *Afghanistan.ru*, 5 April 2018, http://afghanistan.ru/doc/119817.html.
49 'Tajikistan Inches Toward Making Capital from Prison Massacre', *Eurasianet*, 19 November 2018, https://eurasianet.org/tajikistan-inches-toward-making-capital-from-prison-massacre.
50 Khudoberdi Kholiqnazar, 'Afganistan-2018: novye vyzovy i ugrozy dlia stran Tsentralnoi Azii', *Tojikiston va jahoni imruz* 2, 61 (2018): p. 13..
51 Khudoberdi Kholiqnazar, 'Afganistan-2018: novye vyzovy i ugrozy dlia stran Tsentralnoi Azii', *Tojikiston va jahoni imruz* 2, 61 (2018): p. 13.
52 Quoted in 'Rossiia peredala Tadzhikistanu partiiu voennogo oborudovaniia', *TASS*, 19 December 2017, https://tass.ru/armiya-i-opk/4823384.
53 Aleksandr Sternik, 'Rossiia usilila voennye bazy v Srednei Azii', *RIA Novosti*, 7 February 2018, https://ria.ru/interview/20180207/1514082705.html.
54 Quoted in 'Uzbekistan i Tadzhikistan postroiat dve GES na reke Zarafshan', *Gazeta.uz*, 17 August 2018, https://www.gazeta.uz/ru/2018/08/17/agreement/.
55 'Uzbekistan i Tadzhikistan – forpost Tsentralnoi Azii', *Narodnoe slovo*, 26 September 2018, http://xs.uz/ru/post/vmeste-sila.
56 'Tajikistan: Trucks resume Turkmenistan transit', *Eurasianet*, 4 October 2018, https://eurasianet.org/tajikistan-trucks-resume-turkmenistan-transit.
57 Mehrinisa Sulaimanova, 'IGIL otkryto zaiavliaet o namerenii napast' na Tsentralnuiu Aziiu', *Kabar*, 19 June 2018, http://www.kabar.kg/news/igil-otkryto-zaiavliaet-o-namerenii-napast-na-tcentral-nuiu-aziiu-sekretar-sovbeza-kr/.
58 Anna Matveeva, 'Radicalisation and Violent Extremism in Kyrgyzstan', *The RUSI Journal* 163, 1 (2018): pp. 40–41.
59 Dmitrii Orlov, 'Tsel' etoi voiny – ne pobeda, a sama . . . voina', *Delo No*, 23 May 2018, https://delo.kg/tsel-etoj-vojny-ne-pobeda-a-sama-vojna/.
60 'Tashkent–Andijan–Osh–Irkeshtam–Kashgar route will kick off on Feb. 25', *Kabar*, 19 February 2018, http://kabar.kg/eng/news/first-highway-convoy-route-of-tashkent-andijan-osh-irkeshtam-kashgar-will-kick-off-on-feb.25/.

61 Erlan Abdyldaev quoted in 'Kirgiziia obespokoena rasprostraneniem ideologii IGIL v regione – MID', *Interfax*, 4 October 2018, http://interfax.az/view/745481.

62 Quoted in Vadim Neshkumai, 'Prezident Kirgizii: sotrudnichestvo s Rossiei imeet osobuiu znachimost', *TASS*, 14 May 2018, http://tass.ru/opinions/interviews/5195365.

63 'Kul-Antiterror-2018"Issyk-Kul-Antiterror-2018"', *General Staff of the Armed Forces of the Kyrgyz Republic*, 26 September 2018, http://www.genstaff.gov.kg/ru/русский-антитеррористическое-учени/#more-4078.

64 Quoted in 'Turkmenistan mozhet stat' mestom provedeniia obshchenatsionalnogo afganskogo dialoga pod egidoi OON', *Turkmenistan segodnia*, 23 April 2018, http://tdh.gov.tm/news/articles.aspxarticle12468&cat11.

65 Serdar Durdyev, 'Afghanistan: Questions and Answers', *Turkmenistan* 1–2, 154–155 (2018): p. 37.

66 Luca Anceschi, 'Turkmenistan and the Virtual Politics of Eurasian Energy: the Case of the TAPI Pipeline Project', *Central Asian Survey* 36, 4 (2017): p. 422.

67 Viktoria Panfilova, 'V RF mogut poiavitsia novye migranty – iz Turkmenii', *Nezavisimaia gazeta*, 13 April 2018, http://www.ng.ru/cis/2018-04-13/1_7211_turkmenia.html.

68 Nikita Mendkovich, 'Turkmenia pod udarom. Proizoidet li v strane ekstremistskaia revoliutsiia?' *Regnum*, 21 June 2018, https://regnum.ru/news/2434765.html.

69 'Turkmenistan: s gazom, no bez edy', *Rezonans.kz*, 28 June 2018, https://rezonans.kz/mir/6626-turkmenistan-s-gazom-no-bez-edy.

70 'Tysiachi etnicheskikh turkmen iz-za boevykh deistvii pokinuli svoi sela na granitse s Turkmenistanom', *Radio Azatlyk*, 18 May 2018, https://rus.azathabar.com/a/29232625.html.

71 Vitalii Volkov, 'Turkmenskaia armiia: na pod'eme ili v upadke?' *Deutsche Welle*, 2 June 2018, https://p.dw.com/p/2yhoj.

72 'Sovmestnoe uchenie s Mirotvorcheskimi silami ODKB', *CSTO Official Portal*, 2 November 2018, http://www.odkb-csto.org/news/detail.php?ELEMENT_ID=13996&SECTION_ID=91.

73 Nursultan Nazarbaev, 'Ot chistogo serdtsa prinimaem vas zdes', *Tengri News*, 15 March 2018, https://tengrinews.kz/kazakhstan_news/ot-chistogo-serdtsa-prinimaem-vas-zdes-nazarbaev-jeenbekovu-339948/.

74 Georgi Gotev, 'Astana Hosts Little-Publicised Central Asia Summit', *EURACTIV.com*, 16 March 2018, https://www.euractiv.com/section/central-asia/news/fri-astana-hosts-little-publicised-central-asia-summit/.

75 S. Frederick Starr and Svante E. Cornell, 'Modernization and Regional Cooperation in Central Asia: A New Spring?' (Report, Central Asia–Caucasus Institute & Silk Road Studies Program, Washington D.C., 2018), p. 63.

76 Nazarbaev quoted in 'Prezident Kazakhstana podvel itogi sammita glav gosudarstv Tsentralnoi Azii', *News.tj*, 15 March 2018, https://news.tj/ru/news/tajikistan/

politics/20180315/prezident-kazahstana-podvel-itogi-sammita-glav-gosudarstv-tsentralnoi-azii.

77 Nursultan Nazarbaev quoted in 'Prezident RK ob otnosheniiakh s Tashkentom', *Kapital.kz*, 15 March 2018, https://kapital.kz/gosudarstvo/67639/prezident-rk-ob-otnosheniyah-s-tashkentom-nastroenie-izmenilos.html.

78 Shaimergenov and Abisheva. *Tsentralnaia Aziia 2027*, p. 55..

79 Roy Allison, 'Protective Integration and Security Policy Coordination: Comparing the SCO and CSTO', *The Chinese Journal of International Politics* 11, 3, (2018): pp. 297–338.

80 Allison, 'Protective Integration and Security Policy Coordination', pp. 297–338.

81 B. Zh Somzhurek, A.M. Yessengaliyeva, Zh.M. Medeubayeva and B.K. Makangali, 'Central Asia and Regional Security', *Communist and Post-Communist Studies* 51, 2 (2018): pp. 161–171.

82 Tomohiko Uyama, 'Sino-Russian Coordination in Central Asia and Implications for U.S. and Japanese Policies', *Asia Policy* 13, 1 (2018): p. 30.

Conclusion

Since the US-led military intervention in October 2001, Afghanistan has made little progress towards becoming a stable and secure state. Today, the insurgency in the country progresses at an all-time high. The Afghan government remains weak and internally divided, and the insurgents, led by the Taliban – coupled, since 2016, with the rival Islamic State's Khorasan branch (ISIS-K) – have grown increasingly robust. The investment of the United States and its allies in blood and money, and the Afghan people's civilian and military casualties, as well as property losses, provide little confidence about Afghanistan's future. 'While American and NATO politicians, military strategists, academics and the Western press engage in post-conflict heart-searching about what went wrong with the Afghanistan "experiment" and whether it was worth the cost in cash and lives', observed Jonathan Lee, 'it is Afghans who have to face the consequences of a foreign intervention poorly conceived and badly executed. For Afghans and Afghanistan, Enduring Freedom remains a very distant dream.'[1]

US-led peacemaking efforts since September 2018 have not produced any tangible results as yet. Afghanistan remains in a state of limbo, despite the fact that a certain amount of infrastructural development, improvements in media freedoms and empowerment of minorities have bestowed a veneer of change on the country. In May 2019, Brigadier Ed Butler, who commanded the first UK troops on the ground in southern Afghanistan, spoke wistfully about 'the glimmers of a better life' promised by the international community which could be snuffed out with ease.[2]

Afghanistan's neighbours, the Central Asian republics, have felt an acute sense of security discomfort, in respect of possible 'spill-over'. They perceive a threat posed by the reassertion of radical Islamism in Afghanistan and from the outflow of drugs, given Afghanistan's notorious reputation as the largest producer of narcotics in the world.[3] Meanwhile, policy choices in addressing Central Asian concerns in relation to the Afghan situation are influenced and limited by a number of complex factors; most importantly Russia's determination to be an assertive power in its former Soviet Central Asian republics in order to secure its southern flank, along with the emerging Russo–American competition for geopolitical influence and China's attempt to carve out a role for itself in pursuit of its security and economic interests in the region. The republics are also cognisant of the critical role played in Afghanistan by the country's other two neighbours – Pakistan and the Islamic Republic of Iran – and their respective regional rivals, India and Saudi Arabia, as well as the Russo–Iranian de facto alliance, the Chinese–Pakistani and Pakistani–Saudi partnerships, and American–Iranian hostilities. All these variables have cumulatively contributed to the formation of a complex zone of menacing indeterminacy, leaving the Central Asian republics with no easy choices in dealing with the 'Afghan threat' in its various manifestations.

Constructing the Afghan Threat and Policy Responses in Central Asia

All of Afghanistan's northern neighbours have securitised its dire situation using six basic discourses of danger: the spread of Islamic militancy; narcotics trafficking; fighting spillover; refugee flows; and the potential for manipulation by superpowers. The intensity of specific articulations of threat and their reflection in the actual policy outcomes has oscillated among the five countries depending on the variables of physical proximity/border configuration and regime type and capacity. Afghanistan's role as a recruitment depot, safe haven and propaganda site for local militants is the universal trope that is shared across the region. Presently even in the relatively remote and secular Kazakhstan authorities speak about 20,000 followers of 'destructive religious ideologies' who might be susceptible to the call of jihad spruiked by those who started to leave for Afghanistan back in 2008.[4] In May 2019, the Pentagon's assessment of the strength of ISIS-K in Afghanistan (where Central Asians are widely represented) quintupled compared to 2018 reaching 5,000 fighters. Curiously, this figure converged with the Russian estimates which theretofore were regarded in the West as vastly exaggerated.[5] ISIS-K claimed responsibility for an attack on a Tajik military post on the border with Uzbekistan in November 2019. While details of the incident remain murky, twenty jihadis based in Kunduz apparently travelled more than 100 kilometres across the border without being detected.[6] This revived uneasy memories of the 1999 and 2000 IMU incursions in the Central Asian media and public imagination.

Drug trafficking from Afghanistan is an undeniable security problem for all Central Asian republics. Yet, it stays muted in the official discourse of Turkmenistan and Uzbekistan where opiate transit has been a taboo subject for many years. Seizures of heroin increased in Tajikistan and Uzbekistan in 2018; the latter also continues to lead the region in terms of narco-related crimes (4,779 vs 2,457 in Kazakhstan, 1,424 in Kyrgyzstan, and 812 in Tajikistan; no statistics is available for Turkmenistan).[7] The perception that a narco-mafia is becoming the number one threat to regime stability is widely shared by local security intellectuals.[8]

The frontline states – Tajikistan, Uzbekistan and Turkmenistan – are expected to securitise the spillover of fighting from the Afghan soil robustly; yet this is the case only for Tajikistan. The Uzbek–Afghan border is short and heavily fortified while the reclusive regime in Ashgabat chooses to maintain silence over numerous clashes on the border.

Despite the presence of consanguinal ethnic communities in Afghanistan, ethnofidelity does not play a big role in securitising acts by the Central Asian republics. The only and partial exception is Tajikistan where due to a peculiar official mythology of nation-building pan-Aryan solidarity has some traction among members of the intelligentsia who resent the spectre of Pushtun ethnocracy should the Taliban come back to power in Afghanistan. This doesn't mean that the government or the people of Tajikistan are prepared to defend Tajik brethren south of the border through all means possible. However, the precarious situation of Afghan Tajiks is often used to bolster domestic legitimacy of President Emomali Rahmon. As a government-friendly journalist and singer put it, 'every Tajik [from Tajikistan] should visit Afghanistan at least once in order to appreciate fully what our President [Rahmon] has achieved by way of providing peace, security and comfortable life for us'.[9]

Only Kyrgyzstan and Tajikistan securitise Afghanistan as a zone of geopolitical competition into which they can be drawn against their will. As the weakest countries in the region, they lack the capacity to pursue a genuinely multi-vector foreign policy and have to defer to the Russian (and increasingly Chinese) framing of Afghanistan's international context, including the rationale for the continuing presence of US and NATO forces there. Kazakhstan, Uzbekistan and Turkmenistan are much more confident engaging with the big players on their own terms and formulating policies that reflect their idiosyncratic national interests.

At the highest level of generalisation, all policies based on the securitisation of Afghanistan in Central Asia seek to achieve one paramount objective: enhance statehood in the former Soviet republics. The local governments have been involved in a baffling array of bilateral, regional and international efforts ostensibly aiming at stabilizing their southern neighbour. The number of summits, ministerials, expert meetings and public fora where they raise concerns and offer solutions is astounding, and so is the alphabet soup of schemes where they participate: HoA, RECCA, CAREC, RATS and AKT to name but a few. It doesn't matter that the vast majority of these initiatives has resulted in little or no improvement of the situation on the ground. In pursuing these initiatives, the Central Asian leaders obtain global recognition as legitimate and relevant actors in resolving the Afghanistan conflict. Kazakhstan's rotating membership in the United Nations Security Council in 2017–2018 was particularly illustrative of this goal. While no breakthrough on Afghanistan was accomplished then, President Nursultan Nazarbaev received a lot of kudos as a global statesman setting the agenda and caused the UN Secretary-General to comment that 'the entire international community has a stake in peace, stability and development in Afghanistan, and the countries of Central Asia have a particularly important role to play'.[10] Taking stock of grandiloquent rhetoric, feverish diplomatic initiatives and tokenistic aid, Kristin Fjæstad and Heidi Kjærnet convincingly argued that 'the case of Central Asian performance and Afghanistan indicates that processes and participation have always been valuable in themselves for states, regardless of the actual results or functions'.[11]

The Central Asian policy response to security threats from Afghanistan can be divided into three broad categories: economic, military and expediting intra-Afghan dialogue. On the economic front, their verbal commitment to the principle of 'peace through economic development' notwithstanding, the republics have proved stingy in providing aid to the government and people of Afghanistan. Kazakhstan has made a one-off contribution of US$50 million to Afghanistan's reconstruction which is by no means commensurate with its capacity as a moderately affluent country. Others have confined themselves to symbolic gestures such as building a school or a clinic, offering a few scholarships, or donating vehicles. Central Asian investment in Afghanistan is virtually non-existent. The republics have proved useful in the running of the Northern Distribution Network (NDN) providing vital supplies to US and Afghan security forces. They continue to lobby external donors for infrastructure projects connecting Central Asia and Afghanistan but the enthusiasm of the early 2000s has distinctly waned. Regional leaders are not in a hurry to commit their own money to erecting the joint economic space of prosperity. A case in point is the Turkmenistan–Afghanistan–Pakistan–India pipeline (TAPI). Turkmenistan's state monopoly Turkmengaz assumed the leadership of the pipeline consortium in 2015, reported the completion of the pipeline section on its territory in 2018, and announced that gas deliveries through Afghanistan would commence in 2020. In late 2019 it transpired that not much work had actually been done on Turkmen soil and the project continued to exist in virtual reality. The new Energy Strategy adopted by the Central Asia Regional Economic Cooperation Program (CAREC) in November 2019, envisages that by 2030 'ongoing negotiations for possible modalities to realise the TAPI gas pipeline shall be accelerated' where 'dialogue on the implementation of TAPI project intensified' is the sole criterion of success.[12] Translated from the turgid bureaucratic language this probably means 'forget about it'. Kazakhstan, Turkmenistan and Uzbekistan have emerged as important trading partners of Afghanistan but the balance of trade is extremely skewed against the latter which implies that if the United States and other donors scale down assistance to Kabul it won't be able to import food and energy from Central Asia at inflated prices.

'The Afghan Conundrum: Everyone Wants Peace but Is Preparing for War' is a snappy headline from a June 2019 Kazakhstani publication which sums up the attitude of the Central Asian leaders towards Afghanistan.[13] Since 2014, all countries in the region have invested heavily in bolstering the capacity of their military and security apparata to deal with the Afghan threat. Turkmenistan and Uzbekistan have done so largely under their own steam and using multiple formats of international cooperation and procurement sources, while the remaining three republics have prioritised collaboration under the aegis of the Collective Security Treaty Organization (CSTO). Large-scale rearmament, enhanced border protection, counterterrorism and counter-insurgency training, intelligence sharing and increased Russian military presence at the 201st and 999th bases are some of the hallmarks of the process. Nonetheless, there is still apprehension that such measures may not be sufficient. Three weeks before the 2019 ISIS-K incursion into Tajikistan the country's deputy commander of border guards testified before the lower house of the parliament and said: 'As a result of clashes between the Taliban and government forces of Afghanistan in territories adjacent to our land a lengthy stretch of the border with Tajikistan became unprotected.'[14] He also predicted a growth in the activity of jihadist cells in Tajikistan and 'an increased likelihood of border violation on the part of criminal, terrorist and extremist groups as well as armed smugglers'. The tense situation on the Tajik–Afghan border was one of the reasons for China's decision to increase military assistance to Dushanbe and set up a small border guard post in the Badakhshan region of Tajikistan in 2018.

The Central Asian republics are unique among Afghanistan's neighbours in that they don't operate proxy factions in the war-torn country, largely abstain from interfering in its domestic affairs and maintain cordial, if not particularly deep, relations with the sitting government in Kabul. Since 2014, all of them bar Tajikistan have offered themselves as mediators in the intra-Afgfhan peace dialogue. All of them including Tajikistan have also established and maintained low-level contacts with the Taliban, primarily for the pragmatic reason of helping the latter fight ISIS-K and other Islaimst groups that are considered a greater threat to their national security. Uzbekistan has progressed further than its Central Asian neighbours in desecuritisng the Taliban whose first official delegation was invited to Tashkent in 2018. In August 2019, a visit by the co-founder of the group Mullah Abdul Ghani Baradar drew criticism from the Afghan Foreign Ministry which refused to accept it as 'facilitating peace talks' and called on Uzbekistan 'to respect the leadership and ownership of the people and government of the Islamic Republic of Afghanistan in the Peace Process'.[15]

Lack of policy coordination is a prominent feature of the Central Asian republics' stance on Afghanistan. There is no such thing as a consolidated regional response to the crises south of the common border. On rare occasions when the five countries can agree on collective action this is done through the good offices of an external broker within formats such as the Shanghai Cooperation Organization (SCO) or C5 + 1. The 2016 power transit in Uzbekistan and subsequent reforms of President Mirziyoyev have lessened intra-regional tensions but it is still a long way before a critical mass of trust and the realisation of mutual interests is attained so as to enable Central Asia to speak in a single voice on the issue of Afghanistan. The Second Consultative Meeting of Central Asian leaders in November 2019 did not produce much beyond ritual platitudes to the effect that 'only the Afghan people should decide the fate of their country' and 'our neighbour has economic potential'; a renewed suggestion by Mirziyoyev to invite Afghanistan future annual gatherings as an observer was not met with enthusiasm.[16]

Great Powers and Political Settlement in Afghanistan

The formulation of Afghan policies by the Central Asian governments does not occur in a vacuum, of course. As Bruce Pannier put it, 'there are outside governments that are ready to offer, or force, their help to keep Afghanistan's problems inside Afghanistan'.[17] Pannier's quip refers to Russia and China who would prefer Central Asia to adopt an isolationist stance and act as a cordon sanitaire of sorts. The same logic can be stretched to the United States which, for the better part of the past two decades, has tried to merge Central Asia and Afghanistan into an awkward whole. Such pressures don't sit comfortably with the Central Asian republics' desire to see a stable and secure Afghanistan – as neither a menacing 'other' nor an intimate friend, but a regular neighbour with whom they can do business.

As the protracted Afghan conflict has so far defied any military solution, the need for a political settlement has increasingly become paramount, not only for the warring Afghan groups but also for those outside actors with a geopolitical stake in the country. The Central Asian republics have found themselves in a position where they are impelled to deal with two parallel, and often competing, diplomatic efforts: one led by the United States and the other by Russia.

The American search for a political settlement began under President Barack Obama as part of an exit strategy. But it has lately gained momentum under President Donald Trump, who had promised during his 2016 election campaign to end America's very costly Afghan military adventure. Although he was initially persuaded by his military advisors and Congressional advocates not to embark on a hasty troop withdrawal, from September 2018 he nonetheless tasked Zalmay Khalilzad, the Afghan-American diplomat, who has advised and served various Republican administrations since Ronald Reagan's presidency (1981–1989), with securing a political solution to the conflict.

As Special Representative for Afghanistan Reconciliation, Khalilzad commenced an intense shuttle diplomacy to build a national and regional consensus in support of a negotiated settlement. Over nine months, he held several rounds of discussion with Taliban representatives in Qatar and the United Arab Emirates (UAE), which amounted to America's virtual recognition of the group as a legitimate partner in peacemaking. This represented a sharp about-face, given that Washington had previously condemned the Taliban for harbouring Al Qaeda during the group's rule in Afghanistan and designated it a terrorist organisation. Khalilzad's efforts were undertaken with the backing of the main patron of the Taliban – Pakistan – which Trump has subjected to increased pressure to cooperate. Other regional and international actors were consulted, with the notable exception of the Islamic Republic of Iran (and, to some extent, Russia). President Trump has castigated Tehran as a regional menace, despite Iran being an important player in the region, and without whose cooperation (and that of Russia) it will be very difficult to ensure a lasting peace in Afghanistan.[18] Tehran and Moscow have formed a strong axis not only in relation to Syria, but also in regard to a number of other regional issues, including the Afghanistan conflict, where they closely cooperate to ensure that the US intervention and peacemaking in the country does not evolve contrary to their interests.

Khalilzad announced progress in his talks with the Taliban in late January 2019, tweeting that in principle the United States and the Taliban had agreed on a peace framework, involving primarily the issue of a withdrawal of foreign troops from Afghanistan in return for a Taliban undertaking not to allow Afghanistan to be used by extremist groups against the United States and its allies.[19] This was followed by several more rounds of talks, including an important meeting in late February in Doha, where the Taliban delegation was led, for the first time, by a senior co-founder of the movement, Mullah Abdul Ghani Baradar, who had recently been released from a Pakistani jail.

The ninth and final round of negotiations took place in early September 2019, at the conclusion of which Khalilzad contended that a US–Taliban peace agreement had been reached, pending President Trump's approval. The deal met only two of the four objectives that Khalilzad had been pursuing: the United States would withdraw 5,400 of its some 14,000 troops within 130 days, to be followed by a pullout of the rest of the forces according to the conditions in Afghanistan; and the Taliban pledged to prevent any terrorist activities against the United States from occurring in Afghanistan.[20] The other two objectives – negotiations between the Taliban and other Afghan parties, most importantly the Afghan government, and a nation-wide ceasefire – were supposed to follow the signing of the agreement. Yet, there was no guarantee that the Taliban would implement either of the latter objectives; they had persistently rejected the Afghan government as illegitimate and a 'puppet'; and there was little evidence that they could or would control other armed opposition groups, most importantly ISIS–K.

To seal the agreement, President Trump secretly invited the Taliban negotiators and President Ashraf Ghani to meet with him separately in Camp David in early September. However, when the Taliban executed a suicide bombing in Kabul, killing twelve people including an American soldier, Trump abruptly called off the meeting with an expression of anger over the Taliban's actions. He announced that there was not going to be a peace deal.[21] The President was criticised not only by his Democratic opponents, but also by some senior members of his Republican Party, especially in light of the fact that the Taliban had carried out violent operations throughout the negotiation period. The Taliban claimed that Trump's move would damage the United States, but at the same time they left the door open for signing the agreement at a future date.[22] All the optimism that the negotiations and the draft agreement had generated, rapidly dissipated. With no ongoing peace process, the killing fields in Afghanistan continued with greater intensity.

Meanwhile, Moscow, backed by its Central Asian allies in the CSTO – Kyrgyzstan and Tajikistan – as well as by Tehran, pursued its own diplomatic track in support of an Afghan political settlement, parallel to US efforts. It held several regional conferences, with the participation of the Taliban, Pakistan and India. The Moscow process started well before Khalilzad's mission, and initially neither Kabul nor Washington were invited to participate. However, after Kabul's protest, the Afghan government found it expedient to attend the November 2018 Moscow conference, as did the United States, by sending a junior diplomat from its Moscow embassy to observe the meeting. As Khalilzad's mission gathered pace, the Afghan government, in step with Washington, increasingly viewed Moscow's initiatives with scepticism and refused to participate in its February 2019 conference; it denounced it as unhelpful to the cause of peacemaking. Yet Abbas Stanikzai (one of the Taliban's senior figures and head of the group's office in Doha, with a history of contacts with Moscow), and a number of Afghan political personalities – including former President Karzai, Hanif Atmar (former National Security Advisor and now political rival to President Ghani) and Yunus Qanooni (former Afghan vice-president under Karzai and now an ally of Atmar) – along with representatives of all regional actors, attended the conference.[23] This underlined the complexity of the Afghan situation and of the region. It also clearly showed that the Moscow track has real potential to compete with the US track, and that few Afghan leaders have much trust in either Khalilzad or the US-led peace process. Following Trump's termination of peace talks with the Taliban, the latter's negotiators visited Moscow, playing their Russia card and putting pressure on Trump to resume the negotiation process.[24]

Beijing's position approximated that of Moscow on account of its concerns about ISIS-K, regime vulnerability in Central Asia, and containment by the United States.[25] Given that neither the American nor Russian efforts had paid off so far, it recognised an opportunity to pursue its own track for assisting the divided Afghan parties to unite in reaching a settlement. Beijing invited the Kabul government and the Taliban to send delegations to a meeting to pave the way for a peace agreement between them. The meeting was originally planned to be held in Beijing on 29–30 October 2019, but was postponed at the request of Kabul until it was able to form an all-inclusive delegation – something that failed to materialise.[26]

However, Trump's cancellation of negotiations pleased the Afghan government.[27] Despite publicly supporting Khalilzad's peacemaking mission, President Ghani and Chief Executive Abdullah Abdullah, especially the former, had not been entirely happy with the envoy's conduct of his mission. They preferred all peace negotiations to be channelled through their government. Yet, this was never going to be the case. Although Khalilzad regularly briefed the Afghan leaders, he managed his talks in deference to the Taliban's refusal to recognise the Afghan government. He had publicly said that his objective was to make the process Afghan-owned by bringing the National Unity Government, plus other major Afghan stakeholders, and the Taliban together to negotiate directly. Yet, with the United States dealing directly with the Taliban, the group and its main backer, Pakistan, had all along been elevated to a stronger position than the Afghan government. The fear in Kabul was that ultimately the United States would bypass the Afghan government in striking a deal with the Taliban, thereby leaving it high and dry. The similarity between the Doha peace process for Afghanistan and the Paris peace talks for Vietnam fifty years ago is pertinent. The Paris talks involved United States and North Vietnam without participation of the US-backed South Vietnam. The Paris Accords, which were signed between the two parties, primarily provided a cover for US troop withdrawal from the South. The end result was the overrunning of the South by the North, and humiliation of the United States.

Soon after calling off peace talks with the Taliban, Trump once again found it expedient to backtrack, especially in view of his domestic problems being compounded by the Congressional process of impeachment. Khalilzad resumed his mission, re-starting peace talks with the Taliban delegation in Doha in early December 2019. After a period of intense negotiations, he finally managed to pull off a bilateral US-Taliban deal, called the 'Agreement for Bringing Peace to Afghanistan', which he and Mullah Baradar signed on 5 March 2020. Under the deal, the US agreed to two key demands of the Taliban: a withdrawal of all foreign forces from Afghanistan within 14 months and the immediate release of 5,000 Taliban prisoners in Afghan jails. In return, the Taliban pledged to prevent Afghan soil from being used for hostile actions against the US and to release 1,000 captured Afghan soldiers. The Agreement also stipulated direct negotiations between the Taliban and other Afghan parties, including the government, by 10 March 2020.

However, the Agreement came against the backdrop of deepening political turmoil in Afghanistan, threatening to derail the deal. After a year's delay and growing disunity within the NUG, the government held presidential elections on 28 September 2019. Given the level of insecurity, people's disillusionment with their leaders and the Taliban's warning to the public not to participate in the ballot, the result was a very poor voter turnout. Of the 9 million voters registered (from an estimated 16 million eligible in a population of some 37 million), less than 1.8 million cast their votes. However, the election results remained unannounced because of irregularities claimed by different parties until 18

February 2020 when the Afghan Independent Electoral Commission (IEC) declared Ghani as the winner with 50.52 per cent (or 923,592 votes). The result was immediately rejected as fraud by Ghani's main political rival, Abdullah, who claimed that Ghani had stacked the IEC with his supporters and that the Commission counted some 300,000 non-biometric votes in favour of Ghani. While backed by several other presidential candidates, Abdullah declared himself as the victor and promised to form a parallel government.[28] Ghani and Abdullah held separate swearing-in ceremonies on 9 March. This development was set to scuttle the US–Taliban peace agreement, as the chances of forming an all-inclusive Afghan delegation, representing the socially and politically mosaic makeup of Afghanistan, to negotiate with the Taliban, dramatically declined.

As Khalilzad's mediation, along with that of former President Karzai and former mujahideen leader Abdul Rasul Sayyaf, for some form of unity government between the two protagonists failed, US Secretary of State Mike Pompeo found it necessary to pay an unannounced urgent visit to Kabul on 22 March to prompt the Afghan rivals to reconcile as critical to the implementation of the US–Taliban deal, especially in the light of Ghani's assertion that the release of the 5,000 Taliban prisoners was the responsibility of his government and should be part of peace negotiations with the Taliban. Pompeo basically sought to achieve what his Democratic predecessor, John Kerry, had accomplished in the wake of the disputed results of the 2014 election: another national unity government. Yet, this time the Ghani-Abdullah rift was so deep that it could not be bridged easily, given Ghani's orchestrations to remain at the helm and Abdullah's determination not to bow out. Pompeo tried to cajole the two sides to form what he called an 'inclusive' government: 'In an unusually harsh statement, Pompeo slammed the two men for being unable to work together and threatening a potential peace deal that could end America's longest-running conflict'. As a result, the Trump administration announced that it was slashing $1 billion in its critical assistance to Afghanistan and threatened further reductions in all forms of cooperation, if the Afghan rivals failed to resolve their differences.[29] While ultimately under US pressure Ghani and Abdullah reached a resolution with Ghani confirmed as president and Abdullah as Chair of the Council of National Reconciliation outside the executive power, this may not bring stability to the highly fractured Afghan politics. At the time of writing, Afghanistan was potentially edging towards a Vietnam-type fiasco with the Taliban as the main winner who, as David Petraeus and Vance Serchuk have noted, could not be trusted to uphold its end of the bargain against terrorism and control such entities as Al-Qaeda and ISIS–K that operate in Afghanistan.[30]

In this context, the Central Asian republics appear to be befuddled by the sheer fluidity and complexity of the Afghan predicament. They are wary of the possibility that the downward spiral in US–Russian relations might indeed lead to 'an indirect war by proxy' on the diplomatic arena, pitting the Taliban against the government in Kabul.[31] The region's leaders have essentially adopted the stance of masterly inactivity awaiting further developments. They became noticeably more reticent in their statements on Afghanistan in 2019, compared to a year before, and abstained from commenting on the presidential campaign there beyond the 'let the people decide' adage. The aforementioned visit by Baradar to Tashkent in August 2019 that drew opprobrium from Kabul was also met with displeasure in Russia where some interpreted the move as a direct challenge to the Moscow format of negotiations and a '100 per cent American-conceived scenario'.[32] This is not necessarily the Kremlin's official view but it certainly stands in contrast to the coverage of the Taliban's initial appearance in Uzbekistan in 2018, which was uniformly seen as complementary to the Kremlin's objectives. The increased paranoia about being seen as partial to the conflict was illustrated by an incident in March 2019, when the authorities in Turkmenistan quietly pushed back a company of Afghan servicemen who had been chased by the Taliban across the border. As a result, the Taliban took 150 soldiers prisoner.[33] Previously Ashgabat's standard operational procedure was to provide safe passage to the Taliban and the ANSF alike.

The March 2020 deal between the US and the Taliban divided the region's experts and politicians into two camps: pessimists and optimists. The former's opinion was summarised by the head of a strategic think tank in Kyrgyzstan: Ghani's government is a spent force; the US will disengage completely leaving China, Russia and the Central Asian republics to clean up the mess; and the Taliban need to be befriended quickly as the only actor in Afghanistan capable of stopping ISIS-K.[34] The Foreign Minister of Uzbekistan was more sanguine about the deal noting that in his opinion it signified a growing convergence of positions between Washington, Moscow and Beijing who might potentially act as joint guarantors of the internal search for peace in Afghanistan.[35]

Whatever the final outcome of the US, Russian and Chinese diplomatic efforts, no viable Afghan political settlement could be concluded and executed without addressing satisfactorily a number of major hurdles: the Taliban's persistent rejection of the Afghan government as illegitimate; their key demands for the departure of all foreign forces and the disbanding of the Afghan security forces – the support of which the Afghan government's survival depends; and their wish that the Afghan constitution be changed to conform with a strict version of *shari'a*. In addition, the Taliban have remained adamant that the name of Afghanistan should be changed from the 'Islamic Republic of Afghanistan' to the 'Islamic Emirate of Afghanistan' as it was under their rule.

For a settlement to be successful, it would need to be acceptable to a cross-section of the mosaic Afghan population, and to Afghanistan's neighbours and major powers. As such, it would need to be couched within the frame of an interlocking regional and international consensus, guaranteed and closely monitored by the five permanent members of the United Nations Security Council. Afghanistan should be returned to its traditional position of neutrality in world politics, and if any outside actors seek to violate Afghanistan's stability and sovereignty in pursuit of its regional interests, that actor should be subject to penalty under the United Nations' Chapter VII. Meanwhile, this should be accompanied by the formation of an all-inclusive transitional government of national unity, with participation of the mainstream Taliban, to hold free and fair presidential and parliamentary elections within two years. All foreign combat and civilian assistance to the transitional government and its elected successor should be tied to the promotion of good governance, national unity and economic development. The question is who should take the lead for such an initiative to make it a reality? The United States as the dominant and most resourceful power in Afghanistan is the obvious choice, but it must have a shared goal with the other permanent members of the Security Council, plus the European Union as an important contributor to the process.

To achieve such an objective is by no means easy. It requires binding cooperation among the Afghan leadership, irrespective of their political, ideological, ethno-tribal, cultural and sectarian differences, and between those regional and international actors which have patronised various Afghan groups in support of their conflicting agendas. As the situation stands, Afghanistan suffers from a multiplicity of internal and external actors fuelling its conflict. There is not a sufficient degree of cooperation and commitment on the part of these actors to generate the necessary foundations for transition of the country into a stable, functional and sovereign state. The Central Asian republics cannot play a decisive role in the process of normalisation but they can help in a meaningful way through acting as honest brokers and making small material contribution to the development of Afghanistan. Their relative weakness compared to Afghanistan's other neighbours who have vested interests in its factional struggles paradoxically is their greatest asset. It would be unfortunate if their agency is once again reduced to the rigid binary geopolitical choice between the United States on the one hand and Russia and China on the other, which seems increasingly likely at present.

Notes

1. Jonathan L. Lee, *Afghanistan: A History from 1260 to the Present* (London: Reaktion Books, 2019), p. 683.
2. Butler cited in David Reynolds, 'Enduring Hope: NATO Operations in Afghanistan', *Jane's Defence Weekly*, 16 May 2019, https://janes.ihs.com/DefenceWeekly/Display/FG_1973589-JDW
3. For details, see 'Record-high Opium Production in Afghanistan Creates Multiple Challenges for Region and Beyond, UN warns', *UN News*, 21 May 2018, https://news.un.org/en/story/2018/05/1010332.
4. Tamara Vaal, 'Bolee 20 tys. posledovatelei destruktivnykh religioznykh ideologii zhivut v Kazakhstane – KNB', *Vlast.kz*, 6 November 2019, https://vlast.kz/novosti/35957-bolee-20-tys-posledovatelej-destruktivnyh-religioznyh-ideologij-zivut-v-kazahstane-knb.html.
5. Jeff Seldin, 'Islamic State in Afghanistan Growing Bigger, More Dangerous', *Voice of America*, 21 May 2019, https://www.voanews.com/south-central-asia/islamic-state-afghanistan-growing-bigger-more-dangerous.
6. Kirill Krivosheev, 'Tadzhiksko-uzbekskuiu granitsu atakovali iz Afganistana', *Kommersant*, 6 November 2019, https://www.kommersant.ru/doc/4149850.
7. CARICC, 'Infografika po ofitsialnym dannym za 2017-2018gg', (report, Central Asian Regional Information and Coordination Centre for Combating Illicit Trafficking of Narcotic Drugs, Psychotropic Substances and their Precursors, Almaty, 2019), https://caricc.org/index.php/infografika/po-ofitsialnym-dannym.
8. See, for instance, Sh. Amanbekova, 'Afganskii narkotrafik i problem regionalnoi bezopasnosti v Tsentralnoi Azii', *Postsovetskie issledovaniia* 2, 3 (2019): pp. 1103–1110.
9. Shoirai Rahimjon, 'Dasti Prezidentu khoki Tojikistonro mebusam!' *SSSR.tj*, 14 November 2019, http://www.cccp.tj/tj/2016-02-23-16-45-52/mehmonhona/item/6647-dasti-prezidentu-hok.html?tmpl=component&print=1.
10. António Guterres, 'Secretary-General's remarks to the Security Council on Building Regional Partnership in Afghanistan and Central Asia, to Link Security and Development', *United Nations Secretary-General*, 19 January 2018, https://www.un.org/sg/en/content/sg/statement/2018-01-19/secretary-general%E2%80%99s-remarks-security-council-building-regional.
11. Kristin Fjæstad and Heidi Kjærnet, 'Performing Statehood: Afghanistan as an Arena for Central Asian States', *Central Asian Survey* 33, 3 (2014): p. 324.
12. Sarin Abado, 'CAREC Energy Strategy 2030: Common Borders. Common Solutions. Common Energy Future', (institutional document, Asian Development Bank, Manila, 2019), p. 30.
13. Saule Isabaeva, 'Afganskaia golovolomka: vse khotiat mira, no gotoviatsia k voine', *Central Asia Monitor*, 6 June 2019, https://camonitor.kz/33129-afganskaya-golovolomka-vse-hotyat-mira-no-gotovyatsya-k-voyne.html.

14 Abdusattor Shohiyon cited in Payrav Chorshanbiyev, 'GKNB Tadzhikistana: rastet veroiatnost' proryva tadzhiksko-afganskoi granitsy terroristami', *Asia-Plus*, 16 October 2019, https://asiaplustj.info/news/tajikistan/security/20191016/gknb-tadzhikistana-rastet-veroyatnost-proriva-tadzhiksko-afganskoi-granitsi-terroristami.

15 'Afghan Foreign Ministry Criticizes the Warm Reception of Taliban Leaders in Uzbekistan', *The Tashkent Times*, 12 August 2019, https://tashkenttimes.uz/national/4249-afghan-foreign-ministry-criticizes-the-warm-reception-of-taliban-leaders-in-uzbekistan.

16 'O chem govorili lidery Tsentralnoi Azii', *Gazeta.uz*, 30 November 2019, https://www.gazeta.uz/ru/2019/11/30/ca-partnership/

17 Bruce Pannier, 'Keeping Afghanistan in Afghanistan', *The Cairo Review of Global Affairs*, Summer 2019, https://www.thecairoreview.com/essays/keeping-afghanistan-in-afghanistan/.

18 For a detailed background discussion, see Amin Saikal, *Iran Rising: The Survival and Future of the Islamic Republic* (Princeton: Princeton University Press, 2019), pp. 208–224.

19 See Mujib Marhal, 'US and Taliban Agree in Principle to Peace Framework, Envoy Says', *New York Times*, 28 January 2019.

20 For details, see 'US Envoy says Agreement "in principle" for Afghanistan Peace Deal Reached with Taliban', *CBS News*, 2 September 2019, https://www.cbsnews.com/news/us-taliban-afghanistan-agreement-in-principle-partial-withdrawal-forces-zalmay-khalilzad-today-2019-09-02/.

21 Michael Crowley, Lara Jakes and Mujib Mashal, 'Trump Says he's Called off Negotiations with Taliban after Afghanistan Bombing', *New York Times*, 7 September 2019.

22 For a detailed account, see '"More Losses to US", says Taliban as Trump Cancels Afghan Talks', *al-Jazeera*, 9 September 2019, https://www.aljazeera.com/news/2019/09/losses-taliban-trump-cancels-afghan-talks-190908133847765.html.

23 For a discussion, see Amin Saikal, 'The Afghanistan Conundrum', *Project Syndicate*, 13 June 2019, https://www.project-syndicate.org/commentary/afghanistan-america-russia-political-settlement-by-amin-saikal-2019-06?barrier=accesspaylog.

24 See Samuel Ramani, 'In the Demise of the Taliban Peace Talks, Russia is the Winner', *Foreign Policy*, 11 September 2019, https://foreignpolicy.com/2019/09/11/in-the-demise-of-the-taliban-peace-talks-russia-is-the-winner/.

25 Niklas Swanstrom and Julian Tucker, 'China in Afghanistan – A New Force in the War in Afghanistan?' in *Rebuilding Afghanistan in Times of Crisis: A Global Response*, edited by Adenrele Awotona (Abingdon: Routledge, 2019), pp. 156–173.

26 'Govt Has Finalized Participant List for China Meeting', *Tolo News*, 6 November 2019, https://tolonews.com/afghanistan/govt-has-finalized-participant-list-china-meeting.

27 Pamela Constable, 'Afghans Welcome Trump's Cancellation of Taliban Peace Talks', *Washington Post*, 9 September 2019.

28 Emma Graham-Harrison, 'Ghani Declared Winner of Afghan Election – But Opponent Rejects Result', *The Guardian*, 19 February 2020, https://www.theguardian.com/world/2020/feb/18/ashraf-ghani-wins-afghan-presidential-election.
29 Matthew Lee, 'US Slashes Aid to Afghanistan after Pompeo Visit to Kabul', Associated Press, 24 March 2020, https://apnews.com/649879924a532522e51291955170c034.
30 David Petraeus and Vance Serchuk, 'Can America Trust the Taliban to Prevent Another 9/11? A Dangerous Asymmetry Lies at the Heart of the Afghan Peace Deal', *Foreign Affairs*, 1 April 2020, https://www.foreignaffairs.com/articles/afghanistan/2020-04-01/can-america-trust-taliban-prevent-another-911.
31 K. A Golubev, 'Constructing Narratives about the Taliban by Russia's Ministry of Foreign Affairs', *Vestnik of Saint Petersburg University: International Relations* 12, 2 (2019): p. 240.
32 Russian political analyst Alexander Knyazev quoted in Isabaeva, 'Afganskaia golovolomka'.
33 Najim Rahim and Rod Nordland, 'Taliban Capture about 150 Afghan Soldiers after Chase into Turkmenistan', *The New York Times*, 17 March 2019, https://www.nytimes.com/2019/03/17/world/asia/afghanistan-soldiers-taliban-turkmenistan.html.
34 Dmitrii Orlov, 'Bez paniki – eto 'Taliban'', *Nezavisimaia Gazeta*, 15 March 2020, http://www.ng.ru/dipkurer/2020-03-15/11_7817_asia.html
35 Abdulaziz Kamilov, 'Soglashenie mezhdu SShA i talibami – eto tolko nachalo puti k miru', Gazeta.uz, 29 February 2020, https://www.gazeta.uz/ru/2020/02/29/kamilov/

Bibliography

Abado, Sarin. 'CAREC Energy Strategy 2030: Common Borders. Common Solutions. Common Energy Future'. Institutional document, Asian Development Bank, Manila, 2019.

Abdrakhmanov, Kairat. 'Afganistan dolzhen byt' integrirovan v ekonomicheskie sviazi v TsA'. *Kursiv*, 5 September 2018. https://kursiv.kz/news/politika/2018-09/kayrat-abdrakhmanov-afganistan-dolzhen-byt-integrirovan-v-ekonomicheskie.

Abdullohi Rahnamo, Hakim. 'Novoe pokolenie ekstremistov i novye vyzovy bezopasnosti Tsentralnoi Azii'. In *Tsentralnaia Aziia v usloviiakh globalnoi transformatsii*, edited by Z.K. Shaukenova, pp. 63–73. Astana: KISI, 2017.

Abdykarieva, S. 'Sotrudnichestvo v deistvii'. *Chegarada* 9, 163 (2017): p. 2.

Achilov, B. 'O predprinimaemykh Uzbekistanom merakh po dalneishemu ukrepleniiu regionalnogo vzaimodeistviia, razvitiu torgovo-ekonomicheskogo sotrudnichestva'. In *Sbornik dokladov mezhdunarodnoi konferentsii 'Tsentralnaia Aziia—glavnyi prioritet vneshnei politiki Uzbekistana'*. pp. 100–108. Tashkent: Ministry of Foreign Affairs of Uzbekistan, 2017.

Adilkhodzhaeva, Suraye. 'Obostrenie situatsii v Afganistane: novye ugrozy miru i puti ikh predotvrashcheniia' *Sravnitelnaia politika* 8, 4 (2017): pp. 73–82.

Afghanistan Today, 'Kyrgyzstan, Afghanistan i Tadzhikistan obsudili "severnyi marshrut" narkotrafika'. 31 May 2016. http://afghanistantoday.ru/hovosti/kyrgyzstan-afghanistan.

Ahmad Rahim, Shoaib. 'The Geopolitics of the Lapis Lazuli Corridor'. *The Diplomat*, 22 December 2017. http://thediplomat.com/2017/12/the-geopolitics-of-the-lapis-lazuli-corridor/.

Ahmadzaia, Saadatullah and Alastair McKinna. 'Afghanistan Electrical Energy and Transboundary Water Systems Analyses: Challenges and Opportunities'. *Energy Reports* 4 (2018): pp. 435–69.

Ahmed, Azam. 'Taliban Justice Gains Favor as Official Afghan Courts Fail'. *The New York Times*, 31 January 2015. http://www.nytimes.com/2015/02/01/world/asia/taliban-justice-gains-favor-as-official-afghan-courts-fail.html.

Akbaralieva, Nodira. 'UNHCR and Sheraton Hotel in Tajikistan Offer Afghan Refugees Chance to Shine'. *UNHCR*, 25 October 2017. https://www.unhcr.org/en-au/news/latest/2017/10/59edc3de4/unhcr-sheraton-hotel-tajikistan-offer-afghan-refugees-chance-shine.html.

Akhantaev, Erbol. 'V Kazakhstane rastet chislo storonnikov IGIL'. *Eurasia News*, 20 April 2017. http://eurasianews.info/analitika/v-kazaxstane-rastet-chislo-storonnikov-igil.html.

Akimbekov, S.M. *Afganskii uzel i problemy bezopasnosti Tsentralnoi Azii*. Almaty: KISI, 2003.

Akseer, Tabasum and John Rieger, eds. 'Afghanistan in 2018: A Survey of the Afghan People'. Report, The Asia Foundation, Washington, DC, 2018.

Al Jazeera. 'Russia, Taliban "Laughed" at US Claims of Moscow Arming Fighters'. 31 March 2018. https://www.aljazeera.com/news/2018/03/russia-taliban-laughed-claims-moscow-arming-fighters-180330113642328.html.

Al Jazeera. '"More Losses to US", says Taliban as Trump Cancels Afghan Talks', 9 September 2019. https://www.aljazeera.com/news/2019/09/losses-taliban-trump-cancels-afghan-talks-190908133847765.html.

Alamshozoda, A.A., K. Kh. Soliev and M.G. Bukhorizoda. 'Obzor narkosituatsii v Afganistane'. *Narkofront* 1 (2017): p. 18–24.

Ali, Obaid. 'Qari Hekmat's Island: A Daesh Enclave in Jawzjan?' *Afghanistan Analysts Network*, 11 November 2017. https://www.afghanistan-analysts.org/qari-hekmats-island-a-daesh-enclave-in-jawzjan/.

Aliyeva, Kamila. 'Volumes of Tajik Electricity Exports to Afghanistan Disclosed'. *AzerNews*, 1 February 2018. https://www.azernews.az/region/126427.html.

Allison, Roy. 'Protective Integration and Security Policy Coordination: Comparing the SCO and CSTO'. *The Chinese Journal of International Politics* 11, 3 (2018): pp. 297–338.

Amanbekova, Sh. 'Afganskii narkotrafik i problem regionalnoi bezopasnosti v Tsentralnoi Azii'. *Postsovetskie issledovaniia* 2, 3 (2019): pp. 1103–1110.

Amin, Mohsin. 'Power to the People: How to Extend Afghans' Access to Electricity'. Report, Afghanistan Analysts Network, Kabul, 3 February 2015. https://www.afghanistan-analysts.org/power-to-the-people-how-to-extend-afghans-access-to-electricity/.

Amineh, Mehdi Parvizi and Henk Houweling. 'IR-Theory and Transformation in the Greater Middle East: The Role of the United States'. *Perspectives on Global Development and Technology* 6, 1 (2007): pp. 57–86.

Aminjonov, Farkhod. 'Limitations of the Central Asian Energy Security Policy: Priorities and Prospects for Improvement'. *CIGI Papers* 103, 2016.

Aminjonov, Farkhod. 'Afghanistan's Energy Security: Tracing Central Asian Countries' Contribution'. Report, Friedrich-Ebert-Stiftung Afghanistan Office, Kabul, 2017.

Aminjonov, Farkhod. 'Stability Over Prosperity and Security over Development in Republic of Uzbekistan'. In *Current Challenges to Central Asia and Afghanistan: Towards a Better World*, edited by Anna Gusarova, pp. 58–57. Almaty: Friedrich-Ebert-Stiftung, 2017.

Amirov, Temur. 'Afganskie bezhentsy. V poiskah luchshei doli'. *Asia-Plus*, 7 April 2017. https://www.news.tj/ru/news/tajikistan/society/20170407/afganskie-bezhentsi-v-poiskah-luchshei-doli.

Amnesty International. 'Threats of Expulsion of Loya Jirga Delegate Unacceptable'. 29 November 2003. http://asiapacific.amnesty.org/library/Index/ENGASA110292003?open&of=ENG-AFG.

Analytical Center on Drug Control. 'O narkosituatsii v Respublike Uzbekistan v 2017 godu'. *NCDC.uz*, 2018. http://www.ncdc.uz/ru/protivodeystvie-nezakonnomu-oborotu-narkoticheskikh-sredstv/analiticheskie-obzory/.

Analytical Center on Drug Control. *Natsionalnyi otchet o narkosituatsii v Respublike Uzbekistan 2012*. Prague: ResAd s.r.o, 2012.

Anceschi, Luca. 'Turkmenistan's Export Crisis: Is TAPI the Answer?' Policy brief 27. Central Asia Program, Washington, D.C., June 2015. http://centralasiaprogram.org/wp-content/uploads/2015/06/Policy-Brief-27-June-2015.pdf.

Ariana News. 'Afghanistan Would Be Used as Substrate to Shift Terrorism into Russia: Karzai'. 18 March 2017. https://ariananews.af/afghanistan-would-be-used-as-substrate-to-shift-terrorism-into-russia-karzai/.

Asef, N. 'Vozvrashchenie Rossii v Afganistan: perspektivy dvustoronnego ekonomicheskogo sotrudnichestva'. *Vestnik RUDN* 17, 4 (2017): pp. 781–92.

Ashikbaev, Erzhan. 'Afganistan ne dolzhen rassmatrivat'sia iskliuchitelno kak ugroza miru'. *Tengri news*, 4 January 2018. https://tengrinews.kz/kazakhstan_news/afganistan-doljen-rassmatrivatsya-isklyuchitelno-ugroza-miru-334683/.

Ashna – Voice of America Dari Service. 'TV interview with Kunduz MP Engineer Kamal'. 4 April 2018. https://www.darivoa.com/a/4331976.html.

Asian Development Bank. 'Unstoppable: The Hairatan to Mazar-e-Sharif Railway Project'. Report, ADB, Manila, February 2014.

Asian Development Bank. 'Afghanistan: Hairatan to Mazar-e-Sharif Railway Project'. Validation report PVR-439. ADB, Independent Evaluation Department, Manila, December 2015. https://www.adb.org/sites/default/files/evaluation-document/178419/files/pvr-439.pdf.

Asian Development Bank. 'Corridor Performance Measurement and Monitoring'. Annual Report, CAREC, ADB, Manila, 2015. https://www.carecprogram.org/uploads/2015-CAREC-CPMM-Annual-Report.pdf.

Asian Development Bank. 'RRP Sector Assessment (Summary): Energy'. Report, ADB, Manila, 2015. https://www.adb.org/sites/default/files/linkeddocuments/47282-001-ssa.pdf.

Asian Development Bank. 'CAREC 2030: Connecting the Region for Shared and Sustainable Development'. Report, ADB, Manila, 2017.

Asia-Plus. 'Afghanistan Reportedly Refuses to Receive Electricity through CASA 1000 Project'. 12 May 2016. http://www.news.tj/en/news/afghanistan-reportedly-refuses-receive-electricity-through-casa-1000-project.

Asia-Plus. 'Tajik Envoy Denies Reports that Russia Allegedly Sells Weapons to the Taliban as Baseless'. 14 February 2017. https://www.asiaplus.tj/tj/node/236627.

Asia-Plus. 'Tadzhikistan otvetil na obvineniia Afganistana v obstrele mirnykh zhitelei: eto porozhdenie bolnogo razuma'. 13 November 2017. https://news.tj/ru/news/tajikistan/security/20171113/tadzhikistan-otvetil-na-obvineniya-afganistana-v-obstrele-mirnih-zhitelei-eto-porozhdenie-bolnogo-razuma.

Atambaev, Almazbek. 'Ekskjliuzivnoe interview telekanalu "Mir"'. *Mir 24*, 31 March 2017. https://mir24.tv/news/15910069/eksklyuzivnoe-intervyu-almazbeka-atambaeva-telekanalu-mir-video.

Atambaev, Almazbek. 'Ekskliuziv: o EAES, Afganistane i "Mire"'. *TV Mir*, 31 March 2017. https://mir24.tv/news/15903439/eksklyuziv-almazbek-atambaev-o-eaes-afganistane-i-mire.

Auelbaev, B.A., S.K. Kushkumbayev, K.L. Syroezhkin and V.Y. Dodonov, *Central Asia – 2020: Four Strategic Concepts*. Astana: KISI, 2015.

Avesta. 'Emomali Rahmon obratil vnimanie glav gosudarstv ODKB na voprosy ukrepleniia tadzhiksko-afganskoi granitsy'. 9 November 2018. http://avesta.tj/2018/11/09/emomali-rahmon-obratil-vnimanie-glav-gosudarstv-odkb-na-voprosy-ukrepleniya-tadzhiksko-afganskoj-granitsy/.

Azamy, Hekmatullah. 'Challenges and Prospects for Daesh in Afghanistan and its Relations with the Taliban'. In *Countering Daesh Extremism*, edited by Beatrice Gorawantschy, Rohan Gunaratna, Megha Sarmah and Patrick Rueppel, pp. 43–60. Singapore: Konrad-Adenauer-Stiftung, 2016.

Babanov, Omurbek. 'Tsentralnoaziatskie vyzovy dlia Rossii'. *Russian International Affairs Council*, 13 September 2017. http://russiancouncil.ru/analytics-and-comments/analytics/tsentralnoaziatskie-vyzovy-dlya-rossii/.

Bakhtar News. 'JICA Supports the Effective Management of Tajikistan's Common Border with Afghanistan'. 28 November 2018. http://bakhtarnews.com.af/eng/business/item/35783-jica-supports-the-effective-management-of-tajikistan%E2%80%99s-common-border-with-afghanistan.html.

Balzacq, Thierry. 'Enquiries into Methods: A New Framework for Securitisation Analysis'. In *Securitisation Theory: How Security Problems Emerge and Dissolve*, edited by Thierry Balzacq, pp. 31–53. London and New York: Routledge, 2011.

Balzacq, Thierry. 'The "Essence" of Securitization: Theory, Ideal Type, and a Sociological Science of Security'. *International Relations* 29, 1 (2015): pp. 103–112.

BBC News. 'Minister Voices Afghan Opium Fear'. 2 May 2008. http://news.bbc.co.uk/2/hi/health/7377817.stm.

BBC News. 'Afghan Blast Kills NATO Soldiers'. 1 August 2008. http://news.bbc.co.uk/2/hi/south_asia/7537674.stm.

BBC News. 'Aid Warning over Afghan Violence'. 1 August 2008. http://news.bbc.co.uk/2/hi/south_asia/7536422.stm.

BBC News. 'Wedding Carnage in Afghan Blast'. 2 August 2008. http://news.bbc.co.uk/2/hi/south_asia/7538905.stm.

Bell, Arvid. *Afghanistan and Central Asia in 2015. An Overview of Actors, Interests, and Relationships*. Frankfurt: Peace Research Institute, 2015.

Bernard, Cheryl and Nina Hachigan, eds. *Democracy and Islam in the New Constitution of Afghanistan*. Santa Monica: RAND, 2003.

Bhadrakumar, M. K. 'The Afghan War: Trump and Putin Battle for Uzbek Support'. *Asia Times*, 25 December 2017. http://www.atimes.com/article/afghan-war-trump-putin-battle-uzbek-support/.

Bhutta, Zafar. 'CASA-1000 Project: US to Pour Millions into Afghan Support Programmes'. *The Express Tribune*, 30 March 2014. https://tribune.com.pk/story/688934/casa-1000-project-us-to-pour-millions-into-afghan-support-programmes/.

Biddle, Stephen. 'Ending the War in Afghanistan: How to Avoid Failure on the Plan'. *Foreign Affairs* 92, 5 (2013): pp. 49–58.

Bird, Tim and Alex Marshall. *Afghanistan: How the West Lost its Way*. New Haven and London: Yale University Press, 2011.

Blank, Stephen and Younkyoo Kim. *Making Sense of Russia's Policy in Afghanistan*. Paris: IFRI, 2018.

Bleuer, Christian. 'Kyrgyzstan and Afghanistan's Diminishing Relationship'. In *Afghanistan and Its Neighbors after the NATO Withdrawal*, edited by Amin Saikal and Kirill Nourzhanov, pp. 129–46. New York: Lexington Books, 2016.

Bleuer, Christian. 'To Syria, not Afghanistan: Central Asian Jihadis "Neglect" their Neighbour'. *Afghanistan Analysts Network*, 8 October 2014. https://www.afghanistan-analysts.org/to-syria-not-afghanistan-central-asian-jihadis-neglect-their-neighbour/.

Bleuer, Christian and Said Reza Kazemi. *Between Co-operation and Insulation: Afghanistan's Relations with the Central Asian Republics*. Kabul: Afghanistan Analysts Network, 2014.

Bojor, Laviniu and Mircea Cosma. 'Afghanistan after NATO Withdrawal'. *Scientific Bulletin* 20, 1 (2015): pp. 29–34.

Boone, Jon. 'WikiLeaks Cables Portray Hamid Karzai as Corrupt and Erratic'. *The Guardian*, 3 December 2010. http://www.theguardian.com/world/2010/dec/02/wikileaks-cables-hamid-karzai-erratic.

Borger, Julian and Ewen MacAskill. 'US will Appoint Afghan "Prime Minister" to Bypass Hamid Karzai'. *The Guardian*, 23 March 2009. http://www.theguardian.com/world/2009/mar/22/us-afghan-plan-to-bypass-karzai.

Botobaev, A.A. 'Kharakteristika narkosituatsii v Kyrgyzstane na sovremennom etape'. *Problemy sovremennoi nauki i obrazovaniia* 9, 91 (2017): pp. 79–84.

Brattvoll, Joakim. 'Uzbekistan's Ambiguous Policies on Afghanistan'. *PRIO Policy Brief* 1, 2016. https://www.files.ethz.ch/isn/196758/Brattvoll%20-%20Uzbekistans%20ambiguous%20policies%20on%20Afghanistan,%20PRIO%20Policy%20Brief%201-2016.pdf.

Bromley, Simon. 'Connecting Central Eurasia to the Middle East in American Foreign Policy towards Afghanistan and Pakistan: 1979–Present'. In *The Greater Middle East in Global Politics*, edited by M. Parvizi Amineh, pp. 75–96. Leiden: Brill, 2007.

Burnashev, Rustam. 'Afganistan: chto Kazakhstanu daleko, to Germanii—blizko'. *Ostkraft*, 2 June 2014. http://ostkraft.ru/ru/documents/1482.

Burnashev, Rustam and Irina Chernykh. *Bezopasnost' v Tsentralnoi Azii: metodologicheskie ramki analiza*. Almaty: Kazakhstansko-nemetskii universitet, 2006.

Burnett, Victoria. 'Afghan Constitution Ready for Public Debate: Draft would Establish an Islamic Republic'. *The Boston Globe*, 2 October 2003. http://www.boston.com/

news/world/middleeast/articles/2003/10/02/afghan_constitution_ready_for_public_debate/.

Burns, Robert and Lolita C. Baldor. 'Amid Taliban Gains, US Military Favors Longer Presence'. *Associated Press*, 30 September 2015. http://bigstory.ap.org/article/259db99 1199d4b6a8652aeb6878eb976/us-military-favors-keeping-troops-afghanistan-past-2016.

Burns, William J. 'Deputy Secretary of State William J. Burns on Economic Connectivity in Central Asia. Remarks at Asia Society New York'. *Asia Society Policy Institute*, 23 September 2014. https://asiasociety.org/policy-institute/deputy-secretary-state-william-j-burns-economic-connectivity-central-asia.

Bush, George, W. 'Statement on the Parliamentary Elections in Afghanistan'. *Weekly Compilation of Presidential Documents* 41, 38 (26 September 2005).

Bush, George W. and Hamid Karzai, 'Remarks by President Bush and President Karzai of the Islamic Government of Afghanistan'. *The White House*, 12 September 2002. https://georgewbush whitehouse.archives.gov/news/releases/2002/09/20020912-6.html.

Buzan, Barry and Lene Hansen. *The Evolution of International Security Studies*. Cambridge: Cambridge University Press, 2009.

Buzan, Barry, Ole Wæver, and Jaap de Wilde. *Security: A New Framework for Analysis*. Boulder: Lynne Rienner Publishers, 1998.

Byman, Daniel L. 'What Happens when ISIS Goes Underground?' *Brookings Institution*, 18 January 2018. https://www.brookings.edu/blog/markaz/2018/01/18/what-happens-when-isis-goes-underground/.

Calamur, Krishnadev. 'Is Russia Really Arming the Taliban?' *The Atlantic*, 25 August 2017. https://www.theatlantic.com/international/archive/2017/08/russia-taliban-weapons/537807/.

Caravan.kz. 'Afganskii geroin prodolzhaiut vezti v Kazakhstan'. 14 June 2017. https://www.caravan.kz/news/afganskijj-geroin-prodolzhayut-vezti-v-kazakhstan-396339/.

CARICC. 'Infografika po ofitsialnym dannym za 2017–2018gg'. Report, Central Asian Regional Information and Coordination Centre for Combating Illicit Trafficking of Narcotic Drugs, Psychotropic Substances and their Precursors, Almaty, 2019. https://caricc.org/index.php/infografika/po-ofitsialnym-dannym.

CBS News. US Envoy says Agreement "in principle" for Afghanistan Peace Deal Reached with Taliban', 2 September 2019. https://www.cbsnews.com/news/us-taliban-afghanistan-agreement-in-principle-partial-withdrawal-forces-zalmay-khalilzad-today-2019-09-02/.

Central Asia Institute for Strategic Studies. 'Top Security Concerns in Central Asia – 2017'. *CAISS Paper* 1 (2017): http://caiss.expert/top-security-concerns-in-central-asia-2017/top-10-ca/.

Central Asia Regional Economic Cooperation Program. 'Energy Sector Progress Report and Work Plan (June 2017–May 2018)'. Report, CAREC Senior Officials' Meeting, Bangkok, 27–28 June 2018. https://www.carecprogram.org/uploads/S3b_Energy-Sector-Progress-Report.pdf.

Chan, Minnie. 'China Is Helping Afghanistan Set up Mountain Brigade to Fight Terrorism'. *South China Morning Post*, 28 August 2018. https://www.scmp.com/news/china/diplomacy-defence/article/2161745/china-building-training-camp-afghanistan-fight.

Chaziza, Mordechai. 'China's Peace-Maker Role in Afghanistan: Mediation and Conflict Management'. *Middle East Policy* XXV, 3, (2018): pp. 143–54.

Chorshanbiyev, Payrav. 'Construction of the TAT Railway Remains Questionable, says Tajik Railway Official'. *Asia-Plus*, 26 July 2016. https://asiaplustj.info/en/news/tajikistan/economic/20160726/construction-tat-railway-remains-questionable-says-tajik-railway-official.

Chorshanbiyev, Payrav. 'GKNB Tadzhikistana: rastet veroiatnost' proryva tadzhiksko-afganskoi granitsy terroristami'. *Asia-Plus*, 16 October 2019. https://asiaplustj.info/news/tajikistan/security/20191016/gknb-tadzhikistana-rastet-veroyatnost-proriva-tadzhiksko-afganskoi-granitsi-terroristami.

Clark, Kate. '"Not nation-building," but "killing terrorists": Trump's "New" Strategy for Afghanistan'. *Afghanistan Analysts Network*, 23 August 2017. https://www.afghanistan-analysts.org/not-nation-building-but-killing-terrorists-trumps-new-strategy-for-afghanistan/.

Clarke, Colin P. 'Russia Is Not a Viable Counterterrorism Partner for the United States'. *RAND*, 28 February 2018. https://www.rand.org/blog/2018/02/russia-is-not-a-viable-counterterrorism-partner-for.html.

Clarke, Michael. '"One Belt, One Road" and China's Emerging Afghanistan Dilemma'. *Australian Journal of International Affairs* 70, 5, (2016): pp. 563–79.

Clinton, Hillary Rodham. 'Remarks at the New Silk Road Ministerial Meeting'. *US Department of State*, 22 September 2011. https://2009-2017.state.gov/secretary/20092013clinton/rm/2011/09/173807.htm.

Coburn, Noah. *Losing Afghanistan: An Obituary for the Intervention*. Stanford: Stanford University Press, 2016.

Collective Security Treaty Organization. 'Strategiia kollektivnoi bezopasnosti ODKB na period do 2025 goda'. *CSTO Official Portal*, 14 October 2016. http://odkb-csto.org/documents/detail.php?ELEMENT_ID=8382.

Collective Security Treaty Organization. 'Rabochie gruppy po Afganistanu pri SMID ODKB i po bor'be s terrorizmom pri KSSB'. *CSTO Official Portal*, 19 April 2018. http://www.odkb-csto.org/news/detail.php?ELEMENT_ID=12568&SECTION_ID=91.

Collective Security Treaty Organization. 'Operatsiia ODKB "Kanal – Krasnyi barkhan"'. *CSTO Official Portal*, 15 September 2018. http://www.odkb-csto.org/news/detail.php?ELEMENT_ID=13166&SECTION_ID=91.

Collective Security Treaty Organization. 'Sovmestnoe uchenie s Mirotvorcheskimi silami ODKB'. *CSTO Official Portal*, 2 November 2018. http://www.odkb-csto.org/news/detail.php?ELEMENT_ID=13996&SECTION_ID=91.

Constable, Pamela. 'Afghans Welcome Trump's Cancellation of Taliban Peace Talks'. *Washington Post*, 9 September 2019.

Cooley, Alexander. *Great Games, Local Rules: The New Great Power Contest in Central Asia*. Oxford: Oxford University Press, 2012.

Cordesman, Anthony. 'Afghanistan Desertion in the U.S.: Assessing the Desertion and 'Ghost Soldier' Problems in Afghan National Security Forces'. Report, Center for Strategic and International Studies, Washington, 30 October 2017.

Cordesman, Anthony. 'Are Russia and China Sabotaging American Policy in Afghanistan?' *The Hill*, 9 January 2018. https://thehill.com/opinion/international/404716-are-russia-and-china-sabotaging-american-policy-in-afghanistan#bottom-story-socials.

Cordesman, Anthony. 'America's "Chaos Strategy" in the Middle East and South Asia'. *Centre for Strategic and International Studies*, 26 February 2018. https://www.csis.org/analysis/americas-chaos-strategy-middle-east-and-south-asia.

Cornell, Svante E. 'Central Asia: Where Did Islamic Radicalization Go?' In *Religion, Conflict, and Stability in the Former Soviet Union*, edited by Katya Migacheva and Bryan Frederick, pp. 65–98. Santa Monica: RAND, 2018.

Crisis Group. 'The Afghanistan Transitional Administration: Prospects and Perils'. Briefing Paper 19. International Crisis Group, Kabul/Brussels, 30 July 2002.

Crisis Group. 'Afghanistan: The Constitutional Loya Jirga'. Report, International Crisis Group, Kabul/Brussels, 12 December 2003.

Crisis Group. 'Rivals for Authority in Tajikistan's Gorno-Badakhshan'. Briefing paper 87. International Crisis Group, Europe and Central Asia, Brussels, 2018.

Crowley, Michael, Lara Jakes and Mujib Mashal. 'Trump Says he's Called off Negotiations with Taliban after Afghanistan Bombing'. *New York Times*, 7 September 2019.

Dabiq. 'A New Era Has Arrived of Might and Dignity for the Muslims'. Ramadan 1435/July 2014. https://www.trackingterrorism.org/system/files/chatter/Dabiq%201.compressed_0.pdf, pp. 8–9.

Daily Outlook Afghanistan. 'TAT Railway Has Strategic Importance'. 22 April 2014. http://outlookafghanistan.net/national_detail.php?post_id=9953.

Davis, Julie and Mark Landler. 'Trump Outlines New Afghanistan War Strategy with Few Details'. *The New York Times*, 21 August 2017. https://www.nytimes.com/2017/08/21/world/asia/afghanistan-troops-trump.html.

De Danieli, Filippo. 'Counter-narcotics Policies in Tajikistan and their Impact on State Building'. *Central Asian Survey* 30, 1 (2011): pp. 129–45.

Decamme, Guillaume. 'No Work, no Trade on Empty Silk Road in Northern Afghanistan'. *Business Insider*, 25 May 2016. https://www.businessinsider.com/afp-no-work-no-trade-on-empty-silk-road-in-northern-afghanistan-2016-5/?r=AU&IR=T.

Dirkx, Toon. 'The Unintended Consequences of US Support on Militia Governance in Kunduz Province, Afghanistan'. *Civil Wars* 19, 3 (2017): pp. 377–401.

The Dispatch News Desk. 'CPEC is now Connected with Central Asia by Road Network while Bypassing Afghanistan'. 17 February 2018. https://dnd.com.pk/pakistan-is-linked-now-with-central-asia-by-road-network-while-bypassing-afghanistan/139428.

Dominguez, Gabriel, Jeremy Binnie and Samuel Cranny-Evans. 'Update: Turkmenistan Parades Ground Vehicles for Special Forces'. *Jane's Defence Weekly*, 1 November 2017. https://janes.ihs.com/DefenceWeekly/Display/FG_675609-JDW.

Dorigo, Linda. 'ISIL Continues to Wreak Havoc in Syria's Deir Az Zor'. *Al-Jazeera*, 14 November 2018. https://www.aljazeera.com/indepth/inpictures/isil-continues-wreak-havoc-syria-deir-ez-zor-181028182030798.html.

Driscoll, Jesse. *Warlords and Coalition Politics in Post-Soviet States*. Cambridge: Cambridge University Press, 2015.

Dubnov, Arkady. 'Dustum idet v nastuplenie'. *Institute for War and Peace Reporting*, 21 February 2005. https://goo.gl/hfR5lB.

Dubovtsev, G.F. *Voennaia bezopasnost' Respubliki Kazakhstan: Opyt, aktualnye problemy, osnovnye napravleniia obespecheniia*. Astana: KISI, 2018.

Dzhuraev, Emilbek and Shairbek Dzhuraev. 'The Kazakh and Kyrgyz Sides of Afghanistan: So Near and Yet So Far'. In *The Regional Dimensions to Security: Other Sides of Afghanistan*, edited by Aglaya Snetkov and Stephen Aris, pp. 173–88. Basingstoke: Palgrave Macmillan, 2013.

The Economic Times. 'US Congress Passes Bill to Slash Pakistan's Security Aid to USD 150 million', 3 August 2018. https://economictimes.indiatimes.com/news/international/world-news/us-congress-passes-bill-to-slash-pakistans-security-aid-to-usd-150-million/videoshow/65258721.cms.

Egorov, Ivan. 'Ugroza s iuga'. *Rossiiskaia gazeta*, 25 November 2018. https://rg.ru/2018/11/25/sekretari-sovbezov-sng-rasskazali-kto-pomogaet-boevikam-v-afganistane.html.

Eikenberry, Karl W. 'The Limits of Counterinsurgency Doctrine in Afghanistan: The Other Side of the COIN'. *Foreign Affairs*, September/October 2013. https://www.foreignaffairs.com/articles/afghanistan/2013-08-12/limits-counterinsurgency-doctrine-afghanistan.

Entekhabi-Fard, Camelia. 'Accusations of American Meddling Mar Afghan Council'. *EurasiaNet*, 6 December 2002. http://www.eurasianet.org/departments/insight/articles/eav061202a.shtml.

Entekhabi-Fard, Camelia. 'As Afghan Council Proceeds, America Predicts a Strong President: A EurasiaNet Q & A with US Ambassador Zalmay Khalilzad'. *EurasiaNet*, 22 December 2003. http://www.eurasianet.org/departments/qanda/articles/eav122203.shtml.

Ermekov, Aidar. 'SShA pereshli k planu 'B' po destabilizatsii Tsentralnoi Azii'. *MK Kazakhstan*, 14 November 2018. https://mk-kz.kz/politics/2018/11/14/ssha-pereshli-k-planu-b-po-destabilizacii-centralnoy-azii.html.

Esenalieva, Diana. 'Migratsionnaia sluzhba: v Kyrgyzstane naschityvaetsia 169 bezhnetsev'. *Knews.kg*, 3 February 2016. http://www.knews.kg/society/75036_migratsionnaya_slujba_v_kyrgyizstane_naschityivaetsya_169_bejentsev.

Esipova, Neli and Julie Ray. 'Eastern Europeans, CIS Residents See Russia, U.S. as Threats'. *Gallup*, 4 April 2016. https://news.gallup.com/poll/190415/eastern-europeans-cis-residents-russia-threats.aspx?version=print.

EurAsia Daily. 'FSB: Na sever Afganistana perebrosheny 8000 boevikov iz Sirii'. 5 April 2018. https://eadaily.com/ru/news/2018/04/05/fsb-na-sever-afganistana-perebrosheny-8000-boevikov-iz-sirii.

EurAsia Daily. 'GKNB Tadzhikistana: na granitse s respublikoi sosredotocheny 7 tys. Talibov'. 3 May 2018. https://eadaily.com/ru/news/2018/05/03/gknb-tadzhikistana-na-granice-s-respublikoy-sosredotocheny-7-tys-talibov.

Eurasianet. 'Turkmenistan's Plan B: Electricity Exports'. 28 February 2018. https://eurasianet.org/turkmenistans-plan-b-electricity-exports.

Evseev, V.V. and A.A. Kuznetsov. 'Rekomendatsii po optimizatsii deiatelnosti Shankhaiskoi organizatsii sotrudnichestva'. In *Aktualnye problemy razvitiia Shakhaiskoi organizatsii sotrudnichestva*, pp. 68–71. Moscow: Institut stran SNG, 2018.

Ewing, Philip and Brian Naylor. '"We Are not Nation-Building Again," Trump says while Unveiling Afghanistan Strategy'. *NPR*, 21 August 2017. https://www.npr.org/2017/08/21/545044232/trump-expected-to-order-4-000-more-troops-to-afghanistan.

Fair, Christine. '"Clear, Build, Hold, Transfer": Can Obama's Afghan Strategy Work'. *Asian Affairs: An American Review* 37 (2010): pp. 113–34.

Fair, Christine. 'Afghanistan in 2017: Another Year of Running in Place'. *Asian Survey* 58, 1 (2018): pp. 110–119.

Fazendeiro, Bernardo Teles. 'Uzbekistan's Defensive Self-Reliance: Karimov's Foreign Policy Legacy'. *International Affairs* 93, 2 (2017): pp. 409–27.

Fazilov, G. 'O podkhodakh Uzbekistana v otnoshenii uregulirovaniia konflikta v Afganistane, predprinimaemykh merakh i usiliiakh po sodeistviiu sotsialno-ekonomicheskomu vosstanovleniiu IRA'. In *Sbornik dokladov mezhdunarodnoi konferentsii 'Tsentralnaia Aziia—glavnyi prioritet vneshnei politiki Uzbekistana'*, pp. 92–96. Tashkent: Ministry of Foreign Affairs of Uzbekistan, 2017.

Fedorov, Iurii. 'Afganistan v novykh voenno-politicheskikh realiiakh: chto eto znachit dlia ego sosedei v Tsentralnoi Azii?' *Index bezopasnosti* 21, 1, 112 (2015): pp. 29–46.

Felbab-Brown, Vanda. 'President Trump's Afghanistan Policy: Hopes and Pitfalls'. Report, The Brookings Institution, Washington, DC, September 2017.

Fergana News Agency. 'Tajikistan Border Guards Accused of Killing Afghan Civilians', 10 November 2017. http://enews.fergananews.com/news.php?id=3597&mode=snews.

Fergana News Agency. 'Na peregovorakh Mirzieeva i Gani podnimalas' "tema Dustuma" i uproshchenie rezhima na granitse', 7 December 2017. https://www.fergananews.com/news/27471.

Fjæstad, Kristin and Heidi Kjærnet. 'Performing Statehood: Afghanistan as an Arena for Central Asian States'. *Central Asian Survey* 33, 3 (2014): pp. 312–328.

Forbes.kz. 'Ministry oborony Kazakhstana i Afganistana obsudili sotrudnichestvo v voennoi sfere'. 10 April 2013. https://forbes.kz/news/2013/04/10/newsid_24726.

Fowler, Jeffrey T. 'Afghanistan: Has "The Great Game" Returned Between Russia and the US?' *In Homeland Security*, 1 March 2018. https://inhomelandsecurity.com/afghanistan-great-game/.

Gadoury, Christopher L. 'Should the United States Officially Recognize the Taliban?' *Houston Journal of International Law* 23, 1 (2000): pp. 385–428.

Gafarlı, Orhan. 'Multi-Faceted Linkages between Afghanistan and Central Asian States'. In *Evolving Situation in Afghanistan: Role of Major Powers and Regional Countries*, edited by Sarah Siddiq Aneel, pp. 127–142. Islamabad: IPRI, 2016.

Gafurova, G. 'Tadzhiksko-afganskoe sotrudnichestvo v oblasti transportnoi kommunikatsii v gody nezavisimosti'. *Uchenye zapiski Khudzhandskogo gosudarstvennogo universiteta* 4, 37 (2013): pp. 149–62.

Gall, Carlotta. 'Former Afghan King Rules Out all but Symbolic Role'. *New York Times*, 11 June 2002. http://query.nytimes.com/gst/fullpage.html?res=9F04E1D8113DF932A25755C0A9649C8B63&sec=&spon=&pagewanted=2.

Gall, Carlotta. 'New Afghan Constitution Juggles Koran and Democracy'. *New York Times*, 19 October 2003. http://query.nytimes.com/gst/fullpage.html?res=9C06E2DC133EF93AA25753C1A9659C8B63&sec=&spon=&pagewanted=2.

Gall, Carlotta. 'As the Fighting Swells in Afghanistan, so Does a Refugee Camp in its Capital'. *The New York Times*, 2 August 2008. http://www.nytimes.com/2008/08/03/world/asia/03afghan.html?scp=5&sq=afghanistan%20&st=cse.

Gall, Carlotta. 'Ragtag Taliban Show Tenacity in Afghanistan'. *The New York Times*, 4 August 2008. http://www.nytimes.com/2008/08/04/world/asia/04taliban.html?_r=1&scp=2&sq=afghanistan%20&st=cse&oref=slogin.

Gannon, Kathy. 'Afghanistan Unbound'. *Foreign Affairs,* May/June 2004. https://www.foreignaffairs.com/articles/asia/2004-05-01/afghanistan-unbound.

Gaston, Erica and Lillian Dang. 'Addressing Land Conflict in Afghanistan'. Special Report 372. United States Institute of Peace, June 2015. http://www.usip.org/sites/default/files/SR372-Addressing-Land-Conflict-in-Afghanistan.pdf.

Gates, Robert M. *Duty: Memoirs of a Secretary at War*. New York: Vintage, 2015.

Gavrilis, George. *Afghan Narcotrafficking: The State of Afghanistan's Borders*. New York: East West Institute, 2015.

Gazeta.uz. 'Uzbekistan predlozhil sozdat' transportnuiu strategiiu Tsentralnoi Azii'. 20 September 2018. https://www.gazeta.uz/ru/2018/09/20/transport/.

Gazeta.uz. 'O chem govorili lidery Tsentralnoi Azii', 30 November 2019. https://www.gazeta.uz/ru/2019/11/30/ca-partnership/.

Gezitter. 'Vneshnie i vnutrennie ugrozy aktualny i dlia Kyrgyzstana'. 22 December 2015. http://m.gezitter.org/politic/46369_vneshnie_i_vnutrennie_ugrozyi_aktualnyi_i_dlya_kyirgyizstana/.

Ghiasy, Richard and Maihan Saeedi. *The Heart of Asia Process at a Juncture: An Analysis of Impediments to Further Progress*. Kabul: Afghan Institute for Strategic Studies, 2014.

Ghufran, Nasreen. 'The Taliban and the Civil War Entanglement in Afghanistan'. *Asian Survey* 41, 3 (2001): pp. 462–87.

Giustozzi, Antonio. *Koran, Kalashnikov and Laptop: The Neo-Taliban Insurgency in Afghanistan*. New York: Columbia University Press, 2000.

Giustozzi, Antonio. 'Daesh Moves House: Settling in to Life in Afghanistan'. News brief. Royal United Services Institute, London, May 2018. https://rusi.org/publication/newsbrief/daesh-moves-house-settling-life-afghanistan.

Giustozzi, Antonio. *The Islamic State in Khorasan: Afghanistan, Pakistan and the New Central Asian Jihad*. London: Hurst and Company, 2018.

Glanz, James and Richard A. Oppel Jr. 'U.N. Officials Say American Offered Plan to Replace Karzai'. *The New York Times*, 16 December 2009. http://www.nytimes.com/2009/12/17/world/asia/17galbraith.html.

Goldstein, Joseph. 'Afghan Security Forces Struggle Just to Maintain Stalemate'. *The New York Times*, 22 July 2015. http://www.nytimes.com/2015/07/23/world/asia/afghan-security-forces-struggle-just-to-maintain-stalemate.html.

Golubev, K. A. 'Constructing Narratives about the Taliban by Russia's Ministry of Foreign Affairs'. *Vestnik of Saint Petersburg University: International Relations* 12, 2 (2019): pp. 229–241.

Goodson, Larry. *Afghanistan's Endless War: State Failure, Regional Politics and the Rise of the Taliban*. Seattle: University of Washington Press, 2001.

Goodson, Larry. 'Afghanistan in 2003: The Taliban Re-surface and a New Constitution is Born'. *Asian Survey* 41, 1 (2004): pp. 14–22.

Goodson, Larry. 'Bullets, Ballots and Poppies in Afghanistan'. *Journal of Democracy* 16, 1 (2005): pp. 24–38.

Goodson, Larry and Thomas H. Johnson. *U.S. Policy and Strategy toward Afghanistan after 2014*. Carlisle: U.S. Army War College Press, 2014.

Gorenburg, Dmitry. 'External Support for Central Asian Military and Security Forces'. Report, SIPRI, Stockholm, 2014.

Gotev, Georgi. 'Astana Hosts Little-Publicised Central Asia Summit'. *EURACTIV.com*, 16 March 2018. https://www.euractiv.com/section/central-asia/news/fri-astana-hosts-little-publicised-central-asia-summit/.

Graham-Harrison, Emma. 'Ghani Declared Winner of Afghan Election – But Opponent Rejects Result'. *The Guardian*, 19 February 2020. https://www.theguardian.com/world/2020/feb/18/ashraf-ghani-wins-afghan-presidential-election.

Gritsan, Konstantin. 'Nachalniki shtabov sveriaiut chasy'. *Pogranichnik Sodruzhestva* 4, 88 (2016): pp. 6–13.

Gul, Ayaz. 'US Military Rejects Russian Claims About Number of IS Fighters in Afghanistan'. *Voice of America*, 24 February 2018. https://www.voanews.com/a/us-military-rejects-russia-numbers-of-islamic-state-fighters-in-afghanistan/4268999.html.

Gundarov, Vladimir. 'Kyrgyzstan pereshel pod rossiiskuiu zashchitu'. *Nezavisimaia gazeta*, 3 February 2017. http://nvo.ng.ru/nvoevents/2017-02-03/2_935_news.html.

Gutcher, Lianne. 'Afghanistan's Anti-Corruption Efforts Thwarted at Every Turn'. *The Guardian*, 20 July 2011. https://www.theguardian.com/world/2011/jul/19/afghanistan-anti-corruption-efforts-thwarted.

Guterres, António. 'Secretary-General's remarks to the Security Council on Building Regional Partnership in Afghanistan and Central Asia, to Link Security and Development'. *United Nations Secretary-General*, 19 January 2018. https://www.un.org/sg/en/content/sg/statement/2018-01-19/secretary-general%E2%80%99s-remarks-security-council-building-regional.

de Haas, Marcel. 'Security Policy and Developments in Central Asia: Security Documents Compared with Security Challenges'. *The Journal of Slavic Military Studies* 29, 2 (2016), pp. 203–226.

de Haas, Marcel. 'War Games of the Shanghai Cooperation Organization and the Collective Security Treaty Organization: Drills on the Move!' *The Journal of Slavic Military Studies* 29, 3 (2016): pp. 378–406.

Hadley, Ed and Christopher D. Kolenda. 'Political Process in Afghanistan. What Role for International Partners?' In *Incremental Peace in Afghanistan*, edited by Anna Larson and Alexander Ramsbotham, pp. 85–90. London: Conciliation Resources, 2018.

Haidari, M. Ashraf. 'Afghanistan's Parliamentary Election Results Confirm Stunning Gains for Women'. *Eurasianet.org,* 28 October 2005. http://www.eurasianet.org/departments/civilsociety/articles/eav102805b.shtml.

Hanifi, M. Jamil. 'Editing the Past: Colonial Production of Hegemony through the "Loya Jerga" in Afghanistan'. *Iranian Studies*, 37, 2 (2004): pp. 295–322.

Hanks, Reuel R. '"Multi-Vector Politics" and Kazakhstan's Emerging Role as a Geo-Strategic Player in Central Asia'. *Journal of Balkan and Near Eastern Studies* 11, 3 (2009): pp. 257–267.

Hanks, Reuel R. *Global Security Watch: Central Asia*. Santa Barbara: Praeger, 2010.

Hansen, Lene. 'Reconstructing Desecuritisation: The Normative-Political in the Copenhagen School and Directions for how to Apply it'. *Review of International Studies* 38, 3 (2012), pp. 525–46.

Hansen, Lene. *Security as Practice: Discourse Analysis and the Bosnian Wa*r. Abingdon: Routledge, 2006.

Harpviken, Kristian Berg and Shahrbanou Tadjbakhsh. *A Rock between Hard Places: Afghanistan as an Arena of Regional Insecurity*. London: Hurst and Company, 2016.

Hatef, Azeta and Luwei Rose Luqiu. 'Where Does Afghanistan Fit in China's Grand Project? A Content Analysis of Afghan and Chinese News Coverage of the One Belt, One Road Initiative'. *The International Communication Gazette*, 80, 6 (2017): pp. 551–69.

Hoagland, Richard E. 'Central Asia: Not in Our Backyard, Not a Hot Spot, Strategically Important'. *CIGI Papers* 87 (2016): https://www.cigionline.org/sites/default/files/cigi_paper_no.87web_3.pdf.

Huasheng, Zhao. 'What Is Behind China's Growing Attention to Afghanistan?' *Carnegie Endowment for International Peace*, 8 March 2015. https://carnegieendowment.org/2015/03/08/what-is-behind-china-s-growing-attention-to-afghanistan-pub-59286.

Huasheng, Zhao. 'Afghanistan and China's New Neighbourhood Diplomacy'. *International Affairs* 92, 4 (2016): pp. 891–908.

Hui, Wang. 'SCO Meeting Likely to Deepen Regional Security Cooperation'. *China Daily*, 22 June 2016. http://www.chinadaily.com.cn/opinion/2016-06/22/content_25798646.htm.

Human Rights Watch. 'Q & A on Afghanistan's Loya Jirga Process', 15 April 2002. http://www.hrw.org/press/2002/04/qna-loyagirga.htm.

Human Rights Watch. 'Afghanistan: Loya Jirga off to a Shaky Start'. 13 June 2002. http://hrw.org/english/docs/2002/06/13/afghan4039.htm.

Human Rights Watch. 'Afghanistan: Analysis of New Cabinet, Warlords Emerge from Loya Jirga More Powerful Than Ever'. 20 June 2002. http://hrw.org/english/docs/2002/06/20/afghan4051.htm.

Human Rights Watch. 'Afghanistan: Constitutional Process Marred by Abuses'. 8 January 2004. http://hrw.org/english/docs/2004/01/07/afghan6914.htm.

Hussainkhail, Faridullah. 'TAPI Seen as a Project of Empathy and Integrity for Afghans'. *Tolo News*, 24 February 2018. https://www.tolonews.com/business/tapi-seen-project-empathy-and-integrity-afghans.

Huysmans, Jef. *The Politics of Insecurity. Fear, Migration and Asylum in the EU*. London: Routledge, 2006.

Ihsas, Zabihullah. 'Trade Barriers Linked to Political Tiffs'. *Pajhwok*, 16 July 2013. https://www.pajhwok.com/en/2013/07/16/trade-barriers-linked-political-tiffs.

Iksanova, Gulnar. 'Zasedanie komiteta po sottsialno-kulturnomu razvitiiu sovmestno s sotsialnym sovetom pri fraktsii "Nur Otan"'. *Mazhilis of the Parliament of the Republic of Kazakhstan*, 27 February 2018. http://www.parlam.kz/ru/blogs/iksanova/Details/6/58025.

Imanaliev, M.S. 'Problemy bezopasnosti v Tsentralnoi Azii i kyrgyzsko-afganskie otnosheniia'. *Vestnik Diplomaticheskoi Akademii MID KR* 4, 4 (2014) pp. 49–55.

Imanaliev, Zhanibek. 'ODKB: obespechenie natsionalnoi bezopasnosti Kazakhstana cherez instrumenty kollektivnogo sotrudnichestva'. *Ministry of Foreign Affairs of Kazakhstan*, 12 April 2018. http://mfa.gov.kz/ru/content-view/znibek-imanliev-kszymdyk-yntymaktastyk-kraldary-arkyly-kazakstanny-lttyk-kauipsizdigin-kamtamasyz-etu.

Indyk, Martin S., Kenneth G. Lieberthal and Michael E. O'Hanlon. 'Scoring Obama's Foreign Policy: A Progressive Pragmatist Tries to Bend History'. *Foreign Affairs* 29, 91 (2012): pp. 29–43.

InformBuro. 'Afganistanu predlozhili gotovit' voennykh spetsialistov v Kazakhstane'. 18 July 2017. https://informburo.kz/novosti/afganistanu-predlozhili-gotovit-voennyh-specialistov-v-kazakhstane.html.

Interfax. 'Dushanbe Objects to Afghan Ambassador in Moscow's Remarks on Tajik People'. 12 January 2017. http://www.interfax.com/newsinf.asp?d=1&id=726895.

International Crisis Group. 'Afghanistan's Flawed Constitutional Process'. Briefing paper 56, Kabul/Brussels (12 June 2003): p. 10.

Ionova, E. 'Turkmeniia: poisk novykh gazoeksportnykh marshrutov'. *Rossiia i novye gosudarstva Evrazii* 3 (2018): pp. 83–96.
Irgaliev, Ermek. 'Boeviki iz Sirii nachali vozvrashchatsia v Kyrgyzstan'. *365info.kz*, 2 November 2017. https://365info.kz/2017/11/boeviki-iz-sirii-nachali-vozvrashhatsya-v-kyrgyzstan/.
Isabaeva, Saule. 'Afganskaia golovolomka: vse khotiat mira, no gotoviatsia k voine'. *Central Asia Monitor*, 6 June 2019. https://camonitor.kz/33129-afganskaya-golovolomka-vse-hotyat-mira-no-gotovyatsya-k-voyne.html.
Isamatova, A.T. 'Tsentralnaia Aziia v politike Rossii, SShA i Kitaia'. *Vestnik KRSU* 17, 2 (2017): pp. 152–55.
Iskandarov, Akbarsho, Kosimsho Iskandarov and Ivan Safranchuk. *Novyi etap krizisa v Afganistane i bezopasnost' Tadzhikistana*. Moscow: Valdai Discussion Club, 2016.
Iskandarov, Q. 'Tojikoni Afghoniston dar ravandi raqobathoi qavmiu siyosii kishvar'. *Payomi donishgohi millii Tojikiston* 3, 6 (2017): pp. 12–195.
Islamic Republic of Afghanistan. 'The Constitution of Afghanistan'. 2004. http://www.afghan-web.com/politics/current_constitution.html#chapterone.
Islamic Republic of Afghanistan. 'Afghanistan National Development Strategy 1387–1391 (2008–2013): A Strategy for Security, Governance, Economic Growth & Poverty Reduction'. Report, Afghanistan National Development Strategy Secretariat, Kabul, 2008.
Islamic Republic of Afghanistan, Ministry of Economy. 'Electricity Imports'. Report, Afghanistan Inter-Ministerial Commission for Energy, Kabul, 2016. https://sites.google.com/site/iceafghanistan/electricity-supply/electricity-imports.
Islamic Republic of Afghanistan, Ministry of Foreign Affairs. 'The Heart of Asia–Istanbul Process Progress Assessment 2011–2015'. Report, Kabul, 2016.
Iuldasheva, Ava. 'S nachala goda na tadzhiksko-afganskoi granitse proizoshli 26 boestolknovenii, 13 kontrabandistov ubity'. *Asia-Plus*, 14 November 2017. https://news.tj/ru/news/tajikistan/security/20171114/s-nachala-goda-na-tadzhiksko-afganskoi-granitse-proizoshli-26-boestolknovenii-13-kontrabandistov-ubiti.
Jalali, Ali A. 'The Legacy of War and the Challenge of Peace Building'. In *Building a New Afghanistan*, edited by Robert I. Rotberg, pp. 22–55. Washington: Brookings Institution Press, 2007.
Johnson, Casey Garret, Masood Karokhail and Rahmatullah Amiri. 'The Islamic State in Afghanistan: Assessing the Threat'. Briefing paper. United States Institute of Peace, Washington, DC, 7 April 2016. https://www.usip.org/publications/2016/04/islamic-state-afghanistan-assessing-threat.
Joint Electoral Management Body. Website. http://www.jemb.org/index.html.
Jones, Seth G. 'The Rise of Afghanistan's Insurgency: State Failure and Jihad'. *International Security* 32, 4 (2008): pp. 7–40.
Joshi, Rohan. 'Trump's Afghanistan Policy: The Good, the Bad, and the Ugly'. *The Diplomat*, 25 August 2017. https://thediplomat.com/2017/08/trumps-afghanistan-policy-the-good-the-bad-and-the-ugly/.

Journal of Democracy. 'Election Watch'. 17, 1 (2006): pp. 177–80.
Juraev, Farrukh. 'Ekspet: Uzbekistan vosprinimaet Afganistan kak perspektivnogo partnera, a ne istochnik opasnosti'. *Podrobno.uz*, 12 June 2017. https://podrobno.uz/cat/politic/ekspert-uzbekistan-vosprinimaet-afganistan-kak-perspektivnogo-partnera-a-ne-istochnik-opasnosti/.
Kabar.kg. 'Kyrgyzstan i Afganistan dogovorilis' prodolzhit' rabotu po aktivizatsii dvustoronnikh sviazei'. 12 November 2017. http://kabar.kg/news/kyrgyzstan-i-afganistan-dogovorilis-prodolzhit-rabotu-po-aktivizatcii-dvustoronnikh-sviazei/.
Kabar.kg. 'Stats-sekretar' MID KR i posol Afganistana obsudili voprosy rasshireniia sotrudnichestva'. 9 August 2018. http://kabar.kg/news/stats-sekretar-mid-kr-i-posol-afganistana-obsudili-voprosy-dal-neishego-rasshireniia-i-uglubleniia-sotrudnichestva/.
Kamilov, Abdulaziz. 'Soglashenie mezhdu SShA i talibami – eto tolko nachalo puti k miru'. *Gazeta.uz*, 29 February 2020 https://www.gazeta.uz/ru/2020/02/29/kamilov/.
Kapital.kz. 'Kazakhstan i Afganistan dolzhny ukrepliat' sotrudnichestvo'. 3 August 2018. https://kapital.kz/business/71132/kazahstan-i-afganistan-namereny-ukreplyat-sotrudnichestvo.html.
Karimov, Islam. 'Edinstvennoe reshenie afganskoi problemy—mirnye peregovory s talibami'. *FerganaNews*, 13 December 2015. https://www.ferganews.com/news/24249.
Karimov, Tulkinzhon. 'Vooruzhennye Sily Uzbekistana–nadezhnyi garant bezopasnosti i stabilnosti, blagopoluchnoi zhizni naroda'. *UzDaily*, 25 November 2016. https://www.uzdaily.uz/articles-id-30630.htm.
Karin, Erlan. 'Afganistan dlia kazakhstantsev–chernaia dyra'. *Tengri News*, 31 January 2014. https://tengrinews.kz/kazakhstan_news/erlan-karin-afganistan-dlya-kazakhstantsev-chernaya-dyira-249762/.
Karin, Erlan. *The Soldiers of the Caliphate: The Anatomy of a Terrorist Group*. Astana: KISI, 2016.
Karin, Erlan. *Dilemmy bezopasnosti Tsentralnoi Azii*. Paris: IFRI, 2017.
Karin, Erlan. 'V 2017 aktualiziruetsia ugroza vozvrata terroristov v Tsentralnuiu Aziiu'. *KazInform*, 9 January 2017. http://www.inform.kz/ru/v-2017-godu-aktualiziruetsya-ugroza-vozvrata-terroristov-v-central-nuyu-aziyu-erlan-karin_a2987055.
Karin, Erlan. 'Vliianie IGIL v Afganistane rastet'. *Atameken Business TV*, 8 January 2018. https://abctv.kz/ru/last/vliyanie-igil-v-afganistane-rastet-%E2%80%93-politolog.
Karmon, Ely. 'Central Asian Jihadists in the Front Line'. *Perspectives on Terrorism* 11, 4 (2017): pp. 78–86.
Kassenova, Nargis. 'Kazakhstan's Policy toward Afghanistan: Context, Drivers and Outcomes'. In *Afghanistan and Its Neighbors after the NATO Withdrawal*, edited by Amin Saikal and Kirill Nourzhanov, pp. 98–110. New York: Lexington Books, 2016.
Katzman, Kenneth. 'Afghanistan: Post-Taliban Governance, Security, and U.S. Policy'. *Congressional Research Service*, 17 August 2015.

Kaura, Vinay. 'China, US Differ on Road to Peace in Afghanistan'. *Middle East Institute*, 9 January 2018. https://www.mei.edu/publications/china-us-differ-road-peace-afghanistan.

Kazakhstanskaia Pravda. 'Samye glavnye ugrozy v sovremennom mire nazval Nazarbaev'. 11 April 2017. http://www.kazpravda.kz/news/prezident1/samie-glavnie-ugrozi-v-sovremennom-mire-nazval-nazarbaev/.

Kazanin, M.V. *Kitai–Pakistan:voenno-tekhnicheskoe i ekonomicheskoe sotrudnichestvo v nachale XXI veka*. Moscow: Institut Blizhnego Vostoka, 2017.

Kazantsev, A.A. 'Tsentralnaia Aziia: sleduiushchii akt dramy?' In *Groza s Vostoka. Kak otvetit mir na vyzov IGIL?* Edited by F.A. Lukyanov, pp. 127–133. Moscow: EKSMO, 2016.

Kazantsev A.A. and L. Iu. Gusev, *Ugroza religioznogo ekstremizma na postsovetskom prostranstve*. Moscow: TsIPI MGIMO, 2017.

Kazantsev A.A. and I.N. Panarin. *Ugroza mezhdunarodnogo terrorizma i religioznogo ekstremizma gosudarstvam–chlenam ODKB na tsentralnoaziatskom i afganskom napravleniiakh*. Moscow: MGIMO, 2017.

Kembaev, Zh. 'The Implementation of the Commitments Undertaken by the Republic of Kazakhstan within the Framework of the Collective Security Treaty'. In *Collective Security Treaty Organisation and Contingency Planning after 2014*, edited by A.F. Douhan and A.V. Rusakovich, pp. 145–154. Geneva and Minsk: The Geneva Centre for the Democratic Control of Armed Forces, 2016.

Khalilzad, Zalmay. 'Democracy Bubbles Up'. *The Wall Street Journal*, 25 March 2004. http://www.state.gov/p/sca/rls/rm/30811.htm.

Khalilzad, Zalmay and Daniel Byman. 'Afghanistan: The Consolidation of a Rogue State'. *The Washington Quarterly* 23, 1 (1999): pp. 65–78.

Kheel, Rebecca. 'Mattis: More Evidence Needed on Russian Support for Taliban'. *The Hill*, 10 March 2017. https://thehill.com/policy/defense/353702-mattis-more-evidence-needed-on-how-deep-russian-support-for-taliban-is.

Khodzhaeva, Aliia. 'Kazakhstan: KTZh predlagaet eksportirovat' muku v Afganistan cherez Turkmenistan'. *Agrarny Sektor*, 4 December 2018. https://agrosektor.kz/agriculture-news/kazakhstan-ktzh-predlagaet-eksportirovat-muku-v-afganistan-cherez-turkmenistan.html.

Kholbek, Fakhriddin. 'Gotovte ruzhia! Ili pochemu Nur ne dolzhen uiti?' *Asia-Plus*, 21 December 2017. https://news.tj/ru/news/tajikistan/security/20171221/gotovte-ruzhya-ili-pochemu-nur-ne-dolzhen-uiti.

Khramchikhin, Aleksandr. 'Mnogovektornyi tupik'. *Voenno-promyshlennyi kurier* 14, 629 (2016).

Khramchikhin, Aleksandr. 'Afganskaia lovushka Ameriki'. *Nezavisimaia gazeta*, 27 April 2018. http://nvo.ng.ru/concepts/2018-04-27/1_994_afgan.html.

Khrolenko, Aleksandr. 'Bronia krepka: dinamika voenno-tekhnicheskogo sotrudnichestva Moskvy i Tashkenta'. *Sputnik.tj*, 16 October 2018. https://tj.sputniknews.ru/columnists/20181016/1027123825/Bronya-krepka-dinamika-voenno-tekhnicheskogo-sotrudnichestva-Moskvy-i-Tashkenta.html.

Kippen, Grant. 'The 2004 Presidential Election: On the Road to Democracy in Afghanistan'. Briefing Paper. Centre for Study of Democracy, Queen's University, Kingston, 2006.

Knyazev, Alexander. *Istoriia Afganskoi voiny 1990-kh gg. i prevrashchenie Afganistana v istochnik ugroz dlia Tsentralnoi Azii*. Bishkek: KRSU, 2002.

Knyazev, Alexander, ed. *Afganistan i bezopasnost' Tsentralnoi Azii*. Bishkek: Friedrich Ebert Foundation, 2010.

Kohi, Qutbuddin. 'Turkmenistan Extends Power Export to Afghanistan for a Month'. *Pajhwok*, 2 January 2018. https://www.pajhwok.com/en/2018/01/02/turkmenistan-extends-power-export-afghanistan-month.

Kommersant. 'MID Rossii zaiavil o gotovnosti k vzaimodeistviiu s SShA po Afganistanu'. 23 December 2017. https://www.kommersant.ru/doc/3507622.

Kommersant. 'Rossiia usilila voennye bazy v Tsentralnoi Azii v sviazi s "ugrozami iz Afganistana"'. 7 February 2018. https://www.kommersant.ru/doc/3541501.

Konarovsky, M.A. 'Afganistan posle 2014 goda'. *Vestnik mezhdunarodnykh organizatsii* 12, 3 (2017): pp. 242–253.

Krambs, Timothy A. 'Central Asia and the Afghanistan Security Dilemma: Amelioration, Retrograde, or Status Quo? Central Asia's Role in Regional Security Regarding Afghanistan after 2014'. *Connections* 12, 2 (2013): pp. 1–26.

The Kremlin. 'Meeting with President of Afghanistan Ashraf Ghani'. *Official Portal of the President of Russia*, 10 July 2015. http://en.kremlin.ru/events/president/news/49910.

The Kremlin. 'Sovmestnoe zaiavlenie Rossiiskoi Federatsii i Kitaiskoi Narodnoi Respubliki o tekushchei situatsii v mire i vazhnykh mezhdunarodnykh problemakh'. *Official Portal of the President of the Russian Federation*, 4 July 2017. http://kremlin.ru/supplement/5219.

Krivosheev, Kirill. 'Tadzhikso-uzbekskuiu granitsu atakovali iz Afganistana'. *Kommersant*, 6 November 2019. https://www.kommersant.ru/doc/4149850.

Kucera, Joshua. 'Turkmenistan Big Beneficiary of Pentagon Money, While Uzbekistan Lags'. *Eurasianet*, 3 December 2012. https://eurasianet.org/turkmenistan-big-beneficiary-of-pentagon-money-while-uzbekistan-lags.

Kuchins, Andrew C., Thomas M. Sanderson and David A. Gordon. *The Northern Distribution Network and the Modern Silk Road: Planning for Afghanistan's Future*. Washington, DC: Center for Strategic and International Studies, 2009.

Kun-uz.com. 'Uroven' trevogi zhitelei Uzbekistana iz-za rasprostraneniia religioznogo ekstremizma snizhaetsia'. 18 November 2017. http://kun-uz.com/ru/uroven-trevogi-zhitelei-uzbekistana/.

Kuo, Lily. 'Kazakh Court Frees Woman who Fled Chinese Re-education Camp'. *The Guardian*, 2 August 2018. https://www.theguardian.com/world/2018/aug/01/kazakh-court-frees-woman-who-fled-chinese-re-education-camp.

Laruelle, Marlene. 'The US Silk Road: Geopolitical Imaginary or the Repackaging of Strategic Interests?' *Eurasian Geography and Economics* 56, 4 (2015): pp. 360–375.

Laruelle, Marlene. 'Assessing Uzbekistan's and Tajikistan's Afghan Policies: The Impact of Domestic Drivers'. In *The Central Asia–Afghanistan Relationship: From Soviet Intervention to the Silk Road Initiatives*, edited by Marlene Laruelle, 115–140. Lanham: Lexington Books, 2017

Laruelle, Marlene. 'Introduction'. In *The Central Asia–Afghanistan Relationship: From Soviet Intervention to the Silk Road Initiatives*, edited by Marlene Laruelle, pp. i–xvi. Lanham: Lexington Books, 2017.

Laumulin, Murat. 'Bezopasnost' Tsentralnoi Azii v kontekste situatsii v Afganistane posle 2014 goda'. *Tsentralnaia Aziia i Kavkaz* 16, 3 (2013): pp. 7–23.

Laumulin, Murat. 'Central Asia–2025. Part 2'. *Central Asia's Affairs* 5 (2017): pp. 7–20.

Lavrov, Sergei. 'Partnerstvo, ispytannoe vremenem'. *Rossiskaia gazeta*, 4 October 2017. https://rg.ru/2017/10/04/lavrov-pomoshch-rf-centralnoj-azii-prevysila-6-milliardov-dollarov.html.

Lawrence, J.P. 'Russia Using ISIS Fears to Undermine NATO's Afghan Mission, Analysts Say'. *Stars and Stripes*, 28 March 2018. https://www.stripes.com/news/russia-using-isis-fears-to-undermine-nato-s-afghan-mission-analysts-say-1.519163.

Lee, Graham. *The New Silk Road and the Northern Distribution Network: A Golden Road to Central Asian Trade Reform?* New York: Open Society Foundations, 2012.

Lee, Jonathan L. *Afghanistan: A History from 1260 to the Present*. London: Reaktion Books, 2019.

Lee, Matthew. 'US Slashes Aid to Afghanistan after Pompeo Visit to Kabul'. *Associated Press*, 24 March 2020. https://apnews.com/649879924a532522e51291955170c034.

Lo, Bobo. *Russian Foreign Policy in the Post-Soviet Era Reality, Illusion and Mythmaking*. Basingstoke: Palgrave Macmillan, 2002.

Lobell, Steven E. 'Threat Assessment, the State, and Foreign Policy: A Neoclassical Realist Model'. In *Neoclassical Realism, the State, and Foreign Policy*, edited by Steven E. Lobell, Norrin M. Ripsman, and Jeffrey W. Taliaferro, pp.42–74. Cambridge: Cambridge University Press, 2009.

Lockie, Alex. 'ISIS has been Militarily Defeated in Iraq and Syria'. *Business Insider*, 22 November 2017. https://www.businessinsider.com.au/isis-military-defeat-iraq-syria-2017-11?r=US&IR=T.

Lord, Montague. 'Regional Economic Integration in Central Asia and South Asia'. Munich Personal RePEc Archive, Paper No. 66436, Munich, 15 May 2015. https://mpra.ub.uni-muenchen.de/66436/1/MPRA_paper_66436.pdf.

Lubold, Gordon, Margherita Stancati and Habib Khan Totakhil. 'Taliban Offensive in Afghanistan Tests U.S'. *The Wall Street Journal*, 29 September 2015. http://www.wsj.com/articles/u-s-warplanes-carry-out-airstrike-in-northern-afghanistan-1443526964.

Lushenko, Paul. 'ISKP: Afghanistan's New Salafi Jihadism'. *Middle East Institute*, 26 October 2018.

Magnus, Ralph H. 'Afghanistan in 1996: The Year of the Taliban'. *Asian Survey* 37, 2 (1997): pp. 111–117.

Majidyar, Ahmad. 'Iran and Russia Team up with Taliban to Undermine U.S.-led Mission in Afghanistan'. *Middle East Institute*, 24 March 2017. https://www.mei.edu/publications/iran-and-russia-team-taliban-undermine-us-led-mission-afghanistan.

Maley, William. *Rescuing Afghanistan*. Sydney: University of NSW Press, 2006.

Mamatkulov, Mukhammadsharif. 'Uzbekistan says won't Rejoin Russia-led Security Bloc'. *Reuters*, 6 July 2017. https://www.reuters.com/article/us-uzbekistan-russia-bloc/uzbekistan-says-wont-rejoin-russia-led-security-bloc-idUSKBN19Q2DL.

Mamyshev, Zhanbolat. 'Kazakhstanu rekomendovali rasseliat' bezhentsev v gorodakh, a ne v lageriakh'. *Zakon.kz*, 26 February 2018. https://www.zakon.kz/4777441-kazakhstanu-rekomendovali-rasseljat.html.

Mamytov, Tokon. 'Doklad'. In *Afganistan i Tsentralnaia Aziia v 2014 godu: rol' ODKB v obespechenii regionalnoi bezopasnosti*, pp. 4–5. Bishkek: Region, 2013.

Manenti, Francesca. 'The Competition between al-Qaeda and Daesh for the Asian Stronghold'. In *The Evolution of Jihadist Radicalization in Asia*, edited by Gabriele Iacovino and Francesca Manenti, pp. 25–37. Rome: Centro Studi Internazionali/European Foundation for Democracy, 2018.

Marat, Erica. *The Military and the State in Central Asia: From Red Army to Independence*. London: Routledge, 2010.

Marhal, Mujib. 'US and Taliban Agree in Principle to Peace Framework, Envoy Says'. *New York Times*, 28 January 2019.

Markey, Daniel S. and James West. 'Behind China's Gambit in Pakistan'. *Council on Foreign Relations*, 12 May 2016. https://www.cfr.org/expert-brief/behind-chinas-gambit-pakistan.

Martinez, Luis. '13,000 Afghan Security Forces Killed in Last Three Years'. *USA Today*, 14 August 2015. http://abcnews.go.com/Politics/13000-afghan-security-forces-killed-years/story?id=33094534.

Mashal, Mujib and Jawad Sukhanyar. 'Afghanistan's Approach to Russian Diplomacy: Keep it in the Family'. *The New York Times*, 27 February 2017. https://www.nytimes.com/2017/02/27/world/asia/afghanistan-moscow-putin-ghani-kochai.html.

Mazzetti, Mark and Eric Schmitt. 'In Secret, Obama Extends U.S. Role in Afghan Combat'. *The New York Times*, 22 November 2014. http://www.nytimes.com/2014/11/22/us/politics/in-secret-obama-extends-us-role-in-afghan-combat.html.

McCrisken, Trevor. 'Justifying Sacrifice: Barack Obama and the Selling and Ending of the War in Afghanistan'. *International Affairs* 88, 5 (2012): pp. 993–1007.

McLeary, Paul. 'Top U.S. Commander: American Troops Need to Stay in Afghanistan'. *Foreign Policy*, 6 October 2015. http://foreignpolicy.com/2015/10/06/top-u-s-commander-american-troops-stay-afghanistan/.

Mehl, Damon. 'The Islamic Movement of Uzbekistan Opens a Door to the Islamic State'. *CTC Sentinel* 8, 6 (2015): pp. 11–14.

Melibaev, Navruz. 'Chto sviazyvaet Uzbekistan i Afghanistan krome obshchei granitsy i voprosov bezopasnosti?' *CABAR*, 6 April 2018. https://cabar.asia/ru/chto-svyazyvaet-uzbekistan-i-afganistan-krome-obshhej-granitsy-i-voprosov-bezopasnosti/.

Metrinko, Michael J. 'Elections in Afghanistan: Looking to the Future'. Issue Paper 20. US Army Peacekeeping and Stability Operations Institute, January 2008.

Meyer, Henry. 'Now Putin Is Being Asked to Bring Peace to Afghanistan'. *Bloomberg*, 23 November 2017. https://www.bloomberg.com/news/articles/2017-11-23/russia-must-pressure-taliban-to-seek-peace-afghanistan-says.

Michel, Casey. 'The Obama Administration Is Gifting War Machines to a Murderous Dictator'. *The New Republic*, 4 February 2015. https://newrepublic.com/article/120911/obama-administration-gives-uzbekistans-karimov-military-machines.

Mirsaidov, Negmatullo 'Rahmon–Votel Meeting Highlights Tajikistan's Key Role in Central Asia'. *Caravanserai*, 15 May 2018. http://central.asia-news.com/en_GB/articles/cnmi_ca/features/2018/05/15/feature-01.

Mirzoev, Saimuddin. *Afganistan; vyzovy i ugrozy*. Dushanbe: Irfon, 2017.

Mogilevskii, Roman. *Trends and Patterns in Foreign Trade of Central Asian Countries*. Bishkek: UCA, 2012.

Mohammadi, Zarmina. 'MoF Collected 11 Billion AFs From Balkh Customs'. *Tolo News*, 2 January 2018. https://www.tolonews.com/business/mof-collected-11-billion-afs-balkh-customs.

Mokii, Andrei. 'Bolee 8000 narkozavisimykh sostoiat na uchete v Uzbekistane'. *Gazeta.uz*, 16 February 2018. https://www.gazeta.uz/ru/2018/02/16/drugs/.

The Moscow Times. 'Russia Dismisses as "Idle Gossip" Claims it Is Helping Afghan Taliban'. 25 March 2018. https://themoscowtimes.com/news/russia-calls-claims-it-is-aiding-taliban-in-afghanistan-idle-gossip-60931.

Mukhin, Vladimir. 'Rossiia speshno narashchivaet voennuiu pomoshch' Tadzhikistanu'. *Nezavisimaia gazeta*, 19 December 2017. http://www.ng.ru/world/2017-12-19/2_7140_tajikistan.html.

Müllerson, Rein. *Central Asia: A Chessboard and Player in the New Great Game*. London: Routledge, 2007.

Muratalieva, Z.T. 'Proekt SShA po demokratizatsii Tsentralnoi Azii: teriia na praktike'. *Vestnik KRSU* 15, 5 (2015): pp. 20–23.

National Post. 'The General in Charge of the Afghanistan War Said Russia Is Arming the Taliban'. 22 March 2018. https://nationalpost.com/news/world/us-will-have-role-in-afghan-reconciliation-with-taliban.

National Public Radio. 'Top U.S. Commander in Afghanistan Accuses Russia of Aiding Taliban', 26 March 2018. https://www.npr.org/sections/thetwo-way/2018/03/26/596933077/top-u-s-commander-in-afghanistan-accuses-russia-of-aiding-taliban.

NATO. 'ISAF–Chronology'. *International Security Assistance Force*. http://www.nato.int/ISAF/topics/chronology/index.html.

NATO. 'The Afghanistan Compact'. 31 January–1 February 2006. http://www.nato.int/isaf/docu/epub/pdf/afghanistan_compact.pdf.

Naumkin, Vitaly V. *Militant Islam in Central Asia: The Case of the Islamic Movement of Uzbekistan*. Berkeley: University of California, 2003.

Nazarbaev, Nursultan. 'Voennaia doktrina Respubliki Kazakhstan'. Decree No 161 by the President of Kazakhtsan, 11 October 2011. http://bap.prokuror.kz/rus/o-prokurature/normativnye-pravovye-akty/voennaya-doktrina-respubliki-kazahstan.

Nazarbaev, Nursultan. 'Ob utverzhdenii osnovnykh napravlenii gosudarstvennoi politiki Respubliki Kazakhstan v sfere ofitsialnoi pomoshchi razvitiiu na 2017–2020 gody'. Presidential Decree No. 415, 31 January 2017. http://nomad.su/?a=3-201702100039.

Nazarbaev, Nursultan. 'Ekskliuzivnoe interviu prezidenta kazakhstana (telekanal "Mir")'. *Zakon.kz*, 12 April 2017. https://www.zakon.kz/4853349-jekskljuzivnoe-intervju-prezidenta.html.

Nazarbaev, Nursultan. 'Ob utverzhdenii Voennoi doktriny Respubliki Kazakhstan'. Decree No 554 by the President of Kazakhtsan, 29 September 2017. https://tengrinews.kz/zakon/prezident_respubliki_kazahstan/obopona/id-U1700000554/.

Nazarbaev, Nursultan. '400 kazakhstantsev zaverbovany v "Islamskoe gosudarstvo"'. *Nur.kz,* 16 November 2017. https://www.nur.kz/1679518-nazarbaev-400-kazakhstancev-zaverbovany.html.

The New York Times. 'Guns and Poppies'. Editorial, 5 August 2008. http://www.nytimes.com/2008/08/05/opinion/05tue1.html?scp=1&sq=poppy%20afghanistan&st=cse.

Newberg, Paula R. 'Neither War nor Peace'. In *Afghanistan: Challenges and Prospects*, edited by Srinjoy Bose, Nishank Motwani and William Maley, pp. 28–40. London: Routledge, 2018.

News18. 'Afghanistan will Collapse within Six Months without US Support and Money: President Ashraf Ghani', 18 January 2018. https://www.news18.com/news/world/afghanistan-will-collapse-within-six-months-without-us-support-and-money-president-ashraf-ghani-1635539.html.

Nikitina, Yulia. 'Cooperative Transregionalism and the Problem of the "In Betweens"'. In *Getting Out from 'In-Between': Perspectives on the Regional Order in Post-Soviet Europe and Eurasia*, edited by Samuel Charap, Alyssa Demus and Jeremy Shapiro, pp. 41–48. Santa Monica: RAND, 2018.

Nixon, Hamish and Richard Ponzio. 'Building Democracy in Afghanistan: The Statebuilding Agenda and International Engagement'. *International Peacekeeping* 14, 1 (2004): pp. 26–40.

Nochevkin, Vadim. 'Afganistan: ugroza Kyrgyzstanu rastet s kazhdym dnem'. *Delo No*, 30 August 2017. https://delo.kg/afganistan-ugroza-kyrgyzstanu-rastjot-s-kazhdym-dnjom/.

Nojumi, Neamatollah. *Rise of the Taliban in Afghanistan: Mass Mobilization, Civil War, and the Future of the Region*. New York: Palgrave Macmillan, 2002.

Norchi, Charles H. 'Toward the Rule of Law in Afghanistan: The Constitutive Process'. In *Beyond Reconstruction in Afghanistan: Lessons from Development Experience*, edited by John D. Montgomery and Dennis A. Rondinelli, pp. 115–131. New York: Palgrave Macmillan, 2004.

Norov, Vladimir. 'V stabilnosti Afganistana zainteresovan ves' region'. *EurAsia Daily*, 30 March 2018. https://eadaily.com/ru/news/2018/03/30/vladimir-norov-v-stabilnosti-afganistana-zainteresovan-ves-region.

Nourzhanov, Kirill. 'Central Asia's Domestic Stability in Official Russian Security Thinking under Yeltsin and Putin: From Hegemony to Multilateral Pragmatism'. In *China, Xinjiang and Central Asia: History, Transition and Crossborder Interaction into the 21st Century*, edited by Colin Mackerras and Michael Clarke, pp. 151–172. London and New York: Routledge, 2009.

Nourzhanov, Kirill. 'Russia's Afghanistan Policy after 2014: Staying at an Arm's Length and Preparing for the Worst'. In *Afghanistan and Its Neighbors after the NATO Withdrawal*, ed. Amin Saikal and Kirill Nourzhanov, pp. 163–78. New York: Lexington Books, 2016.

Nourzhanov, Kirill. 'Tajikistan's Multi-Vector Foreign Policy: Constructing Relations with Russia, China, and the United States'. In *Tajikistan on the Move: Statebuilding and Societal Transformations*, edited by Marlene Laruelle, pp. 87–110. Lanham: Lexington Books, 2018.

Numonzoda, R.I. and H.D. Muhammadzoda. 'Sravnitelnyi analiz situatsii s prestupnostiu v sfere nezakonnogo oborota narkoticheskikh sredstv, psikhotropnykh veshchestv i prekursorov'. *Narkofront* 4 (2017): pp. 65–83.

O'Hanlon, Michael. 'Improving Afghanistan Policy'. *The Brookings Foreign Policy Brief*, 2, 1 (2016): pp. 1–8.

Ó Tuathail, Gearóid and Simon Dalby. 'Geopolitics and Discourse: Practical Geopolitical Reasoning in American Foreign Policy'. In *The Geopolitics Reader*, edited by Gearóid Ó Tuathail, Simon Dalby and Paul Routledge, pp. 78–91. London: Routledge, 1998.

Oates, Lauryn and Isabelle Solon Helal. 'At the Cross-Roads of Conflict and Democracy: Women and Afghanistan's Constitutional Loya Jirga'. Report, International Centre for Human Rights and Democratic Development, Montreal, 2004. http://www.wraf.ca/documents/consLoyaJirgaE.pdf.

Obama, Barack. 'Remarks by the President in Address to the Nation on the Way Forward in Afghanistan and Pakistan'. The White House Office of the Press Secretary, 1 December 2009. https://www.whitehouse.gov/the-press-office/remarks-president-address-nation-way-forward-afghanistan-and-pakistan.

The Observer. 'Poorly Directed Aid Increases Afghanistan's Woes'. Editorial, 20 July 2008. http://www.guardian.co.uk/commentisfree/2008/jul/20/afghanistan.internationalaidanddevelopment.

Oehme III, Chester G. 'Terrorists, Insurgents and Criminals—Growing Nexus?' *Studies in Conflict and Terrorism* 31, 1 (2008): pp. 80–93.

Olimov, M.A. 'Religioznaia situatsiia v Tadzhikistane: novye vyzovy'. In *Evraziiskii perekrestok*, Vyp. 7, edited by V.V. Amelin, pp. 27–32. Orenburg: IPK 'Universitet', 2017.

Omelicheva, Mariya. 'Eurasia's CSTO and SCO: A Failure to Address the Trafficking/Terrorism Nexus'. PONARS Policy Memo No. 455, January 2017. http://www.ponarseurasia.org/memo/eurasia-csto-and-sco-failure-address-trafficking-terrorism-nexus.

Omelicheva, Mariya. 'U.S. Security Assistance to Central Asia: Examining Limits, Exploring Opportunities'. PONARS Policy Memo No. 487, October 2017. http://www.ponarseurasia.org/memo/us-security-assistance-central-asia.

Omid, Haidarshah. 'Afghan Goods to Arrive in Turkey via Lapis Lazuli Corridor'. *Tolo News*, 25 December 2018. https://www.tolonews.com/business/afghan-goods-arrive-turkey-%C2%A0lapis-lazuli-corridor.

Orazbekova, Sholpan. 'O zhizni bezhnentsev v Kazakhstane rasskazal predstavitel OON'. *Bnews.kz*, 9 December 2016. https://bnews.kz/ru/dialog/interview/o_zhizni_bezhentsev_v_kazahstane_rasskazal_predstavitel_oon_.

Orazgaliyeva, Malika. 'Kazakhstan Launches First ODA Project in Afghanistan, with Support from UNDP and Japan'. *Astana Times*, 23 February 2017. https://astanatimes.com/2017/02/kazakhstan-launches-first-oda-project-in-afghanistan-with-support-from-undp-and-japan/.

Organization for Security and Co-operation in Europe. 'Tajik and Afghan Border Officers Complete OSCE Training-of-Trainers Course'. Programme Office, Dushanbe, 7 September 2017. https://www.osce.org/programme-office-in-dushanbe/338251.

Orlov, Dmitrii. 'Bez paniki – eto "Taliban"'. *Nezavisimaia Gazeta*, 15 March 2020. http://www.ng.ru/dipkurer/2020-03-15/11_7817_asia.html.

Osmonaliev, K.M. *Trafik afganskikh opiatov cherez territoriiu Kyrgyzstana*. Bishkek: NISI KR, 2014.

Osmonaliev, K.M and A. Isamatova. 'Nekotorye problem obespecheniia bezopasnosti v Tsentralnoi Azii: geopoliticheskie factory i riski'. *Mezhdunarodnoe sotrudnichestvo evraziiskikh gosudarstv* 2, 7 (2016): pp. 82–88.

Ospanova, Aygul. 'Kazakhstan, Russia Back Afghanistan's Transportation System'. *Caspian News*, 13 December 2018. https://caspiannews.com/news-detail/kazakhstan-russia-back-afghanistans-transportation-system-2018-12-13-59/.

Ovsiannikov D.V. and D.G. Popov. 'Sunnitskii Islam i gosudarstvennaia vlast' v Tadzhikistane: voprosy vzaimodeistviia i identifikatsii'. *Musulmanskii mir* 2 (2017): pp. 6–25.

Panarin, I.N. and A.A. Kazantsev. *Ugroza mezhdunarodnogo terrorizma i religioznogo ekstremizma gosudarstvam – chlenam ODKB na tsentralnoaziatskom i afganskom napravleniiakh*. Moscow: IMI MGIMO, 2017.

Panfilova, Viktoria. 'General Dustum s'ezdil na istoricheskuiu rodinu'. *Nezavisimaia gazeta*, 31 January 2014. http://www.ng.ru/cis/2014-01-31/7_dustum.html.

Panfilova, Viktoria. 'Tashkent i Moskva dogovorilis' na 16 milliardov dollarov'. *Nezavisimaia gazeta*, 5 April 2017. http://www.ng.ru/cis/2017-04-05/6_6967_uzbekistan.html.

Panfilova, Viktoria. 'Tashkent i Kabul sodaiut zonu svobodnoi torgovli'. *Nezavisimaia gazeta*, 18 July 2018. http://www.ng.ru/cis/2018-07-18/6_7269_uzbiekistan.html.

Panfilova, Viktoria. 'Armiiu Uzbekistana podniali po trevoge'. *Nezavisimaia gazeta*, 26 November 2018. http://www.ng.ru/cis/2018-11-26/6_7448_training.html.

Pannier, Bruce. 'Majlis Podcast: Turkmenistan's Afghan Dilemma'. *RFE/RL*, 2 July 2016. https://www.rferl.org/a/majlis-podcast-turkmenistan-afghan-dilemma/27834187.html.

Pannier, Bruce. 'Insurgent Activities at the Afghan–Turkmen and Afghan–Tajik Borders'. In *The Central Asia–Afghanistan Relationship: From Soviet Intervention to the Silk Road Initiatives*, Marlene Laruelle, pp. 141–158. Lanham: Lexington Books, 2017.

Pannier, Bruce. 'Analysis: TAPI and Other Turkmen Tales'. *RFE/RL*, 1 December 2018. https://www.rferl.org/a/tapi-turkmen-tales-pipeline-qishloq-ovozi-pannier/29632356.html.

Pannier, Bruce. 'Keeping Afghanistan in Afghanistan'. *The Cairo Review of Global Affairs*, Summer 2019. https://www.thecairoreview.com/essays/keeping-afghanistan-in-afghanistan/.

Pantucci, Raffaello. 'China in Afghanistan: A Reluctant Leader with Growing Stakes'. *ISPI*, 18 October 2018. https://www.ispionline.it/en/pubblicazione/china-afghanistan-reluctant-leader-growing-stakes-21456.

Parto, Saeed, Jos Winters, Ehsan Saadat, Mohsin Usyan and Anastasiya Hozyainova. *Afghanistan and Regional Trade: More, or Less, Imports from Central Asia?* Bishkek: University of Central Asia, 2012.

Patrushev, Nikolai. 'V Afganistane idet terroristicheskaia voina, za god pogibli tysiachi chelovek'. *TASS*, 28 September 2018. https://tass.ru/politika/5605150.

Petraeus, David and Vance Serchuk, 'Can America Trust the Taliban to Prevent Another 9/11? A Dangerous Asymmetry Lies at the Heart of the Afghan Peace Deal'. *Foreign Affairs*, 1 April 2020. https://www.foreignaffairs.com/articles/afghanistan/2020-04-01/can-america-trust-taliban-prevent-another-911.

Peyrouse, Sebastien. 'Political and Economic Pragmatism: Turkmenistan and Afghanistan since 1991'. In *Afghanistan and Its Neighbors after the NATO Withdrawal*, edited by Amin Saikal and Kirill Nourzhanov, pp. 111–128. New York: Lexington Books, 2016.

Peyrouse, Sebastien and Gaël Raballand. 'Central Asia: The New Silk Road Initiative's Questionable Economic Rationality'. *Eurasian Geography and Economics* 56, 4 (2015): pp. 405–20.

Pincus, Walter. 'Red Star's Bagram Contract Extended Again'. *The Washington Post*, 20 March 2012. https://www.washingtonpost.com/blogs/checkpoint-washington/post/red-stars-bagram-contract-extended-again/2012/03/20/gIQAN91cPS_blog.html?utm_term=.3d8a7a9dca25.

Ponzio, Richard and Christopher Freeman. 'Rethinking Statebuilding in Afghanistan'. *International Peacekeeping* 14, 1 (2007): pp. 173–184.

Popov, Dmitrii. 'Dvustoronnie otnosheniia SShA i Tadzhikistana na sovremennom etape'. *Novaia Evraziia* 5, 50 (2018): pp. 87–106.

President of the Kyrgyz Republic. 'Kontseptsiia natsionalnoi bezopasnosti Kyrgyzskoi Respubliki', Decree No. 120, 9 June 2012. http://cbd.minjust.gov.kg/act/view/ru-ru/61367?cl=ru-ru.

President of the Kyrgyz Republic. 'Voennaia doktrina Kyrgyzskoi Respubliki'. Decree No. 165, 15 July 2013. http://cbd.minjust.gov.kg/act/view/ru-ru/900232.

Public Opinion Survey: Residents of Kyrgyzstan. Washington, DC: Center for Insights in Survey Research, 2017.

Putin, Vladimir. 'Vstrecha s Prezidentom Tadzhikistana Emomali Rahmonom'. *Official Portal of the President of Russia*, 6 October 2015. http://www.kremlin.ru/events/president/news/50453.

Putin, Vladimir. 'Esli by v Afganistane ne bylo SShA, bylo by khuzhe'. *Kommersant*, 26 December 2017. https://www.kommersant.ru/doc/3508527.

Putz, Catherine. 'Will Kazakhstan be a Game-Changer in Afghanistan?' *The Diplomat*, 24 November 2015. http://thediplomat.com/2015/11/will-kazakhstan-be-a-game-changer-in-afghanistan/.

Qassem, Shayeq. 'Afghanistan: Imperatives of Stability Misperceived'. *Iranian Studies* 42, 2 (2009): pp. 247–274.

Qiu, Xiaofen. 'Kontseptualnye podkhody Rossii i Kitaia v Tsentralnoi Azii: skhodstvo i razlichiia'. *Problemy postsovetskogo prostranstva* 4 (2015): pp. 74–83.

Rahim, Najim and Rod Nordland. 'Taliban Capture about 150 Afghan Soldiers after Chase into Turkmenistan'. *The New York Times*, 17 March 2019. https://www.nytimes.com/2019/03/17/world/asia/afghanistan-soldiers-taliban-turkmenistan.html.

Rahimjon, Shoirai. 'Dasti Prezidentu khoki Tojikistonro mebusam!' *SSSR.tj*, 14 November 2019. http://www.cccp.tj/tj/2016-02-23-16-45-52/mehmonhona/item/6647-dasti-prezidentu-hok.html?tmpl=component&print=1.

Rahmon, Emomali. 'Poslanie Prezidenta Respubliki Tadzhikistan, Lidera natsii Emomali Rahmona Majlisi Oli Respubliki Tadzhikistan'. *Official Portal of the President of Tajikistan*, 22 December 2017. http://president.tj/ru/node/16772.

Rahmonov, A.S., H. Hojaev and B. Rahmonov. 'Tahdidhoi nav ba amniyati Jumhurii Tojikison: ta'mini rushdi ustuvori kishvar'. *Tojikiston va jahoni imruz* 2, 57 (2017): pp. 62–72.

Rakisheva, Botagoz. 'Integratsionnye orientiry molodezhi Tsentralnoi Azii (rezultaty sotsiologicheskogo issledovaniia)'. In *Tsentralnaia Aziia v usloviiakh globalnoi transformatsii*, edited by Z. K. Shaukenova, pp. 101–110. Astana: KISI, 2017.

Rakisheva, Botagoz. *Molodezh' Tsentralnoi Azii. Sravnitelnyi obzor*. Almaty: Friedrich Ebert Stiftung, 2017.

Ramachandran, Sudha 'Is China Bringing Peace to Afghanistan?' *The Diplomat*, 20 June 2018. https://thediplomat.com/2018/06/is-china-bringing-peace-to-afghanistan/.

Ramani, Samuel. 'In the Demise of the Taliban Peace Talks, Russia is the Winner'. *Foreign Policy*, 11 September 2019. https://foreignpolicy.com/2019/09/11/in-the-demise-of-the-taliban-peace-talks-russia-is-the-winner/.

Rasanayagam, Angelo. *Afghanistan: A Modern History*. London: I.B. Tauris, 2003.

Rashid, Ahmed. *Taliban: Militant Islam, Oil and Fundamentalism in Central Asia*. New Haven: Yale University Press, 2000.

Rashid, Ahmed. *Islam, Oil and the New Great Game in Central Asia*. London: I.B. Tauris, 2002

RECCA. 'The Seventh Regional Economic Cooperation Conference on Afghanistan'. Conference Report, Ashgabat, 14–15 November 2017. http://recca.af/wp-content/uploads/2017/12/RECCA-VII-Report-27-12-2017-1300.pdf.

Reeves, Madeleine. *Border Work: Spatial Lives of the State in Rural Central Asia*. Cornell University Press: Ithaca and London, 2014.

Republic of Kazakhstan, Ministry of Foreign Affairs. 'Pozitsiia Respubliki Kazakhstan po Afganistanu'. *MFA.gov.kz*, 9 May 2014. http://mfa.gov.kz/ru/content-view/uregulirovanie-situatsii-v-afganistane.

Republic of Kazakhstan, Ministry of Foreign Affairs. 'MID RK raz'iasnil prioritety Kazakhstana v SB OON'. *BNews.kz*, 3 January 2017. https://bnews.kz/ru/news/mid_rk_razyasnil_prioriteti_kazahstana_v_sb_oon.

Republic of Kazakhstan, Ministry of Foreign Affairs. 'Mnogostoronnee ekonomicheskoe sotrudnichestvo'. 26 April 2018. http://mfa.gov.kz/ru/content-view/mnogostoronnee-ekonomiceskoe-sotrudnicestvo.

Republic of Kazakhstan, Ministry of Foreign Affairs. 'Kazakhstan prinial uchastie v zasedanii moskovskogo formata konsultatsii po Afganistanu'. 9 November 2018. http://www.mfa.kz/ru/content-view/kazahstan-prinal-ucastie-v-zasedanii-moskovskogo-formata-konsultacij-po-afganistanu.

Republic of Kyrgyzstan, Government. Directive No 196-r, 10 May 2016. http://cbd.minjust.gov.kg/act/view/ru-ru/215822.

Republic of Kyrgyzstan, Ministry of Justice. 'Programma pravitelstva Kyrgyzskoi Respubliki po protivodeistviiu ekstremizmu i terrorizmu na 2017–2022 gody'. 21 June 2017. http://cbd.minjust.gov.kg/act/view/ru-ru/100104.

Republic of Tajikistan, Ministry of Transport. *Investitsionnyi proekt na stroitelstvo zheleznodorozhnoi linii, soediniaiushchei Respubliku Tadzhikistan s Islamskoi Respublikoi Afganistan i Turkmenistanom (cherez Beshkent)*. Dushanbe: Ministry of Transport of the RT, 2014.

Republic of Uzbekistan. 'Oboronnaia doktrina Respubliki Uzbekistan'. Law of the Republic of Uzbekistan No. ZRU-458, 9 January 2018. http://www.lex.uz/docs/3495906.

Republic of Uzbekistan, Ministry of Foreign Affairs. 'Uzbekistan i Afganistan vykhodiat na kachestvenno novyi uroven' sotrudnichestva'. 1 February 2017. https://mfa.uz/ru/press/smi/2017/02/10085/?print=Y.

Republic of Uzbekistan, Ministry of Foreign Affairs. 'Provodimye v Uzbekistane voennye reform v tsentre vnimaniia voenno-politicheskikh krugov SShA i diplomaticheskogo korpusa v g. Vashingtone'. 5 December 2018. https://mfa.uz/ru/press/news/2018/12/16950/.

Republic of Uzbekistan, Ministry of Foreign Affairs. 'Transportno-kommunikatsionnaia strategiia Uzbekistana predstavlena v Vashingtone'. 16 December 2018. https://mfa.uz/ru/press/news/2018/12/17089/.

Reshetniak, Anastasiia. *Terrorizm i religioznyi ekstremizm v Tsentralnoi Azii: problemy vospriiatiia*. Astana: KISI, 2016.

Reynolds, Andrew and Andrew Wilder. 'Free, Fair or Flawed? Challenges for Legitimate Elections on Afghanistan'. Report, Afghanistan Research and Evaluation Unit, Kabul, 2004.

Reynolds, David. 'Enduring Hope: NATO Operations in Afghanistan'. *Jane's Defence Weekly*, 16 May 2019. https://janes.ihs.com/DefenceWeekly/Display/FG_1973589-JDW.

RGP Kazspetseksport. 'Turkmenistan: Vooruzhennye Sily i razvitie voenno-tekhnicheskogo sotrudnichestva kak osnovy obespecheniia boevogo potentsiala armii'. 7 September 2017. http://kaspex.kz/ru/news/118-turkmenistan-vooruzhennye-sily-i-razvitie-voenno-tekhnicheskogo-sotrudnichestva-kak-osnovy-obespecheniya-boevogo-potentsiala-armii.html.

RIA Novosti. 'Ministry oborony Rossii i Turkmenistana obsudili sotrudnichestvo na Kaspii'. 9 June 2016. https://ria.ru/20160609/1444885718.html.

RIA Novosti. 'Shoigu nazval glavnuiu ugrozu v Tsentralnoi Azii dlia bezopasnosti Rossii'. 25 May 2018. https://ria.ru/20180525/1521394049.html.

RIA Novosti. 'Rossiia ne sorevnuetsia s SShA v Afganistane, zaiavili v MID'. 12 November 2018. https://ria.ru/20181112/1532592756.html.

Riphenburg, Carol J. 'Electoral Systems in a Divided Society: The Case of Afghanistan'. *British Journal of Middle Eastern Studies* 34, 1 (2007): pp. 1–21.

Roashan, G. Raif. 'Afghan Constitution an Exercise in Nation Building: A Test in Social Organisation'. Report, Institute for Afghan Studies, 27 July 2004. http://www.institute-for-afghan-studies.org/Contributions/Commentaries/DRRoashan/.

Rosenblum, Daniel. 'Remarks at Ashgabat Media Event'. *US Department of State*, 5 September 2014. https://2009-2017.state.gov/p/sca/rls/rmks/2014/231328.htm.

Roy, Olivier. *Islam and Resistance in Afghanistan*. Cambridge: Cambridge University Press, 1986.

Rubin, Barnett. *A Nation is Dying: Afghanistan under the Soviets 1979–1987*. Evanston: Northwestern University Press, 1988.

Rubin, Barnett. 'Crafting a Constitution for Afghanistan'. *Journal of Democracy* 15, 3 (2004): pp. 5–19.

Rubin, Barnett and Jake Sherman. 'Counter Narcotics to Stabilize Afghanistan: The False Promise of Crop Eradication'. Report, Center for International Co-operation, New York University, New York, February 2008. http://www.cic.nyu.edu/afghanistan/docs/counternarcoticsfinal.pdf.

Rumer, Eugene, Richard Sokolsky and Paul Stronski. *U.S. Policy toward Central Asia 3.0*. Washington, DC: Carnegie Endowment for International Peace, 2016.

Russian Federation, Ministry of Defence. 'Intensivnost sotrudnichestva TsVO so stranami Tsentralnoi Azii v 2018 godu vozrosla na tret'. *Official Portal of the Ministry of Defence of Russia*, 25 December 2018. https://function.mil.ru/news_page/country/more.htm?id=12209621@egNews.

Russian Federation, Ministry of Foreign Affairs. 'Foreign Policy Concept of the Russian Federation (approved by President of the Russian Federation Vladimir Putin on November 30, 2016)'. 1 December 2016. http://www.mid.ru/en/foreign_policy/official_documents/-/asset_publisher/CptICkB6BZ29/content/id/2542248.

Russian Federation, Ministry of Foreign Affairs. 'Press Release on Regional Consultations on Afghanistan in Moscow'. 14 April 2017. http://www.mid.ru/foreign_policy/news/-/asset_publisher/cKNonkJE02Bw/content/id/2726953.

Russian Federation, Ministry of Foreign Affairs. 'Joint Statement by the Member States of the Collective Security Treaty Organisation on the Situation in Afghanistan and the Threat of the Strengthening of International Terrorist and Extremist Organisations in the Northern Provinces of Afghanistan, issued during the 72nd session of the UN General Assembly'. 4 October 2017. http://www.mid.ru/en_GB/foreign_policy/international_safety/conflicts/-/asset_publisher/xIEMTQ3OvzcA/content/id/2886857.

Russian Federation, Ministry of Foreign Affairs. 'Press Release on a Meeting of the SCO-Afghanistan Contact Group'. 12 October 2017. http://www.mid.ru/en/foreign_policy/news/-/asset_publisher/cKNonkJE02Bw/content/id/2898520.

Ruttig, Thomas. 'The 2004 Afghan Presidential Elections and Challenges for the Forthcoming Parliamentary Elections'. In *The Challenge of Rebuilding Afghanistan*, edited by Moonis Ahmar, pp. 61–71. Karachi: Bureau of Composition, Compilation and Translation, University of Karachi Press, 2005.

Ruttig, Thomas 'Climbing on China's Priority List: Views on Afghanistan from Beijing'. *Afghanistan Analysts Network*, 10 April 2018. https://www.afghanistan-analysts.org/climbing-on-chinas-priority-list-views-on-afghanistan-from-beijing/.

Safranchuk, Ivan. 'Islamistskaia ugroza dlia Tsentralnoi Azii: Afganistan i globalnyi kontekst'. *Indeks bezopasnosti* 4, 111 (2014), pp. 103–106.

Safranchuk, Ivan. *Afghanistan and its Central Asian Neighbours: Toward Dividing Insecurity*. Lanham: CSIS and Rowman & Littlefield, 2017.

Safronov, Ivan. 'Frants Klintsevich postradal "za otkrytost"'. *Kommersant*, 12 February 2018. https://www.kommersant.ru/doc/3547099.

Said, Sharif. *Kurs na partnerstvo*. Dushanbe: Orbita, 2013.

Saidzoda, Shohruh. 'Nezakonnyi oborot narkotikov–prestupleniia, predstavliaiushchie ugrozu bezopasnosti Respubliki Tadzhikistan'. *Narkofront* 4 (2017): pp. 32–6.

Saikal, Amin. 'Dimensions of State Disruption and International Responses'. *Third World Quarterly* 21, 1 (2000): pp. 39–49.

Saikal, Amin. 'The Role of Outside Actors in Afghanistan'. *Middle East Policy* 7, 4 (2000): pp. 50–57.

Saikal, Amin. *Modern Afghanistan: A History of Struggle and Survival*. London: IB Tauris, 2004.

Saikal, Amin. 'The United Nations and Democratization in Afghanistan'. In *The UN Role in Promoting Democracy: Between Ideals and Reality*, edited by Edward Neman and Roland Rich (Tokyo: Institute of Samoan Studies, 2004), pp. 320–338.

Saikal, Amin. 'Afghanistan: A Turbulent State in Transition'. In *Modern Afghanistan: The Impact of 40 Years of War*, edited by M. Nazif Shahrani, pp. 21–36. Bloomington: Indiana University Press, 2018.

Saikal, Amin. 'The Afghanistan Conundrum'. *Project Syndicate*, 13 June 2019. https://www.project-syndicate.org/commentary/afghanistan-america-russia-political-settlement-by-amin-saikal-2019-06?barrier=accesspaylog.

Saikal, Amin. *Iran Rising: The Survival and Future of the Islamic Republic*. Princeton: Princeton University Press, 2019.

Saikal, Amin and Kirill Nourzhanov, eds. *Afghanistan and Its Neighbors after the NATO Withdrawal*. Lanham: Lexington Books, 2016.

Schweich, Thomas. 'Is Afghanistan a Narco-State?' *The New York Times,* 27 July 2008. http://www.nytimes.com/2008/07/27/magazine/27AFGHAN-t.html?scp=10&sq=afghanistan%20&st=cse.

Schwelmlein, James. 'The U.S. and Afghan Government Must Re-engage With the Peace Process'. *Carnegie Endowment for International Peace*, 19 November 2018. https://carnegieendowment.org/2018/11/19/u.s.-and-afghan-government-must-re-engage-with-peace-process-pub-77752.

Seldin, Jeff. 'US General: Russia Trying to "Undercut" Progress in Afghanistan'. *Voice of America*, 1 September 2018. https://www.voanews.com/a/us-general-russia-trying-to-undercut-progress-in-afghanistan/4554004.html.

Seldin, Jeff. 'Islamic State in Afghanistan Growing Bigger, More Dangerous'. *Voice of America*, 21 May 2019. https://www.voanews.com/south-central-asia/islamic-state-afghanistan-growing-bigger-more-dangerous.

Shams, Biloli. 'Imenem pogibshego na granitse polkovnika Akhtamova khotiat nazvat' shkolu v ego kishlake'. *Asia-Plus*, 6 December 2017. https://news.tj/news/tajikistan/society/20171206/imenem-pogibshego-na-granitse-polkovnika-ahtamova-mogut-nazvat-shkolu-v-ego-kishlake.

Shams, Shamil. 'China and Russia Want US out of Afghanistan'. *Deutsche Welle*, 14 June 2017. https://www.dw.com/en/china-and-russia-want-us-out-of-afghanistan/a-39250894.

Shanghai Cooperation Organisation Secretariat. 'Qingdao Declaration of the Council of Heads of State of Shanghai Cooperation Organisation'. 10 June 2018. http://eng.sectsco.org/load/443667/.

Sharifali, Sohibi. 'Nahzat va "Davlati Islomi" – du jodai yak paimon!' *Jumhuriyat* 168, 24 August 2018. http://jumhuriyat.tj/index.php?art_id=34802.

Smagulov, Agybai. *Ekspertnaia otsenka vliianiia afganskogo protivostoianiia na politicheskuiu i ekonomicheskuiu situatsiiu v Tsentralnoi Azii*. Bishkek: University of Central Asia, 2013.

Snetkov, Aglaya. *Russia's Security Policy under Putin: A Critical Perspective*. London: Routledge, 2015.

Sokolov, Boris. 'Ni chisla, ni umeniia'. *Voenno-promyshlennyi kurier* 19, 487 (2013).

Sokov, Kirill. 'Afganskii narkotrafik kak sredstvo voiny s Rossiei'. *Ritm Evrazii*, 13 July 2016. https://www.ritmeurasia.org/news--2016-07-13--afganskij-narkotrafik-kak-sredstvo-vojny-s-rossiej-24638.

South China Morning Post. 'China to Build Outposts for Tajik Guards on Tajikistan–Afghanistan Border'. 26 September 2016. https://www.scmp.com/news/china/diplomacy-defence/article/2022718/china-build-outposts-tajik-guards-tajikistan.

Special Inspector General for Afghanistan Reconstruction. 'Afghan National Security Forces: Actions Needed to Improve Weapons Accountability'. Audit Report, SIGAR 14-84, Arlington, July 2014. https://www.sigar.mil/pdf/Audits/SIGAR-14-84-AR.pdf.

Special Inspector General for Afghanistan Reconstruction. 'Afghanistan's Banking Sector: Central Banks Ability to Regulate Commercial Banks Remains Weak'. Audit Report, SIGAR, Arlington, 2014. http://www.sigar.mil/pdf/audits/SIGAR%2014-16-AR.pdf.

Special Inspector General for Afghanistan Reconstruction. 'Quarterly Report to the United States Congress'. Report, SIGAR, 30 April 2018. https://www.globalsecurity.org/military/library/report/sigar/sigar-report-2018-04-30.pdf.

Standish, Reid. 'Kazakhstan Eyes Prestige in Afghanistan's Uncertain Future'. *Foreign Policy*, 16 December 2014. http://foreignpolicy.com/2014/12/16/kazakhstan-eyes-prestige-in-afghanistan-after-2014-drawdown/.

Stanzel, Angela. *Fear and Loathing on the New Silk Road: Chinese Security in Afghanistan and Beyond*. London: The European Council on Foreign Relations, 2018.

Starr, S. Frederick. 'A Partnership for Central Asia'. *Foreign Affairs* 84, 4 (2005): pp. 164–178.

Starr, S. Frederick. 'Introduction'. In *The New Silk Roads: Transport and Trade in Greater Central Asia*, edited by S. Frederick Starr, pp. 5–32. Washington, DC: Johns Hopkins University–SAIS, 2007.

Starr, S. Frederick and Svante E. Cornell. *Modernization and Regional Cooperation in Central Asia: A New Spring?* Report, Central Asia–Caucasus Institute and Silk Road Studies Program, Washington, DC, 2018.

Starr, S. Frederick and Marin J. Strmecki. 'Afghan Democracy and its First Missteps'. *New York Times*, 14 June 2002. http://query.nytimes.com/gst/fullpage.html?res=9F06E1DF123CF937A25755C0A9649C8B63.

Stein, Matthew. 'The History of Central Asian Peacekeepers: The Development of Kazakhstan, Kyrgyzstan, and Tajikistan's Peacekeeping Units by Fits and Starts'. *The Journal of Slavic Military Studies* 31, 2 (2018): pp 257–271.

Stepanova, Ekaterina. 'Faktor IGIL i dvizhenie Taliban v politike Rossii po Afganistanu i v bolee shirokom regione'. In *Problemy terrorizma, nasilstvennogo ekstremizma i radikalizatsii*, edited by Ekaterina Stepanova, pp. 213–237. Moscow: IMEMO RAN, 2017.

Stepanova, Ekaterina. *Russia's Afghan Policy in the Regional and East–West Contexts*. Paris: IFRI, 2018.

Stratfor. 'China's Increasing Security Buffer on Its Western Frontier'. 11 January 2018. https://worldview.stratfor.com/article/chinas-increasing-security-buffer-its-western-frontier.

Strmecki, Marin. 'Creating a Government'. Interview, *Newshour with Jim Lehrer*, PBS, 21 December 2001.

Subbotin, Igor. 'Status Afganistana v ShOS: situatsiia mozhet izmenitsia'. *Afghanistan.ru*, 9 June 2018. http://afghanistan.ru/doc/121292.html.

Suhrke, Astri. 'Democratizing a Dependent State: The Case of Afghanistan'. *Democratization* 15, 3 (2008): pp. 630–648.

Suhrke, Astri. 'Reconstruction as Modernisation: The "Post-Conflict" Project in Afghanistan'. *Third-World Quarterly* 28, 7 (2007): pp. 1304–1306.

Swanstrom, Niklas and Julian Tucker. 'China in Afghanistan – A New Force in the War in Afghanistan?' In *Rebuilding Afghanistan in Times of Crisis: A Global Response*, edited by Adenrele Awotona, pp. 156–173. Abingdon: Routledge, 2019.

Syroezhkin, Konstantin. *Nuzhno li Kazakhstanu boiatsia Kitaia: mify i fobii dvustoronnikh otnoshenii*. Astana-Almaty: IMEP, 2014.

Syroezhkin, Konstantin. *Sintzian: bolshoi vopros dlia Kitaia i Kazakhstana*. Almaty: IMEP, 2015.

Sysoev, Evgenii. 'IG stremitsia sozdat' novoe kvazigosudarstvo na territoriiakh Afganistana, Pakistana i stran Tsentralnoi Azii'. *RATS SCO*, 28 February 2018. http://ecrats.org/ru/situation/status/7083.

Szczudlik-Tatar, Justyna. 'China's Evolving Stance on Afghanistan: Towards More Robust Diplomacy with "Chinese Characteristics"'. *Strategic File* 22, 58 (2014): https://www.pism.pl/files/?id_plik=18261.

Tadjbakhsh, Shahrbanou, Kosimsho Iskandarov and Abdul Ahad Mohammadi. 'Strangers across the Amu River: Community Perceptions along the Tajik–Afghan Borders'. Working paper. SIPRI, Stockholm, 2015.

The Tashkent Times. 'Central Asia–Afghanistan Dialogue Format to Be Created'. 12 December 2017. http://tashkenttimes.uz/world/1793-central-asia-afghanistan-dialogue-format-to-be-created.

The Tashkent Times. 'Afghan Foreign Ministry Criticizes the Warm Reception of Taliban Leaders in Uzbekistan', *The Tashkent Times*, 12 August 2019, https://tashkenttimes.uz/national/4249-afghan-foreign-ministry-criticizes-the-warm-reception-of-taliban-leaders-in-uzbekistan.

TASS. 'Putin: Russia's Military Base in Tajikistan to Ensure Security of Border with Afghanistan'. 27 February 2017. http://tass.com/politics/932980.

Tellis, Ashley J. and Jeff Eggers. *U.S. Policy in Afghanistan: Changing Strategies, Preserving Gains*. Washington DC: Carnegie Endowment for International Peace, 2017.

Temirkhanova, A.E. 'Bezhentsy: Tsentralnaia Aziia vmesto Evropy?' *Uspekhi sovremennoi nauki i obrazovaniia* 1, 4 (2016): pp. 130–132.

Tiulegenov, M. and U. Omuraliev. *Regionalnoe sotrudnichestvo v Tsentralnoi Azii s uchastiem Afganistana posle 2014 goda: perspektivy dlia Kyrgyzskoi Respubliki*. Bishkek: NISI, 2013.

Tritten, Travis J. 'US Surprised by Kunduz, Weighing More Troops in 2016'. *Stars and Stripes*, 6 October 2015. http://www.stripes.com/news/us/us-surprised-by-kunduz-weighing-more-troops-in-2016-1.371913.

Trump, Donald J. @realDonaldTrump. Twitter Post, 22 August 2012, 12:05am. https://mobile.twitter.com/realdonaldtrump/status/237913235045638144?lang=en.

Trump, Donald. 'Remarks by President Trump and President Nursultan Nazarbayev of Kazakhstan in Joint Press Statements'. *The White House*, 16 January 2018. https://www.whitehouse.gov/briefings-statements/remarks-president-trump-president-nursultan-nazarbayev-kazakhstan-joint-press-statements/.

Tsentr-1. 'Pamirtsy opasaiutsia perekhoda talibov na territoriiu Tadzhikistana'. 3 May 2017. https://centre1.com/tajikistan/pamirtsy-opasayutsya-perehoda-talibov-na-territoriyu-tadzhikistana/.

Tsoy, Elena. 'Za chetyre goda s rosiiskoi storony v KR postupila voennaia tekhnika na summu bolee $125 mln'. *Kabar*, 19 June 2018. http://www.env.kabar.kg/news/za-chetyre-goda-s-rossiiskoi-storony-v-kr-postupila-voennaia-tekhnika-na-summu-bolee-125-mln/.

Tuhbatulin, Ruslan. 'Why Does Turkmenistan Provide Ammunition to the Taliban Movement?' *Chronicles of Turkmenistan*, 16 March 2017. https://en.hronikatm.com/2017/03/why-does-turkmenistan-provide-ammunition-to-the-taliban-movement/.

Tuleev, M.S. 'Tsentralnaia Aziia: Afganistan i sovremennye aspekty geopolitiki'. *Vestnik KRSU* 16, 6 (2016): pp. 185–188.

Turkmen Business. 'Razrabotana Kontseptsiia razvitiia elektroenergeticheskoi otrasli Turkmenistana na 2013–2020 gody'. 14 April 2013. http://www.turkmenbusiness.org/news/razrabotana-kontseptsiya-razvitiya-elektroenergeticheskoi-otrasli-turkmenistana-na-2013-2020-go.

Turkmenistan Ministry of Foreign Affairs. 'Message for the Media', 14 November 2018. https://www.mfa.gov.tm/en/news/1094.

Turkmenistan segodnia. 'Turkmeno-afganskie peregovory na vysshem urovne'. 27 August 2015. http://tdh.gov.tm/news/articles.aspx&article2416&cat11.

Turkmenportal. 'Informatsiia o zhertvakh sredi soldat na turkmeno-afganskoi granitse ne sootvetstvuet deistvitelnosti'. 3 July 2018. https://turkmenportal.com/blog/15087/informaciya-o-zhertvah-sredi-soldat-na-turkmenoafganskoi-granice-ne-sootvetstvuet-deistvitelnosti.

TV Zvezda. 'SShA gotoviat "novyi proekt" po destabilizatsii Srednei Azii – Klintsevich'. 13 September 2017. https://tvzvezda.ru/news/vstrane_i_mire/content/201709131818-9qjs.htm.

Umarov, Akram. 'Assessing China's New Policy in Afghanistan'. *Central Asian Affairs* 4, 4, (2017): pp. 384–406.

Umarov, Kairat 'Letter dated 17 January 2018 from the Chair of the Security Council Committee pursuant to resolutions 1267 (1999), 1989 (2011), and 2253 (2015) concerning Islamic State in Iraq and the Levant (Da'esh), Al-Qaida and associated individuals, groups, undertakings and entities addressed to the President of the

Security Council'. *United Nations Security Council*, 26 January 2018. http://daccess-ods.un.org/access.nsf/GetFile?OpenAgent&DS=S/2018/14&Lang=E&Type=DOC.

Umarov, Khojamahmad. *Torgovo-ekonomicheskie otnosheniia mezhdu Respublikoi Tadzhikistan i Islamskoi Respublikoi Afganistan*. Bishkek: University of Central Asia, 2013.

UN News. 'Record-high Opium Production in Afghanistan Creates Multiple Challenges for Region and Beyond, UN warns', 21 May 2018. https://news.un.org/en/story/2018/05/1010332.

UN News. 'Civilian Deaths in Afghanistan hit Record High – UN', 15 July 2018. https://news.un.org/en/story/2018/07/1014762.

United Nations. 'Agreement on Provisional Arrangements in Afghanistan Pending the Re-Establishment of Permanent Government Institution (Bonn Agreement)', 2001. http://www.un.org/News/dh/latest/afghan/afghan-agree.htm

United Nations Economic and Social Commission for Asia and the Pacific. 'Afghanistan and Central Asia: Strengthening Trade and Economic Ties'. Report, UNESCAP, Bangkok, 27 March 2015. https://www.unescap.org/sites/default/files/Afghanistan%20and%20Central%20Asia-Strengthening%20Trade%20and%20Economic%20Ties.pdf.

United Nations General Assembly. 'Tashkent Declaration on Fundamental Principles for a Peaceful Settlement of the Conflict in Afghanistan'. Document A/54/174 S/1999/812. UNGA, New York, 22 July 1999. https://peacemaker.un.org/sites/peacemaker.un.org/files/AF_990719_TashkentDeclaration%28en%29.pdf.

United Nations Office of Drugs and Crime. 'Afghanistan Opium Survey 2017: Cultivation and Production'. Report, UNODP, New York, November 2017. https://www.unodc.org/documents/crop-monitoring/Afghanistan/Afghan_opium_survey_2017_cult_prod_web.pdf.

United Nations Office on Drugs and Crime. 'Afghan Opiate Trafficking along the Northern Route'. Report, UNODC, Vienna, 2018.

United States Committee for Refugees and Immigrants. 'USCR Country Report Tajikistan: Statistics on Refugees and Other Uprooted People, June 2001'. *ReliefWeb*, 19 June 2001. https://reliefweb.int/report/afghanistan/uscr-country-report-tajikistan-statistics-refugees-and-other-uprooted-people-jun.

United States Department of State. 'International Narcotics Control Strategy Report'. Vol. I. Report, Bureau for International Narcotics and Law Enforcement Affairs, Washington, DC, March 2017. https://www.state.gov/documents/organization/268025.pdf.

United States Mission Uzbekistan, 'C5+1 Fact Sheet: Central Asian–U.S. Forum to Enhance Regional Economic, Environmental, and Security Cooperation'. 24 July 2018. https://uz.usembassy.gov/c51-fact-sheet-central-asian-u-s-forum-to-enhance-regional-economic-environmental-and-security-cooperation/.

US House of Representatives. Statement of General Joseph L. Votel, Commander, U.S. Central Command before the House Armed Services Committee on the Posture of

U.S. Central Command Terrorism and Iran: Defense Challenges in the Middle East'. 27 February 2018. https://docs.house.gov/meetings/AS/AS00/20180227/106870/HHRG-115-AS00-Wstate-VotelJ-20180227.pdf.

US Senate Committee on Armed Services. 'Statement for the Record by General John W. Nicholson, Commander, U.S. Forces–Afghanistan before the Senate Armed Services Committee on the Situation in Afghanistan'. 9 February 2017. https://www.armed-services.senate.gov/imo/media/doc/Nicholson_02-09-17.pdf.

UzReport. 'Uzbekistan peredal Afganistanu 25 avtobusov, 3 traktora i navesnuiu tekhniku'. 12 January 2018. https://www.uzreport.news/society/uzbekistan-peredal-afganistanu-25-avtobusov-3-traktora-i-navesnuyu-tehniku.

Vaal, Tamara. 'Bolee 20 tys. posledovatelei destruktivnykh religioznykh ideologii zhivut v Kazakhstane – KNB'. *Vlast.kz*, 6 November 2019. https://vlast.kz/novosti/35957-bolee-20-tys-posledovatelej-destruktivnyh-religioznyh-ideologij-zivut-v-kazahstane-knb.html.

van der Kley, Dirk. *China's Foreign Policy in Afghanistan*. Sydney: Lowy Institute, 2014.

Vasiliev, Alexey. *Russia's Middle East Policy: From Lenin to Putin*. Abingdon: Routledge, 2018.

Verkhoturov, Dmitrii. 'Dan' *Gundogar*, 4 May 2016. http://gundogar.org/?02340516865000000000000011000000.

Vesti.kg. 'Turkmenskie siloviki provodiat reidy protiv bandformirovanii IGIL'. 9 June 2015. https://vesti.kg/analitika/item/34248-turkmenskie-siloviki-provodyat-reydy-protiv-bandformirovaniy-igil.html.

Vesti.uz. '"Dushanbinskaia chetverka" priniala "dorozhnuiu kartu"'. 5 September 2011. https://vesti.uz/2011-09-05-13-05-09/.

Vesti.uz. 'Glava uzbekskikh spetssluzhb nazval vragov gosudarstva'. 2 April 2018. https://vesti.uz/glava-uzbekskih-spetssluzhb-nazval-vragov-gosudarstva/.

Vinogradov, A.O. *Resheniia XIX s'ezda KPK i perspektivy rossisko-kitaiskikh otnoshenii*. Moscow: IDV RAN, 2018.

Vohidov, Karim. 'Na mezhdunarodnoi konferentsii RATS ShOS terroristichesko-ekstremistskaia organizatsiia PIVT priznana ugrozoi regionalnoi bezopasnosti'. *Narodnaia gazeta*, 17 November 2017. https://www.narodnaya.tj/index.php?option=com_content&view=article&id=5448:--------lr----&catid=57:bezopasnost&Itemid=53.

Volkov, Vitalii. 'Ashkhabad uzhestochaet bor'bu s narkooborotom–shou ili vser'ez?' *Deutsche Welle*, 4 February 2015. https://p.dw.com/p/1EUwJ.

Volkov, Vitalii. 'Bezopasnost' v regione: sila i slabost' armii Uzbekistana'. *Deutsche Welle*, 10 May 2016. https://p.dw.com/p/1Ikuf.

Volkov, Vitalii. 'O chem "seryi kardinal" Afganistana dogovorilsia s Kremlem'. *Deutsche Welle*, 20 March 2017. https://p.dw.com/p/2ZYAg.

Volkov, Vitalii. 'Pomogut li kontakty s talibami stabilizirovat' Tsentralnuiu Aziiu?' *Deutsche Welle*, 13 June 2018. https://p.dw.com/p/2zOLv.

Wardak, Ali. 'Building a Post-War Justice System in Afghanistan'. *Crime, Law and Social Change* 41 (2004): pp. 319–341.

Warren, Zach. *Afghanistan in 2014: A Survey of the Afghan People*, San Francisco: The Asia Foundation, 2014. http://asiafoundation.org/resources/pdfs/Afghanistanin2014final.pdf.

Weitz, Richard. 'Almaty Hosts "Heart of Asia" Conference'. *Eurasia Daily Monitor* 10, 84 (2013) https://jamestown.org/program/almaty-hosts-heart-of-asia-conference/.

Wellman, Phillip Walter. 'ISIS Flees Taliban Onslaught, Surrenders to Afghan Government Forces'. *Stars and Stripes*, 1 August 2018. https://www.stripes.com/news/isis-flees-taliban-onslaught-surrenders-to-afghan-government-forces-1.540428.

White, Jeremy. 'Taliban Urges Americans to Pressure Trump and Congress to Pull Troops from Afghanistan'. *The Independent*, 14 February 2018. http://www.independent.co.uk/news/world/asia/taliban-us-donald-trump-congress-troops-afghanistan-soldiers-war-a8211081.html.

The White House. *The National Security Strategy of the United States of America*. Washington, DC: The White House, 2006.

The White House. *National Security Strategy of the United States of America*. Washington, DC: The White House, 2017.

The White House. 'The United States and Uzbekistan: Launching a New Era of Strategic Partnership', 16 May 2018. https://www.whitehouse.gov/briefings-statements/united-states-uzbekistan-launching-new-era-strategic-partnership/.

Wikileaks. 'Powering Afghanistan: Considering the Contribution of Central Asia to Stability and Growth'. Astana Embassy, Wikileaks Cable 09ASTANA1373_a, 11 August 2009. https://wikileaks.org/plusd/cables/09ASTANA1373_a.html.

Wishnick, Elizabeth. 'Post-2014 Afghanistan Policy and the Limitations of China's Global Role'. *Central Asian Affairs* 1, 1 (2014): pp. 133–152.

The World Bank. 'Islamic Republic of Afghanistan Energy Security Trade-Offs under High Uncertainty: Resolving Afghanistan's Power Sector Development Dilemma'. Report, ACS19167, Washington, DC, 25 April 2016. http://documents.worldbank.org/curated/en/136801488956292409/pdf/ACS19167-WP-PUBLIC-P146249.pdf.

The World Bank. 'Afghanistan Renewable Energy Development: Issues and Options', 26 June 2018. http://documents.worldbank.org/curated/en/352991530527393098/pdf/Afghanistan-Renewable-Energy-Development-Issues-and-Options.pdf.

The World Bank. 'Central Asia South Asia Electricity Transmission and Trade Project (CASA-1000) (P145054)'. The World Bank Implementation Status & Results Report, WB, Washington, D.C., 22 December 2018. http://documents.worldbank.org/curated/en/565831545491068302/pdf/Disclosable-Version-of-the-ISR-Central-Asia-South-Asia-Electricity-Transmission-and-Trade-Project-CASA-1000-P145054-Sequence-No-09.pdf.

Yi, Wang. 'Push for New Steps and New Breakthroughs in Afghanistan's Reconciliation Process at an Early Date'. *Ministry of Foreign Affairs of the People's Republic of China*, 12 December 2018. https://www.fmprc.gov.cn/mfa_eng/zxxx_662805/t1624843.shtml.

Yongbiao, Zhu. 'China's Afghanistan Policy since 9/11 Stages and Prospects'. *Asian Survey* 58, 2 (2018): pp. 281–301.

Yuldashev, Avaz. 'Ekspert: v Afganistane nabiraet oboroty pushtunskii natsionalizm'. *Asia-Plus*, 23 November 2017. https://news.tj/news/tajikistan/security/20171123/ekspert-v-afganistane-nabiraet-oboroti-pushtunskii-natsionalizm.

Yuldasheva, Nigora. 'Chernaia ten' na zelenykh sklonakh'. *Delovaia nedelia*, 4 May 2015. http://www.dn.kz/index.php?option=com_content&view=article&id=2751:2015-05-04-05-00-03&catid=2:2011-10-23-11-43-45&Itemid=17.

Zahid, Noor. 'Officials: Son of Slain Uzbek Militant Promotes So-called Islamic State in Afghanistan'. *VOA*, 7 February 2017. https://www.voanews.com/a/son-slain-uzbek-militant-promotes-islamic-state-afghanistan-officials-say/3710083.html.

Zakharova, Maria. 'Russia Records Unidentified Helicopters Delivering Weapons to Taliban, IS in Afghanistan'. *TASS*, 23 August 2018. http://tass.com/defense/1018368.

Zarifi, Sam and Charmain Mohamed. 'Afghan Election Diary'. Human Rights Watch, 19 September 2005. http://www.hrw.org/campaigns/afghanistan/blog.htm.

Zenz, Adrian. '"Thoroughly Reforming them towards a Healthy Heart Attitude": China's Political Re-education Campaign in Xinjiang'. *Central Asian Survey* (2018): DOI: 10.1080/02634937.2018.1507997.

Zimmerman, Erin. *Think Tanks and Non-Traditional Security Governance Entrepreneurs in Asia*. Basingstoke: Palgrave Macmillan, 2016.

Zimmerman, Thomas. *The New Silk Roads: China, the U.S., and the Future of Central Asia*. New York: New York University, 2015.

Zoli, Corri and Emily Schneider. 'Privacy in Muslim Constitutions and Karzai's Refusal to Sign the Bilateral Security Agreement'. *The Washington Post*, 2 January 2014. https://www.washingtonpost.com/news/monkey-cage/wp/2014/01/02/privacy-in-muslim-constitutions-and-karzais-refusal-to-sign-the-bilateral-security-agreement/.

Zubov, Andrei. 'Pochemu Turkmeniia nedovolna slovami Nazarbaeva'. *365info.kz*, 16 October 2015. https://365info.kz/2015/10/pochemu-turkmeniya-nedovolna-slovami-nazarbaeva/.

Index

6+2 talks 71

Abdrakhmanov, Kairat 152, 156
Abdullah Abdullah 3, 27, 34, 38, 187
    see also NUG
Abdyldayev, Erlan 152
ADB 85, 89, 92, 93, 94, 96, 104, 123, 161
Adeeb, Shah Waliullah 92
Adnani, Abu Muhammad al- 53
aid 8, 26, 29, 56, 61, 85, 88, 90, 95, 96, 98, 99, 102, 124, 130, 137, 157, 180
AKN 92
Al Qaeda 14, 15, 19, 28–29, 34, 35, 54, 59, 125, 183, 187
    see also bin Laden
Anceschi, Luca 166
Andijan massacre 158
ANSF 83, 85, 91, 97, 104, 109, 122, 126, 127, 130, 136, 188
Arbaki 98
arms, trafficking of 3, 52, 108, 126, 130, 131, 155, 162
Atambaev , Almaz 60, 101–102
Atmar, Mohammad Hanif 34, 129–130, 185

Babanov, Omurbek 132
Baghdadi, Abu Bakr al- 53
    see also ISIS
Baradar, Mullah Ghani 182
Berdimuhammedov, Gurbanguly 66, 68, 92–93, 94, 95, 98, 99, 165–166
bin Laden, Osama 14, 15, 16, 34
    see also Al Qaeda
Bleuer, Christian 1
Bonn Agreement 6, 17–18, 19, 20, 24, 25
BRI 97, 135, 137–138
Brooking Institution 34
Brzezinski, Zbigniew 60
Bush, George W. 13, 14, 15, 16–27, 28, 31, 34, 36, 37, 40
Butler, Ed 177

CAREC 89, 91, 92, 105, 180, 181
CASA-1000 89, 91, 123, 161
China 1, 8, 40, 53, 57, 66, 71, 72, 89, 91, 94, 99, 103, 105, 109, 121, 123, 124, 125, 127, 128, 132, 134–140, 141, 142, 154, 155, 158, 161, 165, 166, 168, 169, 178, 179, 181, 182, 188, 189
    Central Asian perceptions of 51, 58, 60
    Xinjiang 62, 135, 138–139, 140–141, 164
Clarke, Michael 138
Clinton, Bill 15
Clinton, Hillary 122, 123, 137
Constitution, Afghanistan 17, 18, 19–22, 38, 188–189
Cooley, Alexander 8, 122, 140
Cordesman, Anthony 128, 141
Corridor 5 91–92
corruption 6, 26, 28, 29–31, 38, 123, 159
counter-insurgency 26, 30, 100, 107, 122–124, 132, 136, 159, 181
    people-centered (COIN) 28, 32–33
CPEC 137–138, 140
CSTO 52, 56, 58, 72, 100–103, 105, 131, 132, 140, 141, 155, 157, 167, 168, 181, 185

democracy (Afghanistan) 13, 17, 21, 23, 24, 25, 26, 134, 141
diplomacy 8, 9, 56, 57, 66, 67, 104–108, 109, 132, 135, 138, 139, 140, 153, 156, 157, 158, 164, 169, 180, 183, 185, 188
Dostum, Abdul Rashid 20, 21, 71
Dunford, Joseph 126

education 55, 90, 92, 104, 157, 180
    university 56
Eikenberry, Karl 28, 29, 32, 33
elections, Afghanistan 17–18, 19, 22–27, 38, 186–187, 189
    2019, in 7, 186–187

fraudulent 34, 187
energy sector 84, 85, 109, 122, 135, 166, 181
   electricity 86–89, 91–96, 122, 164
   gas 67, 67, 87, 93–94, 122, 123, 136, 137, 138, 161, 166, 180–181
   oil 15
   regional cooperation 87–89, 93, 96, 122, 181
ethnofidelity 8, 16, 53, 61, 65, 70, 72, 109, 179
Europe 16, 26, 34, 52, 55, 57, 58, 91, 93, 94, 102, 153, 156, 189

Fahim, Muhammad 65
Fair, Christine 124–125
Farooqi, Aslam 54–55
Fazendeiro, Bernardo Teles 99
Faryab 66–67, 94, 166–167
Ferghana Valley 60, 62, 97–98
Fjæstad, Kristin 180
foreign policy executives (FPEs) 4, 5

Galbraith, Peter W 34
GBAO 63, 162
Ghani, Ashraf 3, 20, 35, 36, 38, 39, 65, 71, 95, 108, 125, 128, 129, 153, 155, 158, 160, 184, 185, 187, 188
   see also NUG
Ghazi, Usman 54
Ghulomov, Shuhrat 159
Giustozzi, Antonio 26, 54, 55
Great Game, The 2, 60, 121, 128, 132

Haqqani network 39, 60
Heart of Asia (HoA) *see* Istanbul Process
Helmand 31, 39
Herat 21, 66, 94, 96, 123, 126, 161
Hijab 21
Hoagland, Richard 137

IMU 54, 59, 67, 68–69, 70, 95, 107, 159, 166, 178
India 36, 39, 51, 93, 94, 104, 123, 125, 138, 152, 161, 178, 185
infrastructure 2, 60, 83, 85, 92, 98, 104, 106, 122–123, 128, 130, 137, 140, 154, 157, 161, 177, 180
   ports 85, 90, 92, 94, 96, 137, 155
   railways 90–91, 92–93, 96, 106, 122, 123, 137, 138, 160, 161, 164–165
   roads 85, 86, 90, 94, 123, 138
Interim Authority 17–18, 19, 20, 38
Iran 1, 2, 39, 51, 53, 71, 94, 109, 125, 126, 136, 138, 140, 155, 164, 166, 178, 183–184, 185
   rivalry with Saudi Arabia 39, 104, 153, 178
Iraq 53, 54, 62, 98
   ISIS fighters from 100, 130
   US invasion of 13, 27, 28, 34, 35
IRPT 62, 131
ISAF 3, 16, 56, 66, 85, 91, 94, 96, 98, 107, 121, 122, 123, 132, 136
ISIS 35, 39, 52, 53–55, 57, 59, 60, 62, 65, 66, 69, 101, 126, 129, 131, 134, 159, 163, 164, 165, 166
   Caliphate, defeat of 54, 56
   in Iraq 53–54, 130
   in Syria 53–54, 130
ISIS-K 39, 52, 53–55, 62, 67, 70, 72, 107, 126, 127, 129–130, 132, 136, 137, 138, 139, 177, 178, 181, 182, 184, 185, 187, 188
   alleged US support of 131
   IMU and 54, 67
   Taliban and 5, 54, 55, 127
Istanbul Process 56, 71, 104–105, 160, 180

Jaihun-2018 158
Jeenbekov, Sooronbay 164, 165
JIA 20, 21
JICA 98
JEMB 22, 23
JMIA 20
Jund al-Khilafa 56–57

Kabul 15, 16, 24, 26, 40, 87, 91, 97, 138, 184
Kabul Bank scandal 30
Kabul Process 153, 160
Kabulov, Zamir 133
Karimov, Islam 68, 69, 71, 89, 95, 99, 107, 125, 158
   death of 95, 99, 151
Karin, Erlan 56–57, 132
Karzai, Hamid 17, 19, 20, 21, 23, 27, 28, 29, 30, 32, 33–34, 38, 65, 92, 124, 129, 131, 185, 187

Karzai, Hekmat Khalil 151
Kassenova Nargis 56
Kazakhstan 1, 2, 5, 6, 8, 9, 40, 51, 52, 53,
    55–58; 67, 69, 70, 72, 85, 86, 92, 98,
    100, 101,, 105, 107, 110, 121, 124,
    124, 125, 126, 132, 138, 151, 152,
    153, 154–157, 158, 160, 162, 168,
    169, 178, 179, 181
  aid to Afghanistan 56, 90–91, 130, 180
  China, relationship with 103, 135, 137,
    140–141
  drugs trafficked to 101, 179
  trade with Afghanistan 157, 181
  UN Security Council seat 151, 156, 180
Kazemi, Said Reza 1
Khalilzad, Zalmay 18, 19, 22, 183, 184,
    185–186, 187
Khan, Ismail 21, 126
Khorasan 39, 53–54, 177
Kjærnet, Heidi 180
Klintsevich, Frants 133, 134
Konarovsky, Mikhail 129, 132
Kshimovsky, Alexandr 163
Kyrgyzstan 1, 6, 7, 8, 40, 51–52, 53, 55,
    58–61, 69, 70, 72, 86, 89, 91–92, 100,
    101–102, 103, 105, 106, 110, 121,
    123, 124, 125, 132, 135, 138, 140,
    151–152, 158, 161, 164–165, 185,
    188
  drugs smuggled to 179

Lapis Lazuli Corridor 93, 94–95
Language 1, 16, 65
Laruelle, Marlene 1, 65
Laumulin, Murat 141
Lavrov, Sergei 130, 152
LeT 54
Loya jirga 17, 24, 34
  Constitutional (CLJ) 17, 19–22
  Emergency (ELJ) 17, 18–19, 21

McChrystal, Stanley 28, 30
Mamytov, Tokon 59
Manas Air Base 58, 123, 140
Massoud, Ahmad Shah 19, 38, 65
MCTFA 30
migration 4, 52, 56, 58, 61, 101, 129, 168
  to Europe 57
  see also refugees

minorities 8, 21, 24, 40, 135, 177
  Kazakh 57
  Kyrgyz 61
  Tajik 38, 65–66, 71, 84, 179
  Turkmen 72, 84
  Uzbek 59–60, 70, 71, 72, 84, 160
Mirziyoyev, Shavkat 69, 71, 95, 96, 100,
    105, 106, 151, 158–161, 163, 167,
    182
Moawiya 54–55
Moscow format 125–126, 138, 139, 160,
    188
Mujahideen 4, 14, 15, 20, 55, 59, 67, 70, 71,
    126, 187
multi-vectorism 154–155, 157, 159, 179

narcotics 4, 25, 26, 28, 38–39, 52, 56, 60, 63,
    68, 125, 136, 140, 177
  counter- 60, 68, 69, 99, 100, 101, 103,
    104, 106–107, 123, 124, 136, 153,
    161, 162
  heroin 56, 63, 69, 101, 134, 179
  trafficking 3, 7, 25, 26, 52, 53, 56, 60,
    63–64, 68, 71, 72, 92, 100, 101, 109,
    126, 129, 130, 132, 135, 154, 155,
    159, 162, 165, 177, 178, 179
NATO 13, 16, 26, 28, 36, 56, 58, 97, 124,
    127, 155, 177, 179
  bases 122
  Iraq mission 98
  withdrawal from Afghanistan 2, 51, 96,
    108–109, 122, 129, 132, 134, 151,
    152
Nazarbaev, Nursultan 56, 57, 67, 90, 98,
    101, 155–157, 167–168, 180
NDN 85, 86, 90, 96, 97, 122, 123, 137, 155,
    180
Nicholson, John 125, 126, 127
Northern Alliance 19, 27
  see also Massoud, Ahmad Shah
NSR 105, 106, 122–123, 128, 137, 140, 142
NUG (National Unity Government) 3, 8,
    20, 21, 38, 97, 109, 124, 125, 129,
    132, 138, 139
  failure of 7, 186–187
Nur, Atta Mohammad 65, 92

Obama, Barack 2, 13, 27–36, 40, 106, 183
O'Hanlon, Michael 124

Organised crime 26, 30, 84, 103, 104, 130, 155, 157, 159, 162
OSCE 56, 98, 101, 155, 156, 162, 165

Pakistan 1, 2, 34, 36, 37, 39, 54, 56, 57, 59, 60, 62, 71, 89, 91, 93–94, 102, 104, 106, 109, 123, 125, 128, 133, 135, 137, 138, 139, 178, 185
   India, rivalry with 39
   Taliban, relationship to 14–15, 16, 19, 26, 27, 28, 29, 33, 36, 39, 125, 128, 136, 139, 183, 184, 186
Pannier, Bruce 182
Pantucci, Raffaello 137
Petraeus, David 32, 187
Pompeo, Mike 187
Putin, Vladimir 5, 102, 103, 129, 133, 134, 139

Qanooni, Yunus 185
Qatar 183, 184

Rabbani, Burhanuddin 65
Rahmon, Emomali 62–63, 92, 103, 140, 162–163, 179
Rahmonali, Rajobali 163
Reeves, Madeleine 97
refugees 8, 53, 57, 61, 64–65, 72, 178
Rouhani, Hassan 53
Russia 4, 40, 58, 71, 72, 86, 91, 93, 105, 106, 109, 121, 123, 124, 125, 128–134, 135, 136, 137, 138, 139, 141, 142, 151, 152, 153, 155, 156, 157, 158, 160, 163, 165, 166, 167, 168, 179, 182, 183, 188
   201st base 102, 123, 131, 163, 181
   Central Asian perceptions of 51–52
   China, cooperation with 8, 103, 141, 189
   CSTO and 52, 101, 103
   counterterrorism exercises 159
   drugs trafficked to 26, 63, 68, 129, 133–134
   foreign policy of 5, 129
   geo-political containment of 1, 94
   –India transport corridor 161
   Iran, cooperation with 39
   ISIS and 62, 127, 129, 130–131, 134, 163, 178
   Kazakhstan and 57–58, 101
   Kyrgyzstan and 58, 101–102
   Tajikistan and 63, 65–66, 101, 102–103
   Taliban and 108, 126–127, 129, 130, 185
   Turkmenistan and 67
   US and 39, 94, 126, 127, 131, 132–134, 139, 140, 169, 177–178, 188
   Uzbekistan and 106
   weapons supply from 99, 100, 101, 104, 108, 126, 163

Saeed Khan, Hafiz 54
Safranchuk, Ivan 97
Saleh, Mohammad Zia 29
sanctions 15, 130
Saudi Arabia 15, 21, 39, 104, 153, 178
SCO 58, 97, 101, 103, 105, 135–136, 141, 159, 168, 182
   Afghanistan Contact Group 160
September 11 14, 15, 19, 84, 168
Serchuk, Vance 187
Sharīʿa 20, 21, 189
Shoigu, Sergei 131
single non-transferable voting (SNTV) 23–24
Shi'a 55
Soviet 87, 100, 103, 178, 179
   Afghanistan, occupation of 1, 14–15, 19, 38, 109, 127, 130, 133
   equipment 69, 70, 87, 127, 130
Stepanova, Ekaterina 129, 130
Syria 52, 53, 54, 62, 126, 134, 156
   ISIS fighters from 54, 100, 130, 161, 163
Syroezhkin, Konstantin 141, 142

Tajikistan 1, 7, 8, 51–52, 53, 55, 58, 61–66, 69, 70, 71, 72, 86, 87, 88, 89, 91–92, 101, 105, 106, 108, 109, 121, 123–124, 125, 131, 132, 135, 138, 151, 153, 154, 158, 162–164, 178, 179, 181, 182, 185
   border with Afghanistan 39, 59, 61–62, 63, 64, 65, 72, 98, 100, 101, 102–103, 124, 136, 162–163, 165, 166–167, 181
   civil war 1, 61, 108
   Uzbekistan, thaw in relations with 93, 95–96, 158, 164

Taliban 4, 14–15, 17, 19, 31, 32, 33, 35, 38, 51, 53, 55, 59, 60, 62, 64, 65, 66, 70, 71, 84, 93, 98, 126, 128, 136, 139, 140, 162, 163, 181, 188
   Al Qaeda and 15, 28
   alleged Russian support of 126–127, 129–131, 132–134, 139
   China and 138–139
   defeat of (2001) 2, 6, 14, 16, 85
   negotiations with 3, 5–6, 7, 8, 36, 37, 107–109, 124–126, 133, 153, 160, 182, 183, 184, 185, 186, 187, 188–189
   resurgence of 16, 26, 31, 35–36, 39, 64, 67, 103, 152, 166–167, 177, 179
TAP-500 93, 94
TAPI 68, 93–94, 108, 123, 161, 166, 180, 181
Tashkent conference 153, 160, 166
TAT 92, 93, 123, 164
Trade 8, 83, 84, 85–86, 89, 90, 91, 95, 96, 104, 122, 123, 130, 138, 157, 160, 161, 164, 166, 169, 181
   routes 85, 91–95, 105, 109, 122–123, 128, 137–138, 140, 158, 161, 164–165
Trump, Donald 7, 13, 16, 36–37, 40, 98, 106, 124–126, 128, 133, 134, 139, 141–142, 183, 184, 185–186, 187
TTP 53
Turkey 71, 84, 94, 99, 156
Turkmenistan 1, 6, 7, 8, 39–40, 52, 53, 66–68, 71, 72, 85, 86, 87–88, 91, 92, 93–95, 96, 99, 103, 109, 123–124, 125–126, 132, 138, 151, 154, 158, 165–167, 179
   border with Afghanistan 66–67, 102, 155, 188
   gas fields 67, 94, 167
   TAPI and 68, 93, 94, 98, 108, 123, 161, 166, 180–181
   TAT and 164
   TUTAP and 123
TUTAP 123

UAE 15, 183
UIFSA *see* Northern Alliance
United States 4, 8, 13, 15, 16–41, 58, 60, 68, 71, 84, 85, 88, 91, 93, 99, 104, 105, 106, 109, 122–128, 129, 130, 131, 132–134, 136, 138, 139, 140–142, 155, 158, 169, 181, 182–183, 185, 186
   Afghanistan, invasion of 14, 16, 26, 177
   Al Qaeda attack against 14, 15, 19, 29
   Central Asian perceptions of 51–52, 58, 60, 65–66, 98, 155, 156, 158, 160
   Iran, animosity towards 39, 94, 178
   Iraq, invasion of 28, 35
   ISIS attacks against 55
   Karzai, relationship with 17, 19–21, 23, 27, 29, 30, 32
   mujahideen and 14
   surge 7, 28, 37, 124, 133
   training of Afghan troops and/or police by 3, 40, 98, 102
   withdrawal from Afghanistan 7, 29, 34, 35, 36, 70, 99, 109, 121, 122, 125, 184–184, 187
UNHCR 65
United Kingdom 16, 93
Uyghur *see* China
Uzbekistan 1, 8, 51–52, 53, 55, 68–71, 72, 85, 86, 87–88, 89, 92, 94, 95–96, 99–100, 105–108, 110, 123–124, 125, 131, 132, 136, 137, 138, 140, 153, 154, 157–161, 163–164, 167, 169, 179, 181, 182, 188
   border with Afghanistan 39, 58, 69–70, 178, 179
   thaw in regional relations 9, 93, 151, 158–159, 168
   TUTAP and 123

Votel, Joseph L 123

War on Terror 13, 14, 17, 122
Waziristan 57, 66
Wishnick, Elizabeth 134
Wolesi jirga 22, 23, 24
women's rights 22, 24, 38, 90, 157

Xi Jinping 135, 137, 139

Yamamoto, Tadamichi 153

Zahir Shah 18, 19